ADVANCES IN
EXPERIMENTAL SOCIAL PSYCHOLOGY

VOLUME 23

ADVANCES IN

Experimental Social Psychology

EDITED BY

Mark P. Zanna
DEPARTMENT OF PSYCHOLOGY
UNIVERSITY OF WATERLOO
WATERLOO, ONTARIO, CANADA

VOLUME 23

ACADEMIC PRESS, INC.
Harcourt Brace Jovanovich, Publishers
San Diego   New York   Berkeley   Boston
London   Sydney   Tokyo   Toronto

This book is printed on acid-free paper. ∞

COPYRIGHT © 1990 BY ACADEMIC PRESS, INC.
All Rights Reserved.
No part of this publication may be reproduced or transmitted in any form or by any means, electronic or mechanical, including photocopy, recording, or any information storage and retrieval system, without permission in writing from the publisher.

ACADEMIC PRESS, INC.
San Diego, California 92101

United Kingdom Edition published by
ACADEMIC PRESS LIMITED
24-28 Oval Road, London NW1 7DX

LIBRARY OF CONGRESS CATALOG CARD NUMBER: 64-23452

ISBN 0-12-015223-1 (alk. paper)

PRINTED IN THE UNITED STATES OF AMERICA
90 91 92 93   9 8 7 6 5 4 3 2 1

CONTENTS

Contributors ix
Preface xi

A Continuum of Impression Formation, from Category-Based to Individuating Processes: Influences of Information and Motivation on Attention and Interpretation

Susan T. Fiske and Steven L. Neuberg

I.	Introduction	1
II.	A Continuum Model of Impression Formation Processes	3
III.	Premise 1: Perceivers Give Priority to Category-Based Processes	13
IV.	Premise 2: Interpretation of Fit between Category and Attributes Determines Use of the Continuum	22
V.	Premise 3: Use of the Continuum Is Mediated by Changes in Attention to Attributes	33
VI.	Premise 4: Motivation Influences Impression Formation According to the Interdependence Structure, Specifically, the Motivating Agent's Criteria	36
VII.	Premise 5: Motivational Influences Are Also Mediated by Attentional and Interpretive Responses to Attributes	47
VIII.	Alternatives to the Continuum Model	57
IX.	Conclusions	60
	References	63

Multiple Processes by Which Attitudes Guide Behavior: The MODE Model as an Integrative Framework

Russell H. Fazio

I.	Introduction	75
II.	Current State of the Literature	75
III.	A Spontaneous Processing Model of the Attitude–Behavior Relation	78
IV.	A Deliberative Processing Model of the Attitude–Behavior Relation	88

V.	An Integrative Model: Conditions That Promote Each Process	91
VI.	Mixed Models of the Attitude–Behavior Process	96
VII.	Conclusions	102
	References	105

PEAT: An Integrative Model of Attribution Processes

John W. Medcof

I.	Introduction	111
II.	PEAT	112
III.	Kelley's Theories	128
IV.	Correspondent Inference Theory	162
V.	PEAT, Kelley, and CIT	193
VI.	Other Theories	196
VII.	Conclusions	205
	References	207

Reading People's Minds: A Transformation Rule Model for Predicting Others' Thoughts and Feelings

Rachel Karniol

I.	Predicting Others' Psychological Experiences	211
II.	Procedural Knowledge	218
III.	Declarative Knowledge	227
IV.	Role of Self-Knowledge	233
V.	Situational Influences on Transformation Rule Use	239
VI.	Individual Differences	239
VII.	Conclusions	241
	References	241

Self-Attention and Behavior: A Review and Theoretical Update

Frederick X. Gibbons

I.	Introduction	249
II.	"Original" Self-Awareness Theory: A Review	250
III.	Assessments and Modifications	252
IV.	Alternative Approaches: A Review	263
V.	Points of Distinction between Original Theory and Others	269
VI.	The Nature of Standards	282

| VII. | Revised Model | 286 |
| | References | 295 |

Counterfactual Thinking and Social Perception: Thinking about What Might Have Been

Dale T. Miller, William Turnbull, and Cathy McFarland

I.	Introduction	305
II.	Mentally Undoing Actions	306
III.	Mentally Undoing Outcomes	313
IV.	Mentally Replicating Outcomes	318
V.	Discussion	325
	References	330

Index 333
Contents of Other Volumes 345

CONTRIBUTORS

Numbers in parentheses indicate the pages on which the authors' contributions begin.

RUSSELL H. FAZIO (75), Department of Psychology, Indiana University, Bloomington, Indiana 47405

SUSAN T. FISKE (1), Department of Psychology, University of Massachusetts, Amherst, Massachusetts 01003

FREDERICK X. GIBBONS (249), Department of Psychology, Iowa State University, Ames, Iowa 50011

RACHEL KARNIOL (211), Department of Psychology, Tel Aviv University, Ramat Aviv, Israel

CATHY MCFARLAND (305), Department of Psychology, Simon Fraser University, Burnaby, British Columbia, Canada V5A 1S6

JOHN W. MEDCOF (111), Faculty of Business, McMaster University, Hamilton, Ontario, Canada L8S 4M4

DALE T. MILLER (305), Department of Psychology, Princeton University, Princeton, New Jersey 08544

STEVEN L. NEUBERG (1), Department of Psychology, Arizona State University, Tempe, Arizona 85287

WILLIAM TURNBULL (305), Department of Psychology, Simon Fraser University, Burnaby, British Columbia, Canada V5A 1S6

PREFACE

In founding and editing 22 volumes of *Advances in Experimental Social Psychology,* Leonard Berkowitz created something unique and special for social psychology. Since becoming the new editor, I am more aware than ever of the extraordinary number of important citations in our field that have come from the "Berkowitz" series. Simply stated, my goal (and hope) is to be able to maintain that tradition of quality.

Following the procedure established by Professor Berkowitz, I plan to invite approximately one-half of the articles for each volume and to entertain submissions for the remaining half. Ideally, most submissions will be completed manuscripts; in some instances they may be outlines of proposed manuscripts. In either case, submissions should represent substantial theoretical and/or empirical contributions to the field.

Although I do not plan to have an editorial board (at least, not at first), I do intend to use reviewers for all the manuscripts I receive. The reviewers and I will strive to provide the sort of useful feedback that will make the articles accessible to the widest possible audience. It is my intention to make the editorial process constructive, collegial, and nonadversarial.

Because articles in *Advances* tend to be long, I will ask reviewers to provide a substantial amount of commentary. If the series continues to attract as high a quality of manuscript as it has in the past, reviewers will be pleased to be the first to see the articles. To put it another way, I will try my best to send reviewers manuscripts they will want to read.

On behalf of the authors and myself I thank Gene Borgida, Tom Gilovich, Tory Higgins, John Holmes, Ned Jones, Mel Lerner, Dale Miller, and Mike Ross for their timely and constructive reviews of the articles in Volume 23.

Mark P. Zanna

A CONTINUUM OF IMPRESSION FORMATION, FROM CATEGORY-BASED TO INDIVIDUATING PROCESSES: INFLUENCES OF INFORMATION AND MOTIVATION ON ATTENTION AND INTERPRETATION

Susan T. Fiske
Steven L. Neuberg

I. Introduction

> I just want to know how you can work on that schema stuff at the same time that you do work on information integration theory. The two just don't go together, do they? (Anonymous Ohio State University graduate student, question at a colloquium, 1979)

As implied by the graduate student's question, social psychologists have typically pursued different models of impression formation (for example, schematic and categorical approaches versus fully attribute-oriented approaches) in complete isolation from each other. However, common sense suggests that people do not use just one strategy to understand other people; they use a variety of strategies. People often make sense of other people by categorizing them, and, consequently, people's impressions of others are often primarily based on stereotypes and prejudices about familiar social groups. Alternatively, people sometimes make sense of other people by focusing instead on the others' own particular individuating characteristics, forming impressions based on the others' attributes that go beyond category membership. As a third possibility, people also make sense of other people by combining category membership and target attributes to recategorize others; in such cases, impressions are intermediate between fully category-based and fully individuating impressions. This article attempts an integrated understanding of these various impression formation processes.

Specifically, we address the following questions: What kinds of processes do people use to form impressions of others? Do any of these processes have priority over the others? What informational and motivational factors influence the use of these various processes? How do they do so? And when are people more likely to forgo category-based, stereotypic impression formation for more attribute-oriented, individuating impression formation?

In this article, we propose a model of impression formation that integrates social cognition research on stereotyping with traditional research on person perception. According to this model, people form impressions of others through a variety of processes that lie on a continuum reflecting the extent to which the perceiver utilizes a target's particular attributes. Toward one end of this continuum are category-based processes that use a target's category membership to the relative exclusion of the target's particular attributes. Toward the other end of the continuum are individuating processes that use a target's particular attributes to the relative exclusion of category membership. This model, then, implies that impression formation does not represent one type of process or the other exclusively. Moreover, the continuum implies that the distinctions among these processes are matters of degree, rather than discrete shifts.

The model's first premise posits that *category-based processes have priority over attribute-oriented processes* in two respects: Perceivers attempt category-based impression formation before they use more attribute-oriented impression formation, and if relatively category-oriented processes are successful, then the perceiver goes no further toward more attribute-oriented processes. The sequential priority of processes goes from category confirmation, to recategorization, to piecemeal integration of attributes. We will review research that indicates this variety of processes and supports the priority of the more category-based processes.

The second premise states that *progress along the impression formation continuum depends on the ease with which perceivers can interpret the target's attributes as fitting an available category*. To the extent that a perceiver can interpret a target's attributes to fit a category, either an initial category or one the perceiver subsequently constructs, the more category-based impression formation processes will occur. To the extent, however, that a perceiver is not able to fit a target's attributes to an appropriate category, the more attribute-oriented processes will occur. Accordingly, we will present research that specifies the informational conditions that typically elicit different interpretations of the fit between category and attributes, leading to different impression formation processes.

Third, the model proposes that attention is a necessary mediator through which the different types of impression formation take place. Specifically, the model posits that differential *attention to attribute information mediates the use of the impression formation continuum;* increased attention is necessary for more individuating impression formation. Supporting research by ourselves and others will also be reviewed here.

The fourth premise assumes that motivation influences impression formation outcomes. In a given situation, the particular *interdependence structure, specifically, the motivating agent's criteria for providing the perceiver's desired outcomes, will determine the likely goal of impression formation*. The motivating agent may be a third party to the interaction, may be the target, or may be the perceiver's self. Perceivers can be pushed toward the categorizing or individuating ends of the continuum, under circumstances in which they would ordinarily do otherwise, depending on the motivations resulting from a particular interdependence structure. We will review research supporting this analysis.

The fifth premise is that *motivational influences are also mediated by attentional and interpretive responses to attributes*. Variations in the perceived type of interdependence should directly affect the perceiver's attention and interpretation. As with the impact of various informational circumstances on the continuum of impression formation (Premise 3), attention is the necessary mediating mechanism, and interpretation determines the degree of perceived fit between category and attributes (Premise 2). Available research again supports this framework.

One of the model's fundamental purposes is to integrate diverse perspectives on impression formation, as indicated by the opening quotation. It is also designed to generate predictions about basic impression formation processes and to help generate interventions that can lessen the impact of stereotypes on impression formation. We begin by presenting the model, and next we define our terms in more detail. We then discuss research that supports each of the five basic premises. Competing models and hypotheses for further research are presented throughout.

II. A Continuum Model of Impression Formation Processes

A simple model of impression formation can reflect the balance between category-based and individuating processes, as influenced by informational and motivational factors (building on Fiske, 1982; Fiske & Pavelchak, 1986). As will be supported by our own and by other people's research, the model proposes the following sequence, components 4–6 being characterized as a continuum of impression formation: (1) Perceivers initially categorize others, and their immediate responses may be triggered by this category; (2) if the target is at least minimally relevant, perceivers' further attention to attribute information will be determined by informational and motivational factors; (3) attention to attributes in turn mediates use of the processes along the continuum that follows; (4) when possible, perceivers will confirm the initial category; (5) when an initial category cannot be confirmed, perceivers will recategorize according to a subcategory, new category, exemplar, or self-category; (6) when recategorization fails, perceivers will use fully individuated, attribute-by-attribute, piecemeal integration processes. Finally, perceivers may decide that further assessment is needed, in which event they attend further to the target's attributes, and the cycle repeats (see Fig. 1).

A. THE CONTINUUM MODEL

1. Initial Categorization

Perceivers initially categorize others immediately upon encountering information sufficient for cuing a meaningful social category. This information may be in the form of a physical feature (e.g., skin color, clothing, hair style), a verbalized or written category label (e.g., "Melissa is a banker"), a configuration of category-consistent attributes that cue a label in memory (e.g., young, male, disheveled, defiant expression, carries a knife), or some other form of information that becomes accessible concurrently with the initial perception of the target individual. Perceiving the most dominant of these immediately noticeable cues brings to mind an apparently appropriate social category. The relative dominance of various cues may be determined by their temporal primacy, physical manifestation, contextual novelty, relative accessibility, or relationship to the perceiver's mood (as will be reviewed below). Once the category is cued, category-relevant cognitions, affect, and behavioral tendencies become accessible, although the perceiver will not necessarily act upon them. This initial categorization stage occurs immediately upon encountering any target individual, is extremely rapid, and is essentially perceptual (cf. Bruner, 1957b). This initial stage reflects the findings of the cognitive stereotyping literature, to be reviewed, indicating the pervasiveness of social categorization. The most basic types of categories to be accessed for virtually any target include age, sex, ethnicity, and social class. Other types of categorization, for example, occupation, may or may not occur at this initial step depending on how obvious they are in context. A neatly dressed female, typing at a desk facing the hallway, outside the door leading to another office, may be rapidly categorized as "secretary" even though there is no label on her desk.

2. Degree of Personal Relevance

Following rapid initial categorization, the perceiver quickly determines whether the target is minimally interesting or personally relevant enough to warrant further processing (cf. Brewer, 1988). If not, then no additional process-

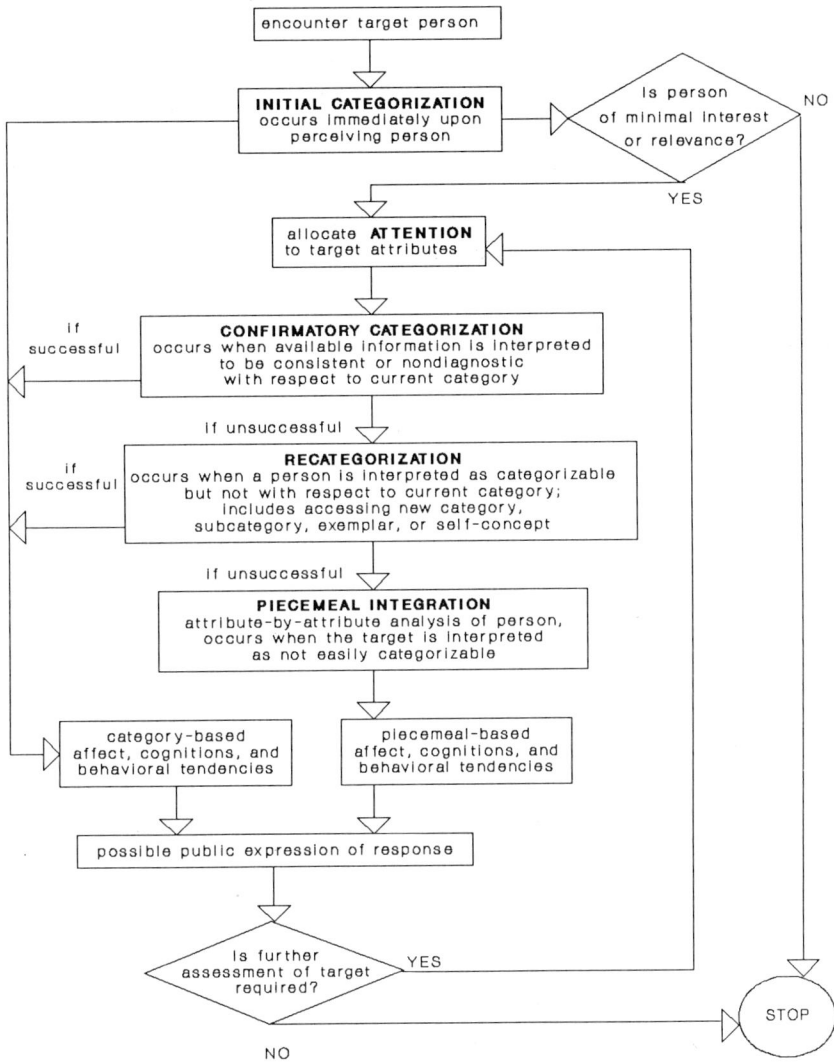

Fig. 1. The continuum model of impression formation. It shows the range from category-based to individuating impression formation processes, as a function of attention and interpretation. Informational and motivational conditions determine the attentional and interpretive processes that result in the various impression formation processes. Copyright © Susan T. Fiske, 1986.

ing will take place. If the target is at least minimally interesting or relevant, then the perceiver will attend to other noticeable information, information necessary to form an impression beyond the essentially perceptual, rapid, initial categorization. Thus, for example, while walking along a busy corridor, a perceiver may categorize a woman typing at a desk facing an open door as a secretary, but if the woman is neither interesting nor relevant to the perceiver, the perceiver's attention will move elsewhere. Alternatively, if the woman is in some way relevant to the perceiver, say, particularly attractive to a male or of particular social comparison relevance to a female, the perceiver instead will move on to the next stage of the model and attend to additional information at hand. If motivations extend beyond a minimal level of interest or relevance, then the interdependence structure between perceiver and target will determine the processes that follow; a later section will elaborate on the proposed operation of motivation.

3. Allocating Attention to Additional Target Attributes

If the perceiver has determined that the target individual is of sufficient personal relevance, the person will begin attending to, or collecting, additional information about the target. Attention to this information is necessary in order to assess the target in a manner beyond the essentially perceptual, rapid, initial categorization. The attention stage is especially important because it provides the raw material that heavily influences which of the alternative processes is utilized. Hence, attention to attributes mediates the extent to which people use relatively stereotypic or relatively more individuating processes. This single mediator is posited to transmit the effect of both informational and motivational influences on subsequent impression-formation processes. Hence, if the secretary is informationally incongruent (wearing a clown suit) or motivationally relevant (holds the keys to the xerox room), the perceiver will attend to her more than if she is neither interesting nor relevant.

4. Confirmatory Categorization

Interpretive processes come into play as the perceiver attends to information beyond the initial categorization. As the perceiver attends to additional information about the target, the perceiver will attempt to judge the target's typicality with regard to the initial categorization (cf. Bruner, 1957b). The exact criteria for interpreting whether an instance fits a category are clearly important but cannot be our primary concern here (for models of such processes see Brooks, 1978; Cantor & Mischel, 1979; Kahneman & Miller, 1986; Medin & Schaffer, 1978; Murphy & Medin, 1985; Rosch, 1978; Smith & Medin, 1981; Tversky, 1977).

If the additional information is interpreted to be either consistent with or adaptable to the initially determined category label, then the perceiver's affects, cognitions, and behavioral tendencies are likely to be based on the initial category. People often attempt to assimilate information to an initial category by a variety of interpretive processes to be described later. For example, if one observes the "secretary" running a meeting, which would be informationally incongruent, one might view her role there as that of entertaining people who are waiting for her boss, rather than attribute it to her intrinsic role in the meeting. This and similar strategies enable the perceiver to retain the initial categorization, and they reflect the difficulty of engaging in individuating processes. On the other hand, if the perceiver is unable to fit the target's attributes to the initial category, then the perceiver will move on to recategorization.

5. Recategorization

Recategorization represents an attempt to find a different category that can be interpreted as adequately organizing the bulk of current information. It may entail accessing a subcategory (e.g., a female administrative assistant; see Brewer, Dull, & Lui, 1981; Deaux & Lewis, 1984; Taylor, 1981; Weber & Crocker, 1983); subcategories allow the perceiver to retain many features of the initial category, while including some exceptional features. Recategorization may, instead, entail accessing an exemplar (e.g., "this woman reminds me of my sister Suzy"); exemplars clearly represent a common basis for judgment (Brooks, 1978; Kahneman & Miller, 1986), and their use fits with people's frequent reliance on low-level categories and subcategories rather than on abstract, global categories. Alternatively, the perceiver may access a self-schema ("this person reminds me of myself in certain ways"; Markus, 1977; Markus, Smith, & Moreland, 1985); reference to self-categories can organize the perception of others through social comparison processes. Or recategorization may entail accessing an entirely new category (e.g., changing one's category for Andre Watts from "famous black performer" to "classical musician"). Whether the perceiver accesses a subcategory, exemplar, self-category, or an altogether new category is not important here, as we assume that these different recategorization processes have fundamentally similar effects on impression formation.

If the perceiver can successfully recategorize the target, then the perceiver's affects, cognitions, and behavioral tendencies in relation to the target are likely to be those relevant to the new category. On the other hand, if the perceiver cannot recategorize the target, then the perceiver moves on to piecemeal integration. Note that the recategorization process is neither purely category-based nor entirely devoid of the initial category influence. That is, the initial categorization surely affects the selection of a new category, exemplar, or self-reference. But this process is also attribute-oriented to the extent that the new category is determined largely by the particular attributes of the target. Also note that we have posited that recategorization processes dominate piecemeal integration processes. Given the demonstrated strength of people's tendency to categorize others, this seems a reasonable assumption.

6. Piecemeal Integration

If the perceiver is unable either to confirm the initial categorization or to recategorize the target, and if the perceiver has sufficient time, resources, and motivation to understand that particular person, then the perceiver must integrate the available information in some sort of piecemeal, attribute-by-attribute fashion (N. H. Anderson, 1974; Fishbein & Ajzen, 1975). That is, the perceiver must average or add in some manner all of the target's particular characteristics in order to arrive at a final assessment of the individual. The perceiver's affects, beliefs, and behavioral tendencies will thus be heavily influenced by the results of this integration process, and the perceiver then will determine whether additional assessment is required. Note that this is the most individuating stage of all; the perceiver considers the target's attributes with minimal influence of any category. The category label at most counts as just another attribute, so the perceiver's responses will be relatively uncontaminated by category-based generalizations. Piecemeal processes occur, for example, when perceivers have to evaluate many individuals on the basis of a few specific dimensions, as in preliminary screening of clerical job applicants, or when one simply cannot meaningfully categorize the other on the basis of prior experience (e.g., a secretary who is black, Danish, and quantitatively oriented and who believes in the genetic determination of intelligence).

7. Public Expression of Internal Responses

Throughout, the model has posited that several processes result in category-based or attribute-based affects, cognitions, and behavioral tendencies. These responses need not be manifested behaviorally (as in public displays of prejudice, stereotyping, or discrimination), although quite obviously they often are. Unfortunately, a discussion of the factors that initiate or inhibit the public expression of these internal states is beyond the scope of this article. Others, however, have addressed this and similar issues (e.g., Abelson, 1981; Ajzen & Fishbein, 1977, 1980; Fazio, 1986; Kuhl, 1984; Saltzer, 1981; Snyder, 1982; Warshaw & Davis, 1985).

8. Is Further Assessment of the Target Required?

We have seen that, beyond the initial categorization stage, responses to the target can be elicited through successful confirmatory categorization processes, recategorization processes, or piecemeal integration processes. There are instances, however, in which these responses seem inadequate. For example, the need to reassess a target may arise from an inconsistency between one's assessment and the expectations one might have for future interactions. Suppose a perceiver's early assessment of a new, highly recommended secretary is negative; given the perceiver's hopes for teamwork, it seems unlikely that many perceivers are going to accept that discouraging assessment without first making an attempt to acquire additional information that better conforms to the initial expectations. When perceivers decide their conclusions are unsatisfactory, we posit that they will search for additional information, returning to the attention stage of the model. This time, however, instead of attempting to fit the target's attributes to an initial category, perceivers attempt to fit the attributes to the currently most accessible category. Thus, the loop of attending to target information and generating responses based on confirmatory categorization, recategorization, or piecemeal integration processes is continuous, until the perceiver makes an implicit decision that no more assessment is needed.

B. A CLARIFICATION: WHAT'S A CATEGORY AND WHAT'S AN ATTRIBUTE?

We have described a continuum model in which impression formation proceeds from relatively category-based processes to relatively attribute-based processes, and the bulk of this article is devoted to the relationships among these types of impression formation, as influenced by informational and motivational factors. However, we have yet to differentiate formally what we mean by categories and attributes. Individuals possess many features that potentially provide information useful for impression formation. These features may be observed (e.g., body size, skin color, voice tone), communicated by a third party (e.g., "Frank is a schizophrenic"; "Alan is brilliant"), or inferred by the perceiver through attributions from behavior in context (e.g., telling the truth, despite strong temptation to lie, suggests honesty).

The feature that a perceiver uses to organize and understand the remaining features defines the category label; the other features are defined here as attributes. Suppose, for example, that a bigoted white perceiver encounters an individual who is black, well dressed, and outgoing. To the extent the perceiver organizes the bulk of the target's features in terms of skin color (e.g., assumes that the person cannot be well off, so the expensive clothes reflect money obtained illegally), the perceiver is using "black" as the category label and the remaining features as attributes. Thus, operationally, the category label has more and stronger links to the attributes than any single attribute has to the other attributes; hence, the category label can be said to organize the attributes. The other attributes may have links to each other, but not strong links. Moreover, category–attribute linkages may be asymmetric (Andersen & Klatzky, 1987), with categories cuing attributes more easily than the converse. This analysis has several implications (see Lingle, Altom, & Medin, 1984, for a discussion of other issues related to the category–attribute distinction).

First, the category label may or may not be a verbal label, such as "black" or "Jewish." It may be a single feature treated as a label, for example, dark skin treated as a label for blackness. Or it may be a combination of a few critical features that cue a category label (e.g., secondary sex characteristics). For example, Deaux and Lewis (1984) found that a target's physical characteristics correlate as strongly as gender labels with other stereotype elements, suggesting the role of physical features in categorization (cf. McArthur, 1982).

Second, the category label is more likely to be a social grouping (demographic category, role, job) than a single personality trait. Recent research demonstrates the greater distinctiveness, richness, and vividness of social stereotype groupings compared to traits (Andersen & Klatzky, 1987), as well as their superior efficiency in cuing memory for acquaintances (Bond & Brockett, 1987; Bond & Sedikides, 1988). Accordingly, they are likely candidates for organizing a target's other features.

Third, the model proposes that perceivers initially categorize others rapidly, so the feature used as a category label does not have to organize the attributes *ideally* in any sense; rather, to serve the function of a category label, a feature must only organize the remaining features well enough, compared to the other initially noticeable features. Broad social categories, roles, and jobs are proposed to be the categories with which perceivers start out, although if the target is even minimally relevant, they rapidly move on to confirmatory categorization and recategorization, which provide more differentiated categories.

Finally, the same feature may or may not cue a category, depending on the context and the other features present. People potentially are classifiable into multiple social groupings, based on their many features. Hence, it is crucial to determine which category is likely to predominate in the perceiver's impression. If one cannot do this, arguments for the distinction between category and attributes cannot predict much about the actual impressions likely to be formed in any given case. Accordingly, we will address this last point in some detail.

Several characteristics of the environment and the perceiver combine with the target's features to determine which of many potential categories are likely to be used initially as a category label. Specifically, features that possess temporal primacy, have physical manifestations, are contextually novel, are chronically or acutely accessible in memory, or are related in particular ways to a perceiver's mood will tend to serve the role of category label, especially during the initial categorization stage. For example, the contextual primacy, or temporal priority, of a particular feature can heavily influence the social group into which an individual is categorized. The individual is more likely to be categorized in terms of features encountered initially, rather than those encountered later, because initial features typically have the most influence on impressions (Asch, 1946; Jones & Goethals, 1972).

A feature that is physically manifested is a likely basis for categorization because physical appearance is immediately apparent upon encountering someone in person. A target's physical appearance often cues stereotypes (McArthur, 1982; Secord, 1958). And many of the most pervasive social categories in our culture—race, age, sex, class—are a function of easily perceived physical features (Milord, 1978). Moreover, visual cues may dominate nonvisual cues when both are simultaneously present (Fiske & Cox, 1979; Posner, Nissen, & Klein, 1976). Thus, physically manifested features heavily influence how individuals are categorized.

An individual's contextual novelty also affects how he or she will be categorized. Whatever dimension is made salient by the surrounding environment will tend to be the one used for categorization (Taylor, 1981). For example, the race of a lone black in an otherwise all-white group, or the gender of a lone woman (man) in an otherwise all-male (all-female) group is especially salient (Taylor, Fiske, Close, Anderson, & Ruderman, 1977). People perceive the lone individual as playing special roles, often quite stereotypic, compared to the same behavior in a mixed group (cf. Kanter, 1977; Pettigrew & Martin, 1987; Wolman & Frank, 1975). Similar novelty effects even occur for relatively meaningless interpersonal categories (e.g., a red shirt among a group of blue shirts or vice versa; McArthur & Post, 1977). Therefore, the target's novelty in context can substantially influence the basis for categorization.

The relative accessibility of social categories available to the perceiver can also influence which category among many will be utilized for understanding a target. A category's accessibility depends partly on the recency of its activation (Higgins, Rholes, & Jones, 1977; Srull & Wyer, 1979; Wyer & Srull, 1980, 1981). For example, if one has just returned from a conference on aging, one may be especially likely to categorize an older Hispanic woman as a member of the category "elderly" than as a member of the category "Hispanic." Moreover, a category can be chronically accessible, or permanently primed, based on its frequency of activation in the past (Bargh & Pratto, 1986; Bargh, Bond, Lombardi, & Tota, 1986; Higgins & King, 1981; Higgins, King, & Maven, 1982). The relevant cues need not be in conscious awareness in order to prime categories (Bargh et al., 1986; Bargh & Pietromonaco, 1982; Neuberg, 1988). Thus, the recency and frequency of exposure to events in the past can significantly influence which categories perceivers are most likely to use.

Finally, one's mood at the time of encountering a target can influence the category selected. Mood activates mood-congruent knowledge in memory (Bower, 1981; Clark & Isen, 1982; Isen, 1984). Furthermore, mood can influence which among several available features will be utilized by the perceiver to form an impression (Erber, 1985). For example, people in a positive mood will tend to categorize the target with respect to positive features.

In sum, temporal primacy, physical manifestation, contextual novelty, relative accessibility, and perceiver mood will influence which among the many possible features a perceiver will use to categorize a target. However, certain types of information (social roles, jobs, demographic categories) appear more likely to be used as categories than others, based on their ability to organize other target information in memory.

C. SUMMARY OF THE MODEL

The model proposes four general impression-formation processes: the rapid, "perceptual," initial categorization process that requires no attention to potentially individuating attributes, and three "thoughtful" processes—confirmatory categorization, recategorization, and piecemeal integration—that do require attention to and interpretation of potentially individuating target information. Of these three processes, which together constitute a continuum of impression formation, confirmatory categorization is hypothesized to occur when available information can be interpreted to fit the initial categorization; recategorization is hypothesized to occur when the available information is categorizable but does not fit the initial categorization; and piecemeal integration is hypothesized to occur when the available information as a whole does not seem to fit any particular category. Motivational factors also influence the use of each process, as will be described later.

The vital premises of this model are all supported by previous research findings, to be reviewed in the sections that follow: First, the model posits that perceivers give priority to category-based processes over more individuating processes. Second, the model posits that interpretation of category–attribute fit determines use of the continuum. Accordingly, information configuration, specifically, ease of confirmatory categorization, influences the use of alternative impression-formation processes along the continuum. Third, the allocation of attention to attributes is the key mechanism underlying the utilization of various impression formation processes. Fourth, the model posits that motivations can alter how the perceiver forms impressions and, specifically, that the particular interdependence structure moves the perceiver's impression formation goals toward one or the other end of the continuum. Finally, attention to and interpretation of attributes are also posited to mediate the effects of motivations on impression formation. Alternatives to the continuum model are discussed in the penultimate section of this article.

III. Premise 1: Perceivers Give Priority to Category-Based Processes

The model's first premise is that category-based processes typically have priority over more attribute-oriented processes. This section reviews literature on the cognitive orientation toward stereotyping in order to support this position. This review does not attempt to represent thoroughly the entire contribution of the cognitive orientation to our understanding of stereotyping. Rather, it focuses on the work most relevant to supporting the claim that category-based processes have priority over individuating processes.

A. SOCIAL CATEGORIZATION IS AN ADAPTIVE AND PERVASIVE PROCESS

The normal cognitive process of categorization is central to social as well as to nonsocial perception. Just as people possess cognitive categories for furniture, automobiles, and birds, they also possess cognitive categories for social groups (e.g., black women, blue-collar workers, politicians, the physically handicapped). People's general knowledge about the attributes of a category is assumed to be well organized and to facilitate the understanding of new information; such organized knowledge is termed a schema (Cantor & Mischel, 1979; Fiske & Dyer, 1985; Fiske & Linville, 1980; Fiske & Taylor, 1984, chap. 6; Hastie, 1981; Markus & Zajonc, 1985; Taylor & Crocker, 1981). A schema by definition is a cognitive structure that contains knowledge about the expected attributes of a certain category and the links among these attributes (Rumelhart & Ortony, 1977). Social categories and schemas can thus be conceptualized as instances of a more general phenomenon, for they serve to organize knowledge, in this instance, knowledge about a certain group of people.

Social categorization—the process of matching a target person to a prior social category—is important for several reasons. First, people gain meaning from new elements in their environment by relating these new elements to past experiences, that is, by categorizing them. Certainly, none of this is new: Bartlett (1932) discussed the role of past experiences in the process of understanding events and introduced the schema concept; Gestalt psychology emphasized the effects that perceptual configurations and expectations have on the perception of objects and people (cf. Asch, 1946); and Bruner (1957a) discussed going "beyond the information given" via the active construction of reality, drawing heavily on one's previous experiences. Moreover, it seems safe to state that people cannot gain an understanding of new information in the environment without first relating it in some way to previous experiences (Vinacke, 1957; but cf. Gibson, 1979; McArthur & Baron, 1983). Thus, psychologists have long viewed categorization as a necessary and pervasive cognitive process (Bruner, 1958; Rosch & Lloyd, 1978; Smith & Medin, 1981). In the social world, categorization is likely to be especially important because immediate responses are required and one's verbal and nonverbal behavior depend on each person's role.

Furthermore, people must categorize others for the additional reason that we are exposed to so much information that we must in some manner simplify our social environment (Allport, 1954; Lippmann, 1922; Tajfel, 1969). We have neither the cognitive capacity nor the time to deal with all the interpersonal information we have available to us. Hence, the perceiver has been characterized as a "cognitive miser" (Fiske & Taylor, 1984; cf. Mischel, 1979). For reasons of cognitive economy, we categorize others as members of particular groups— groups about which we often have a great deal of generalized, or stereotypic, knowledge. Given our limited cognitive resources, it is both simpler (requires less effort) and more efficient (requires less time) for a perceiver to use stereotypic information to make inferences about individuals belonging to a group than it is to analyze each person on an individual basis without benefit of this integrated, prior information. For example, it typically takes longer to form an attribute-oriented impression than a category-oriented impression (Fiske, Neuberg, Beattie, & Milberg, 1984; see Fiske & Pavelchak, 1986, for a review of relevant research). Moreover, attribute-oriented processes seem to require greater attentional resources than do category-based processes (e.g., Bechtold, Naccarato, & Zanna, 1986). But some implications of the adaptability argument still need to be tested more directly. Additional studies measuring response time, subjective effort, capacity, and the like should show that categorization is easier than more attribute-oriented processing.

Research on stereotyping thus assumes that social categorization is a necessary, if unfortunate, byproduct of our cognitive makeup. For example, Allport (1954, p. 19) wrote, "Open-mindedness is considered to be a virtue. But, strictly speaking, it cannot occur. A new experience must be redacted into old categories." More recently, Ashmore and Del Boca (1981, p. 29) stated that "cognitive limitations make humans susceptible to systematic biases in processing information about people and events, and these biases contribute significantly to the formation and maintenance of stereotypes regarding social groups." Moreover, Hamilton (1979, p. 80) extends the argument for the necessity and naturalness of such cognitive biases by noting that these biases are adaptive: "The cognitive mechanisms we use [in stereotyping] continue to be employed because, in some sense, they work. The biases . . . help reduce the complexity of the stimulus world which may otherwise be overwhelming and hence are in many circumstances quite adaptive" (cf. Hamilton, 1981; A. G. Miller, 1982).

Thus, social categorization is in one sense a necessary and adaptive process given the logic of human cognition. Moreover, category-based processes minimally deplete cognitive resources, compared to more attribute-oriented processes. Because social categorization is adaptive and efficient, then, it should have priority in impression formation over an attribute-by-attribute examination of each person as a unique individual.

B. IMMEDIATELY ACCESSIBLE, CATEGORY-RELEVANT RESPONSES POTENTIALLY PREEMPT ATTRIBUTE-ORIENTED RESPONSES

Although perceivers categorize frequently, and perhaps unavoidably, the priority of social categorization would not matter except for its immediate consequences: Category-relevant responses are accessible immediately upon classifying an individual as a member of some social group (Allport, 1954; Cauthen, Robinson, & Krauss, 1971; Secord, 1959; Tajfel, 1969). As Gordon Allport (1954, p. 20) noted, "A person with dark brown skin will activate whatever concept of Negro is dominant in our mind. If the dominant category is one composed of negative attitudes and beliefs we will automatically avoid him, or adopt whichever habit of rejection is most available to us." For example, when people categorize an individual in a photograph as being a member of the "Negro" category, they ascribe stereotypic traits to the individual (Secord, Bevan, & Katz, 1956). Likewise, categorizing someone by gender (Taylor, Fiske, Etcoff, & Ruderman, 1978), mental illness (Langer & Abelson, 1974), occupation (C. E. Cohen, 1981), and personality traits (Cantor & Mischel, 1979) also can result in stereotypic beliefs about the target individual. Moreover, affect toward the target can result from the category to which the target has been assigned (Fiske, 1982; Fiske, Neuberg, Beattie, & Milberg, 1987; Fiske & Pavelchak, 1986; Pavelchak, 1989). Finally, the category in which a target individual is placed can have significant consequences for the perceiver's behavior toward the target (Hilton & Darley, 1985; Snyder, Tanke, & Berscheid, 1977; Word, Zanna, & Cooper, 1974; for reviews of the above work see Brigham, 1971; Fiske & Taylor, 1984, chap. 6; Hamilton & Trolier, 1986).

In many situations, then, perceivers relate the target individual to preexisting categories, and they utilize the contents of these categories to form their beliefs, feelings, and behavioral possibilities. However, the mere process of categorization has significant effects even when there are no preexisting categories (for reviews see Brewer, 1979; Wilder, 1981). For example, even when target stimuli (objects or people) are arbitrarily assigned to an explicitly random group label (e.g., "A" or "B"), people overestimate both the similarities of members within a particular category and the differences between members of different categories (Tajfel, 1969; Tajfel & Wilkes, 1963; Taylor, 1981; Wilder, 1978).

Furthermore, striking effects of social categorization are found when people are separated into an "ingroup" and "outgroup" on the basis of such trivial tasks as estimating the number of dots presented on a slide (cf. Tajfel, Billig, Bundy, & Flament, 1971). People assume that members of their own group have beliefs more similar to their own than do members of other groups (Allen & Wilder, 1975). Moreover, people preferentially treat members of an arbitrarily determined ingroup, whether in assigning positive traits or in allocating rewards (Allen & Wilder, 1975; Billig & Tajfel, 1973; Brewer & Silver, 1978; Rabbie & Wilkins, 1971; Tajfel & Billig, 1974).

Thus, one's cognitive, affective, and behavioral responses to an individual are heavily influenced by social categorization. Once one categorizes an individual, either as belonging to a particular category about which one has specific knowledge or as merely belonging to an outgroup, one immediately has accessible category-based responses to the individual. The important point here is that, because category-relevant responses are activated immediately, the information required to form category-based impressions is potentially more accessible to perceivers than is the attribute information needed to form more individuated impressions. Consequently, category-based impression formation may well occupy a position of priority over more individuating types of impression formation.[1]

C. CATEGORIES FUNCTION TO DISCOURAGE INDIVIDUATION

Once a perceiver has accessed a social category, it becomes more difficult for the perceiver to respond accurately to a target's particular characteristics; this makes individuating impression formation less likely. We will discuss how categories influence what one perceives, remembers, and infers about a target. All else being equal, one's perceptions, memories, and inferences become consistent with one's expectations about the particular category accessed. For example, if one passes a male construction worker, without any particular need to think about him, and if one believes that construction workers are beer-guzzling rednecks, then regardless of this particular individual's attributes, one will tend to notice the tattoo on his upper arm, remember him ogling the attractive woman walking past on the sidewalk (whether he did or not), and infer that he is not very

---

[1]Although social categorization clearly makes accessible a variety of stereotypic, prejudicial, and discriminatory responses, this is certainly not to say that perceivers inevitably form category-based impressions of targets upon categorizing them. Indeed, the bulk of this article is devoted to explicating the informational and motivational circumstances that elicit more individuating kinds of impression formation.

intellectual. However, there are important limits on the extent to which categories override potentially individuating, inconsistent information. As our model predicts, the more attention one pays to the target, the more likely one is to notice, remember, and use information inconsistent with the initial category (cf. Higgins & Bargh, 1987).

First, social categorization doubtless influences one's perception of a target. For example, once a target has been categorized, that target may be perceived as having category-appropriate attributes, regardless of how representative the individual is of typical category members (Secord, 1959; Secord et al., 1956). In other words, the perceiver minimizes the variability of members within the particular category (Park & Rothbart, 1982; Quattrone & Jones, 1980; Tajfel & Wilkes, 1963; Wilder, 1981). The phenomenon "they all look alike to me" (Malpass & Kravits, 1969; Malpass, Lavigueur, & Weldon, 1973) is an example of minimizing within-group variability. At low levels of contact between groups, perceivers may look for similarities among outgroup members, thereby enhancing the perception of homogeneity (Quattrone, 1986). Moreover, contact with outgroup members is likely to be limited to a few constrained roles and settings and to a few subtypes, all of which would limit the outgroup's perceived variability (Quattrone, 1986).

Moreover, categorization also influences interpretations of the individual's actions. For example, a child taking an eraser from another may be perceived as mean and threatening if black, but not so if white (Duncan, 1976; Sagar & Schofield, 1980). An identical comment may be seen as spiteful coming from a woman and cynical coming from a man (Taylor et al., 1978). Stereotypic perceptions thus occur even when the same behavior is performed by members of different categories (Ruble & Ruble, 1982; Stephan & Rosenfield, 1982). Furthermore, stereotypic interpretations influence perception at its earliest moments (Devine, 1989; Dovidio, Evans, & Tyler, 1986; Gaertner & McLaughlin, 1983; Klatzky, Martin, & Kane, 1982). These findings seem to suggest, then, that people do not necessarily perceive the potentially individuating information presented to them as actually being individuating. To date, research on perception (as apart from memory and inference) has not explored the limits on category-consistent interpretation at encoding. However, because our model posits that attention must precede any process beyond the rapid initial categorization, the model predicts that increased attention to the target is necessary to undercut category-consistent perceptions. All else being equal (attention not being increased), categorization encourages category-consistent perception.

One's memory for target-relevant information is also heavily influenced by the category applied to the target. Again, under ordinary circumstances, categories can bias memory in the direction of category-consistent attributes (Cantor & Mischel, 1979; C. E. Cohen, 1981; O'Sullivan & Durso, 1984; Rothbart, Evans, & Fulero, 1979; Snyder & Uranowitz, 1978; Tsujimoto, 1978; Tsujimoto, Wilder & Robertson, 1978). In particular, people may guess or infer that bogus category-consistent events are more likely, given the target's category.

This is not to say that people ignore category-inconsistent information—information that seems especially suited for eliciting more individuating impression formation (cf. Alba & Hasher, 1983; Hastie, 1981). Two reviews have concurrently concluded that memory for consistent and inconsistent information depends on the degree to which an expectancy has already developed (Higgins & Bargh, 1987; Ruble & Stangor, 1986). When perceivers are initially developing an impression, they recall expectancy-inconsistent information, but when the expectancy is well developed, they recall expectancy-consistent information. Because social stereotypes are generally well-developed categories, our model favors recall for consistent information. Moreover, as indicated in our own review of the informational conditions of stereotyping and individuating processes (below, under Premise 2 of the model), we have independently come to a similar conclusion.

As our model predicts, attentional processes again are key in memory for inconsistency, even in a developing impression. Inconsistency is well remembered only when the perceiver spends time attending to it (Bargh & Thein, 1985; Brewer et al., 1981; Hastie & Kumar, 1979; Sentis & Burnstein, 1979; Srull, 1981; see Higgins & Bargh, 1987, for a review), but not so much otherwise. Attention appears necessary, first, for expectancy-inconsistent information to be actually perceived as inconsistent. Second, attention apparently allows perceivers to integrate the inconsistent information into their impression of a meaningful person or group, thereby linking the inconsistency to the other information and thus making it more retrievable (Srull, Lichtenstein, & Rothbart, 1985). Such attention, however, takes time, on-line, as perceivers initially encounter information about the target. Because in real-life interactions people rarely have the opportunity to stop the rapid flow of interpersonal information, paying attention may be difficult, thereby making memory for inconsistent information less likely (cf. Bargh & Thein, 1985).

Third, another attentional factor discourages memory for inconsistency. Having extra time, after the actual encounter, to integrate inconsistent information into an impression also reduces the memorability of inconsistency (Wyer & Martin, 1986). Poststimulus thought tends to increase the coherence of impressions (Tesser, 1978), for people are quite facile at resolving inconsistency and forming overall impressions (e.g., Asch & Zukier, 1984). Notably, many of those studies that do show a memory advantage for category-inconsistent information have interpolated a distraction task between stimulus presentation and recall, perhaps making it difficult for perceivers to resolve the inconsistency and thereby rendering it especially memorable. Thus, the results of these studies might not generalize to situations in which people have time afterwards to think about what they have perceived, as is often the case.

Expectancy-inconsistent information is, thus, particularly recalled only under certain constraining circumstances: When the expectancy is first developing, but before it becomes a well-established category; when one has time to integrate it on-line; and when one does not have time to dwell on the inconsistency later. These would seem to be fairly limited circumstances for inconsistency to be recalled well.

Of course, even when inconsistency is incorporated into memory, it can be incorporated in ways that support an initial categorization. For example, people can attribute inconsistencies to temporary situational factors, making them irrelevant to the target's enduring disposition (Crocker, Hannah, & Weber, 1983; Hastie, 1984; Kulik, 1983). Whether this happens depends partly on the particular configuration of information and partly on motivational factors, both of which we will discuss later. Overall, however, the "default option" does not seem to favor a major role for inconsistency under many everyday circumstances.

Finally, one's inferences about an individual are also influenced by the particular category to which the individual has been assigned. For example, ingroup members are inferred to have better personalities, less responsibility for failure, more responsibility for success, and greater similarity to oneself than are outgroup members (Allen & Wilder, 1975; Billig & Tajfel, 1973; Brewer & Silver, 1978; Hamilton & Trolier, 1986). Moreover, the perceiver infers characteristics of an individual that are consistent with the individual's ascribed category. Thus, referring to a previous example, although one might not have any information about the intellectual capabilities of a particular construction worker, one would tend to infer that this construction worker was not an intellectual on the basis of one's stereotypes of construction workers in general.

In sum, perception, memory, and inference are clearly shaped by the social category to which an individual is assigned. Furthermore, in the absence of increased attention, these processes emphasize information consistent with the perceiver's category-based expectations. Hence, it might seem difficult for a person to respond to another in an individuating manner, once the person has been initially categorized. These findings, too, then suggest that category-based impression formation may have priority over more individuating impression-formation processes.

D. ISSUES RELATED TO THE PRIORITY OF CATEGORY-BASED PROCESSES

We hope to have made the point that category-based processes are likely to have priority in impression formation. First, social categorization processes are basic, adaptive, and efficient. Second, social categorization makes immediately accessible the category-relevant responses (cognitions, affect, and behavioral tendencies) that potentially preempt attribute-oriented responses. Finally, the functions of categories tend to discourage the use of other, more potentially individuating information. However, all this evidence is open to a pair of critical misinterpretations, which we address now.

1. Do Social Perceivers Categorize without Intent?

One might mistakenly assume that stereotyping, prejudice, and discrimination operate unintentionally because perceivers apparently have few options to respond otherwise. Category-based social responses might be seen as an inevitable side effect of necessary and adaptive cognitive processes, driven by the exigencies of the environment. Unfortunately, the cognitive stereotyping evidence has all too easily led some readers to the erroneous and pessimistic conclusion that people are essentially "wired" to categorize others, either through innate or overlearned cognitive factors, and thus that people will inevitably stereotype others. If people essentially have no other options, then people stereotype others without intent, and thus without responsibility. For example, in reviewing this literature, Jones *et al.* (1984) note that "if stereotypes are normal by-products of the inevitable selecting and packaging of data from a complex world, . . . will stigma not always be with us? Contemporary cognitive approaches to stereotyping . . . [project] a rather weary fatalism. The subprocesses involved in stigmatization are seen as . . . ingrained human proclivities" (p. 300). In his review, Hamilton (1979, p. 80) calls the implications of the cognitive approach "a rather depressing dilemma." The assumption that cognitive explanations for stereotyping imply a lack of intent also surfaces frequently in original empirical articles, including those involving the senior author: "Race is used as an encoding strategy . . . regardless of whether a perceiver is intentionally trying" (Taylor *et al.*, 1978, p. 782). Another cognitively oriented empirical article even states that "stereotypes operate unconsciously as automatic expectations" (V. Brown & Geis, 1984, p. 812).

These conclusions are both unnecessarily depressing and inaccurate. People do initially categorize others according to normal, predictable cognitive principles, without the explicit operation of motivation. Moreover, category-based impression formation may dominate, at least under many of the circumstances in which most research has been conducted so far. But people also individuate under specifiable circumstances, as we will see, and they appear to have some control over these processes. In short, if perceivers create options to override their initial categorizations by paying more attention, as our model and supporting research indicate, then stereotyping is amenable to intentional control. Hence, it is premature to assume that social perceivers stereotype wholly without intent (see Fiske, 1989, for a detailed discussion of these issues).

2. Are Category-Based Processes the Most Common Type of Impression Formation?

Based on the cognitive stereotyping literature, the proposed model makes a fundamental assumption about the priority of category-oriented processes. Category-based processes seem to be the default option. First, people initially categorize others. Second, perceivers often form their impressions on the basis of the category when they do not pay enough attention to individuate and when they are not explicitly motivated to do otherwise—common conditions in everyday life. People frequently need to form rapid impressions of others; it is abundantly clear that people cannot routinely form well-differentiated impressions of most of the others with whom they interact. Moreover, in addition to the research evidence, the importance of category-based responses is further suggested by the persistence of gender-based, race-based, class-based, and similarly stereotypic responses in our society. For example, although people's verbally expressed racial attitudes have improved, subtle forms of race-based responses are still commonly documented (Crosby, Bromley, & Saxe, 1980).

On the other hand, there clearly exist alternative, more individuating impression-formation processes that people utilize every day. The remainder of this article is devoted to explicating them. Social psychologists have insufficiently studied the cognitive processes underlying individuation, probably because they are not perceived to be a pressing problem in the same way that stereotyping is. We concur with researchers who argue that individuating processes have been neglected (e.g., Higgins & Bargh, 1987; Locksley, Borgida, Brekke, & Hepburn, 1980; Nisbett, Zukier, & Lemley, 1981). But we do not agree with the implication, sometimes made, that individuating processes typically dominate category-based processes or that stereotypes only matter under the most trivial circumstances. The evidence simply does not indicate that category-based processes are less important than individuating processes. Categories clearly do matter; individuation clearly also occurs. In an attempt to integrate these two factors, we will describe some conditions under which each occurs.

Note that one cannot ultimately resolve the overall question of whether category-based or individuating processes are more common in daily life. One cannot feasibly do a representative sample survey of people's impression formation processes; one can merely demonstrate that category-based and individuating processes occur under specifiable circumstances and then argue that those circumstances are more or less representative of life outside the lab. Assertions about actual frequencies of each process are simply not provable. This is not to discourage research on these issues. Our own position is that under ordinary conditions, people simply do not pay enough attention to individuate each other. This is testable by specifying what constitutes "ordinary conditions," and researchers can certainly disagree about the operationalizing of daily life circumstances.

Accordingly, rather than asserting simply that one process or the other is more common, it seems more profitable to specify some likely conditions of each type of process, to argue for their ecological validity, and then to concentrate on the processes by which category-based and individuating impressions each occur.

To that end, we will next discuss various types of impression formation—ranging from the category-based processes discussed above to some more individuating alternatives—as we discuss the different informational conditions that elicit them.

IV. Premise 2: Interpretation of Fit between Category and Attributes Determines Use of the Continuum

Although category-based processes have high priority, as just discussed, and people do categorize other people in order to simplify the complexity of the social world, people also go beyond their categorizations to form impressions of others in ways that have not received as much research attention lately. The model explicitly posits that impression formation processes constitute a continuum and that various informational conditions tend to elicit the various processes because they lend themselves more easily or less easily to interpreting the target's attributes as fitting an initial category. Perceivers actively use the available information, and its configuration importantly determines whether they form impressions based on an individual's category membership, whether they form impressions based on the individual's particular attributes, or whether they do something in-between. The ease of fitting attributes to a given category, as interpreted by the perceiver, locates impressions along the category-based versus individuating continuum. Targets whose attributes easily fit their category membership elicit responses toward the category-based end. Other targets, whose attributes are more difficult to interpret as fitting their category, elicit responses toward the fully individuated end. Accordingly, the information configurations that affect the perceived ease of categorization are critical.

Our model therefore predicts, and considerable research now supports, both the various alternative impression-formation processes available to perceivers and the informational conditions that tend to elicit them. The discussion is organized from most to least category-based processes. The section first discusses initial categorization, as well as when it occurs. Second, the section describes informational conditions that facilitate confirmatory categorization processes, whereby part of the available information suggests a category and perceivers interpret the remaining information as subjectively validating the category. The section next discusses the intermediate mode of response, recategorization, which modifies the available category in light of the individual's other particular attributes. And last, we discuss the individuating, attribute-by-attribute response that comparatively neglects category membership and relies on a piecemeal integration of the other attribute information. Throughout, the discussion emphasizes how information configurations influence the ease of interpreting category–attribute fit.

A. INITIAL CATEGORIZATION

Initial categorization occurs (1) upon access to a category label and no immediately accessible additional target attributes and (2) upon access to a set of target attributes that easily cue a particular category label. Upon initial categorization, perceivers necessarily form impressions of the target on the basis of the category only because no additional, nonredundant target attributes are present. This is thus the purest form of category-based impression formation. Although these are fairly obvious configurations for category-based processing, these conditions do provide a useful baseline for comparison to the other informational conditions that elicit confirmatory categorization, intermediate recategorization, or piecemeal integration.

It may be helpful to recall that initial categorization is, strictly, off the continuum of the other impression-formation processes described in this section. That is, the model specifies initial categorization as an essentially perceptual process, preceding attention, while the processes that fall on the continuum itself—confirmatory categorization, recategorization, and piecemeal integration—presuppose attention. Nevertheless, in another sense, initial categorization is the purest category-based process, so it anchors the continuum in that respect despite its qualitative differences from the other processes.

1. Category-Label Only

Not surprisingly, when people are provided with a social category label or a single feature that easily elicits categorization, essentially without any other information, and are asked to make a judgment, they use the label. When subjects are asked to specify the attributes of various ethnic groups (D. Katz & Braly, 1933; Gilbert, 1951; Karlins, Coffman, & Walters, 1969), they have generally been able and willing to do so.[2] And, as discussed earlier, when

---

[2]This research has been justifiably criticized as not showing that subjects necessarily believe or use category-based processes. For one, many subjects refuse to answer these questions, and the number of refusals has grown over time. Second, just because subjects can report cultural stereotypes does not mean that they personally subscribe to them. Nevertheless, subsequent research suggests that cultural stereotypes are indeed accessible and influential immediately upon the perceiver's encountering such labels (e.g., Devine, 1989; Dovidio, Evans, & Tyler, 1986; Gaertner & McLaughlin, 1983; Klatzky, Martin, & Kane, 1982).

perceivers see a photograph of a black person, they often ascribe stereotypic traits to the individual (Secord *et al.*, 1956).

Moving to more recent research, when asked how generally assertive Susan and Paul are, subjects reported that she is less assertive than he (Locksley *et al.*, 1980, Study 2; Rasinski, Crocker, & Hastie, 1985). Similarly, when told simply that Lou A. is a night person, subjects inferred that he is rebellious, unconventional, not responsible, not healthy, and not self-controlled (Locksley, Hepburn, & Ortiz, 1982, Study 1). When told that John V. is an engineering major planning a career in aerospace engineering, subjects inferred that he would tolerate more electric shock than would Alan H., a music major planning to be either a professional musician in an orchestra or band or a teacher of music (Nisbett *et al.*, 1981, Studies 1–2, cf. Study 3; for a contrasting finding see Darley & Gross, 1983, control condition). All of these category-based responses came solely from labeling information (see Ruble & Ruble, 1982; Stephan & Rosenfield, 1982, for other examples). Thus, it seems clear that perceivers generate category-based impressions upon encountering a category label alone.

2. Easily Categorized Attributes

Furthermore, when no explicit label is available, but the attributes together strongly suggest an organizing category, subjects also respond in a category-based manner. For example, when a target was described as being quick-tempered and aroused by sadomasochistic fantasies, subjects easily judged the person as likely to be a child abuser (Nisbett *et al.*, 1981, Studies 4–5). When a student was described as often starting things he does not finish, subjects easily judged him to be a low achiever (Zukier, 1982). This evidence indicates only that subjects are capable of generating a social category from target attributes. However, previous evidence strongly suggests that once a category label is cued, without the presence of any additional target information, category-based impression formation is likely to follow.

B. CONFIRMATORY CATEGORIZATION

What happens when perceivers encounter attributes in addition to a noticeable or accessible category label? We propose that the perceiver will first attempt to use the additional target attributes to confirm the accessible category. Successful category confirmation is most likely to occur (1) when the additional target attributes are consistent with the category label; (2) when the additional attributes are nondiagnostic because they are mixed (i.e., some category-consistent and some category-inconsistent); and (3) when the attributes are nondiagnostic because they are irrelevant to both the category label and the judgment at hand, but when the category label represents a relatively strong stereotype.

1. Label plus Category-Consistent Attributes

When subjects encounter a social category label plus category-consistent attributes, they not surprisingly form category-based impressions. Category-consistent stimuli have included campus categories (e.g., an engineer photographed wearing nerd clothes and working at a computer terminal; Fiske, 1982, Study 3), occupations (e.g., a loan shark described as opportunistic, shady, greedy, shrewd, and heartless; Fiske et al., 1987, Study 1), mental patient categories (e.g., a schizophrenic described as out-of-touch, obsessive, hallucinating, and bizarre; Fiske, Neuberg, Pratto, & Allman, 1986, Studies 1–2), and gender (e.g., John Stevens described as a business major and economics minor; Heilman, 1984; or Paul, who forcefully tells a seedy pest to go away, prevents the teacher's pet from monopolizing the class, and also breaks into a group conversation at a party; Locksley et al., 1980, Study 1).

Of course, in these studies, it is not clear whether subjects were responding on the basis of the ascribed category or on the basis of the category-consistent attributes, given that both bases for response would yield similar outcomes. Results of other work, however, seem congruent with the notion that, given a category label and category-consistent attributes, subjects use the consistent attributes to confirm the validity of the label. In a series of studies by Fiske et al. (1984; also described in Fiske & Pavelchak, 1986), subjects invariably took less time to form impressions of targets when the attributes were consistent with a category label than when the attributes were either inconsistent with a label or when the same attributes were present without a label. Because inconsistent and attribute-only conditions typically lead to more attribute-oriented impression formation, as will be discussed later, the point here is that subjects encountering category-consistent attributes apparently were not spending enough time to form more individuating, attribute-oriented impressions. Rather, the latency data support the idea that subjects were merely checking the fit of the consistent attributes to the category, confirming its validity, and subsequently responding on the basis of the category and its contents.

In addition, more detailed analyses (i.e., having perceivers think aloud as they form impressions) have more directly revealed the existence of confirmatory categorization processes (Erber & Fiske, 1984; Fiske et al., 1987). Most of the time, perceivers spontaneously test the consistency of the target's attributes with the category label. Moreover, perceivers often confirm the category by interpreting attributes that had pretested as category-inconsistent to be consistent instead. Thus, the attribute "strong" was generally perceived by subjects to refer to physical strength when the category label was "construction worker," although strong was interpreted as meaning "strong-minded" when the label provided was "professor." Hence, it appears that perceivers mainly respond to the label, once they quickly confirm its fit to the category-consistent attributes.

2. Label plus Mixed Attributes

When perceivers encounter a label and mixed (category-consistent plus category-inconsistent) attributes, they also appear to make category-based judgments (e.g., Bodenhausen, 1988; Bodenhausen & Lichtenstein, 1987; Dipboye, Fromkin, & Wiback, 1975; Duncan, 1976; Heneman, 1977; Sagar & Schofield, 1980). In fact, some evidence suggests that this is indeed the case even when the label is not explicit. In one study, subjects viewed a videotape that provided easily categorizable social class information (the implicit label) showing a child's school, home, and playground environments (Darley & Gross, 1983). When provided with additional information showing the child's test performance to be mixed, subjects rated the wealthier child has having higher ability than the poorer child. These data seem to indicate a stereotype-confirming interpretative bias, in line with other evidence of expectancy confirmation (see Darley & Fazio, 1980, for a review). A range of studies show that subjects' judgments of ambiguous, mixed information are heavily influenced by stereotypic labels (Fiske & Taylor, 1984; Higgins & Bargh, 1987; Markus & Zajonc, 1985). We posit that this is the case because these types of mixed attribute information enable the perceiver to confirm the validity of the category label.

One well-known study, however, failed to reliably find such an effect. Subjects were given male or female names for targets, along with assertive or passive labels for their behavior in four psychology experiments (Locksley, Hepburn, & Ortiz, 1982, Experiment 2). Five of the conditions were balanced: they depicted two passive and two assertive behaviors in varying sequences. Two of the five balanced conditions showed category-based judgments, and three did not. Hence, those conditions that would be most telling for category-confirmation biases, conditions in which the information was objectively neutral because it was balanced, were inconclusive in this study. We are left with the general conclusion from the rest of the literature that mixed information typically allows or even reinforces stereotypic responses.

3. Strong Category Label plus Judgment-Irrelevant, Category-Irrelevant Attributes

When attributes are interpreted as irrelevant to both the category label and the judgment at hand, and when the category label represents well-established stereotypes (e.g., gender, ethnicity), perceivers tend to confirm the category again. As will be seen in the next section, strong category labels encourage category-based responses more than do less well-established category labels (cf. Higgins & Bargh, 1987; Ruble & Stangor, 1986). For example, some studies have presented gender labels (male or female names) along with additional attribute information that was nondiagnostic with regard to both category membership and the judgment at hand (e.g., got a haircut early in the day, with regard to judged assertiveness; physically attractive, with regard to judged suitability for a job; a high score on a test of low validity, with regard to judged suitability for a job; and simply entered an art contest, with regard to artistic ability). Category-based responses were made in each case (Locksley *et al.*, 1980, Experiment 2; Rasinski *et al.*, 1985; Dipboye *et al.*, 1975; Heneman, 1977; Pheterson, Kiesler, & Goldberg, 1971). Another study, focusing on ethnicity rather than on gender, found similar results (Bodenhausen & Wyer, 1985). Subjects were provided with category labels indicating ethnicity and status (e.g., Ashley Chamberlaine of Cambridge, Massachusetts or Carlos Ramirez of Albuquerque, New Mexico) and category-consistent criminal behavior (embezzlement or assault, respectively). A variety of individuating information was provided, including crime-relevant or crime-irrelevant life circumstances. Regardless of the relevance of the additional information, judgments were stereotypic: The category-consistent crime was judged more likely to be repeated, while the category-inconsistent crime was not. In all of these studies, the irrelevant information was unable to undercut the category-based stereotypes, and thus category-based responses ensued.

To summarize, category confirmation typically succeeds when (1) the category label is accompanied by attributes interpreted as consistent; (2) the category label is accompanied by attributes interpreted as mixed (i.e., consistent and inconsistent); or (3) a well-established category label is accompanied by attributes interpreted as irrelevant to both the category label and the judgment at hand. We now turn to information configurations that typically do not enable category confirmation but instead enable somewhat more individuating impression-formation processes.

C. RECATEGORIZATION

The attribute-oriented processes of recategorization and piecemeal integration appear to be elicited in reaction to those information configurations that do not easily allow for confirmatory categorization: (1) When target attributes are interpreted as irrelevant to both the ascribed category and the judgment at hand (thus being nondiagnostic) but when the category is not strongly established; (2)

when the target attributes are interpreted as clearly inconsistent with the category label; or (3) when target attributes are present in the absence of any clearcut category and do not cue one easily.

We will discuss the informational conditions that tend to elicit both the intermediate process of recategorization and the fully individuating process of piecemeal integration. Of the two processes, recategorization should be more common because piecemeal integration should only occur when perceivers simply cannot generate a usable new category or subcategory for the target. This prediction is consistent with our data on the relative rarity of piecemeal integration processes and also conforms to the premise that relatively category-based processes take precedence over more individuating processes.

1. Weak Category Label plus Judgment-Irrelevant, Category-Irrelevant Attributes

Whereas perceivers encountering nondiagnostic attributes in conjunction with a strongly held category label (e.g., gender, ethnicity) appear to generate category-based responses, perceivers encountering nondiagnostic target information in conjunction with relatively weaker categories apparently dilute the impact of the categories. Studies demonstrating this dilution effect have utilized categories that differ from gender and ethnicity in important respects: None are established as early or as consensually, or are based as greatly on physical cues or on direct experience, as are gender and ethnicity. Consequently, such less-established stereotypes may not be as robust and flexible as gender and ethnic stereotypes. A well-established stereotype that has already persisted through exposure to many varied instances of the category is likely to be able to absorb the additional nondiagnostic information more easily. When combined with neutral information, then, the better established categories dominate neutral information, as discussed above.

The impact of less robust categories, however, is typically diluted when combined with additional nondiagnostic attributes. For example, this dilution effect has been found when the available social category consists of a college major, such as engineering or music (Nisbett *et al.*, 1981, Experiments 1–3); one or two easily categorized child-abuser attributes, such as quick temper and sadomasochistic fantasies (Nisbett *et al.*, 1981, Experiments 4–5); or an easily categorized low- or high-achievement attribute, such as often failing to finish things (Zukier, 1982). In addition, dilution effects have been found when the category is an occupation, such as artist (Fiske *et al.*, 1987, Experiment 1), or a personal characteristic serving as a category, such as day person versus night person (Locksley *et al.*, 1982, Experiment 1). In every case, the diluting information was clearly interpreted as nondiagnostic in pretesting. For example, hometown was rated nondiagnostic for judgments of shock tolerance by various college majors, employment as a hardware store manager for judgments of child abuse, or number of siblings for achievement judgments. Nonetheless, the additional target attributes served to limit the impact of the initial category. Nondiagnostic target information thus appears to lead to more individuating impressions when combined with relatively weak categories. Again, from a different perspective on the literature, our conclusions converge with those of others (Higgins & Bargh, 1987; Ruble & Stangor, 1986).

Our model predicts that recategorization predominates here as a relatively category-based process that has priority over a more attribute-based process. Examples of diluting recategorization appeared in our think-aloud data (Fiske *et al.*, 1987), where subjects combined weak category labels (e.g., professor) with uninformative attributes (e.g., normal, nice) to create a "basic, ordinary, everyday, average American professor" and similar subcategories. Additional research is needed to illuminate the subprocesses involved in the dilution effect.

2. Category plus Clearly Inconsistent Attributes

When target attributes are perceived as inconsistent with the target's ascribed category, category-based processing tends to yield to more individuated processing, even when the inconsistent information is judgment-irrelevant. For example, males and females described as performing the other sex's role behaviors (e.g., financial provider versus children's caretaker) were much more likely to be viewed as homosexual than were category-congruent targets (Deaux & Lewis, 1984). This suggests recategorization processes; subjects were not responding solely on the basis of the gender label but rather combining the label with the inconsistency to generate a subcategory. Similarly, in another study, females were described as having category-inconsistent academic backgrounds (e.g., biology major, with a political science minor). As applicants for a job in business, they were seen as less suitable than females with no specified background and as less suitable than males with the same background, even though pretesting had indicated that these backgrounds were irrelevant to the job (Heilman, 1984). One plausible account of these data is that subjects recategorized the role-incongruent female as a masculine woman and so penalized her (e.g., Costrich, Feinstein, Kidder, Marecek, & Pascale, 1975).

Clearly counterstereotypic, judgment-relevant information also undercuts category-based responses and causes relative individuation. For example, when female targets engaged in three assertive behaviors (e.g., forcefully telling a seedy pest to go away) or male targets engaged in three passive behaviors (e.g., waiting in frustration to make a point while a favored student monopolizes the class discussion), subjects judged the targets' assertiveness according to the gender-role incongruent behavior, rather than according to gender (Locksley *et al.*, 1980, Experiment 1). Similar results were obtained both when only one behavioral episode was used (Locksley *et al.*, 1980, Experiment 2; Rasinski *et al.*, 1985) and when male and female targets were described as reacting passively or assertively in three out of four psychology experiments (Locksley *et al.*, 1982, Experiment 2). Many other investigations have obtained these effects of dramatically inconsistent information on gender stereotypes (Dipboye & Wiley, 1977; Heilman, 1984; Pheterson *et al.*, 1971; Renwick & Tosi, 1978). Note that in each instance the inconsistent information was completely judgment-relevant; some reviewers have even argued that the inconsistency was essentially redundant with the judgment to be made (Deaux & Lewis, 1984) or that it alerted subjects to the experimental hypotheses (R. Brown, 1986). It seems clear, then, that dramatically inconsistent, judgment-relevant information undercuts the effects of well-established stereotypes on directly relevant judgment dimensions.

This kind of inconsistency, of course, also undercuts the effects of less well-established stereotypes. For example, engineering and art students who behaved inconsistently with respect to their category were evaluated in accord with their behavioral attributes, that is, in a relatively individuating fashion (Fiske, 1982). Holding constant the isolated evaluations of the category and attributes, the consistent or inconsistent combination of target information apparently determined whether the perceiver's affect toward the target was category-based or attribute-based. Similar effects have been obtained with category-inconsistent targets described as various types of mental patients (e.g., a depressive who is clownish and conceited; Fiske *et al.*, 1986) and targets described as having various occupations (e.g., a doctor who is bored, obedient, unenterprising, uneducated, and efficient; Fiske *et al.*, 1987). Thus, category-inconsistent attributes often lead to relatively individuating impression formation.

More detailed analyses of our think-aloud data (Fiske *et al.*, 1987) indicated several types of recategorization when perceivers encountered information configurations interpreted as inconsistent. For example, a person who apparently believed that professors are generally boring, remote, and preoccupied—and then encountered a professor described as energetic, liberal, and aggressive—subcategorized the professor as the "charismatic lecturer" subtype of professor. Other types of recategorization included accessing self-categories (e.g., "this person being opinionated reminds me of myself") and exemplars (e.g., "this person reminds me of my roommate") to make sense of people who did not easily fit an ascribed category label.

In sum, several types of inconsistency appear to disconfirm ascribed category labels and to encourage responses that are at least somewhat more individuating. Note that the individuating effects of dramatic inconsistency are not incongruous with the view, presented in an earlier section, that perceivers encounter difficulties when confronted with category-inconsistent information. The key factors, as the model states, are attention and interpretation. When perceivers have available the proper amount of on-line attentional resources, when they do not reinterpret the inconsistency to be consistent instead, when they are not able to discount the inconsistency, when they do not dwell on their impressions afterwards, and, we argue later, when they have the proper motivation, they seem quite capable of using category-inconsistent information to generate attribute-oriented responses. Hence, in the studies just described, investigators have in a sense stacked the deck by creating an environment that meets all the necessary conditions for individuation. The procedures required a particular combination of circumstances, predicted by the model, for inconsistency effectively to undercut category-based impressions.

The point is merely that when people do interpret information as being inconsistent, they can utilize relatively individuating processes. We want to stress, though, that we have not presented any evidence that perceivers ignore the ascribed categories when they do perceive inconsistency or when they dilute relatively weak category labels encountered in conjunction with nondiagnostic information. Rather, the evidence indicates the use of category information even when difficulty in category confirmation leads to more attribute-oriented impressions (Fiske *et al.*, 1987; Rasinski *et al.*, 1985). We thus do not claim that inconsistency and nondiagnosticity in these studies necessarily elicited fully individuated responses but rather just relatively individuated responses, intermediate between fully category-based and fully attribute-based responses.

D. PIECEMEAL INTEGRATION

1. Uncategorizable Attributes Only

When perceivers are confronted with target attributes in the absence of any category label, and these attributes do not easily elicit an implied category label, perceivers necessarily must form impressions of the target in a relatively individuating manner (Fiske *et al.*, 1987). For example, in one study (Pavelchak, 1989), subjects were presented with trait lists that had been pretested as not easily categorized. Some subjects were asked to rate the people so described and then to categorize them according to college major. Other subjects first categorized and then rated the targets. Their ratings of the targets were compared to their own prior, separate ratings of the trait lists and the categories. When subjects were instructed to categorize first, their overall rating of the target was better predicted by the category. When subjects did not categorize first, but responded to the attributes alone, their rating was better predicted by the average of the attributes. The point here is that when perceivers encounter a group of attributes that are not easy to categorize, they are likely to respond to them in a relatively individuating manner (unless explicitly told to generate a particular kind of category). The model predicts that such piecemeal processes will occur if target attributes are interpreted as an uncategorizable list.

Two other kinds of research support this point. First, the paradigm of information-integration research frequently entails numerous rapid judgments of targets whose attributes are drawn from a master list, in multiple combinations and recombinations (e.g., N. H. Anderson, 1974). Hence, the attributes usually do not "go together" in any natural way, and they are not easily categorizable. Moreover, it takes time to generate a category when no salient labels are ascribed and no obvious labeling features (e.g., gender, age, race) are present. In this paradigm, subjects do not usually have the time or the motivation to fully understand the target, for all they have to do is generate a likability response. Under such circumstances, attribute-by-attribute integration seems more likely than category-oriented processes (Fiske & Pavelchak, 1986; Wyer & Carlston, 1979).

Second, subjects' responses are indeed impressively well predicted by averaging the isolated evaluations of the attributes, without interactions among the attributes and without inferences that might be category-based. Although this formula suggests some sort of attribute-by-attribute piecemeal process, it does not specify the cognitive properties of the process. Lopes (1982) has proposed a cognitive model of anchoring-and-adjustment processes to account for Anderson's findings. In this view, the perceiver takes the evaluative component of each attribute and combines it with a running average from the impression so far, adjusting the impression up or down from the current anchor. This seems a plausible cognitive account for the empirically predictive algebraic model (cf. Fishbein & Ajzen, 1974), but it remains untested.

Finally, our own think-aloud data (Fiske *et al.*, 1987) are potentially consistent with such a piecemeal integration process of anchoring and adjustment, although it occurs only rarely. Occasionally, subjects would quickly read a list of target attributes and immediately announce a rating, and sometimes they would read an attribute list, reacting evaluatively to each in turn ("selfish—yuk; power hungry—not good; pragmatic—OK"), and culminate in an overall rating. In some few instances, then, an algebraic anchoring-and-adjustment interpretation may approximate the cognitive processes involved in fully individuated impressions. We should note, however, that fully individuated processes were rare in this study, while confirmatory categorization and recategorization were more common. In effect, the anchoring-and-adjustment account of piecemeal integration describes the processes perceivers use when all else fails, which fits the overall continuum model.

E. SUMMARY

Perceivers actively use the information given, and their interpretation of its configuration influences how they use it. As the target's attributes become increasingly difficult for the perceiver to fit to the target's initial category, that is, as category confirmation becomes more difficult, individuating processes become more likely. A continuum of impression formation processes is available to perceivers, and certain information configurations tend to be interpreted in consensual ways that elicit category confirmation, recategorization, or piecemeal integration. As a later section will indicate, the perceiver's motivation also influences the attentional and interpretive processes that mediate use of the impression formation continuum. However, before turning to motivation, we will more explicitly examine the role of attentional processes. In particular, the data presented thus far do not indicate whether use of the category-based versus individuating continuum operates by changing perceivers' attentional focus on attribute information, by changing their attentional focus on category information, or through some combination of the two.

V. Premise 3: Use of the Continuum Is Mediated by Changes in Attention to Attributes

How is a perceiver's use of the various processes along the continuum mediated? The model posits that attention to perceiver attributes is necessary for relatively individuating processes. But why should it be differential attention to attribute information, rather than differential attention to category information or some combination?

One might reasonably predict that differential attention to category information would be the key mediating factor because, when people stereotype, they presumably make heavy use of social category information, and when they individuate, they presumably neglect social category information. Alternatively, one might predict that differential attention to attribute information would be the key mediating factor because, when people stereotype, they presumably do not use the target's nonstereotypic attributes, and when they individuate, they presumably rely mostly on the target's nonstereotypic attributes. Or, as a third alternative, use of both category and attributes might influence the use of different impression-formation processes. As we review studies of information and stereotyping that include indicators of attention, we will see that support for changes in attribute usage will emerge as the critical mediator.

At a minimum, perceivers must have the attention available to take in the more extensive attribute information that goes beyond category membership. When perceivers have only limited attentional resources, category-based impressions typically occur, consistent with the idea that increased use of information about the target's attributes is a necessary component of individuating processes (or other data-driven processes; Jamieson & Zanna, 1988). For example, male perceivers, and female perceivers with conservative attitudes toward women, discriminated more against female job applicants when under time pressure. Conversely, females with liberal attitudes toward women discriminated more against male applicants when under time pressure (Bechtold et al., 1986). Evidently, tendencies toward category-based processes are exaggerated when perceivers are under time pressure and are thus less able to notice and use additional information about the target's attributes.

More direct evidence on the role of attention to attributes comes from the study by Fiske et al. (1987, Study 2), in which subjects read target descriptions containing trait attributes that were either consistent, irrelevant, or inconsistent with regard to job category labels. The subjects' task was to think aloud as they arrived at an overall rating of the targets' likability. If decreased use of category information were responsible for changing impression formation, then use of category information should be highest when the attribute information is consistent with the available category, intermediate when the attribute information is nondiagnostic with respect to the category, and lowest when the attribute information is decidedly inconsistent with the category. Conversely, if increased use of attribute information is responsible for changing impression formation, then use of attribute information should be lowest when the attribute information is consistent with the available category, intermediate when the attribute information is nondiagnostic with respect to the category, and highest when the attribute information is inconsistent with the category.

The results indicated that use of category information did not vary significantly across conditions. The use of the attribute information, however, did significantly differ across informational conditions, and in the direction predicted. This suggests that increases in the degree of individuated processing are mediated by an increased use of attribute information, as opposed to a decreased use of category information.

Another series of studies also supports the specific mediating role of attribute use (Fiske et al., 1986). Subjects read descriptions of targets whose attributes were either consistent or inconsistent with a mental patient category label. The attributes' set size was also varied (e.g., two, four, or six attributes were provided). We predicted that inconsistent stimuli would require longer to read and rate than would consistent stimuli, as in previous research (e.g., Burnstein & Schul, 1982, 1983; Brewer et al., 1981; Fiske & Pavelchak, 1986; Sujan, 1985). More importantly, we predicted that increases in attribute set size would produce a steeper slope for inconsistent sets than for consistent sets. This finding supports the idea that inconsistent sets specifically required more attribute-oriented processing than did consistent sets. It also suggests that, at least within our ranges of inconsistency, the effects of inconsistency cumulate with each additional inconsistent attribute, rather than reaching either a threshold (i.e., an abrupt transition) or a plateau (i.e., leveling off). Experiment 1 showed the predicted effects. Experiment 2 suggested that the effect resulted specifically from attentional processes, for it occurred at reading times separated from judgment times. Experiment 3 used think-aloud protocols as evidence that the inconsistency set-size effect resulted specifically from an increase in attribute-oriented thoughts, rather than from a decrease in category-oriented thoughts.

Although the increased use of attribute information appears necessary to mediate the use of individuating processes, this does not mean that category information has no influence on these impressions. On the contrary, in the first protocol study (Fiske *et al.*, 1987, Study 2), subjects mentioned the average attribute only 0.68 times, and the category label 1.24 times, per target. This suggests that their responses were determined in part by the category, regardless of variations in the degree to which the attributes were used. Hence, the absolute use of category information appears to remain high even when perceivers are adopting relatively individuating processes (cf., Rasinski *et al.*, 1985). This finding is thus inconsistent with the view that perceivers fail to use their stereotypes at all in the presence of individuating behaviors.

In conclusion, use of category information remains relatively high across information conditions. But it is changes in the use of attribute information that apparently mediate changes in impression formation, that is, whether it stays at the category-based end of the continuum or moves toward the fully individuating end. Thus, the model retains important roles for both category and attribute information, but category information has a constant role, while attribute information plays a variable and mediating role.

In addition to mediating perceivers' use of processes along the continuum, attention to attribute information is important to the model in other ways. First, perceivers use the target's attributes to suggest categories that might effectively organize what they know about the other. Not all people come labeled with unambiguous category membership derivable from a single characteristic, such as minority racial characteristics, a job uniform, or a verbal label. Groups of attributes often suggest category labels, as we have noted. Although much of our discussion might seem limited to circumstances under which perceivers encounter an obvious category label, this is not intended, for attributes certainly direct initial categorization in many instances. Second, attribute information is important because, during category confirmation, perceivers examine the fit between an initial category and the data at hand. This potentially allows the data to have additional impact, through the processes discussed in depth earlier. For example, attributes guide the perceiver to more specific subcategories, exemplars, or self-categories that enable the perceiver to respond in a somewhat more individuating manner. Finally, attributes by themselves provide the raw data needed for the more purely individuating, piecemeal integration processes. The importance of attention to target attribute information thus seems clear. For all these reasons, but especially because it mediates the use of alternative impression-formation processes, it is a significant aspect of our model.

VI. Premise 4: Motivation Influences Impression Formation According to the Interdependence Structure, Specifically, the Motivating Agent's Criteria

Up to this point, we have discussed impression formation in terms of the informational circumstances that influence it. We have described informational reasons for the priority of category-based processes, interpretations of information configurations that elicit processes along the continuum, and variations in attention to attribute information that appear to mediate the use of these processes. Clearly, however, understanding informational influences on impression formation is not enough. Why do perceivers sometimes use attribute-oriented processes even when category-based processes would otherwise seem to be dominant (or vice versa)? Why do perceivers sometimes diverge from the most obvious, consensual interpretation of an information configuration? Why do perceivers allocate more or less attention to the target's potentially individuating attributes? Some answers to these questions apparently lie in the perceiver's motivation and, specifically we will suggest, in the perceived interdependence structure.

We begin by defining what we mean by motivation, and how it fits into our model of impression formation. We then review research covering a range of motivational factors, both those that increase perceivers' use of relatively individuating processes as well as those that increase perceivers' use of more category-based processes. The following section then describes how motivation operates, and the conclusion suggests future directions, drawing on the theory of dyadic interdependence developed by Kelley and his colleagues (Kelley & Thibaut, 1978; Kelley *et al.*, 1983).

A. WHAT DO WE MEAN BY MOTIVATION AND HOW IS IT RELEVANT HERE?

According to current views, motivations instigate goal states that attempt to produce desired changes in the environment by way of specific cognitive strategies and goal-relevant actions (Cantor, Markus, Niedenthal, & Nurius, 1986; Kuhl, 1986; Weiner, 1986). The self is inextricably involved in any motivational theory because the environment carries desired or feared possibilities only when it impinges on the self. Hence, motivational manipulations are those that involve the self in important ways. If a perceiver desires or fears some state that may be a consequence of forming an impression of another, and the perceiver attempts to adjust his or her impression formation goals to either attain or avoid that state, then the perceiver can be said to be motivated. Thus, if a perceiver is forming an impression of a new boss, the different possible outcomes of the impression formation process may well have different, and important, implications for the perceiver. These implications may motivate the perceiver to adopt an impression formation goal to, for example, increase the potential accuracy of the impression. We would thus hypothesize that real-world impression formation is subject to motivation when an impression of a particular target has important self-relevant implications for the perceiver. The idea that the target's motivational relevance influences social perception is not new (Jones & deCharms, 1957; Jones & Thibaut, 1958), but we examine it here in light of recent evidence.

Motivations sometimes move perceivers toward individuation and sometimes keep them toward the category-based end of the continuum. Each type of motivation can be analyzed structurally by focusing on the interdependence structure within the situation. First, who is mainly motivating the perceiver? That is, within the structure of the impression formation setting, is the perceiver primarily motivated by the target, by a third party, or by internalized values? This question is answered by examining who mainly controls what the perceiver wants from the situation. It is less important what the perceiver wants (e.g., material reinforcement versus approval) than who controls it. Thus, an analysis focusing on the perceiver's interdependence structure reveals the primary motivating agent. Second, what are the criteria for attaining the desired outcome? The perceiver will presumably try to meet the criteria for attaining a desired outcome or avoiding a feared outcome. These two structural features of interdependence, the motivating agent and the criteria, jointly determine the perceiver's specific goal in the situation.

For example, consider the case of a perceiver whose role is to evaluate job applicants. If the perceiver is mainly motivated by seeking the boss's approval, the boss controls the desired outcome (approval), and the boss's criteria for good applicant evaluation will determine the perceiver's specific impression-formation goals. If the boss is concerned with impression accuracy, the perceiver will adopt a goal of impression accuracy (or apparent impression accuracy), and thus relatively individuating processes are likely to follow. If the boss is instead concerned that certain kinds of people not be hired, the perceiver will adopt a goal of forming specific impressions of certain applicants (e.g., negative impressions of black or female applicants), and thus category-based processes are more likely to follow.

On the other hand, the perceiver may be strongly guided by self-approval. In this case, the perceiver controls the relevant motivator and the criterion for achieving it. As above, a consequence of achieving this criterion may be to form accurate impressions of the applicants or specific impressions of them. The perceiver may also be motivated to form any minimally acceptable impression, again depending on the characteristics of the perceiver's self-criteria.

Finally, if the perceiver seeks the approval of the applicant, the goal will be to form an accurate impression if the applicant's apparent criterion is fairness, or a positive impression if the applicant's criterion is a positive evaluation. The important point, here, is that essentially the same motivation, seeking approval, could generate completely different impression-formation processes, depending on the primary motivating agent, the criterion, and the specific perceiver goals that result from these two factors. We now turn to recent evidence on motivation and impression formation that supports this framework.

B. MOTIVATED CHANGES TOWARD INDIVIDUATION

Although the literature on motivation and impression formation is limited, some studies do indicate that the motivating agent's particular criteria lead perceivers to form more individuated impressions than they would otherwise. What these factors apparently have in common is that they all elicit within the perceiver a goal of forming more accurate impressions, as demanded by the motivating agent's criteria for obtaining something desired.

1. Short-Term, Task-Oriented Outcome Dependency on the Target

Outcome dependency entails the instrumental value of the other in controlling specific reinforcements. Pure outcome dependency, by itself, assumes nothing about personal and social involvement beyond that specific motivation. When people's outcomes depend on another, perceivers need to be able to predict the behavior of the other, as well as their own behavior, to improve their chances of reaching the desired outcome (Berscheid, Graziano, Monson, & Dermer, 1976; Erber & Fiske, 1984). For example, suppose George, who thinks older people are incompetent, is assigned to work with Ron on a company project. If he desires success (the motivator), they must perform effectively as a team (the criterion, controlled by both of them). Accordingly, each must coordinate accurately with the other. George's goal is likely to be the formation of an accurate impression, so that he will be able to predict what Ron will do in response to his actions. George's predictions about Ron are more likely to be accurate if he does not rely on a prior category (e.g., old men cannot do this job) but instead relies on specific knowledge about him (e.g., Ron has not mastered some of the new technology, but he has more experience with people than George does). For these reasons, outcome dependency by itself should promote more individuating impression formation.

The question here is whether a perceiver's outcome dependency on a target might facilitate individuating processes under circumstances in which category-based processes generally dominate, and whether this could result from a change in impression formation goals. In one study (Neuberg & Fiske, 1987, Experiment 1), subjects expected to interact with a former, long-term hospital patient as part of a patient-reintegration program cosponsored by a local hospital and the psychology department. Subjects expected to work with the former patient on a joint task, from which they could personally make $20, based either on their joint performance (outcome-dependent condition) or on their individual contribution to the task (not outcome dependent). All of the subjects were told that Frank, the former patient with whom they were going to interact, had entered the hospital as a schizophrenic. As a category, the schizophrenic label had pretested as affectively negative; as consistent with being nervous, edgy, inconsistent, suspicious, and obsessive; and as inconsistent with being outgoing, determined, and adaptable.

All the subjects then read a personal profile ostensibly written by Frank. Half read a stereotypically and affectively neutral profile. That is, this profile was neither consistent nor inconsistent with the schizophrenic label; the information was essentially neutral, creating a condition that facilitates relatively category-based responses. The remaining subjects read a positive profile that made Frank appear to be outgoing, adaptable, and determined, and not nervous, suspicious, and obsessive. Thus, this profile was inconsistent with the schizophrenic label; in such conditions, perceivers typically individuate. Note that subjects in the neutral and inconsistent conditions received the same label for Frank, only the additional attribute information differed.

To determine whether subjects' impressions were primarily category-based or individuating, subjects rated how likable Frank seemed. When subjects were not outcome dependent, their responses were predicted to be relatively category-based in the neutral cell and more individuating in the inconsistent cell. Thus, their responses were expected to be more negative in the neutral cell, in line with the negative schizophrenic category, and more positive in the inconsistent cell, in line with the positive profile.

Outcome dependency was predicted to eliminate this information-based difference and to facilitate relatively individuating processes. If so, evaluations in the neutral cell should be neutral, based on the neutral profile, and evaluations in the inconsistent cell should be positive, based on the positive profile. In sum, evaluations should be lowest in the non-outcome-dependent/neutral cell, medium in the outcome-dependent/neutral cell, and highest and equal in the two inconsistent cells. Planned contrasts significantly supported the predicted pattern, whereas the residual was nonsignificant. The important point here is that under circumstances in which category-based processes usually dominate (the category-label-plus-neutral-attributes cell), individuating processes were elicited by making the perceiver outcome dependent on the target. The criterion for the $20 prize was successful task performance in each case, but under outcome dependency the target partially controlled whether subjects reached the criterion.

A second study (Neuberg & Fiske, 1987, Experiment 3) supported the idea that short-term, task-oriented outcome dependency encourages individuating processes by evoking within the perceiver a goal of impression accuracy. This study was essentially identical to the study just described, except that the goal of forming accurate impressions was explicitly manipulated instead of outcome dependency. As expected, this direct goal manipulation elicited the same pattern of responses as did outcome dependency within the otherwise identical paradigm. This result supports the proposed mediating role of goals in the continuum model.

These studies suggest further research. We manipulated only one type of interdependence, namely symmetrical outcome dependency involved with peers. In these instances, the motivating agents are both self and other together, for attaining the criterion depends on the actions of both. One would expect that asymmetrical operationalizations of outcome dependency, as long as they evoke a goal of impression accuracy, would also lead to more individuated processing. For example, it is clear that a perceiver's concrete outcomes frequently depend on authorities as well. An authority with power to reward or punish could represent a fairly pure manipulation of asymmetrical outcome dependency. One might well individuate an authority who had such control over one's outcomes. Outcome dependency on authorities thus helps to explain why people in organizations often have individuated impressions of their supervisors and often only vague, categorical impressions of their subordinates.

In addition, perceivers may be motivated by asymmetrical outcome dependency of another kind: when the target's outcomes depend critically on the impression formed by the perceiver (Freund, Kruglanski, & Shpitzajzen, 1985). When the perceiver realizes that the target's future will be importantly affected, the perceiver may be motivated to be more accurate, perhaps through a desire to avoid guilt associated with inadequate attempts at accuracy. In effect, the motivating agent would be the self, the criterion would be a fair judgment, and the desired outcome would be self-respect.

Finally, these accounts of outcome dependency revolve around cooperation in the service of some overriding aim. Such cooperation traditionally has been viewed as conducive to intergroup contact, presumably because it typically encourages individuation. Nevertheless, under some circumstances, competition might also encourage individuation (Ruscher & Fiske, 1988). Self-interest would dictate that perceivers also be able to predict a competitor's behavior, in order to maximize their chances at success. One-on-one competition, in which people's performances are interdependent, would seem to encourage each to accurately size up the other. In a pair of studies designed to test this idea, subjects received expectancy information and read mixed consistent and inconsistent attributes; competitors' impressions were much more variable than were those of noncompetitors, as the competitors attended more to their partners' attributes and more idiosyncratically interpreted those attributes. Note, however, that individuation demonstrably does not occur when groups compete, for ingroup–outgroup membership becomes more salient (e.g., N. Miller & Brewer, 1984). Hence, if outcome dependency leads to individuation in competitive interactions, it may be limited to one-on-one competition and to task-relevant perceptions. The overall point is that the motivating agent is the target and the criterion (besting the target) suggests an individuating goal.

2. Self-Presentation to a Third Party

We have discussed the impact that short-term, task-oriented outcome dependency can have on perceivers' use of individuating impression-formation processes. In that case, the motivation to form more accurate impressions comes from the interdependence between the perceiver and target. Another class of important motivational factors is predicated on the interdependence between the perceiver and some third party. In this case, the motivation to form accurate impressions of a target is based on a perceiver's fear of being evaluated negatively by peers, authorities, etc. For example, authority and neighborhood support of school desegregation seems critical for successful implementation (Amir, 1976), and this may operate partially through perceivers' self-presentational concerns. Although such third-party influences typically have been examined in the context of changing group-level attitudes, there is some relevant research on individual impression-formation processes.

When people expect to have to justify their judgments to another person, they may be more careful in the formation of these judgments than they would be otherwise, in an attempt to avoid negative evaluation by the other. In our structural terms, the motivating agent is the third party, the assumed criterion is apparent accuracy, and the desired outcome is approval. Unless they happen to know that the third party is biased, perceivers will likely have a goal of impression accuracy. One might thus expect accountable perceivers, if they are unaware of any third-party biases, to utilize relatively individuating impression-formation processes. In fact, accountable perceivers do seem particularly receptive to new evidence in impression formation. In one study, perceivers judging evidence from a murder trial showed typical impression-primacy biases (Tetlock, 1983b). However, when they learned before encountering the evidence that they would be accountable for their opinions afterwards, they showed no primacy biases. Moreover, when perceivers expect to have to justify their attitudes to another person with an unknown orientation, their thoughts seem to be more cognitively complex and less one-sided, and their attitudes are more evaluatively variable (Tetlock, 1983a). Similarly, when perceivers expect to check their personality predictions against accurate information, their judgments become more complex, more accurate, and less overconfident (Tetlock & Kim, 1987). Tetlock suggests that, when accountable, perceivers are more vigilant information processors (Janis & Mann, 1977): They consider a variety of alternatives, tolerate inconsistency, and are receptive to new evidence, resulting in generally more complex impressions (Tetlock & Boettger, in press; cf. Weldon & Gargano, 1988). People thus appear to utilize more individuating impression-formation processes when accountable to others, providing they do not have any evidence that the other holds a particular impression bias (a circumstance we will discuss shortly). The critical factors appear to be that third parties (the motivating agents) control the approval, which depends on the perceiver being able to justify the impression (criterion). Hence, the perceiver's likely goal is to form an accurate impression.

Self-presentation to third parties influences other judgments relevant to impression formation. Kruglanski and Freund (1983) operationalized the perceived costs of judgmental error—"fear of invalidity"—by the following compelling combination: Subjects thought their judgments would reflect fundamental abilities that were important to them, they thought they would have to explain their judgments to peers, and they thought their judgments would be compared to public standards. Under these conditions, if subjects were not under time pressure, their stereotypic judgments were eliminated. Thus, self-presentational concerns seemed to be elicited by the scrutiny of peers, even unknown peers, although other factors may also have been operating here (cf. Freund et al., 1985).[3]

---

[3]Research on belief perseverance may also be relevant to self-presentational motivations. People's false beliefs about themselves and others, although often resistant to disconfirming evidence, can be eliminated when the experimenter emphasizes the personal costs of perseverance or emphasizes exactly how it is to be avoided (Ross, Lepper, & Hubbard, 1975). The original interpretation of these results is that perceivers must be given explicit "how-to" knowledge in order to successfully undercut their erroneous impressions; in this view, perceivers simply lack specific enough knowledge about procedural aspects of debiasing.

However, when one examines the operationalizations directly, the various procedures for debiasing people all seem to contain an important self-presentational motivation. Telling people about the costs to themselves clearly arouses a motivation not to appear foolish. Other manipulations can verge on experimental demand and pleasing the experimenter and, at least, require the experimenter to spell out precisely what the perceiver must do to prevent perseverance. Such techniques include instructing perceivers to consider the opposite, apparently counterfactual outcome (Lord, Lepper, & Preston, 1984), making the opposite outcome extremely salient to them (Lord, Lepper, & Preston, 1984), and instructing them to explain how the opposite outcome could have occurred (C. A. Anderson, 1982). In these cases, subjects may well be motivated to follow the instructions simply in order to save face

3. Personal Values

We have presented evidence indicating that motivations elicited in both perceiver–target interdependence and perceiver–third-party interdependence can lead perceivers to utilize more individuating impression-formation processes. It also seems plausible, however, that perceivers' internalized values may induce them to utilize more individuating processes. That is, people can be their own motivating agents, with living up to internalized values as the criterion for self-esteem. For example, most Americans simultaneously hold humanitarian values and work-ethic values; for whites, these values apparently provide conflicting attitudes toward blacks. Priming one set of values or the other creates stronger problack and antiblack sentiments (I. Katz & Hass, 1988). It is a small leap to suggest that priming one or the other would lead to more or less stereotypic impressions as well. This may especially be true when a perceiver encounters a member of a stigmatized group, thus cuing personal values.

4. Summary

Individuation can be elicited by a variety of interdependence structures; sometimes the motivating agent is the target, sometimes a third party, and sometimes the perceiver's own internalized standards. What all the interdependence structures apparently have in common, however, is that the agent's criteria for giving the desired outcome seem to evoke the goal of forming an accurate impression of the target. Each of these motivational factors, however, also has the potential to elicit impression formation goals more amenable to category-based processing, given an altered interdependence structure. Depending on the motivating agent's criteria, these altered circumstances can elicit either the goal to form a specific impression or the goal to form any minimally acceptable impression (cf. Kruglanski, 1989), as will be seen next.

C. MOTIVATED CHANGES TOWARD CATEGORY-BASED IMPRESSIONS

1. Committed Outcome Dependency

Committed outcome dependency elicits the goal to form a particular kind of impression, as opposed to the goal to form an accurate impression. As a conse-

---

and not appear to the experimenter as stupid or insensitive. That is, the experimenter's detailed attention to debiasing may elicit self-presentational concerns, thus motivating perceivers to try harder. Hence, the "how-to" knowledge may be critical but ineffective without the motivation. It is not a large leap to suggest that the same factors that elicit more accurate impressions of the self would also elicit more individuated impressions of others.

quence, category-based impression formation may result. For example, upon meeting one's freshman roommate for the first time, one might be motivated to retain an expectancy (as supplied by the resident advisor) of the individual as easygoing and sociable, even in the face of behavior seemingly to the contrary. The commitment associated with being roommates could conflict with forming a negative impression of that person. In order to reduce this conflict, perceivers may be motivated to form a positive impression of the target. In this instance, outcome dependency is the general motivation, the desired outcome is a pleasant ongoing relationship, both people control that outcome, and one criterion for success includes each communicating an open-minded and positive predisposition toward the other. In fact, when committed to important, social outcome dependency, perceivers often do form categorically positive impressions of others upon whom they depend, when initial exposure to them can be construed as being positive. For example, male perceivers formed more uniformly positive impressions of future dates than of nondates (Berscheid et al., 1976).

On the other hand, outcome dependency may also elicit the goal of confirming negative impressions. For example, if one is involuntarily committed to a blind date with a person who turns out to be the "wrong race," one might immediately assume that the relationship simply will not work out. One possible motivation in this situation is to escape from the relationship as soon as possible, without appearing racist. The primary motivation might well be to perceive oneself as having given the other person a fair chance but, regrettably, having been forced to conclude that the person is not appropriate anyway. Hence, perceivers may be motivated to form more negative impressions of the target than they typically would (Omoto & Borgida, 1988). These cases both suggest that outcome dependency, when committed and social, can motivate category-based rather than individuating processes by evoking the goal to form a particular impression.

2. Self-Presentation to Third Parties

Self-presentation may also lead to more category-based impressions by motivating a perceiver to form a particular impression. For example, a personnel officer whose boss makes public his belief that women are incompetent may find himself "discovering" that the women he interviews really are not suited for the particular job. In this case, wanting to present himself favorably to his boss, the interviewer may adopt his boss' negative expectancy. Self-presentation can plausibly motivate perceivers to form particular category-based impressions of others. Consistent with this notion, when perceivers anticipate having to justify their attitudes to an audience with known opinions, they show strategic attitude shifts (Tetlock, 1983a). Such attitudes show little complexity, suggesting that it is not simply a reporting bias: People are not merely reporting simple audience-pleasing attitudes, while holding more complicated views themselves. Rather, the process through which the attitudes were formed seems more categorical. Presumably, such effects would generalize to impression formation. Having to justify their impressions to a third party with categorical impressions (i.e., a motivating agent with particular criteria), perceivers might well form more category-based impressions than otherwise would be the case.

Moreover, when one's self-esteem is publicly threatened, thus creating self-presentational concerns, one may utilize category-based processes in order to bolster one's image (Crocker & Gallo, 1985). For example, when high self-esteem subjects were presumably threatened by belonging to a low-status group, they showed greater ingroup favoritism (Crocker, Thompson, McGraw, & Ingerman, 1987). Moreover, high self-esteem subjects, following perceived failure, evaluated a variety of targets more negatively than when they had succeeded. It seems, then, that the preservation of their public image can lead perceivers to favor categorically their ingroup. If this is the mechanism operating, then the desired outcome is a positive view of the self, and the motivating agents are probably both self and observers. One possible criterion, then, would be the self being associated with an ingroup that is perceived as better than the outgroup.

Self-presentation, however, is not limited to evoking the goal of forming particular impressions. Self-presentation may also motivate perceivers to adopt any impression in order not to look as though they have no opinion, are unsure of themselves, or are afraid to take a stand. This "need for structure" can lead perceivers to cling to an initial hypothesis and limit their search for additional information (Kruglanski, 1989). One might well expect perceivers to cling to their initial category-based impressions under such circumstances. For example, if a faculty member asks some eager graduate students for their opinion of a visiting job candidate, they may be reluctant to waver in their response, for fear of appearing wishy-washy. As a consequence, they may rapidly categorize the candidate as a "social cognition type" and base their impression on their relevant stereotypes. In this case, the students deem that even a relatively unsubstantiated impression, one based only minimally on the target's individuating attributes, is better than no impression at all. The faculty member, as motivating agent, presumably has a criterion of independent thinking that the student perceivers try to match in order to be evaluated positively (the desired outcome). Thus, again, self-presentation can also elicit more category-based processing than typically would be expected.[4]

---

[4]Research on communication sets can also be interpreted as reflecting the influence of self-presentation on the need to adopt any minimally acceptable impression. Perceivers expecting to communicate information to others form more organized, more polarized, more fixed, and often more category-oriented impressions than do those expecting to receive the information (e.g., A. R. Cohen, 1961; Higgins, McCann, & Fondacaro, 1982; C. Hoffman, Mischel, & Baer, 1984; Leventhal, 1962; Zajonc, 1960). In addition, communicators also tend to utilize stereotypic information more than do receivers (C. Hoffman, Mischel, & Baer, 1984; Zajonc, 1960, raw data, not

3. Personal Values

Perceivers' personal values may also lead them to form impressions in a more category-based manner. For example, for neo-Nazi or Ku Klux Klan members, prejudice against Jews and blacks may be an important component of the self-concept. As a consequence, such perceivers may frequently form stereotypic impressions of Jews and blacks even when confronted with overwhelmingly category-inconsistent target attributes. In a less extreme case, making salient white people's work-ethic values can make them respond in a more prejudiced fashion toward blacks (I. Katz & Hass, 1988). This is a case of a perceiver's personal values leading to a particular impression, with the self as motivating agent and the values as criteria for self-esteem. In addition, personal values may also motivate perceivers to settle for any impression, as opposed to either a particular one or an accurate one. For example, if one considers oneself a rapid judge of character, then one may be willing to accept any impression as long as it is quickly formed. To the extent that category-based impressions are typically formed more rapidly than individuated impressions, this kind of personal value may lead one to form predominantly category-based impressions.

D. CONCLUSION: THE IMPORTANCE OF GOALS INSTIGATED BY INTERDEPENDENCE

Motivation clearly matters to impression formation. Outcome dependency, self-presentation, and personal values can facilitate either category-based or individuating impression formation, depending on the particular interdependence structure. Because motivational factors produce different impression-formation goals under different circumstances, it is misleading to make statements about *the* effects of particular motivations on impression formation. Rather, specifiable goals are elicited by the particular motivation–situation combination. As an analytic tool, we propose that the critical features of the motivation–situation combination lie in the interdependence structure: the motivating agent who controls the desired outcome and the agent's criteria for obtaining it. Knowing these specific features of interdependence enables one to understand the perceiver's likely goals in the situation. These goals subsequently direct the impression

---

percentages). While these results could be interpreted as reflecting communicators' attempts to adhere to a rule of communication that requires them to present information in an organized manner (Higgins, 1981), it may also be the case that the anticipation of public scrutiny makes the communicator more willing than otherwise to adopt initial categories. Because category-based impressions are generally prior to additional, potentially individuating attribute information and are essentially "packaged" as an organized unit, perceivers expecting to communicate their impressions to others are likely to form category-based impressions and thus avoid the risk of appearing incoherent.

formation process. When a particular interdependence structure leads to a goal of impression accuracy, relatively individuating impression formation takes place; when it elicits a goal to form a specific impression, relatively category-based impression formation takes place; and when it elicits a goal to form an impression, any impression, category-based impression formation also tends to occur.

The theory next examines how goals operate. It proposes that goals guide attention to and interpretation of target attributes. Recall that increased attention to target attributes, accompanied by interpretation based on the information configuration, apparently mediates perceivers' use of impression formation processes along the category-based versus individuating continuum in the absence of strong motivations. If goals resulting from particular interdependence structures also determine attentional and interpretive responses to attribute information, then one mediator may account for the effects of both information and motivation on impression formation.

VII. Premise 5: Motivational Influences Are Also Mediated by Attentional and Interpretive Responses to Attributes

The preceding section suggests that motivations result from the perceived interdependence structure, specifically the motivating agent and the relevant criteria. This suggests where they come from, but how do these motivations operate? Our model suggests that attention and interpretation mediate the effects of motivation as well as the effects of information. This prediction follows from an analysis of the motivational implications of interdependence, as well as from our overall continuum model.

A. INDIVIDUATING RESPONSES

Interdependence clearly influences who attends to whom in a dyad, and attention appears to be goal driven. In one study (Erber & Fiske, 1984), subjects believed that they would be working on a joint task with a partner. Half of the subjects were made outcome dependent on the partner, that is, they were told that they could personally win $20 based on their joint performance; and half of the subjects were not made outcome dependent, that is, they were told that they could win $20 based on their individual performance. Perceivers were then led to believe that their partner was likely to be either competent or incompetent at the task. Before the task began, perceivers received specific attribute information about their prospective partner; half of this information was consistent with their expectancy and half was not. If perceivers' outcome dependency affects their goal to better understand the target, then they should pay more attention to expectancy-inconsistent attributes. Consistent attributes would be relatively uninformative, for they merely confirm the expectancy, but inconsistent attributes potentially carry more information, information critical to a sense of prediction and control. Consequently, outcome-dependent perceivers should attend more to inconsistency than should perceivers who are not outcome dependent. Attention to consistent information should be relatively unaffected by outcome dependency.

The results confirmed these predictions. Moreover, a second study demonstrated that perceivers particularly thought about the dispositional implications of the inconsistent information; dispositional inferences might be perceived to facilitate a goal of predictive accuracy about their partners' behavior. Thus, short-term, task-oriented outcome dependency influenced both the quantity and quality of attention to target information. Inconsistent information is perceived to be more informative than consistent information (Jones & McGillis, 1976), so this type of outcome dependency enhances attention to information that might enable perceivers to form a more accurate impression. This indirectly supports the idea that outcome dependency creates accuracy-driven attention.

Moreover, attention to target attributes may well mediate the influence of interdependence on impression formation. Recall that outcome dependency and informational inconsistency led perceivers to form relatively individuating impressions of a negatively labeled target (Neuberg & Fiske, 1987, Experiment 1). In this study, subjects' attention to information about the target was also measured, by timing how long they spent reading the patient's personal profile. The results indicated that the conditions increasing individuated impressions also increased attention to attribute information, and where variance ranges allowed it, they were also correlated.

Another study pursued this possible mediating link (Neuberg & Fiske, 1987, Experiment 2). Subjects viewed a videotape depicting stereotype-relevant patient attributes, behaviors that were independently rated as nervous, suspicious, not at all outgoing, etc. The amount of time subjects spent considering the patient information while making an impression judgment was considered an indicator of attention. Consistent with the results from the first study, attention increased under those conditions predicted to elicit individuated processing. In addition, outcome dependency did not influence subjects' immediate, category-based nonverbal responses to the target prior to the availability of attribute information. This finding fits well with the notion that attention to attributes per se mediates motivational effects, which supports the model.

In another paradigm, cooperatively interdependent perceivers actively sought more individuating information from their interaction partners, resulting in more accurate impressions (Darley, Fleming, Hilton, & Swann, 1988). The type of information gathered is analogous to increased attention to attributes already provided by the experimenter.

However, increasing attention to target attributes by itself should not lead to individuating impression formation. If, for example, the perceiver is attending to the target attributes in order to discount an inconsistency between the attributes and the category, a category-based impression would most likely occur. It would appear, then, that additional attention to attribute information in conjunction with the goal of forming an accurate impression would be needed to elicit individuating processes.

To test more directly whether accuracy-driven attention mediates the effects of outcome dependency on impression formation, Neuberg and Fiske (1987, Experiment 3) conducted an experiment essentially identical to Experiment 1, described earlier. In this study, all subjects had time sufficient for attention to individuating information, as determined by spontaneous attention to patient profiles in the previous experiment's individuating conditions. Half the subjects were told to form an accurate impression, and half were given no explicit goal. Accuracy-driven attention mimicked the effects of outcome dependency on impression formation. This supports the model's premise that outcome dependency increases individuation by increasing accuracy-driven attention to attributes. Note, however, that increased time to attend by itself, without the explicit goal of forming an accurate impression, did not lead to individuated processing. Altogether, accuracy-driven attention apparently enables outcome dependency to have its effects on impression formation (cf. Baxter, Hill, Brock, & Rozelle, 1981; Touhey, 1972).

Accuracy instructions are also interesting for their own sake because they represent interdependence between subject and the experimenter as an authority who gives approval and experimental credits. Such accuracy instructions enhance attention to attributes provided by the experimenter, as just noted. In addition, an explicit accuracy goal causes perceivers to actively seek information from the target, especially if the target is under the shadow of a negative expectancy (Neuberg, 1989). Accuracy-goal perceivers provided more opportunities for targets to reveal potentially individuating information than did no-goal perceivers, resulting in more (accurately) favorable impressions. Instructions to "find out as much as you can about the other person" also have the intriguing side effect of making interactants more comfortable (Leary, Kowalski, & Bergen, 1988).

Other kinds of interdependence encourage individuation via increased attention to attributes as well. For example, when the perceiver is oriented toward an audience as the primary motivating agent, the audience's criteria for approval may determine the perceiver's impression formation goal and consequent attentional and interpretive responses. Thus, self-presentation may affect impressions by increasing attention to the available data. Consistent with this idea, evaluation apprehension only increases individuation when there is sufficient time to consider the information available (Kruglanski & Freund, 1983). In two studies, category-based impressions were undercut only when perceivers had both the time to attend to the target and the goal of making accurate judgments (Kruglanski & Freund, 1983). Fear of invalidity also increases information seeking, again suggesting that attention to attribute information mediates the influences of motivation on individuation (Mayseless & Kruglanski, 1987). Similarly, accountability to third parties increases perceivers' use of additional information, but only if perceived accountability occurs prior to receiving the additional information, thus altering how perceivers attend to it (Tetlock, 1983b, 1985). Moreover, the accountable perceivers' tendency to use more of the attribute information at hand can make them more accurate or less accurate, depending on whether that information is actually useful (Tetlock & Boettger, in press). Finally, people attend to more individuating information when they are explicitly alerted to the possibility of appearing prejudiced (Snyder, Campbell, & Preston, 1982), which presumably raises self-presentational concerns.

The kinds of interdependence discussed so far have all been at least potentially facilitating interdependence. A pair of studies investigated mutually interfering interdependence by examining the effects of competition on impression formation (Ruscher & Fiske, 1988). As noted earlier, competitors' impressions were more variable than noncompetitors' impressions, presumably because they made more use of and more idiosyncratic interpretations of their partner's attributes. Analysis of their attentional patterns provides more direct evidence of their impression formation processes. Competitors attended to the most informative attributes, that is, those inconsistent with their expectancy, and they made more dispositional comments about them, presumably in the service of enhancing their sense of prediction and control. Thus, competitors show the same pattern of attention and interpretation as do cooperatively interdependent perceivers (Erber & Fiske, 1984).

Finally, personal values can also influence attention and interpretation. In a set of studies designed to test this idea (Fiske & Von Hendy, 1989), subjects expected to meet a former hospital patient, depicted by a label and mixed consistent and inconsistent attributes. Subjects were given feedback about categorizing and individuating impression-formation processes, on the assumption that all perceivers have both processes at their disposal. The feedback was tailored to individual differences in self-monitoring, that is, in the extent to which people typically rely on their social situations or their internal states to guide their behavior. High self-monitors (socially oriented perceivers) were most influenced by false feedback about the impression formation strategies used by most other undergraduates in that situation, but low self-monitors (internally oriented perceivers) were most influenced by false feedback about the results of their own personality test. For both sets of perceivers, feedback that emphasized either categorizing or individuating processes produced the respective patterns of attention to attributes. That is, individuating feedback encouraged attention to the more informative inconsistent attributes, compared to categorizing feedback. Because attention was measured unobtrusively and because attention increased only in relation to stereotype-inconsistent attributes, the results support the role of personal values as guiding impression formation processes and attention in particular. Altogether, a promising amount of evidence indicates that the nature of the perceiver's interdependence can increase accuracy-driven attention to attributes, which in turn mediates individuated impressions.

B. CATEGORY-BASED RESPONSES

Types of interdependence that encourage category-based responses can also be mediated by attention and interpretation. For example, as already noted, socially committed outcome dependency can cause categorically positive responses to a future date; it increases attention to target information as well (Berscheid et al., 1976). A perceiver may thus attend primarily to the category information (my ideal date) or to category-consistent attributes (e.g., smiles a lot). Or the perceiver may attend to potentially individuating information (my prospective date's main hobby seems to be collecting bottle tops) merely in order to discount it. Clearly, the goal that one has while attending to target attributes can support more category-based interpretations and final impressions. Interacting with a prospective date would seem to constitute a relatively strong interdependence, leading to the goal of forming a positive impression if possible.

A related dating situation would seem to constitute a different kind of relatively strong interdependence. White males involuntarily committed to dating a black woman subsequently seem to focus their attention on the overall situation, to the detriment of their partner's actual attributes (Omoto & Borgida, 1988). In this instance, the primary motivating agents are presumably third parties (the subject's peers), and the perceiver's concerns revolve around how to handle this apparently awkward situation. There is also suggestive evidence that the target's attributes are interpreted more negatively as a result of the interdependence structure that is apparently perceived to be not altogether facilitating. Again, more data are prescribed, but an analysis of the interdependence structure helps explain perceivers' attentional and interpretive processes.

Moreover, third parties can be motivating agents who demand an impression, any impression, as noted earlier. When the interdependence structure motivates perceivers simply to form an impression, any impression, by time pressure, they cannot attend sufficiently to target attributes, and category-based impressions typically occur. For example, one study already cited indicates that perceivers' tendencies toward category-based impression formation are exaggerated under time pressure (Bechtold *et al.,* 1986; cf. Koller & Wicklund, 1988). Time pressure may prevent data-driven strategies (Jamieson & Zanna, 1988), such as relatively individuating impression-formation processes. Need for structure may specifically influence perceivers' abilities to attend to expectancy-inconsistent information when forming impressions (Holmes, Zanna, & Whitehead, 1986). Thus, factors that reduce one's ability to attend to attribute information apparently also reduce the likelihood of individuating impression formation, again consistent with this premise of the model.

Finally, personal values also contribute to attention that encourages category-based processes (Fiske & Von Hendy, 1989). Although there is less direct evidence, motivational factors can encourage a failure to attend to the target's attributes, creating relatively category-based impression-formation processes.

C. CONCLUSIONS REGARDING ATTENTION AND INTERPRETATION

Several studies indicate that, like informational influences, motivational influences are also mediated by attentional and interpretive responses to attributes. Moreover, interdependence is a central source of motivations that encourage either category-based or individuating responses, depending on the specific motivating agents and their criteria.

Of course, interdependence is not the only source of motivation relevant to impression formation, although we would argue that many motivations result from the various types of interdependence. Even those motivations that less obviously result from interdependence may well be mediated by the same attentional and interpretive responses. Any motivation that elicits a specific impression-formation goal will affect both attention and interpretation. For example, even simple impression-formation goals that result directly from instructions demonstrate this process. In an unpublished study (Neuberg & Fiske, 1986), perceivers were asked to form impressions of profiles consisting of an occupational label (e.g., artist) and a list of traits that were neither clearly consistent nor inconsistent with the label (loyal, dependable, opinionated, productive, hard-working). Some of the perceivers were given the goal of thinking about how much the targets have in common with other members of their occupation (confirmation goal), while others were given the goal of thinking about how little the targets have in common with other members of their occupation (disconfirmation goal). Perceivers were then given either 10 or 20 seconds to think about the targets, after which, in addition to providing their impressions of the targets, they also judged how typical the targets were of their occupational group. As one would expect, confirmation-goal perceivers judged the targets to be more typical of their occupation than did the disconfirmation-goal perceivers, but only when they had 20 seconds to think about the targets. There was no difference in typicality judgments when perceivers had only 10 seconds to form an impression. These findings are consistent with the notion that perceivers' goals can influence the way they interpret ambiguous target information, and that the conjunction of the goal and appropriate attentional resources allows this effect. It thus seems likely that perceiver goals influence impression formation by altering both attentional and interpretive responses to the target.

Recent work by Quattrone (1986) also emphasizes the importance of the perceiver's attentional focus in altering stereotypic perceptions. Quattrone focuses on factors that enhance perceptions of outgroup variability, rather than on individuating processes applied to impressions of a single individual. But, as we do, he notes that attention is key: Perceivers must attend to within-group differences, to factors other than the adequacy of role performance, and to subordinate levels of categorization. Quattrone thus identifies various attentional foci that undercut categorization. Our point is that various motivations can promote accuracy-driven or biased attention to a target's individual attributes in the service of one's goal.

D. OTHER STAGES AT WHICH MOTIVATION LIKELY MATTERS

The remaining stages of the continuum model—from the "automatic" initial categorization and minimal interest–relevance judgment, to the more "thoughtful" confirmatory categorization, recategorization, and piecemeal integration stages—are no doubt influenced by various motivational factors as well, although we have not included those influences as a major part of our model. The continuum model allows one to pinpoint potentially critical junctures that would profit from further research.

1. Initial Categorization

According to the model (again see Fig. 1), the initial categorization stage occurs automatically upon the perception of a target individual, is extremely rapid, and is not influenced by a perceiver's accuracy-driven attention. Some of our outcome-dependency data appear to support this claim. In our patient-reintegration paradigm, there was no influence of outcome dependency on subjects' initial "gut" reactions to the person's category, although outcome dependency did influence impression formation processes after attribute information had been received (Neuberg & Fiske, 1987, Experiment 2). Subjects received the outcome-dependency manipulation described earlier, and then subjects were unobtrusively filmed as they were told that they would be meeting a former schizophrenic (a negative affect-laden category) or a heart patient (an affectively neutral category). In general, affective states can often be reflected in immediate and observable changes in interpersonal nonverbal behavior (e.g., Word et al., 1974). Therefore, the presence or absence of nonverbal changes as a function of category label and motivational state can reveal the influences of each, at the earliest stages of impression formation. As expected, there were greater immediate changes in nonverbal behavior for subjects exposed to the schizophrenic label than for subjects exposed to the heart patient label. Interestingly, however, there were no changes in nonverbal behavior as a function of either outcome dependency or the outcome-dependency-by-label interaction. That is, outcome dependency did not attenuate the initial negative responses to the schizophrenic target. Given that outcome dependency had clearly influenced later processing, this finding supports the notion that an initial categorization occurs prior to potentially individuating attention to target attributes. This is not to say, however, that initial categorization is always unaffected by motivation. A main point of the "New Look" in perception was precisely that people's motivational states affect their initial categorizing of ambiguous stimuli (e.g., Bruner, 1958).

2. Minimal Interest–Relevance

A perceiver's motivations help determine whether or not a particular target will exceed the criterion for minimal relevance or interest. Some people generally are of more natural relevance to us, for example, those of our own age (Rodin, 1987). Other people are relevant given short-term goals of perceivers. Thus, for example, if Assistant Professor Alan's overriding intent at a particular moment is to give an exam on time, the probability that the average person he passes along the corridor will be of sufficient relevance to him at that moment will be reduced. On the other hand, if our Professor Alan is in less of a rush, or thinks the target might enable him to open up the exam room on time, the probability that this person will be of sufficient relevance will be increased. Thus, it seems plausible that a perceiver's motivations can determine whether or not further assessment of a target individual takes place, by influencing that target's relevance or interest to the perceiver at that moment in time.

3. Confirmatory Categorization

Moving to the first stage of the model after attention to attribute information, motivation may influence the probability of confirmatory categorization, not only by altering the salience of information consistent or inconsistent with the initial category, as discussed earlier, but also by altering the criteria for determining inconsistency. For example, motivational factors such as a threat to self-esteem may increase the threshold for considering information to be inconsistent, thus increasing the likelihood that information will be perceived as being consistent with the initial categorization. As a consequence, confirmatory categorization is more likely to be successful. Alternatively, motivational factors such as short-term outcome dependency, fear of invalidity, or accountability may lower the threshold for considering information to be inconsistent, thus making it more likely that information will be perceived as being inconsistent with the initial categorization. As a consequence, individuating processes may be more likely.

To the extent that perceivers view target information as consistent with the category, confirmatory categorization is likely. Nevertheless, it is not at all clear that the presence of information perceived to be inconsistent will necessarily lead to recategorization or piecemeal integration processes. For example, outcome dependency has led some perceivers to reinterpret inconsistent information as supporting the initial categorization (cf. Erber & Fiske, 1984). Thus, the same motivational states that might lead one to initially interpret target information as inconsistent may not be sufficient ultimately to lead one to accept that interpretation.

4. Recategorization

To the extent that one's particular motivation increases the probability of perceiving target information as category inconsistent, it also increases the probability that recategorization processes will be utilized. Moreover, it certainly seems plausible that one's motivation can also influence the judgment of whether any new category, subtype, or exemplar appropriately fits the information one has about a target individual. For example, the greater one's motivation for accurate prediction, the less likely that any particular category will be satisfactory for assessing a particular individual, and the more likely it is that one will access more specific subcategories, exemplars, or self-schemas or even utilize a piecemeal integration process. Alternatively, if one is motivated mainly by time or resource constraints, one will be much less likely to use the more individuating processes. It seems, then, that motivation can influence not only whether a perceiver utilizes recategorization processes but also the specificity of the category selected.

5. Piecemeal Integration

The probability of a perceiver assessing a target via piecemeal integration is increased by those factors that motivate accurate assessment of the target. One likely condition for the use of piecemeal processes involves perceivers who are highly outcome dependent on someone they do not know very well. For example, if one acquired a new boss, whose position entailed a great deal of power, and the previously unknown person began by behaving arbitrarily and capriciously, the subordinates might be unable to categorize the boss easily, but they would acquire substantial quantities of information that they could and would combine in order to generate relatively individuated judgments about the boss. Anther likely condition for piecemeal processing is the repeated judgment of large numbers of people, with highly structured information, where the decisions are important and supposedly objective. Familiar examples include reviewing job applications or graduate admissions folders, cases in which the perceiver may intend to be objective and to combine only a few specific criteria to formulate a judgment.

6. Further Assessment?

Finally, it seems that motivational factors play a large role in determining whether the perceiver restarts the whole impression-formation process. A motivation, for example, to assess others with great accuracy supports a decision to obtain additional information about the target (Mayseless & Kruglanski, 1987), taking the perceiver back to the attention-to-attribute-information stage. People are constantly gathering information about individuals who are important to them, and updating their impressions accordingly. Moreover, if perceivers, for some reason, are not satisfied with their first impressions, perhaps because the impression runs counter to some expectation, perceivers may also be more likely to continue the impression process. On the other hand, a motivation to maintain one's stereotypes—careless or reckless of the consequences to targets—might limit the chance of restarting the impression process.

E. SUMMARY AND CONCLUSIONS

In the preceding sections, we have presented empirical evidence, where available, suggesting how and when interdependence motivations may influence the impression formation process. The findings at this point seem to indicate an especially crucial role for goal-directed attention in mediating the influence of motivational factors in the selection of impression formation processes. Moreover, we presented some reasonable hypotheses concerning other influences of motivation on impression formation processes. One possible direction for future work lies in the careful analysis of the interdependence motivations that influence attention, interpretation, and impression formation. Some basic ideas about interdependence follow from simple but fruitful assumptions: First, people seek prediction and control over positive outcomes. This is noncontroversial; psychologies from Freudianism to behaviorism assert as much. Second, as a consequence of seeking control, people identify others who control their desired outcomes, that is, people identify motivating agents and their criteria. The ensuing impression-formation goals guide people's attention and interpretation. Accordingly, the interdependence structure in any given setting will predict who attends to whom and how perceivers interpret what they take in.

A framework for analyzing interdependence has been developed over time by Kelley and Thibaut (Kelley & Thibaut, 1978; Thibaut & Kelley, 1959). Specific features of interdependence have informed work on close relationships (Kelley *et al.*, 1983), and it seems likely that some of the same features will also clarify how interdependence operates in initial impression formation. Some specific features of interdependence that seem useful here are its symmetry, its degree of facilitation, and its strength; we suggest that together these features will predict the direction of attention in a dyad, as well as the nature of the interpretations that are likely to follow. In particular, interdependence symmetry should motivate who attends to whom, in an effort to control outcomes. Degree of facilitation should motivate the interpretations given to ambiguous information: To the extent that the target is perceived as facilitating the perceiver's outcomes, the target should be interpreted in a positive light; to the extent that the target is perceived as potentially hindering the perceiver's outcomes, the target should be interpreted more negatively. And the strength of interdependence may polarize the preceding responses; the more important the desired outcome, the more extremely the perceiver may respond. In short, various structural features of interdependence likely motivate goal-driven attention and interpretation, which are the proposed processes mediating use of the impression formation continuum.

VIII. Alternatives to the Continuum Model

Having examined the evidence for the five main premises of our model, it is helpful to discuss some related models that raise issues for additional consideration.

A. ARE IMPRESSION FORMATION PROCESSES AND REPRESENTATIONS MUTUALLY EXCLUSIVE?

Brewer (1988), simultaneously with us, has proposed a superficially similar model of cognitive representations and processes involved in stereotyping and individuation. Brewer's dual-process model proposes a dichotomous sequence of processes, which is similar to our continuum mainly in its explicit statement of processing stages and its supposition that the more category-based processes dominate the more individuating processes. Brewer's stages include (1) automatic identification of a primitive category, after which a judgment of relevance and a second judgment of self-involvement determine which of two dichotomous branches is followed. Under relevance but low self-involvement, Brewer's dual-process model posits (2) category-based typing. If the category does not fit, (3) individuation occurs, through subtype or exemplars. Under relevance and high self-involvement, which is the alternative branch, the model posits (4) personalization. Brewer's model thus identifies two primary and mutually exclusive processes: on the one hand, category-based typing or individuation and, on the other, personalization.

Elsewhere, our continuum model has been compared to Brewer's dual-process model in some detail (Fiske, 1988). Similarities between the models are fairly superficial. One of the most central differences is that Brewer's dual-process model posits mutually exclusive types of cognitive representation for each of the different stages: According to that model, automatic identification occurs in multidimensional space, typing occurs in pictoliteral prototypes, individuation occurs as schema-plus-tag, and personalization occurs in propositional networks. Without repeating the arguments in detail, there are logical, empirical, and intuitive reasons not to posit different cognitive representations at different stages. First, there seems to be a logical confusions of types. The techniques researchers use to test their theories are not isomorphic with the cognitive representations in perceivers' heads (e.g., multidimensional scaling and propositions). Second, the distinct types of representation cannot be established empirically as operating uniquely at each stage. Third, it does not make common sense to suppose that perceivers do not have visual representations of personalized others or verbal propositions about stereotyped others.

A second major difference between the two models is that the Brewer dual-process model posits that different decision rules enter at different stages. That is, personalization results from involvement and individuation results when category-based typing fails. This is another sense in which processes are posited to be mutually exclusive. In our continuum model, informational fit and motivational factors both affect attentional and interpretive responses, and through them, all the impression formation processes, not only one stage apiece. In our model, the perceiver judges the target's fit both to an initial category and to new categories. And if confirmatory categorization, recategorization, or piecemeal integration produce results that do not fit expectancies, the perceiver may start the impression cycle over. Similarly, motivation is posited to affect each stage of our continuum model, as described. Thus, the continuum model posits similar informational and motivational decision processes at each stage.

A third difference is that attentional processes are central to our continuum model, mediating both informational and motivational effects on impression formation. We reviewed evidence supporting the central role of attention in determining impression formation processes; the Brewer dual-process model is less explicit about mediating processes.

Finally, we believe the continuum itself provides a more flexible framework than available with a model that posits mutually exclusive representations and processes. The dual-process model does not describe how perceivers might move from typing or subtyping to fully person-based impressions. It assumes that self-involvement primarily produces person-based impressions and that a lack of involvement produces stereotyping, both premises that appear to be weak based on our reading of the literature.

For these and related reasons (Fiske, 1988), our continuum model appears to be more testable, more integrative of previous results, more parsimonious, and more internally consistent. Brewer's model, on the other hand, reminds verbally oriented researchers of the importance of images, emphasizes the possibility of alternative decision rules, and highlights the role of self-involvement. In sum, our efforts and Brewer's are concerned with many overlapping issues, but the models differ dramatically in their proposed representations and processes, in the amount of emphasis on informational and motivational conditions influencing these processes, and in the theme of attention that emerges throughout our model. In broadest outline, certainly, both models concur that impression formation can proceed as relatively more category-oriented or relatively more individuated. But the crux of the differences between the models is that our continuum model does not posit mutually exclusive representations and processes.

B. DO IMPRESSION FORMATION PROCESSES OPERATE IN PARALLEL?

Our continuum model does not posit that impression formation processes are mutually exclusive, as just noted. On the other hand, neither does the continuum model propose that all of the various processes—initial categorization, confirmatory categorization, recategorization, and piecemeal integration—operate in parallel. It proposes a sequence of processes from the more category-oriented to the more attribute-oriented.

One alternative to the continuum model is a model in which some category-based and some individuating processes occur in parallel, with one type or the other taking precedence under specific circumstances (M. L. Hoffman, 1986, p. 252). However, these alternative approaches may not differ as much as they seem. First, both the parallel-processes approach and our continuum model allow a mixture of the two types of process, in the vast middle between fully category-based and fully individuating processes. Second, the parallel-process and continuum approaches may not ultimately differ in the outcomes they predict, for the results of two processes operating in parallel can be represented as a continuum. That is, if category-based processes dominate attribute-based processes, the resulting impressions are located at the category-based end of the continuum, and if attribute-based processes dominate, impressions are located at the individuating end of the continuum. And if both operate equally, then use of the category and attributes together produces intermediate recategorization processes. Third, like the parallel-processes approach, our model specifies important roles for both category and attribute information, separately and together. Data-driven and theory-driven processes operate together (Higgins & Bargh, 1987), but one or the other may have relatively more influence under different circumstances. Finally, our model does posit a priority given to category-based processes, but that could be proposed within either a parallel or a continuum framework. Overall, the comparative strengths of a parallel-processes approach remain to be developed.

IX. Conclusions

We have presented a model that views impression formation as commencing with initial categorization and attention, leading into a continuum of different impression-formation processes—confirmatory categorization, recategorization, and piecemeal integration. These range from relatively category-based processes to relatively individuating processes, with category-based processes occupying a position of priority.

Perceivers typically use both the target's initially accessible category label as well as the target's additional attributes in the impression formation process. The configuration of this information largely determines the interpretive ease of fitting the target's attributes to the category given, which in turn determines where along this category-based versus individuating continuum the perceiver's impressions of the target will eventually lie. Targets whose attributes are perceived as validating the target's category will elicit relatively category-based impressions; targets whose attributes make it more difficult to confirm their initial category will elicit relatively individuating impressions. Moreover, the key mechanism underlying the use of various impression-formation processes is proposed to be attention to target attributes.

In addition to premises regarding informational influences on impression formation, we have also proposed premises regarding how motivational factors might impact upon impression formation. Motivations arise from particular interdependence structures that evoke different impression-formation goals. The perceiver's particular goal depends on the primary motivating agent (self, target, third party) and on that agent's criteria for providing the desired outcome. Perceivers attempt to achieve the criteria by creating what they believe to be appropriate impression-formation goals. Motivating agents and criteria that evoke a goal of impression accuracy will lead to relatively individuating impression formation; agents and criteria that evoke goals of forming either a specific impression or any minimally adequate impression will elicit relatively category-based impression formation. The influence of motivation on impression formation seems to be primarily mediated by goal-driven attention to and interpretation of target attributes, although motivational influences at other stages of impression formation may occur as well. An analysis of interdependence structures seems a promising avenue for future efforts to understand the role of motivation in the use of impression formation strategies.

What does this model buy us? First, it synthesizes previously competing or apparently incompatible approaches. When Asch (1946) asked whether impression formation operates by holistic, gestalt processes or by elemental, algebraic processes, there began a running debate within impression formation research. Asch favored the gestalt idea, N. H. Anderson (1974) favored the elemental idea, and schema researchers represented a return to gestalt principles (see Fiske & Taylor, 1984, chaps. 1 and 6, for an overview of the holistic–elemental debates). Our work represents a synthesis of previous theses and antitheses. As such, we have delineated informational and motivational circumstances that lead perceivers to engage in each type of impression formation. Accordingly, we think this effort captures the accumulated evidence in the field of impression formation, as well as data from other, related areas.

The model also provides a role for motivation, a role that is warranted by empirical findings as well as by common sense. The roles of motivation in impression formation are just now being explored again. In this renewed effort, it will be important to have specific analytic frameworks that allow findings to cumulate. In discussing the roles of motivating agents and their criteria, as well as the perceived symmetry, facilitation, and strength of interdependence, we have suggested one possible framework. Moreover, the model posits a specific mediator for motivation's effects on impression formation: goal-driven attentional and interpretive responses to target attributes.

From a practical perspective, the model provides a conceptual base from which interventions may be designed to decrease the impact of category-based impression formation. One message of the model is that interventions, to elicit effectively individuated processing, must motivate perceivers to search for additional target attributes with the goal of using them to form accurate impressions. In addition, our analysis of motivational factors pointed out a pressing need to understand the particular goals that different interdependence factors elicit under different circumstances. Although a deep understanding of perceivers' surrounding context will be necessary to successfully undercut category-based impression formation, we think that the analysis presented here provides a starting point for such attempts.

This is not to say that category-based impression formation is always undesirable. In effect, we have implied throughout this effort that individuation is preferable to categorization. In part, this is because perceivers categorize outgroups to a greater extent than ingroup members, and outgroup categories are likely to be negative. This propensity is what people in the street commonly mean by stereotyping. It is clearly important to understand how to undercut the use of negative and oversimplified outgroup categorizations, especially when these result in unfair consequences for the targets. In part, we have emphasized individuation also because using any single category is inherently likely to be less accurate than using the individual's whole range of noticeable attributes. Categorization by definition generalizes beyond the individual case and thus introduces error, to the highly likely extent that the individual is not the prototype of the category.

Nevertheless, it is not always good to individuate. It depends on interactions among the category, the attributes, the judgmental goal, and the relative importance of efficiency. Some categories are relatively appropriate and useful, as when one interacts with a gas station attendant in a brief encounter at the pumps. Some attributes may be relatively inappropriate and useless, as when judgments about the attendant's competence are affected by how attractive the individual is. Moreover, one can certainly attempt to use the individual's attributes but misperceive them (e.g., assuming that a new professor knows how to teach because she is a kind person). In that case, the attempt to individuate might be less preferable than the more accurate use of a better fitting, single category (cf. Cronbach, 1955). Finally, in some cases, an approximately accurate category-based answer may be better than a more accurate but less efficient individuated answer, as when one is approached by a potential mugger. Our analysis has focused primarily on cases of unjustified and potentially injurious category-based responses.

We are optimistic that recent efforts, including our own, seek to balance data-driven and theory-driven social cognition. It seems only realistic, moreover, to consider motivational as well as informational factors in this effort. Social perceivers are versatile, flexible human beings, a point we researchers often seem to miss. This article is not alone in advocating that people are remarkably skilled and often quite attuned in their use of situation-appropriate strategies (e.g., Chaiken, 1980; Chaiken, Liberman, & Eagly, 1989; C. E. Cohen & Ebbesen, 1979; Fiske, Kinder, & Larter, 1983; Harkness, DeBono, & Borgida, 1985; C. Hoffman, Mischel, & Mazze, 1981; Petty, Cacioppo, & Goldman, 1981; Zukier & Pepitone, 1984; for reviews see D. T. Miller & Turnbull, 1986; Pittman & Heller, 1987; Showers & Cantor, 1985; Sorrentino & Higgins, 1986; Srull & Wyer, 1986). This renewed interest in the relationships among cognition, affect, motivation, and action creates a favorable prognosis for our appreciation of the social perceiver's healthy ability to function adaptively and effectively.

Acknowledgments

We thank, for their helpful comments, James Averill, John Bargh, Barbara Fiske, Donald Fiske, David Hamilton, Sara Kiesler, George Levinger, Carolyn Mervis, Shelley Taylor, and participants of the fourth annual Nags Head Conference on Social Cognition. Preparation of this chapter was supported by the first author's NSF Grants BNS 8406913 and BNS 8596028, NIMH Grant 1 R01 MH41801, as well as by the second author's NATO Postdoctoral Fellowship.

References

Abelson, R. P. (1981). The psychological status of the script concept. *American Psychologist,* **36**, 715–729.
Ajzen, I., & Fishbein, M. (1977). Attitude–behavior relations: A theoretical analysis and review of empirical research. *Psychological Bulletin,* **84**, 888–918.
Ajzen, I., & Fishbein, M. (1980). *Understanding attitudes and predicting social behavior.* Englewood Cliffs, NJ: Prentice-Hall.
Alba, J. W., & Hasher, L. (1983). Is memory schematic? *Psychological Bulletin,* **93**, 203–231.
Allen, V. L., & Wilder, D. A. (1975). Categorization, belief similarity, and intergroup discrimination. *Journal of Personality and Social Psychology,* **32**, 971–977.
Allport, G. W. (1954). *The nature of prejudice.* Reading, MA: Addison-Wesley.
Amir, Y. (1976). The role of intergroup contact in change of prejudice and ethnic relations. In P. A. Katz (Ed.), *Towards the elimination of racism.* New York: Pergamon.
Andersen, S. M., & Klatzky, R. L. (1987). Traits and social stereotypes: Levels of categorization in person perception. *Journal of Personality and Social Psychology,* **53**, 235–246.
Anderson, C. A. (1982). Inoculation and counter-explanation: Debiasing techniques in the perseverance of social theories. *Social Cognition,* **1**, 126–139.
Anderson, N. H. (1974). Information integration: A brief survey. In D. H. Krantz, R. C. Atkinson, R. D. Luce, & P. Suppes (Eds.), *Contemporary developments in mathematical psychology* (pp. 236–305). San Francisco: Freeman.
Asch, S. E. (1946). Forming impressions of personality. *Journal of Abnormal and Social Psychology,* **41**, 258–290.
Asch, S. E., & Zukier, H. (1984). Thinking about persons. *Journal of Personality and Social Psychology,* **46**, 1230–1240.
Ashmore, R. D., & Del Boca, F. K. (1981). Conceptual approaches to stereotypes and stereotyping. In D. L. Hamilton (Ed.), *Cognitive processes in stereotyping and intergroup behavior* (pp. 1–36). Hillsdale, NJ: Erlbaum.
Bargh, J. A., Bond, R. N., Lombardi, W., & Tota, M. (1986). The additive nature of chronic and temporary sources of construct accessibility. *Journal of Personality and Social Psychology,* **50**, 869–878.
Bargh, J. A., & Pietromonaco, P. (1982). Automatic information processing and social perception: The influence of trait information presented outside of conscious awareness on impression formation. *Journal of Personality and Social Psychology,* **43**, 437–449.
Bargh, J. A., & Pratto, F. (1986). Individual construct accessibility and perceptual selection. *Journal of Experimental Social Psychology,* **22**, 293–311.

Bargh, J. A., & Thein, R. D. (1985). Individual construct accessibility, person memory, and the recall-judgment link: The case of information overload. *Journal of Personality and Social Psychology*, **49**, 1129–1146.

Bartlett, F. A. (1932). *A study in experimental and social psychology*. New York: Cambridge University Press.

Baxter, J. C., Hill, P. C., Brock, B., & Rozelle, R. M. (1981). The perceiver and the perceived revisited. *Personality and Social Psychology Bulletin*, **7**, 91–96.

Bechtold, A., Naccarato, M. E., & Zanna, M. P. (1986). *Need for structure and the prejudice-discrimination link*. Paper presented at the annual meeting of the Canadian Psychological Association, Toronto.

Berscheid, E., Graziano, W., Monson, T., & Dermer, M. (1976). Outcome dependency, attention, attribution, and attraction. *Journal of Personality and Social Psychology*, **34**, 978–989.

Billig, M., & Tajfel, H. (1973). Social categorization and similarity in intergroup behavior. *European Journal of Social Psychology*, **3**, 27–52.

Bodenhausen, G. V. (1988). Stereotypic biases in social decision making and memory: Testing process models of stereotype use. *Journal of Personality and Social Psychology*, **55**, 726–737.

Bodenhausen, G. V., & Lichtenstein, M. (1987). Social stereotypes and information processing strategies: The impact of task complexity. *Journal of Personality and Social Psychology*, **52**, 871–880.

Bodenhausen, G. V., & Wyer, R. S., Jr. (1985). Effects of stereotypes on decision making and information-processing strategies. *Journal of Personality and Social Psychology*, **48**, 267–282.

Bond, C. F., Jr., & Brockett, D. R. (1987). A social context-personality index theory of memory for acquaintances. *Journal of Personality and Social Psychology*, **6**, 1110–1121.

Bond, C. F., Jr., & Sedikides, C. (1988). The recapitulation hypothesis in person retrieval. *Journal of Experimental Social Psychology*, **24**, 195–221.

Bower, G. H. (1981). Emotional mood and memory. *American Psychologist*, **36**, 129–148.

Brewer, M. B. (1979). In-group bias in the minimal intergroup situation: A cognitive-motivational analysis. *Psychological Bulletin*, **86**, 307–324.

Brewer, M. B. (1988). A dual process model of impression formation. In T. K. Srull & R. S. Wyer, Jr. (Eds.), *Advances in social cognition: Vol. 1. A dual model of impression formation* (pp. 1–36). Hillsdale, NJ: Erlbaum.

Brewer, M. B., Dull, V., & Lui, L. (1981). Perceptions of the elderly: Stereotypes as prototypes. *Journal of Personality and Social Psychology*, **41**, 656–670.

Brewer, M. B., & Silver, M. (1978). Ingroup bias as a function of task characteristics. *European Journal of Social Psychology*, **8**, 393–400.

Brigham, J. C. (1971). Ethnic stereotypes. *Psychological Bulletin*, **76**, 15–38.

Brooks, L. (1978). Nonanalytic concept formation and memory for instances. In E. Rosch & B. B. Lloyd (Eds.), *Cognition and categorization* (pp. 169–211). Hillsdale, NJ: Erlbaum.

Brown, R. (1986). *Social psychology: The second edition*. New York: Free Press.

Brown, V., & Geis, F. L. (1984). Turning lead into gold: Evaluations of men and women leaders and the alchemy of social consensus. *Journal of Personality and Social Psychology*, **46**, 811–824.

Bruner, J. S. (1957a). Going beyond the information given. In H. E. Gruber, K. R. Hammond, & R. Jessor (Eds.), *Contemporary approaches to cognition* (pp. 41–69). Cambridge, MA: Harvard University Press.

Bruner, J. S. (1957b). On perceptual readiness. *Psychological Review*, **64**, 123–152.

Bruner, J. S. (1958). Social psychology and perception. In E. E. Maccoby, T. M. Newcomb, & E. L. Hartley (Eds.), *Readings in social psychology* (3rd ed., pp. 85–94). New York: Holt, Rinehart & Winston.

Burnstein, E., & Schul, Y. (1982). The informational basis of social judgments: Operations in

forming impressions of other persons. *Journal of Experimental Social Psychology,* **18,** 217–234.
Burnstein, E., & Schul, Y. (1983). The informational basis of social judgments: Memory for integrated and nonintegrated trait descriptions. *Journal of Experimental Social Psychology,* **19,** 49–57.
Cantor, N., Markus, H., Niedenthal, P., & Nurius, P. (1986). On motivation and the self-concept. In R. M. Sorrentino & E. T. Higgins (Eds.), *Handbook of motivation and cognition: Foundations of social behavior* (pp. 96–121). New York: Guilford Press.
Cantor, N., & Mischel, W. (1979). Prototypes in person perception. In L. Berkowitz (Ed.), *Advances in experimental social psychology* (Vol. 12, pp. 3–52). New York: Academic Press.
Cauthen, N. R., Robinson, I. E., & Krauss, H. H. (1971). Stereotypes: A review of the literature 1926–1965. *Journal of Social Psychology,* **84,** 103–125.
Chaiken, S. (1980). Heuristic versus systematic information processing and the use of source versus message cues in persuasion. *Journal of Personality and Social Psychology,* **39,** 752–766.
Chaiken, S., Liberman, A., & Eagly, A. H. (1989). Heuristic and systematic information processing within and beyond the persuasion context. In J. S. Uleman & J. A. Bargh (Eds.), *Unintended thought: Limits of awareness, intention, and control* (pp. 212–252). New York: Guilford Press.
Clark, M. S., & Isen, A. M. (1982). Toward understanding the relationship between feeling states and social behavior. In A. Hastorf & A. Isen (Eds.), *Cognitive social psychology* (pp. 73–108). New York: Elsevier/North-Holland.
Cohen, A. R. (1961). Cognitive tuning as a factor affecting impression formation. *Journal of Personality,* **29,** 235–245.
Cohen, C. E. (1981). Person categories and social perception: Testing some boundaries of the processing effects of prior knowledge. *Journal of Personality and Social Psychology,* **40,** 441–452.
Cohen, C. E., & Ebbesen, E. B. (1979). Observational goals and schema activation: A theoretical framework for behavior perception. *Journal of Experimental Social Psychology,* **15,** 305–329.
Costrich, N., Feinstein, J., Kidder, L., Marecek, J., & Pascale, L. (1975). When stereotypes hurt: Three studies of penalties for sex-role reversals. *Journal of Experimental and Social Psychology,* **11,** 520–530.
Crocker, J., & Gallo, L. (1985). *The self-enhancing effect of downward comparison.* Paper presented at the meeting of the American Psychological Association, Los Angeles.
Crocker, J., Hannah, D. B., & Weber, R. (1983). Person memory and causal attributions. *Journal of Personality and Social Psychology,* **44,** 55–66.
Crocker, J., Thompson, L., McGraw, K. M., & Ingerman, C. (1987). Downward comparison, prejudice and evaluations of others: Effects of self-esteem and threat. *Journal of Personality and Social Psychology,* **52,** 907–916.
Cronbach, L. J. (1955). Processes affecting scores on "understanding of others" and "assumed similarity." *Psychological Bulletin,* **52,** 177–193.
Crosby, F., Bromley, S., & Saxe, L. (1980). Recent unobtrusive studies of black and white discrimination and prejudice: A literature review. *Psychological Bulletin,* **87,** 546–563.
Darley, J. M., & Fazio, R. H. (1980). Expectancy confirmation processes arising in the social interaction sequence. *American Psychologist,* **35,** 867–881.
Darley, J. M., Fleming, J. H., Hilton, J. L., & Swann, W. B., Jr., (1988). Dispelling negative expectancies: The impact of interaction goals and target characteristics on the expectancy confirmation process. *Journal of Experimental Social Psychology,* **24,** 19–36.
Darley, J. M., & Gross, P. H. (1983). A hypothesis-confirming bias in labeling effects. *Journal of Personality and Social Psychology,* **44,** 20–33.
Deaux, K., & Lewis, L. (1984). The structure of gender stereotypes: Interrelationships among components and gender label. *Journal of Personality and Social Psychology,* **46,** 991–1004.

Devine, P. G. (1989). Stereotypes and prejudice: Their automatic and controlled components. *Journal of Personality and Social Psychology,* **56,** 5–18.
Dipboye, R. L., Fromkin, H. L., & Wiback, K. (1975). Relative importance of applicant sex, attractiveness, and scholastic standing in evaluation of job applicant resumes. *Journal of Applied Psychology,* **60,** 39–43.
Dipboye, R. L., & Wiley, J. W. (1977). Reactions of college recruiters to interviewer sex and self-presentation style. *Journal of Vocational Behavior,* **10,** 1–12.
Dovidio, J. F., Evans, N., & Tyler, R. B. (1986). Racial stereotypes: The contents of their cognitive representations. *Journal of Experimental Social Psychology,* **22,** 22–37.
Duncan, S. L. (1976). Differential social perception and attribution of intergroup violence: Testing the lower limits of stereotyping of blacks. *Journal of Personality and Social Psychology,* **34,** 590–598.
Erber, R. (1985). *Choosing among multiple categories: The effects of moods on category accessibility, inference, and interpersonal affect.* Unpublished doctoral dissertation, Carnegie-Mellon University, Pittsburgh, PA.
Erber, R., & Fiske, S. T. (1984). Outcome dependency and attention to inconsistent information. *Journal of Personality and Social Psychology,* **47,** 709–726.
Fazio, R. H. (1986). How do attitudes guide behavior? In R. M. Sorrentino & E. T. Higgins (Eds.), *Handbook of motivation and cognition: Foundations of social behavior* (pp. 204–243). New York: Guilford Press.
Fishbein, M., & Ajzen, I. (1974). Attitudes toward objects as predictors of single and multiple behavioral criteria. *Psychological Review,* **81,** 59–74.
Fishbein, M., & Ajzen, I. (1975). *Belief, attitude, intention, and behavior: An introduction to theory and research.* Reading, MA: Addison-Wesley.
Fiske, S. T. (1982). Schema-triggered affect: Applications to social perception. In M. S. Clark & S. T. Fiske (Eds.), *Affect and cognition: The 17th Annual Carnegie Symposium on Cognition* (pp. 55–78). Hillsdale, NJ: Erlbaum.
Fiske, S. T. (1988). Compare and contrast: Brewer's dual-process model and Fiske *et al.*'s continuum model. In T. K. Srull & R. S. Wyer, Jr. (Eds.), *Advances in social cognition: Vol. 1. A dual model of impression formation* (pp. 65–76). Hillsdale, NJ: Erlbaum.
Fiske, S. T. (1989). Examining the role of intent: Toward understanding its role in stereotyping and prejudice. In J. S. Uleman & J. A. Bargh (Eds.),*Unintended thought: The limits of awareness, intention, and control* (pp. 253–283). New York: Guilford Press.
Fiske, S. T., & Cox, M. G. (1979). Person concepts: The effects of target familiarity and descriptive purpose on the process of describing others. *Journal of Personality,* **47,** 136–161.
Fiske, S. T., & Dyer, L. M. (1985). Structure and development of social schemata: Evidence from positive and negative transfer effects. *Journal of Personality and Social Psychology,* **48,** 839–852.
Fiske, S. T., Kinder, D. R., & Larter, W. M. (1983). The novice and the expert: Knowledge-based strategies in political cognition. *Journal of Experimental Social Psychology,* **19,** 381–400.
Fiske, S. T., & Linville, P. W. 91980). What does the schema concept buy us? *Personality and Social Psychology Bulletin,* **6,** 543–557.
Fiske, S. T., Neuberg, S. L., Beattie, A. E., & Milberg, S. J. (1984). Unpublished response-time data, Carnegie-Mellon University. Cited in Fiske & Pavelchak (1986).
Fiske, S. T., Neuberg, S. L., Beattie, A. E., & Milberg, S. J. (1987). Category-based and attribute-based reactions to others: Some informational conditions of stereotyping and individuating processes. *Journal of Experimental Social Psychology,* **23,** 399–427.
Fiske, S. T., Neuberg, S. L., Pratto, F., & Allman, C. (1986). *Stereotyping and individuation: The effects of information inconsistency and set size on attribute-oriented processing.* Unpublished manuscript, University of Massachusetts at Amherst.

Fiske, S. T., & Pavelchak, M. A. (1986). Category-based versus piecemeal-based affective responses: Developments in schema-triggered affect. In R. M. Sorrentino & E. T. Higgins (Eds.), *Handbook of motivation and cognition: Foundations of social behavior* (pp. 167–203). New York: Guilford Press.

Fiske, S. T., & Taylor, S. E. (1984). *Social cognition.* New York: Random House.

Fiske, S. T., & Von Hendy, H. (1989). *Categorizing and individuating impression formation strategies resulting from false feedback to perceivers.* Unpublished manuscript, University of Massachusetts at Amherst.

Freund, T., Kruglanski, A. W., & Shpitizajzen, A. (1985). The freezing and unfreezing of impression primacy: Effects of the need for structure and the fear of invalidity. *Personality and Social Psychology Bulletin,* **11,** 479–487.

Gaertner, S. L., & McLaughlin, J. P. (1983). Racial stereotypes: Associations and ascriptions of positive and negative characteristics. *Social Psychology Quarterly,* **46,** 23–30.

Gibson, J. J. (1979). *The ecological approach to visual perception.* Boston: Houghton Mifflin.

Gilbert, G. M. (1951). Stereotype persistence and change among college students. *Journal of Abnormal and Social Psychology,* **46,** 245–254.

Hamilton, D. L. (1979). A cognitive-attributional analysis of stereotyping. In L. Berkowitz (Ed.), *Advances in experimental social psychology* (Vol. 12, pp. 53–84). New York: Academic Press.

Hamilton, D. L. (1981). Stereotyping and intergroup behavior: Some thoughts on the cognitive approach. In D. L. Hamilton (Ed.), *Cognitive processes in stereotyping and intergroup behavior* (pp. 333–353). Hillsdale, NJ: Erlbaum.

Hamilton, D. L., & Trolier, T. K. (1986). Stereotypes and stereotyping: An overview of the cognitive approach. In J. Dovidio & S. L. Gaertner (Eds.), *Prejudice, discrimination, and racism.* New York: Academic Press.

Harkness, A. R., DeBono, K. G., & Borgida, E. (1985). Personal involvement and strategies for making contingency judgments: A stake in the dating game makes a difference. *Journal of Personality and Social Psychology,* **49,** 22–32.

Hastie, R. (1981). Schematic principles in human memory. In E. T. Higgins, C. P. Herman, & M. P. Zanna (Eds.), *Social cognition: The Ontario Symposium* (Vol. 1, pp. 39–88). Hillsdale, NJ: Erlbaum.

Hastie, R. (1984). Causes and effects of causal attribution. *Journal of Personality and Social Psychology,* **46,** 44–56.

Hastie, R., & Kumar, P. A. (1979). Person memory: Personality traits as organizing principles in memory for behavior. *Journal of Personality and Social Psychology,* **37,** 25–38.

Heilman, M. E. (1984). Information as a deterrent against sex discrimination: The effects of applicant sex and information type on preliminary employment decisions. *Organizational Behavior and Human Performance,* **33,** 174–186.

Heneman, H. G. (1977). Impact of test information and applicant sex on applicant evaluations in a selection simulation. *Journal of Applied Psychology,* **62,** 524–526.

Higgins, E. T. (1981). The "communication game": Implications for social cognition and persuasion. In E. T. Higgins, C. P. Herman, & M. P. Zanna (Eds.), *Social cognition: The Ontario Symposium* (Vol. 1, pp. 343–392). Hillsdale, NJ: Erlbaum.

Higgins, E. T., & Bargh, J. A. (1987). Social cognition and social perception. *Annual Review of Psychology,* **38,** 369–425.

Higgins, E. T., & King, G. A. (1981). Accessibility of social constructs: Information-processing consequences of individual and contextual variability. In N. Cantor & J. F. Kihlstrom (Eds.), *Personality, cognition, and social interaction* (pp. 69–121). Hillsdale, NJ: Erlbaum.

Higgins, E. T., King, G. A., & Mavin, G. H. (1982). Individual construct accessibility and subjective impressions and recall. *Journal of Personality and Social Psychology,* **43,** 35–47.

Higgins, E. T., McCann, C. D., & Fondacaro, R. (1982). The "communication game": Goal-directed encoding and cognitive consequences. *Social Cognition*, **1**, 21–37.

Higgins, E. T., Rholes, W. S., & Jones, C. R. (1977). Category accessibility and impression formation. *Journal of Experimental Social Psychology*, **13**, 141–154.

Hilton, J. L., & Darley, J. M. (1985). Constructing other persons: A limit on the effect. *Journal of Experimental Social Psychology*, **21**, 1–18.

Hoffman, C., Mischel, W., & Baer, J. S. (1984). Language and person cognition: Effects of communicative set on trait attribution. *Journal of Personality and Social Psychology*, **46**, 1029–1043.

Hoffman, C., Mischel, W., & Mazze, K. (1981). The role of purpose in the organization of information about behavior: Trait-based versus goal-based categories in person cognition. *Journal of Personality and Social Psychology*, **40**, 211–225.

Hoffman, M. L. (1986). Affect, cognition, and motivation. In R. M. Sorrentino & E. T. Higgins (Eds.), *Handbook of motivation and cognition: Foundations of social behavior* (pp. 244–280). New York: Guilford Press.

Holmes, J. G., Zanna, M. P., & Whitehead, L. A. (1986). *Stress and social perception*. Unpublished manuscript, University of Waterloo, Waterloo, Ontario.

Isen, A. M. (1984). Toward understanding the role of affect in cognition. In R. S. Wyer, Jr. & T. K. Srull (Eds.), *Handbook of social cognition* (Vol. 3, p. 179–236). Hillsdale, NJ: Erlbaum.

Jamieson, D. W., & Zanna, M. P. (1988). Need for structure in attitude formation and expression. In A. R. Pratkanis, S. J. Breckler, & A. G. Greenwald (Eds.), *Attitude structure and function*. Hillsdale, NJ: Erlbaum.

Janis, I. L., & Mann, L. (1977). *Decision making*. New York: Free Press.

Jones, E. E., & deCharms, R. (1957). Changes in social perception as a function of the personal relevance of behavior. *Sociometry*, **20**, 75–85.

Jones, E. E., Farina, A., Hastorf, A. H., Markus, H., Miller, D. T., & Scott, R. A. (1984). *Social stigma: The psychology of marked relationships*. New York: W. H. Freeman.

Jones, E. E., & Goethals, G. (1972). Order effects in impression formation: Attribution context and the nature of the entity. In E. E. Jones, D. E. Kanouse, H. H. Kelley, R. E. Nisbett, S. Valins, & B. Weiner (Eds.), *Attribution: Perceiving the causes of behavior* (pp. 27–46). Morristown, NJ: General Learning Press.

Jones, E. E., & McGillis, D. (1976). Correspondent inferences and the attribution cube: A comparative reappraisal. In J. H. Harvey, W. J. Ickes, & R. F. Kidd (Eds.), *New directions in attribution research* (Vol. 1, pp. 389–420). Hillsdale, NJ: Erlbaum.

Jones, E. E., & Thibaut, J. W. (1958). Interaction goals as bases of interference in interpersonal perception. In R. Tagiuri & L. Petrullo (Eds.), *Person perception and interpersonal behavior*. Stanford, CA: Stanford University Press.

Kahneman, D., & Miller, D. T. (1986). Norm theory: Comparing reality to its alternatives. *Psychological Review*, **93**, 136–153.

Kanter, R. (1977). *Men and women of the corporation*. New York: Basic Books.

Karlins, M., Coffman, T. L., & Walters, G. (1969). On the fading of social stereotypes: Studies in three generations of college students. *Journal of Personality and Social Psychology*, **13**, 1–16.

Katz, D., & Braly, K. N. (1933). Verbal stereotypes and racial prejudice. *Journal of Abnormal and Social Psychology*, **133**, 280–290.

Katz, I., & Hass, R. G. (1988). Racial ambivalence and American value conflict: Correlational and priming studies of dual cognitive structures. *Journal of Personality and Social Psychology*, **55**, 893–905.

Kelley, H. H., Berscheid, E., Christensen, A., Harvey, J. H., Huston, T. L., Levinger, G., McClintock, E., Peplau, L. A., & Peterson, D. R. (1983). Analyzing close relationships. In H. H. Kelley, E. Berscheid, A. Christensen, J. H. Harvey, T. L. Huston, G. Levinger, E.

McClintock, L. A. Peplau, & D. R. Peterson, (Eds.), *Close relationships* (pp. 20–67). New York: W. H. Freeman.

Kelley, H. H., & Thibaut, J. W. (1978). *Interpersonal relations: A theory of interdependence.* New York: Wiley-Interscience.

Klatzky, R. L., Martin, G. L., & Kane, R. A. (1982). Influence of social-category activation on processing of visual information. *Social Cognition,* **1,** 95–109.

Koller, M., & Wicklund, R. A. (1988). Press and task difficulty as determinants of preoccupation with person descriptors. *Journal of Experimental Social Psychology,* **24,** 256–274.

Kruglanski, A. W. (1989). *Motivations for judging and knowing: Implications for causal attribution.* In E. T. Higgins & R. M. Sorrentino (Eds.), *Handbook of motivation and cognition: Foundations of social behavior* (Vol. 2). New York: Guilford Press, in press.

Kruglanski, A. W., & Freund, T. (1983). The freezing and unfreezing of lay-inferences: Effects of impressional primacy, ethnic stereotyping, and numerical anchoring. *Journal of Experimental Social Psychology,* **19,** 448–468.

Kuhl, J. (1984). Volitional aspects of achievement motivation and learned helplessness: Toward a comprehensive theory of action control. In B. Maher (Ed.), *Progress in Experimental Personality Research* (Vol. 13, pp. 99–171). New York: Academic Press.

Kuhl, J. (1986). Motivation and information processing: A new look at decision making, dynamic change, and action control. In R. M. Sorrentino & E. T. Higgins (Eds.), *The handbook of motivation and cognition: Foundations of social behavior* (pp. 404–434). New York: Guilford Press.

Kulik, J. A. (1983). Confirmatory attribution and the perpetuation of social beliefs. *Journal of Personality and Social Psychology,* **44,** 1171–1181.

Langer, E. J., & Abelson, R. P. (1974). A patient by any other name . . . : Clinician group difference in labeling bias. *Journal of Consulting and Clinical Psychology,* **42,** 4–9.

Leary, M. R., Kowalski, R. M., & Bergen, D. J. (1988). Interpersonal information acquisition and confidence in first encounters. *Personality and Social Psychology Bulletin,* **14,** 68–77.

Leventhal, H. (1962). The effects of set and discrepancy on impression change. *Journal of Personality,* **30,** 1–15.

Lingle, J. H., Altom, M. W., & Medin, D. L. (1984). Of cabbages and kings: Assessing the extendibility of natural object concept models to social things. In R. S. Wyer, Jr. & R. K. Srull (Eds.), *Handbook of social cognition* (Vol. 1, pp. 71–117). Hillsdale, NJ: Erlbaum.

Lippmann, W. (1922). *Public opinion.* New York: Harcourt-Brace.

Locksley, A., Borgida, E., Brekke, N., & Hepburn, C. (1980). Sex stereotypes and social judgment. *Journal of Personality and Social Psychology,* **39,** 821–831.

Locksley, A., Hepburn, C., & Ortiz, V. (1982). Social stereotypes and judgments of individuals: An instance of the base-rate fallacy. *Journal of Experimental Social Psychology,* **18,** 23–42.

Lopes, L. L. (1982). *Toward a procedural theory of judgment* (WHIPP 17). Madison, WI: University of Wisconsin, Wisconsin Human Information Processing Program.

Lord, C. G., Lepper, M. R., & Preston, E. (1984). Considering the opposite: A corrective strategy for social judgment. *Journal of Personality and Social Psychology,* **47,** 1231–1243.

Malpass, R. S., & Kravitz, J. (1969). Recognition for faces of own and other race. *Journal of Personality and Social Psychology,* **13,** 330–334.

Malpass, R. S., Lavigueur, H., & Weldon, D. E. (1973). Verbal and visual training in face recognition. *Perception & Psychophysics,* **14,** 285–292.

Markus, H. (1977). Self-schemata and processing information about the self. *Journal of Personality and Social Psychology,* **35,** 63–78.

Markus, H., Smith, J., & Moreland, R. L. (1985). Role of the self-concept in the perception of others. *Journal of Personality and Social Psychology,* **49,** 1494–1512.

Markus, H., & Zajonc, R. B. (1985). The cognitive perspective in social psychology. In G. Lindzey

& E. Aronson (Eds.), *Handbook of social psychology* (3rd ed., Vol. 1, pp. 137–230). New York: Random House.

Mayseless, O., & Kruglanski, A. W. (1987). What makes you so sure? Effects of epistemic motivations on judgmental confidence. *Organizational Behavior and Human Decision Processes,* **39,** 162–183.

McArthur, L. Z. (1982). Judging a book by its cover: A cognitive analysis of the relationship between physical appearance and stereotyping. In A. Hastorf & A. Isen (Eds.), *Cognitive social psychology* (pp. 149–210). New York: Elsevier/North-Holland.

McArthur, L. Z., & Baron, R. (1983). Toward an ecological theory of social perception. *Psychological Review,* **90,** 215–238.

McArthur, L. Z., & Post, D. L. (1977). Figural emphasis and person perception. *Journal of Experimental Social Psychology,* **13,** 520–535.

Medin, D. L., & Schaffer, M. M. (1978). Context theory of classification learning. *Psychological Review,* **85,** 207–238.

Miller, A. G. (Ed.). (1982). *In the eye of the beholder: Contemporary issues in stereotyping.* New York: Praeger.

Miller, D. T., & Turnbull, W. (1986). Expectancies and interpersonal processes. *Annual Review of Psychology,* **37,** 233–256.

Miller, N., & Brewer, M. B. (Eds.). (1984). *Groups in contact.* New York: Academic Press.

Milord, J. T. (1978). Aesthetic aspects of faces: A (somewhat) phenomenological analysis using multidimensional scaling methods. *Journal of Personality and Social Psychology,* **36,** 205–216.

Mischel, W. (1979). On the interface of cognition and personality: Beyond the person–situation debate. *American Psychologist,* **34,** 740–754.

Murphy, G. L., & Medin, D. L. (1985). The role of theories in conceptual coherence. *Psychological Review,* **92,** 289–316.

Neuberg, S. L. (1988). Behavioral implications of information presented outside of conscious awareness: The effect of subliminal presentation of trait information on behavior in the prisoner's dilemma game. *Social Cognition,* **6,** 207–230.

Neuberg, S. L. (1989). The goal of forming accurate impressions during social interactions: Attenuating the impact of negative expectancies. *Journal of Personality and Social Psychology,* **56,** 374–386.

Neuberg, S. L., & Fiske, S. T. (1986). Unpublished data, Carnegie-Mellon University, Pittsburgh, PA.

Neuberg, S. L., & Fiske, S. T. (1987). Motivational influences on impression formation: Outcome dependency, accuracy-driven attention, and individuating processes. *Journal of Personality and Social Psychology,* **53,** 431–444.

Nisbett, R. E., Zukier, H., & Lemley, R. E. (1981). The dilution effect: Non-diagnostic information weakens the implications of diagnostic information. *Cognitive Psychology,* **13,** 248–277.

Omoto, A. M., & Borgida, E. (1988). Guess who might be coming to dinner? Personal involvement and racial stereotypes. *Journal of Experimental Social Psychology,* **24,** 571–593.

O'Sullivan, C. S., & Durso, F. T. (1984). Effect of schema-incongruent information on memory for stereotypical attributes. *Journal of Personality and Social Psychology,* **47,** 55–70.

Park, B., & Rothbart, M. (1982). Perception of out-group homogeneity and levels of social categorization: Memory of the subordinate attributes of in-group and out-group members. *Journal of Personality and Social Psychology,* **42,** 1051–1068.

Pavelchak, M. (1989). Forming impressions of others: A demonstration of two distinct processes using an idiographic measurement technique. *Journal of Personality and Social Psychology,* **56,** 354–363.

Pettigrew, T. F., & Martin, J. (1987). Shaping the organizational context for black American inclusion. *Journal of Social Issues,* **43,** 41–78.

Petty, R. E., Cacioppo, J. T., & Goldman, R. (1981). Personal involvement as a determinant of argument-based persuasion. *Journal of Personality and Social Psychology, 41,* 847–855.

Pheterson, G. I., Kiesler, S., & Goldberg, P. A. (1971). Evaluation of the performance of women as a function of their sex, achievement, and personal history. *Journal of Personality and Social Psychology, 19,* 114–118.

Pittman, T. S., & Heller, J. F. (1987). Social motivation. *Annual Review of Psychology, 38,* 461–489.

Posner, M. I., Nissen, M. J., & Klein, R. M. (1976). Visual dominance: An information processing account of its origins and significance. *Psychological Review, 83,* 157–171.

Quattrone, G. A. (1986). On the perception of a group's variability. In S. Worchel & W. Austin (Eds.), *The psychology of intergroup relations* (Vol. 2, pp. 25–48). New York: Nelson-Hall.

Quattrone, G. A., & Jones, E. E. (1980). The perception of variability within ingroups and outgroups: Implications for the Law of Small Numbers. *Journal of Personality and Social Psychology, 38,* 141–152.

Rabbie, J. M., & Wilkins, G. (1971). Intergroup competition and its effect on intragroup and intergroup religion. *European Journal of Social Psychology, 1,* 215–234.

Rasinski, K. A., Crocker, J., & Hastie, R. (1985). Another look at sex stereotypes and social judgments: An analysis of the social perceiver's use of subjective probabilities. *Journal of Personality and Social Psychology, 49,* 317–326.

Renwick, P. A., & Tosi, H. (1978). The effects of sex, marital status, and educational background on selection decisions. *Academy of Management Journal, 21,* 93–103.

Rodin, M. J. (1987). Who is memorable to whom: A study of cognitive disregard. *Social Cognition, 5,* 144–165.

Rosch, E. (1978). Principles of categorization. In E. Rosch & B. B. Lloyd (Eds.), *Cognition and categorization* (pp. 27–48). Hillsdale, NJ: Erlbaum.

Rosch, E., & Lloyd, B. B. (Eds.). (1978). *Cognition and categorization.* Hillsdale, NJ: Erlbaum.

Ross, L., Lepper, M. R., & Hubbard, M. (1975). Perseverance in self-perception and social perception: Biased attribution process in the debriefing paradigm. *Journal of Personality and Social Psychology, 32,* 880–892.

Rothbart, M., Evans, M., & Fulero, S. (1979). Recall for confirming events: Memory processes and the maintenance of social stereotyping. *Journal of Experimental Social Psychology, 15,* 343–355.

Ruble, D. N., & Ruble, T. L. (1982). Sex stereotypes. In A. G. Miller (Ed.), *In the eye of the beholder: Contemporary issues in stereotyping* (pp. 188–252). New York: Praeger.

Ruble, D. N., & Stangor, C. (1986). Stalking the elusive schema: Insights from developmental and social-psychological analyses of gender schemas. *Social Cognition, 4,* 227–261.

Rumelhart, D. E., & Ortony, A. (1977). The representation of knowledge in memory. In R. C. Anderson, R. J. Spiro, & W. E. Montague (Eds.), *Schooling and the acquisition of knowledge* (pp. 99–135). Hillsdale, NJ: Erlbaum.

Ruscher, J. B., & Fiske, S. T. (1988). *Interpersonal competition can cause individuating impression formation.* Unpublished manuscript, University of Massachusetts at Amherst.

Sagar, H. A., & Schofield, J. W. (1980). Racial and behavioral cues in black and white children's perceptions of ambiguously aggressive acts. *Journal of Personality and Social Psychology, 39,* 590–598.

Saltzer, E. B. (1981). Cognitive moderators of the relationship between behavioral intentions and behavior. *Journal of Personality and Social Psychology, 41,* 260–275.

Secord, P. F. (1958). Facial features and inference processes in interpersonal perception. In R. Tagiuri & L. Petrullo (Eds.), *Person perception and interpersonal behavior* (pp. 300–315). Stanford, CA: Stanford University Press.

Secord, P. F. (1959). Stereotyping and favorableness in the perception of Negro faces. *Journal of Abnormal and Social Psychology,* **59,** 309–321.

Secord, P. F., Bevan, W., & Katz, B. (1956). Perceptual accentuation and the Negro stereotype. *Journal of Abnormal and Social Psychology,* **53,** 78–83.

Sentis, K. P., & Burnstein, E. (1979). Remembering schema-consistent information: Effects of a balance schema on recognition memory. *Journal of Personality and Social Psychology,* **37,** 2200–2211.

Showers, C., & Cantor, N. (1985). Social cognition: A look at motivated strategies. *Annual Review of Psychology,* **36,** 275–305.

Smith, E. E., & Medin, D. L. (1981). *Categories and concepts.* Cambridge, MA: Harvard University Press.

Snyder, M. (1982). When believing means doing: Creating links between attitudes and behavior. In M. P. Zanna, E. T. Higgins, & C. P. Herman (Eds.), *Consistency in social behavior: The Ontario Symposium* (Vol. 2, pp. 105–130). Hillsdale, NJ: Erlbaum.

Snyder, M., Campbell, B. H., & Preston, E. (1982). Testing hypothesis about human nature: Assessing the accuracy of social stereotypes. *Social Cognition,* **1,** 256–272.

Snyder, M., Tanke, E. D., & Berscheid, E. (1977). Social perception and interpersonal behavior: On the self-fulfilling nature of social stereotypes. *Journal of Personality and Social Psychology,* **35,** 656–666.

Snyder, M., & Uranowitz, S. W. (1978). Reconstructing the past: Some cognitive consequences of person perception. *Journal of Personality and Social Psychology,* **36,** 941–950.

Sorrentino, R. M., & Higgins, E. T. (1986). *Handbook of motivation and cognition: Foundations of social behavior.* New York: Guilford Press.

Srull, T. K. (1981). Person memory: Some tests of associative storage and retrieval models. *Journal of Experimental Psychology: Human Learning and Memory,* **7,** 440–463.

Srull, T. K., Lichtenstein, M., & Rothbart, M. (1985). Associative storage and retrieval processes in person memory. *Journal of Experimental Psychology: Learning, Memory, and Cognition,* **11,** 316–345.

Srull, T. K., & Wyer, R. S., Jr. (1979). The role of category accessibility in the interpretation of information about persons: Some determinants and implications. *Journal of Personality and Social Psychology,* **37,** 1660–1672.

Srull, T. K., & Wyer, R. S., Jr. (1986). The role of chronic and temporary goals in social information processing. In R. M. Sorrentino & E. T. Higgins (Eds.), *Handbook of motivation and cognition: Foundations of social behavior* (pp. 503–549). New York: Guilford Press.

Stephan, W. G., & Rosenfield, D. (1982). Racial and ethnic stereotypes. In A. G. Miller (Ed.), *In the eye of the beholder.* New York: Praeger.

Sujan, M. (1985). Consumer knowledge: Effects on evaluation strategies mediating consumer judgments. *Journal of Consumer Research,* **12,** 1–16.

Tajfel, H. (1969). Cognitive aspects of prejudice. *Journal of Social Issues,* **25,** 79–97.

Tajfel, H., & Billig, M. (1974). Familiarity and categorization in intergroup behavior. *Journal of Experimental Social Psychology,* **10,** 159–170.

Tajfel, H., Billig, M., Bundy, R. P., & Flament, C. (1971). Social categorization and intergroup behavior. *European Journal of Social Psychology,* **1,** 149–178.

Tajfel, H., & Wilkes, A. L. (1963). Classification and quantitative judgment. *British Journal of Psychology,* **54,** 101–114.

Taylor, S. E. (1981). A categorization approach to stereotyping. In D. L. Hamilton (Ed.), *Cognitive processes in stereotyping and intergroup behavior* (pp. 88–114). Hillsdale, NJ: Erlbaum.

Taylor, S. E., & Crocker, J. (1981). Schematic bases of social information processing. In E. T. Higgins, C. P. Herman, & M. P. Zanna (Eds.), *Social cognition: The Ontario Symposium* (Vol. 1, pp. 89–134). Hillsdale, NJ: Erlbaum.

Taylor, S. E., Fiske, S. T., Close, M., Anderson, C., & Ruderman, A. (1977). *Solo status as a psychological variable: The power of being distinctive*. Unpublished manuscript, Harvard University, Cambridge, MA.
Taylor, S. E., Fiske, S. T., Etcoff, N. L., & Ruderman, A. J. (1978). Categorical bases of person memory and stereotyping. *Journal of Personality and Social Psychology*, **36**, 778–793.
Tesser, A. (1978). Self-generated attitude change. In L. Berkowitz (Ed.), *Advances in Experimental Social Psychology* (Vol. 11, pp. 289–338). New York: Academic Press.
Tetlock, P. E. (1983a). Accountability and complexity of thought. *Journal of Personality and Social Psychology*, **45**, 74–83.
Tetlock, P. E. (1983b). Accountability and the perseverance of first impressions. *Social Psychology Quarterly*, **46**, 285–292.
Tetlock, P. E. (1985). Accountability: A social check on the fundamental attribution error. *Social Psychology Quarterly*, **48**, 227–236.
Tetlock, P. E., & Boettger, R. (in press). Accountability: A social magnifier of the dilution effect. *Journal of Personality and Social Psychology*.
Tetlock, P. E., & Kim, J. I. (1987). Accountability and judgment processes in a personality prediction task. *Journal of Personality and Social Psychology*, **52**, 700–709.
Thibaut, J. W., & Kelley, H. H. (1959). *The social psychology of groups*. New York: Wiley.
Touhey, J. C. (1972). Role perception and the relative influence of the perceiver and the perceived. *Journal of Social Psychology*, **87**, 213–217.
Tsujimoto, R. N. (1978). Memory bias toward normative and novel trait prototypes. *Journal of Personality and Social Psychology*, **36**, 1391–1401.
Tsujimoto, R. N., Wilde, J., & Robertson, D. R. (1978). Distorted memory for exemplars of a social structure: Evidence for schematic memory processes. *Journal of Personality and Social Psychology*, **36**, 1402–1414.
Tversky, A. (1977). Features of similarity. *Psychological Review*, **84**, 327–352.
Vinacke, W. E. (1957). Stereotypes as social concepts. *Journal of Social Psychology*, **46**, 229–243.
Warshaw, P. R., & Davis, F. D. (1985). Disentangling behavioral intention and behavioral expectation. *Journal of Experimental Social Psychology*, **21**, 213–228.
Weber, R., & Crocker, J. (1983). Cognitive processes in the revision of stereotypic beliefs. *Journal of Personality and Social Psychology*, **45**, 961–977.
Weiner, B. (1986). Attribution, emotion, and action. In R. M. Sorrentino & E. T. Higgins (Eds.), *Handbook of motivation and cognition: Foundations of social behavior* (pp. 281–312). New York: Guilford Press.
Weldon, E., & Gargano, G. M. (1988). Cognitive loafing: The effects of accountability and shared responsibility on cognitive effort. *Personality and Social Psychology Bulletin*, **14**, 159–171.
Wilder, D. A. (1978). Perceiving people as a group: Effects on attributions of causality and beliefs. *Social Psychology*, **1**, 13–23.
Wilder, D. A. (1981). Perceiving persons as a group: Categorization and intergroup relations. In D. L. Hamilton (Ed.), *Cognitive processes in stereotyping and intergroup behavior*. Hillsdale, NJ: Erlbaum.
Wolman, C., & Frank, H. (1975). The solo woman in a professional peer group. *American Journal of Orthopsychiatry*, **45**, 164–171.
Word, C. O., Zanna, M. P., & Cooper, J. (1974). The nonverbal mediation of self-fulfilling prophecies in interracial interaction. *Journal of Experimental Social Psychology*, **10**, 109–120.
Wyer, R. S., Jr., & Carlston, D. (1979). *Social cognition, inference, and attribution*. Hillsdale, NJ: Erlbaum.
Wyer, R. S., Jr., & Martin, L. L. (1986). Person memory: The role of traits, group stereotypes, and specific behaviors in the cognitive representation of persons. *Journal of Personality and Social Psychology*, **50**, 661–675.

Wyer, R. S., Jr., & Srull, T. K. (1980). The processing of social stimulus information: A conceptual integration. In R. Hastie, T. M. Ostrom, E. B. Ebbesen, R. S. Wyer, Jr., D. Hamilton, & D. E. Carlston (Eds.), *Person memory: The cognitive basis of social perception* (pp. 227–300). Hillsdale, NJ: Erlbaum.

Wyer, R. S., Jr., & Srull, T. K. (1981). Category accessibility: Some theoretical and empirical issues concerning the processing of social stimulus information. In E. T. Higgins, C. P. Herman, & M. P. Zanna (Eds.), *Social cognition: The Ontario Symposium* (Vol. 1, pp. 161–197). Hillsdale, NJ: Erlbaum.

Zajonc, R. B. (1960). The process of cognitive tuning in communication. *Journal of Abnormal and Social Psychology,* **61,** 159–167.

Zukier, H. (1982). The role of the correlation and the dispersion of predictor variables in the use of nondiagnostic information. *Journal of Personality and Social Psychology,* **43,** 1163–1175.

Zukier, H., & Pepitone, A. (1984). Social roles and strategies in prediction: Some determinants of the use of base-rate information. *Journal of Personality and Social Psychology,* **47,** 349–360.

MULTIPLE PROCESSES BY WHICH ATTITUDES GUIDE BEHAVIOR: THE MODE MODEL AS AN INTEGRATIVE FRAMEWORK

Russell H. Fazio

I. Introduction

Although the concept of attitude has been a central one in the field of social psychology for decades (Allport, 1935), it is not until relatively recently in this long history that much systematic work has been conducted on the correspondence between expressed attitudes and subsequent behavior. Researchers appear to have been more concerned with issues regarding attitude formation and change and, for the most part, appear to have presumed that attitudes guide later behavior. However, beginning in the late 1960s and running to the present time, a considerable amount of empirical work has addressed the issue of attitude–behavior consistency (see the *Annual Review* chapters by Chaiken & Stangor, 1987; Cialdini, Petty, & Cacioppo, 1981; Cooper & Croyle, 1984; Eagly & Himmelfarb, 1978).

Despite this increased attention over the last two decades, there exists a very fundamental question regarding the attitude–behavior relation that has not been subjected to much theoretical or empirical inquiry. The question concerns an issue of process: How do attitudes guide behavior? By what conceivably multiple processes do individuals' attitudes have impact on their behavior? The present article describes two very different basic processes that link attitudes and behavior, along with variants that amount to a mixture of the essentials of each process. Conditions that promote one process or the other also are discussed.

II. Current State of the Literature

Before presenting the two contrasting models of the attitude-to-behavior process, it is useful to consider the state of the present literature on attitude–

behavior consistency. Historically, the field shifted from virtual neglect of the issue of attitude–behavior correspondence to the more recent intense scrutiny of the issue. With the exception of a few early skeptics (e.g., Corey, 1937; LaPiere, 1934), the question of whether attitudes were predictive of subsequent behavior was largely ignored. Wicker's (1969) widely cited and extremely pessimistic review of the available literature called attention to the lack of supporting evidence, sparking interest and research. Later developments have made it clear that Wicker's conclusion regarding the lack of attitude–behavior consistency was overstated. Indeed, more recent reviews have portrayed the issue far more optimistically (Fazio & Zanna, 1981; Schuman & Johnson, 1976). The optimism stems, in part, from occasional observations of fairly impressive attitude–behavior correlations (e.g., Goodmonson & Glaudin, 1971; Kelley & Mirer, 1974; Seligman et al., 1979). Thus, it appears that attitude–behavior relations can range from zero to the very strong. Zanna and Fazio (1982) have referred to research that has asked "Is there an attitude–behavior relation?" as the first generation of work concerning attitude–behavior consistency. The answer to this "is" question appears to be a resounding "sometimes."

Given the range of outcomes observed across various investigations, researchers began to ask what Zanna and Fazio (1982) characterized as "when" questions. That is, when or under what conditions are attitudes predictive of behavior? In its most general form, the issue that this generation of research focused on was, "Under what conditions do what kinds of attitudes held by what kinds of individuals predict what kinds of behavior?" (Fazio & Zanna, 1981, p. 165). As indicated by the question, researchers began to search for situational factors, personality variables, and classes of attitudes and behaviors that might moderate the attitude–behavior relations.

These efforts to identify moderating variables have been remarkably successful in that the literature now provides documentation for a lengthy list of such moderators. With respect to situational variables, normative constraints or inducements have been shown to affect the attitude–behavior relation (e.g., Ajzen & Fishbein, 1973; Schofield, 1975; Warner & DeFleur, 1969), as does the degree to which individuals hold a vested interest in the behavioral issue (Sivacek & Crano, 1982). Situational cues that suggest that one's attitude is relevant to a behavioral decision also have been found to enhance the attitude–behavior relation (Borgida & Campbell, 1982; Snyder & Kendzierski, 1982). Various personality factors are also known to moderate the relation. For example, self-monitoring (Snyder & Swann, 1976; Zanna, Olson, & Fazio, 1980), self-consciousness (e.g., Scheier, Buss, & Buss, 1978), and level of moral reasoning (Rholes & Bailey, 1983) have each been found to relate to attitude–behavior consistency.

Just as some kinds of people are more apt to display consistency, some kinds of attitudes seem more likely to promote attitude–behavior consistency. Various attitudinal qualities, including the manner of attitude formation (Fazio & Zanna, 1981), the consistency between affective and cognitive components of attitudes (Norman, 1975), the temporal stability of the attitude (Schwartz, 1978), the confidence with which the attitude is held (Sample & Warland, 1973; Fazio & Zanna, 1978a, 1978b), and how clearly defined the attitude is, as measured by the width of the latitude of rejection (Fazio & Zanna, 1978b), have been found to moderate the attitude–behavior relation.

In addition to the variables mentioned above, it has been demonstrated that the prediction of behavior from attitude is improved by the assessment of attitudes and behaviors of equivalent levels of specificity (Ajzen, 1982; Ajzen & Fishbein, 1977; Fishbein & Ajzen, 1974). Essentially, specific behaviors are best predicted by a similarly specific attitude measure. General patterns of behavior or multiple behaviors are best predicted by a general attitude.

One conclusion is quite clear from even this brief summary of the present literature. There can be no doubt that attitudes do sometimes relate to subsequent behavior and that the field has achieved some understanding of just when that sometimes is. However, there are two additional, related observations that can be made. First, it is evident that the "when" approach has been primarily empirical in nature. What we have at this point in time is a fairly lengthy catalog of variables known to moderate the attitude–behavior relation. As commentators on this literature have noted, there has been a marked lack of theory (Cooper & Croyle, 1984). Second, there is the point alluded to earlier about the processes linking attitudes to behavior. Despite the resurgence of research on the attitude–behavior relation and despite the now voluminous literature, little attention has been paid to the very fundamental issue of how attitudes guide behavior. Throughout the literature, mention is made of attitudes guiding or influencing behavior with little or no accompanying explanation of how this might occur. It is this concern that Zanna and Fazio (1982) forecasted as the central issue of a third generation of research on attitude–behavior consistency.[1]

[1]Obviously, this categorization of the attitude–behavior literature into three generations of research was intended as a rough heuristic by which the literature could be organized and considered. It is not always the case that a single endeavor can be neatly characterized as fitting purely into one generation or another—the single best example being the work of Ajzen and Fishbein (1980). Initial efforts (e.g., Fishbein, 1967) appear to have been aimed primarily at indicating that attitudes (or at least, attitudes toward the act) can be predictive of behavior. Indeed, with the focus of attention having been on the value of the construct of attitude toward a specific act (e.g., Abelson, 1982; Schuman and Johnson, 1976), such attempted resolution of the "is" question appears to have been the primary nature of the work's impact on the field. However, given the model's postulate that any impact of attitudes on a behavioral decision can be overpowered by the influence of normative concerns, the work might just as well be characterized as falling within the "when" generation. Finally, as the work evolved into the theory of reasoned action (Ajzen and Fishbein, 1980), it provided specification of one conceivable process by which attitudes guide behavior and, hence, can be considered within the "how" generation. The theory is discussed in this manner at a later point in the present article.

These two points are not unrelated in the sense that models of the attitude–behavior process can provide the needed theoretical perspective. Such models have the potential to provide a conceptual integration of the host of moderating variables, in addition to suggesting how and why these various factors moderate the attitude–behavior relation.

In what follows, two types of models of the attitude–behavior process are discussed. The basic difference between the two types centers on the extent to which deciding on a particular course of action involves conscious deliberation about or a spontaneous reaction to one's perception of the immediate situation. An individual may analyze the costs and benefits of a particular behavior and, in so doing, deliberately reflect on the attitudes relevant to the behavioral decision. These attitudes may serve as one of possibly many dimensions that are considered in arriving at a behavior plan, which may then be enacted. Alternatively, attitudes may guide an individual's behavior in a more spontaneous manner, without the individual having actively considered the relevant attitudes and without the individual's necessary awareness of the influence of the attitude. Instead, the attitude may influence how the person interprets the event that is occurring and, in that way, affect the person's behavior. In either case, attitudes are impacting on behavior, but the process by which they are doing so differs markedly. The spontaneous processing alternative will be developed first and then contrasted to the deliberative process.

III. A Spontaneous Processing Model of the Attitude–Behavior Relation

The class of models based upon spontaneous processing must begin with the presumption that not all social behavior is deliberative or reasoned. Instead, the behavior is more spontaneous in nature. Many daily social behaviors appear to be of this sort (cf. Langer, 1978). For people to do otherwise, that is, for people to rely constantly on reflective reasoning processes in order to decide how to behave, would be enormously dysfunctional for daily living. The ease with which we all engage in normal social discourse in itself suggests that much of our behavior is spontaneous rather than the planned outcome of some reflective process.

How might such spontaneous behaviors be influenced by one's attitude toward the object in question? To the extent that individuals engage in any construal or interpretation of the attitude object and the situation in which the attitude object is encountered, there exists the possibility of attitudes guiding behavior toward the object. By influencing such perceptions, attitudes may have an impact on the eventual behavior. Furthermore, such influence may occur even though the individual does not actively retrieve the attitude from memory and reflect upon it in any way.

This notion forms the crux of a model of the attitude–behavior process that has been proposed recently by Fazio and colleagues (Fazio, 1986; Fazio, Powell, & Herr, 1983). The model is presented in a detailed fashion elsewhere (Fazio, 1986) and will only be summarized here. The model postulates that an individual's social behavior is largely a function of the individual's perceptions in the immediate situation in which the attitude object is encountered. Given that the situations are typically at least somewhat ambiguous and that social stimuli frequently have multiple meanings, some degree of interpretation on the part of the individual is required. Such definition of the event that is occurring is presumed to determine the direction and nature of the individual's behavior in the immediate situation.

Latane and Darley's (1970) analysis of bystander intervention in emergency situations provides an excellent illustration of the importance of perceptions of the event that is occurring. Definition of the event as an emergency is viewed as a critical step if the individual its to intervene. For example, failing to define smokelike vapors as an indicant of fire greatly decreased the likelihood that a subject would report the event to the experimenter. Likewise, failing to define a person's moans following a crash as cries of anguish from a real victim decreased the likelihood that bystanders would intervene.

Definitions of the event obviously can be influenced by cues within the situation itself. Again using the bystander intervention work as an example, the emotional stoicism of other witnesses to the event can have a profound influence on the likelihood that a given individual defines the event as an emergency. If the others available for comparison purposes are not displaying any discernible reaction to a loud crash or to smokelike vapors, then the likelihood that the individual will view the event as an emergency is reduced.

However, the cues that are used to interpret an event also can stem from the activation of relevant constructs from memory. Beginning with the "new look" movement (e.g., Bruner, 1957), which so heavily emphasized the constructive nature of perception, psychology has recognized that such perceptions are dependent upon the knowledge structures, affects, values, and expectations that the individual holds. Advances in the area of social cognition make it evident that such memorial constructs can have an influence through a passive, automatic process. That is, the individual need not consciously reflect upon the construct and its applicability to current information for the construct to affect interpretations. Instead, the recent activation, or priming, of a construct from memory is sufficient for that construct to influence interpretations in a later situation (e.g., Fazio et al., 1983; Higgins, Rholes, & Jones, 1977; Srull & Wyer, 1979). Indeed, such priming can even be subliminal in nature. For example, subjects in an experiment conducted by Bargh and Pietromonaco (1982) unknowingly were exposed to words semantically related or unrelated to hostility during the course of a "vigilance task." The words were presented in a manner that was shown to preclude conscious recognition of the words. Subjects who had been exposed to a large proportion of hostility-related words were subsequently more likely to interpret the ambiguous behaviors of a hypothetical target person as hostile. Thus, hostility-related constructs were primed despite subjects' lack of awareness, and the heightened accessibility of the hostility construct affected subjects' interpretations.

One class of structures that are stored in memory and that might be relevant to construal of the event is the individual's knowledge regarding what behaviors are or are not normatively appropriate in a given situation. Indeed, as suggested earlier when the catalog of variables known to moderate the attitude–behavior relation was reviewed, norms have been found to exert such a moderating influence (e.g., Ajzen & Fishbein, 1973; Schofield, 1975; Warner & DeFleur, 1969). Thus, normative information may be activated from memory and may affect one's definition of the event. To the extent that normative guidelines are counter to the individual's attitude, the definition of the event may not be attitudinally congruent.

According to the model, whether the individual's definition of the event is attitudinally congruent determines the likelihood that the individual will display attitude–behavior consistency. That is, given that one's definition of the event determines behavior, the question of attitudes guiding behavior centers on the extent to which attitudes influence the definition of the event. The individual's attitude is also a construct that can guide perceptions. In particular, the attitude can affect perceptions of the attitude object in the immediate situation in which it is encountered.

The suggestion that attitudes guide perceptions is by no means novel. Allport (1935) argued that "attitudes determine for each individual what he will see and hear. . . . They draw lines about and segregate an otherwise chaotic environment; they are our methods for finding our way about in an ambiguous universe" (p. 806). Indeed, attitude theorists have long considered one of the major functions served by attitudes to be that of organizing and structuring a rather chaotic universe of objects (Katz, 1960; Smith, Bruner, & White, 1956). In the words of Smith et al. (1956), an attitude provides "a ready aid for 'sizing up' objects and events in the environment" (p. 41).

Consistent with these notions, a rich and varied literature exists documenting that attitudes influence perceptions of the attitude object. Just to give a few examples, attitudes have been found to relate to what is perceived in an ambiguous scene (e.g., Hastorf & Cantril, 1954; Proshansky, 1943; Seeleman, 1940), to affect individual's causal interpretation of a target person's behavior (e.g., Regan, Straus, & Fazio, 1974), and to affect individuals' evaluations of attitudinally relevant empirical evidence (e.g., Lord, Ross, & Lepper, 1979). In each of these cases, individuals with differing attitudes toward the target person, object, or issue have been shown to arrive at different perceptions and judgments of the very same stimulus information.

Thus, when one encounters an attitude object, one's attitude can guide perceptions of the object in the immediate situation. These immediate perceptions, congruent as they are with one's attitude, can then prompt attitudinally consistent behavior. According to the model, it is through their mediating impact on perceptions that attitudes guide behavior in a spontaneous fashion. That is, the individual need not consciously reflect upon feelings toward the attitude object for an attitudinally biased perception of the attitude object in the immediate situation to occur. Yet, such differential perceptions on the part of individuals with differing attitudes can lead them to respond very differently toward the attitude object.

According to the spontaneous processing model, whether such differential perceptions occur depends on whether the individuals' attitudes are activated from memory. In many instances, the entire attitude–behavior process described thus far simply may not be initiated. Although the model does not postulate that it is necessary for individuals to reflect upon their attitudes toward the object in question for selective perception to occur, it is necessary that individuals' evaluations of the attitude object be activated from memory when they encounter the attitude object. Unless the attitude is activated from memory, it cannot produce selective perception of the object in the immediate situation. Indeed, an individual may never view the object in evaluative terms. Thus, the key to the model is attitude accessibility. The attitude must be activated from memory when the individual observes the attitude object if the attitude is to in any sense guide subsequent behavior.

A. A MODEL OF ATTITUDES AND THEIR ACCESSIBILITY FROM MEMORY

According to the model, the likelihood of activation of the attitude upon mere observation of the attitude object depends on the chronic accessibility of the attitude. An attitude is viewed as an association in memory between a given object and one's evaluation of that object. This definition implies that the strength of an attitude, like any construct based on associative learning, can vary. That is, the strength of the association between the object and the evaluation can vary. It is this associative strength that is postulated to determine the chronic accessibility of the attitude and, hence, the likelihood that the attitude will be activated automatically when the individual encounters the attitude object. Only if it is strongly associated with the object is it likely that the evaluation will be activated spontaneously upon observation of the attitude object.

Empirical tests of this view of attitudes as object-evaluation associations have yielded confirming results. Subjects who had been induced to express their attitudes repeatedly, which should have the consequence of strengthening the object-evaluation association, have been found to be capable of responding relatively quickly to direct inquiries about their attitudes (Fazio, Chen, McDonel, & Sherman, 1982; Powell & Fazio, 1984). For example, Powell and Fazio (1984) manipulated the number of times that an attitude was expressed by varying the number of semantic differential items that appeared relevant to a given attitude issue. In this way, subjects expressed their attitudes zero, one, three, or six times toward a given attitude object. In a subsequent task, subjects were presented with each attitude issue and instructed to make a good–bad judgment about each object as quickly as possible. Response latency was found to relate to the number of previous attitudinal expressions. The greater the number of expressions, the faster the latency of response to the attitudinal inquiry.

Further evidence regarding the relevance of the strength of the object-evaluation association to the chronic accessibility of the attitude is provided by a recent series of experiments concerning automatic activation (Fazio, Sanbonmatsu, Powell, & Kardes, 1986). These experiments examined the hypothesis that the mere presentation of an attitude object toward which an individual possesses a strong evaluative association would automatically activate the evaluation. Automatic processes are effortless and are initiated spontaneously and inescapably when the individual encounters appropriate stimulus conditions (see Schneider & Shiffrin, 1977; Shiffrin & Schneider, 1977). Indeed, Shiffrin and Dumais (1981) characterize as automatic any process that leads to the activation of some response "whenever a given set of external initiating stimuli are presented, regardless of a subject's attempt to ignore or bypass the distraction" (p. 117). In contrast controlled processes are effortful, requiring the active attention of the individual.

The experiments employed a priming procedure. On each trial, the prime that was presented was the name of an attitude object. Its presentation was followed by the display of a positive or a negative evaluative adjective. The subject's task was to press a key as quickly as possible to indicate whether the adjective had a positive or a negative connotation. The latency with which these responses were made was facilitated on trials that involved evaluatively congruent primes (attitude objects) and targets, provided that the attitude object possessed a strong evaluative association for the subject. For example, if a subject had a strong negative association to the object "cockroach," then presentation of "cockroach" as the prime facilitated the subject's indication that an evaluative adjective such as disgusting had a negative connotation.

Such facilitation was observed only in the case of attitudes characterized by strong object-evaluation associations. In some of the experiments, preexperimentally strong and weak associations were identified via a measurement procedure. The measurement involved latency of response to a direct attitudinal inquiry—the same measure that had been shown in the research described earlier to reflect the strength of the object-evaluation association. Attitude objects for which the subject was able to respond relatively rapidly when faced with an attitudinal inquiry had served as the strong primes and those for which the subject responded relatively slowly served as the weak primes. In an additional experiment, strength of the object-evaluation association was manipulated rather than measured. Attitude objects for which subjects had been induced to express their attitudes repeatedly produced facilitation when the objects later served as primes in the adjective connotation task.

These findings provide corroboration for the hypothesis that the likelihood of automatic activation of an attitude upon mere observation of the attitude object depends on the strength of the object-evaluation association in memory. The existence of facilitation suggests that the subject's attitude toward the object was activated automatically upon its mere presentation as the prime. Such a conclusion regarding automatism appears justifiable for two reasons. The first argument concerns the nature of the adjective connotation task. Subjects were merely exposed to the attitude object and were not asked to consider their attitudes toward the object. Nor was it to the subjects' advantage to do so, for the subjects' major task was simply to respond to the target adjective. Nevertheless, despite this irrelevance of attitudes to the immediate task concerns, exposure to objects for which subjects possessed strong affective associations appears to have prompted activation of the associated evaluation. Thus, the very nature of the task leads to the suggestion that the facilitation observed in the case of strong primes was a result of automatic rather than of controlled processing.

A second basis for this conclusion stems from the fact that facilitation was observed only under conditions that involved a relatively short interval between onset of the attitude object presented as the prime and onset of the target adjective, a timing differential commonly referred to as the stimulus onset asynchrony (SOA). Under conditions involving a longer stimulus onset asynchrony, no facilitation was found. Yet, if the results had been due to a controlled, effortful process, one would have expected that allotting the subjects more time to actively retrieve their attitudes would have produced greater facilitation. Instead, the findings imply that in the case of strong object-evaluation associations the attitude was activated automatically upon presentation of the prime. The level of activation of the associated evaluation was apparently sufficient to facilitate responding to an evaluatively congruent target adjective if the adjective was presented very soon thereafter (SOA = 300 msec). However, this level of activation apparently dissipated quickly (or was actively suppressed) due to the presumed irrelevance of the subject's attitudes to the major task of identifying the connotation of the target adjective. As a result, presentation of the target adjective 1000 msec after presentation of the attitude object appears to have been too

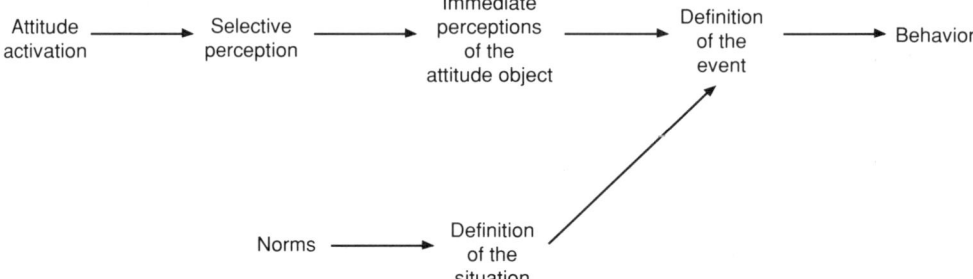

Fig. 1. A schematic diagram of Fazio's (1986) model of the attitude–behavior process.

late for the prime to facilitate response to adjectives of congruent valence. Thus, the results of these experiments indicate that attitudes can be activated from memory automatically and that the strength of the object-evaluation association determines the likelihood of such automatic activation (see Fazio, 1989, for a brief review of additional experiments corroborating this hypothesis).

It is activation of the attitude upon mere observation of the attitude object that forms the crux of the attitude–behavior process based upon automatism. Figure 1 presents a schematic summary of the spontaneous processing model that has been discussed. In essence, the model proposes that a number of steps must occur for behavior toward an object to be influenced in an automatic fashion by one's attitude. First and foremost, the attitude must be activated when the individual encounters the attitude object. Such activation is to be expected only if the object and its evaluation are strongly associated in memory. Once activated, the attitude will serve as a "filter" through which the attitude object will be perceived. A positive attitude that has been activated is likely to lead the individual to notice, attend to, and process primarily the positive qualities that the object is exhibiting in the immediate situation. Likewise, a negative attitude will direct attention to negative qualities of the object. Thus, selective perception produces perceptions of the object in the immediate situation that are consistent with the attitude. These immediate perceptions comprise at least a part of the individual's definition of the event. Normative guidelines may affect the individual's definition of the situation and, if counter to the attitude, may result in a definition of the event that is not attitudinally congruent. In situations where norms do not dictate the definition of the event, however, the definition will be attitudinally congruent if attitude activation and selective perception have occurred. It is this definition of the event that determines the direction and nature of the behavior. Approach behaviors are prompted by a definition of the event that consists primarily of positive perceptions of the attitude object in the immediate situation. Likewise, avoidance behaviors follow from a negative definition of the event.

This entire sequence need not involve any deliberate reflection or reasoning.

Instead, behavior simply follows from a definition of the event that has been biased by the automatically activated attitude. Neither the activation of the attitude from memory nor the selective perception component require conscious effort, intent, or control on the part of the individual. Indeed, it is within an entirely automatic sequence that attitude activation and selective processing take on a necessary role if the attitude is to exert any influence on the behavior. Such an automatic process will operate only to the extent that a strong evaluative association has been established toward the attitude object. If the relevant association is too weak to be activated, then behavior will follow from a definition of the event that is not attitudinally based. Instead, the behavior may be determined by whatever features of the situation and the attitude object are sufficiently salient to influence immediate perceptions.

B. THE MODERATING ROLE OF ATTITUDE ACCESSIBILITY

Some evidence supportive of the model already has been described. Additional confirming research merits a brief summary. Consistent with the model's assertion regarding attitudes that involve a strong object-evaluation association, both experimental and correlational work have provided support for the model's propositions that attitude accessibility serves as a moderator of the relation between attitudes and subsequent perceptions of the attitude object and of the relation between attitudes and subsequent behavior toward the object.

1. Perceptions of the Attitude Object

During the summer preceding the 1984 presidential election, Fazio and Williams (1986) measured attitudes toward Reagan and the accessibility of those attitudes, as indicated by latency of response to the attitudinal inquiry, within a large sample of townspeople. Judgments of the performance of the candidates during the televised debates held later in the fall served as the measure of subsequent perceptions. Just as postulated by the model, correlations between attitudes and perceptions were higher among those individuals who were able to respond relatively quickly to the attitudinal inquiry (the high-accessibility group) than among those who responded relatively slowly (the low-accessibility group).

A similar finding was observed by Houston and Fazio (1989) in a study involving judgments of research evidence concerning the efficacy of capital punishment. This investigation was modeled after the work by Lord *et al.* (1979) that was mentioned earlier. Their research indicated that people's attitudes toward the death penalty were predictive of their judgments regarding the quality of two ostensible empirical investigations—one of which purported to support the deterrent efficacy of capital punishment and the other of which did not. Individuals with attitudes favorable to the death penalty viewed the pro–capital punishment study as better conducted and more convincing (and the anti–capital punishment study as poorer conducted and less convincing) than did individuals with negative attitudes. Houston and Fazio (1989) found this effect to be moderated by the accessibility of subject's attitudes toward the death penalty. The relation between attitudes and judgments of the studies was stronger among individuals whose latencies of response to an attitudinal inquiry regarding the death penalty were indicative of a relatively accessible attitude than it was among individuals whose attitudes were less accessible.

A second investigation (Houston & Fazio, 1989, Experiment 2) experimentally manipulated attitude accessibility as opposed to measuring the preexisting accessibility of the attitude. The associative strength between "death penalty" and the subject's evaluation of this issue was enhanced by inducing some of the subjects to express their attitudes repeatedly. As indicated earlier, past research employing this manipulation (e.g., Fazio et al., 1986; Powell & Fazio, 1984) has shown it to be an effective means of enhancing the accessibility of attitudes. Once again, evidence was obtained that attitude accessibility determined the extent to which the attitude colored judgment of the information. Those subjects who earlier had expressed their attitudes repeatedly judged the empirical evidence in a manner that was more congruent with their attitudes than did those subjects who had expressed their attitudes only a single time. Thus, regardless of whether attitude accessibility was measured or manipulated, the findings indicated that the degree to which an attitude is capable of being activated automatically from memory upon mention of the attitude issue determines the extent to which that attitude biases one's interpretation of the available information.

2. Behavior toward the Attitude Object

The postulated role of attitude accessibility as a moderator of the attitude–behavior relation also has received support in both correlational and experimental studies. Experimental work has indicated that the strength of the object-evaluation association acts as a determinant of the degree to which attitudes guide later behavior (Fazio et al., 1982, Experiment 4). The experiment concerned attitudes and behavior toward a set of intellectual puzzles. Subjects for whom the object-evaluation associations were strengthened through inducement to note and express their attitudes toward the puzzles repeatedly displayed greater attitude–behavior consistency subsequently than did subjects who expressed their attitudes only a single time.

The Fazio and Williams (1986) investigation of the 1984 presidential election also examined attitude–behavior consistency. Immediately following election day, and over 3 months after participating in the initial survey in which attitudes toward Reagan and the accessibility of those attitudes had been assessed, the participants were telephoned and asked to reveal how they had voted. Attitudes were much more predictive of voting behavior among those individuals who had responded relatively quickly to the attitudinal inquiry concerning Reagan. Indeed, within the high-accessibility group, attitudes toward Reagan accounted for nearly 80% of the variance in voting behavior, compared to 44% within the low-accessibility group.

A recent study by Fazio, Powell, and Williams (in press) indicates that this moderating role of attitude accessibility is evident in situations involving actual behavior, as opposed to a self-report of behavior as in the voting study. The study involved attitudes and behavior toward a set of 10 products (e.g., Sun-Maid raisins, Dentyne gum, and Mounds candy bar). In the preliminary phase of the experiment, subjects responded to the names of a large number of products, including the 10 target items, by pressing either a "like" or a "dislike" button. The latency of the responses was recorded and served as the basis for indexing the accessibility of subjects' attitudes toward each of the 10 products. Following this task, subjects rated the extent of their liking along a typical 7-point scale, which constituted the attitude measure. In order to obtain behavioral data, subjects were shown a table on which the 10 target products had been arranged and were informed that they could select 5 products as reimbursement for having participated in the experiment.

The major concern was the extent to which the subjects' selections were related to their attitudes. For each product, subjects were classified into high, moderate, and low attitude-accessibility groups, and the correlation between attitudes and having selected the product or not was examined within each group. Averaged across the 10 products, the correlations displayed a significant linear trend as a function of the level of attitude accessibility. The more accessible a subject's attitude toward a given product was, the more likely it was that product selection behavior was consistent with that attitude.

The spontaneous processing model of the attitude–behavior relation (Fazio, 1986) views behavior as a function of the individual's perceptions of the attitude object in the immediate situation. These immediate perceptions may or may not be congruent with the individual's attitude. If the attitude is highly accessible, then it is likely to be activated automatically from memory upon observation of the attitude object and is likely to result in immediate perceptions that are attitudinally congruent. In contrast, if the attitude is not activated from memory, immediate perceptions are more likely to be based upon momentarily salient features of the attitude object. Because these features may not be representative of the object, the immediate perceptions are less likely to be congruent with the attitude.

The influence of a momentarily salient dimension was apparent in the product selection study. The 10 products had been arranged in two rows of 5. Apparently, the products positioned in the front row were more salient than those in the back row, for row status influenced product selection behavior, especially among individuals whose attitudes toward a given product were relatively low in accessibility. Among the front row products, the lower the accessibility of subjects' attitudes, the more likely they were to select the product. For products in the back row, the lower the accessibility of subjects' attitudes, the less likely they were to choose the product. Thus, the lower the attitude accessibility, the more selection behavior was governed by row status. Products afforded relative salience by virtue of their position in the front row were more likely to be selected and those positioned in the "background" were less likely to be selected.

This finding illustrates the importance of the immediate perceptions of the attitude object. Apparently, individuals with accessible attitudes had immediate perceptions of a given product that were heavily influenced by their attitudes and, hence, tended to behave consistently with those attitudes. In contrast, the immediate perceptions of people with less accessible attitudes appear to have been less attitudinally congruent because these perceptions tended to be governed by the momentarily salient dimension of row position.

Together, the various investigations that have been summarized (see Fazio, 1989, for a fuller review of such work) indicate the importance of the attitude activation component of the model. Both the degree to which selective processing of subsequently presented information about the attitude object occurs and the degree to which attitude–behavior consistency occurs depend on the accessibility of the attitude from memory, just as suggested by the model. Activation of the attitude from memory initiates the spontaneous attitude-to-behavior process. Without such activation, behavior follows from perceptions of the object in the immediate situation that are relatively less likely to be congruent with the attitude.

This spontaneous attitude-to-behavior process is enormously functional for daily life. Attitudes that involve strong object-evaluation associations serve the object-appraisal function described earlier very well. They provide the individual with a "ready aid" for interaction. Because they guide behavior in an automatic manner, they free the individual from having to engage in deliberate, reasoned analyses. Yet, there certainly are instances in which individuals do reflect and deliberate. It is to such a deliberate attitude–behavior process that the discussion now turns.

IV. A Deliberative Processing Model of the Attitude–Behavior Relation

Beyond question, some social behavior is planned and deliberate. Indeed, we sometimes decide how we intend to behave and then follow through on that intention when we enter the situation. Deliberative processing is characterized by considerable cognitive work. It involves the scrutiny of available information and an analysis of positive and negative features, of costs and benefits. The specific attributes of the attitude object and the potential consequences of engaging in a particular course of action may be considered and weighed. Such reflection forms the basis for deciding upon a behavioral intention and, ultimately, behavior.

Unquestionably, the most familiar model of this sort is the Ajzen and Fishbein (1980) theory of reasoned action. Because this model is so well known and so well specified, the present discussion will focus on it as an excellent illustration of deliberative processing. However, it should be kept in mind that any specific model that involves individuals engaging in an effortful analysis of attributes could be considered within the class of deliberative processing models of the attitude–behavior relation. The Ajzen and Fishbein model is clearly based upon deliberative processing.

> Generally speaking, the theory is based on the assumption that human beings are usually quite rational and make systematic use of the information available to them. We do not subscribe to the view that human social behavior is controlled by unconscious motives or overpowering desires, nor do we believe that it can be characterized as capricious or thoughtless. We argue that people consider the implications of their actions before they decide to engage or not engage in a given behavior. For this reason we refer to our approach as "a theory of reasoned action". . . . We make the assumption that most actions of social relevance are under volitional control and, consistent with this assumption, our theory views a person's *intention* to perform (or to not perform) a behavior as the immediate determinant of the action. (Ajzen & Fishbein, 1980, p. 5)

Figure 2 presents a schematic diagram of the model proposed by Ajzen and Fishbein. Behavior stems from the behavioral intention, which is itself the consequence of the individual considering and weighing his or her attitude toward the behavior and subjective norms. This latter term refers to the person's beliefs that significant others think that he or she should or should not perform the behavior and the person's motivation to comply with these specific referents. It is important to note that within this model the attitude under consideration is not a general attitude toward the object in question (e.g., Reagan) but an attitude toward performing the specific behavior in question (e.g., voting for Reagan). According to the model, attitude toward the behavior is itself a function of the person's beliefs concerning the outcomes that are likely to result from performing the behavior and the person's evaluations of those outcomes. Clearly, the theory of reasoned action involves deliberative processing. Individuals are assumed to systematically weigh the available information, including the likely consequences of their engaging in the behavior under consideration and the expectations held by others.

This same focus upon deliberative action is apparent in Ajzen's (1985, 1987)

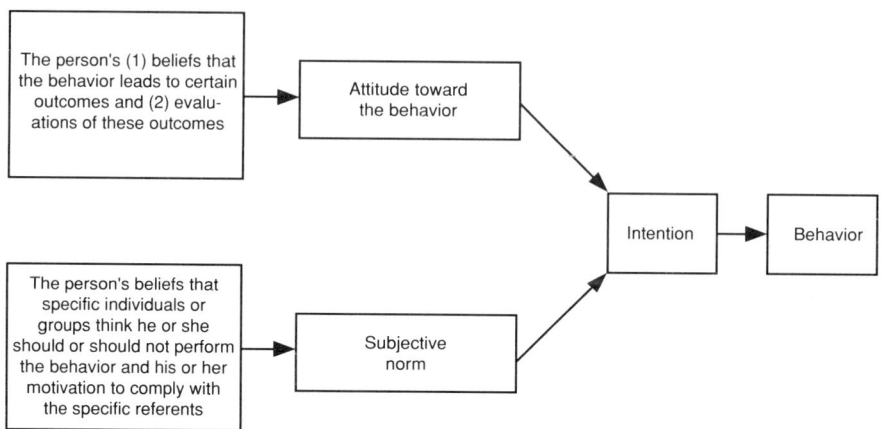

Fig. 2. A schematic diagram of Ajzen and Fishbein's (1980) theory of reasoned action.

recent extension of the theory. This extension, termed the theory of planned behavior, postulates that individuals also consider beliefs concerning their possessing (or lacking) the requisite resources and opportunities necessary to accomplish the behavior. Thus, in formulating a behavioral intention, people examine their perceived control over the behavior in question, in addition to evaluating the likely outcomes of the action (attitude toward the behavior) and considering the expectations of others (subjective norms).

Certainly for any behavior that has not been performed before (and within the Ajzen and Fishbein model this would be virtually any behavior because the behavior always has specific reference to a given context and time), individuals need to "compute" their attitudes toward the behavior. By evaluating the likelihood of the behavior producing various consequences and the desirability of these potential consequences, individuals can arrive at their attitudes toward a specific act in a very deliberate and reasoned manner. These attitudes and information regarding perceived normative pressures are then considered and weighted in order to construct the behavioral intention, which then determines the behavior. The important point is that this process is an effortful one. Reflection and deliberation are required.

The Ajzen and Fishbein model has been subject to some serious criticism at both the conceptual and methodological levels. Concerns have been raised about the value of considering specific attitudes toward the behavior as a remedy for the sometimes poor correspondence between attitudes toward the object and subsequent behavior (Abelson, 1982); about whether additional variables might improve the prediction of behavior beyond what is accomplished via the attitudinal and normative components (e.g., Bentler & Speckart, 1979; Sherman *et al.*, 1982; Songer-Nocks, 1976); and about whether the assessment, in and of itself, of behavioral intention might enhance the likelihood of consistent behavior (Sherman, 1980). Nevertheless, there is little question that the model's attitudinal and normative components generally provide an excellent prediction of behavior. Indeed, investigations conducted by Ajzen and Fishbein and by others have applied the model successfully to a wide variety of domains (see Ajzen & Fishbein, 1980, for a review). Furthermore, there is little doubt that we sometimes do reason about and plan our actions in the manner suggested by Ajzen and Fishbein.

V. An Integrative Model: Conditions That Promote Each Process

It would appear that attitudes can influence individuals' subsequent behavior through either the spontaneous or the deliberative processes described above. The critical distinction between the two models centers on the extent to which the behavioral decision involves effortful reasoning as opposed to spontaneous flowing from individuals' definitions of the event that is occurring. The deliberative process can be viewed as relatively "data driven"; it involves consideration of the specific attributes of the attitude object and of the potential consequences of engaging in a particular behavior. In contrast, focusing as it does on the attitude toward the object and on the activation of this attitude from memory, the spontaneous process can be viewed as "theory driven." The obvious question that arises concerns the conditions under which a spontaneous attitude–behavior process versus a deliberative one might operate.

A. MOTIVATION AND OPPORTUNITY

Given the effortful reflection that is required by the deliberative processing alternative, it would appear that some motivating force is necessary to induce individuals to engage in the reasoning. One such possible force is simply the importance of the behavioral decision. Highly consequential behaviors may prompt a carefully reasoned analysis. Sherman and Fazio (1983) provide examples of deciding what college to attend and what job to pursue as the sort of consequential decisions that may lead individuals to form and consider carefully attitudes toward the behavior in question and to integrate those attitudes with relevant normative beliefs.

A fruitful way of conceptualizing the sort of situations that may foster the deliberative attitude–behavior process is provided by Kruglanski's theory of lay epistemology (Kruglanski, in press; Kruglanski & Freund, 1983). Kruglanski attempts to delineate the general processes and motivating variables relevant to the acquisition of knowledge. In so doing, he discusses the importance of the motivation to avoid reaching an invalid conclusion—motivation that stems from the perceived costliness of a judgmental mistake. The theory suggests that a high "fear of invalidity," as Kruglanski terms this motivating variable, facilitates careful reflection concerning the upcoming judgment. Consistent with this reasoning, Kruglanski and Freund (1983) found that the strength of a number of judgmental biases was reduced in a situation in which subjects were led to view judgmental mistakes as costly to themselves. In three experiments, high fear of invalidity was found to lessen (1) primacy effects in impression formation, (2) the extent of reliance upon ethnic stereotypes, and (3) the extent of influence of an initial numerical anchor in a task involving judgments of probability. In each case, the enhanced fear of invalidity appears to have led subjects to consider more carefully all the information that was available relevant to the judgment that they were required to make rather than rely on some convenient, less effortful shortcut or heuristic.

In the present context, it is such fear of invalidity that likely motivates individuals to undergo the effortful reflection and reasoning involved in a deliberative attitude–behavior process. Without such inducement, individuals have little reason to undertake a deliberative analysis. They perceive little potential cost to permitting behavior to flow spontaneously from however one has interpreted the event. Instead of considering and weighing the potential consequences of the behavior, individuals can allow themselves the effortless luxury of being "theory driven." That is, any attitudinal evaluation that has been activated from memory can guide individuals' definitions of the event and, ultimately, behavior.

Of course, the motivation to engage in the deliberative process is not in and of itself sufficient. The opportunity to do so also must exist. Situations that require one to make a behavioral response quickly can deny one the opportunity to undertake the sort of reflection and reasoning that may be desired. In such cases, individuals may have no alternative to the theory-driven mode characterized by the spontaneous processing model.

The present conceptualization is termed the MODE model of the attitude–behavior relation, referring to both its emphasis on different processing modes for linking attitudes to behavior and its depiction of **m**otivation and **o**pportunity as **de**terminants of which processing mode is likely to operate in any given situation.

Obviously, the MODE model is not the first conceptual framework to consider the importance of motivation and opportunity. Kruglanski's general theory of lay epistemology already has been discussed as an instance in which such constructs have proved useful in distinguishing relatively data-driven processes from relatively theory-driven processes. Within the attitude literature itself, an obvious parallel exists between the present efforts and the work of both Chaiken (1980) and Petty and Cacioppo (1986) regarding modes of processing persuasive communications. These theorists have distinguished (1) an effortful, deliberative analysis of the quality of the persuasive arguments, which has been termed central processing by Petty and Cacioppo and systematic processing by Chaiken, from (2) a relatively easier inference from the cues (e.g., credibility of the source) associated with the persuasive communication, which is referred to as peripheral and heuristic processing by Petty and Cacioppo and by Chaiken, respectively. Only when message recipients are motivated by the personal relevance of the issue at hand do they show evidence of having expended the effort of carefully considering the quality of the presented arguments. Without such motivation, individuals rely upon various cues concerning the source (e.g., source expertise) or the message structure ("length is strength"), as opposed to the quality of the arguments per se, when expressing their opinions. These models of persuasion have been very successful in accounting for a variety of findings concerning the mechanisms underlying persuasion. This success makes one optimistic about the utility of identifying motivation and opportunity as determinants of the mode by which attitudes guide behavior.

The MODE model provides a means of conceptually integrating the automatic processing impact of attitude upon behavior that is inherent to the model proposed by Fazio (1986) and the deliberative processing impact of attitude upon behavior that is central to Ajzen and Fishbein's (1980) theory of reasoned action. The present conceptualization would suggest that people reason and deliberate about their future actions in situations that are characterized by a fear of invalidity. In arriving at a behavioral intention, one of the dimensions that they consider is their attitudes toward the behavior in question. These attitudes are computed on the basis of an examination of the desirability of the likely consequences of the action. Thus, through direct reflection, attitudes can exert some influence on later behavior. The MODE model suggests that the central features of such a deliberative process—retrieving and constructing attitudes toward the behavior and deciding upon a behavior intention—occur only when both the motivation and the opportunity to deliberate exist. Because the perceived costliness of the potential behavior motivates the individual to exert cognitive effort, the degree to which the individual's attitude toward the object is capable of automatic activation from memory becomes irrelevant to the behavior decision process.

However, in situations that are not characterized by this fear of invalidity, or that are so characterized but do not permit the opportunity for deliberation, any effect of attitude on behavior will operate only through the spontaneous processing mode. Individuals will not be sufficiently motivated to deliberate and construct an attitude toward the behavior. Instead, as indicated earlier, the role of attitudes within such a process depends on the extent to which a strong evaluative association has been established toward the attitude object. Only then will encountering the attitude object automatically activate the evaluation from memory. The activated attitude can then color individuals' immediate perceptions and, as a result, influence their behavior toward the attitude object. If the relevant attitudinal association is too weak to be activated, then behavior will follow from a definition of the event that is not attitudinally based. Whatever features of the attitude object and the situation happen to attract individuals' attention at that particular moment in time will serve as the basis for immediate perceptions and behavior.

B. SOME SUPPORTING EVIDENCE

Although not intended as a test of the model, recent research findings by Zanna and colleagues (Bechtold, Naccarato, & Zanna, 1986; Jamieson and Zanna, 1985, 1989) are consistent with the MODE model. For example, Jamieson and Zanna (1985, 1989) conducted two experiments involving simulated court cases. Attitudes toward affirmative action and verdicts in a simulated sex-discrimination suit served as the focus in one experiment, and attitudes toward capital punishment and verdicts in a simulated trial served as the focus in a second experiment. Through instructions, the experimenters emphasized to all subjects that such trial situations require their careful consideration of all the available evidence and that they were to deliver fair and objective decisions and remain as fair and impartial as possible. Thus, all subjects were presumably motivated to process information in a deliberative fashion. However, some subjects were given greater opportunity to do so than were other subjects. Some subjects were under time pressure to read the case material and reach a decision; others were free to study the material at their own pace. Substantially higher correlations between attitudes and judgmental behaviors were observed in both experiments when subjects were under time pressure than when they were not. Thus, even in simulated trial situations, in which deliberative reasoning is expected and in which one is not supposed to be influenced by attitudes, a relation was observed between attitudes and judgments when individuals' opportunity to engage in reflection was restricted.

Furthermore, this attitude–behavior correspondence when under time pressure was observed only among individuals who were classified as low on Snyder's self-monitoring scale. High self-monitoring individuals displayed little attitude–behavior consistency, regardless of the presence or absence of time pressure. Other research indicates that low self-monitoring individuals possess attitudes that are generally more accessible from memory than do high self-monitors (Kardes, Sanbonmatsu, Voss, & Fazio, 1986; Snyder & Kendzierski, 1982). Thus, the findings can be interpreted as indicating the critical moderating role of attitude accessibility in situations in which individuals do not have the opportunity to reason carefully about the data that are available.

A direct test of the MODE model is provided by recent research by Sanbonmatsu and Fazio (1988). This research concerned the degree to which individuals' decisions would be based on their attitudes toward two alternatives (the theory-driven strategy) versus a careful consideration of the specific attributes that had earlier been ascribed to the two alternatives (the data-driven strategy). The experimental stimuli were carefully constructed in such a manner that theory-driven, or attitude-based, decision making would lead to the selection of one of the alternatives, and the data-driven, or attribute-based, strategy would lead to the selection of the other alternative. More specifically, while under instructions to form general evaluations of each of two stores, subjects were exposed to a series of statements (presented in a mixed order) describing a variety of departments (e.g., clothing, jewelry) of each of two fictitious department stores. One such store, Smith's, was described in generally favorable terms; two-thirds of the statements mentioned desirable attributes. The other store, Brown's, was described in predominantly unfavorable terms; two thirds of the statements concerned undesirable attributes. Thus, overall evaluations would lead one to favor Smith's over Brown's. Indeed, when asked to indicate their assessment of each store immediately after the presentation of the stimuli, subjects expressed a more positive attitude toward Smith's than they did toward Brown's.

However, the specific attributes ascribed to the camera departments of the two stores were designed to reverse the direction of this general preference. Brown's, the generally less favorable store, had the better camera department. The two statements describing Brown's camera department were both positive, whereas the two describing Smith's camera department were both unfavorable. The aim underlying the portrayal of the two stores was to create a situation in which subjects had constructed general attitudes toward each store, in addition to having the specific attributes of each store in memory.

At a later point in the experiment, the subjects were asked to imagine that they needed to buy a camera and to consider at which store they would do so. Choice of Brown's (the store with the better camera department) would be indicative of deliberative processing; such subjects would have undertaken the effort to retrieve from memory the specific attributes concerning the camera departments and would have used that information to construct an attitude and a behavioral intention concerning the specific behavior of buying a camera at Brown's versus Smith's. On the other hand, choice of Smith's (the generally superior store with the inferior camera department) would be indicative of a relatively effortless strategy involving simple consideration of the previously formed attitudes toward each store.

The critical concern was with how choice of decision strategy would be affected by the variables postulated to be important by the MODE Model—motivation and opportunity. Prior to the introduction of the camera-buying scenario, both time pressure and fear of invalidity were manipulated. Subjects in the no time-pressure condition were specifically instructed to take their time in answering the question that was to follow. Subjects in the time-pressure condition were warned that they would have only 15 seconds in which to reach a decision about the question that was to follow. Fear of invalidity was manipulated in a manner similar to that employed by Kruglanski and Freund (1983). In the high fear of invalidity condition, the subjects were informed that their decision would be compared to the decisions reached by the other subjects in the group and that they would later have to explain their decision to the other subjects and the experimenter. This information was absent for subjects in the low fear-of-invalidity condition.

The MODE model predicts that both motivation (high fear of invalidity) and opportunity (no time pressure) are prerequisites for deliberative, attribute-based processing. Only then would subjects have the time and desire to retrieve specific bits of information from memory and realize that Brown's, although it might be generally inferior, was the better store at which to shop for a camera. This is precisely what the data revealed. Subjects in this one cell of the design displayed a significantly greater preference for buying a camera at Brown's than did subjects in any of the other three conditions.

Thus, the findings corroborate the hypotheses of the MODE model with respect to motivation and opportunity. Both appear to be necessary conditions for a deliberative, reasoned process to operate. To cast the findings in the language of the Ajzen and Fishbein theory of reasoned action, only subjects who had sufficient motivation and opportunity displayed evidence of having constructed an attitude toward the specific act of buying a camera at each store on the basis of their knowledge regarding the attributes of each store's camera department. In contrast, all the other subjects were guided by their general attitudes toward each store. Much additional research concerning the roles of fear of invalidity and the opportunity to engage in deliberation obviously needs to be conducted. Nevertheless, it appears that these notions may be useful in providing a comprehensive model of the multiple processes by which attitudes can guide behavior.

VI. Mixed Models of the Attitude–Behavior Process

Up to this point, it has been presumed that attitudes guide behavior through a mechanism that can be viewed as involving either essentially spontaneous or essentially deliberative processes. In some ways, this characterization is too simplistic. Although it is possible to consider a purely spontaneous or a purely deliberative sequence, it also is conceivable that components within each basic process are themselves the result of automatic or controlled processing. As Shiffrin (1988) has emphasized, the components of any molar action sequence, for example, a backhand down the line in a tennis match, may involve both automatic and controlled processing. The conscious decision about which stroke to attempt may be the result of a controlled process, whereas the actual stroking of the ball may be automatic.

In the present context, an overall attitude-to-behavior process that is essentially deliberative in nature may still involve some components that are automatized. Likewise, the essentially spontaneous process that has been described may itself sometimes involve some components that are controlled. (See Sherman, 1987, for a similar discussion of automatic and controlled components within various processes of persuasion.) It is to such "mixed models" that we now turn our attention. The potential for automatic subprocesses within the deliberative attitude–behavior process will be discussed first. Then, the discussion will focus on the spontaneous attitude–behavior process and the possible role of controlled components considered.

A. AUTOMATIC COMPONENTS WITHIN A DELIBERATIVE PROCESS

According to Ajzen and Fishbein's theory of reasoned action, individuals construct an attitude toward the behavior in question and consider this attitude, along with normative beliefs, in order to arrive at a behavioral intention. This intention serves as the basis for later behavior. It was argued earlier that attitude toward the behavior typically needs to be computed anew each time an individual attempts to form a behavioral intention because the attitude refers to a specific context and time. The degree to which this is necessary depends upon the similarity of current and past behavioral situations. As Ajzen and Fishbein themselves have pointed out (Ajzen & Fishbein, 1980, chap. 16), an individual may not need to systematically reevaluate beliefs about the behavior. As result of having formed an attitude toward a given behavior in the past, the individual may have a strong evaluative association to the specific behavior available in memory. If this association is sufficiently strong and if the new behavioral situation differs little from the earlier one, the individual's previously formed attitude toward the behavior may be activated automatically from memory. For example, a person who meets another individual for lunch on a monthly basis may have formed an attitude toward this behavior that is capable of being activated from memory automatically when the next luncheon invitation is extended. This previously developed attitude may then be considered in conjunction with any relevant normative guidelines in order to reach a behavioral decision.

Even in situations for which no previously formed attitude toward a behavior exists, automatic processes may be of some relevance. As mentioned earlier, formation of the attitude toward the behavior is presumed to involve consideration of the likely consequences of performing the behavior and evaluation of these consequences. According to the Ajzen and Fishbein formulation, attitude formation can be represented as the summation of salient beliefs about the behavior in question weighted by the evaluation associated with each belief (cf. Anderson & Fishbein, 1965; Fishbein, 1963). There are at least two general ways in which automatic processes might be involved in such attitude formation. First, the chronic accessibility of the beliefs themselves may vary; some may be so strongly associated with the attitude object that they are activated automatically. For example, an individual may strongly associate Ronald Reagan with strengthening national defense, sufficiently so that when the attitude toward voting for Reagan is being developed, beliefs about national defense are activated automatically. Similarly, once the belief about a likely outcome of the behavior has been activated, the accessibility of the evaluation of that outcome comes into play. In some cases, the outcome itself may be so strongly associated with a positive or negative evaluation that the evaluation is activated automatically. Thus, in forming an attitude toward the behavior in question, the chronic accessibility of beliefs about the behavior and the chronic accessibility of evaluations of those beliefs are relevant.

A second manner in which automatic processes may operate in the formation of an attitude toward the behavior stems from the potential influence of attitude toward the object in question. The more accessible this attitude is from memory, that is, the stronger the object-evaluation association, the more likely it is that the attitude toward the object will influence not only the sort of outcomes that one imagines accrue from performance of the behavior but also the valence with which those outcomes are regarded. If the attitude toward the object is activated automatically from memory, it may serve as a retrieval cue that enhances the likelihood that the individual will retrieve and consider a belief that is evaluatively congruent with the attitude. For example, having a negative attitude toward Reagan may increase the likelihood that one retrieves and considers specific beliefs about the probable outcomes of voting for Reagan that also are viewed negatively. Recent research by Ross and his colleagues (Conway & Ross, 1984; Lydon, Zanna, & Ross, 1988; Ross, McFarland, Conway, & Zanna, 1983; Ross, McFarland, & Fletcher, 1981) clearly indicates that such selective retrieval as a function of attitudes is likely. Furthermore, such selective retrieval would appear all the more likely in the case of attitudes toward an object that are capable of automatic activation when individuals are considering how they feel about engaging in a specific behavior toward the object. Thus, through either of the mechanisms that have been mentioned, what is considered while constructing an attitude toward the behavior may be influenced by automatic processes.

An additional linkage of automatic processes to a deliberative, reasoned behavioral decision centers on the stability of the attitude toward the object over time. The more accessible from memory attitudes are, the more likely they are to be resistant to change in the face of contradictory information (Houston & Fazio, 1989; Wood, 1982). Because such attitudes are activated automatically from memory upon mention of the attitude object, they tend to bias individuals' interpretations of information to which they are exposed. Consequently, when an individual faces the need to make a decision about behavioral intention, it is likely that the attitude to be considered is equivalent to one that the individual held at an earlier point in time.

This interrelation between automatic and controlled processes is evident in the investigation of the 1984 presidential election that was described earlier (Fazio & Williams, 1986). Recall that the accessibility of attitudes toward Reagan was found to moderate both the extent to which judgments of performances in the debates and the extent to which actual voting were consistent with those attitudes. Attitudes and their accessibility from memory were measured nearly 4 months prior to the election. Yet, among those with highly accessible attitudes, substantially more selective perception of debate performance was apparent and substantially more consistency between attitudes and voting behavior was apparent than among those respondents whose attitudes were less accessible.

Voting behavior is most likely the result of a deliberative process in which individuals reflect and arrive at a behavioral intention prior to entering the voting booth. Yet, the moderating effect of attitude accessibility implies that automatic processes are relevant to such decisions. The more accessible the attitude is from memory, the more likely it is that the attitude will be activated automatically upon observation or mention of the attitude object. Once activated, the attitude affects the individual's processing of the information. The findings indicate that such differential selective processing on the part of individuals whose attitudes were high or low in accessibility was apparent for perceptions of debate performance. Presumably, the same occurred with respect to other information about the candidates that became available during the course of the campaign. Greater selective processing on the part of those individuals with relatively accessible attitudes is likely to have meant that their final voting decisions were affected by attitudinal positions more equivalent to the ones that they held months earlier than was the case for individuals with less accessible attitudes. Just as implied by this reasoning, the data from this study indicated the existence of an association between attitude–perception congruency and attitude–behavior correspondence. That is, individuals whose perceptions of the debates were not congruent with their initial attitudes were also less likely to vote in a manner that was consistent with those attitudes, presumably because those attitudes were more subject to modification during the course of the campaign.

The mechanism described above, then, constitutes a further manner in which the likelihood of automatic activation of an attitude is relevant to behavioral decisions that are not themselves the immediate outcome of spontaneous processes but instead stem from conscious and deliberative reasoning. Which specific information and evaluations are considered at the time that the behavioral intention is formed may depend on the accessibility of the original attitude.

This discussion has focused upon the relevance of automatic processing to the attitudinal component of the Ajzen and Fishbein model because attitudes are the central focus of this article. Nonetheless, it should be noted that automatism also may be relevant to the normative component. According to the theory of reasoned action, individuals consider their beliefs about what significant others think they should do, in addition to their own attitudes toward the behavior in question, when forming a behavioral intention. What significant others are considered? There are many potentially relevant reference groups or individuals, including parents, spouses, friends, colleagues and so on. Which particular group or groups are considered may itself depend on accessibility from memory. Indeed, recent research by Baldwin and Holmes (1987) indicates that subjects' reactions to a passage describing sexual permissiveness can be influenced by the relative accessibility of different reference groups. In an ostensibly separate experiment prior to exposure to the passage, subjects had been asked to visualize two campus friends or two older members of their family. Subjects for whom the more liberal reference group of campus friends had been primed later reacted more positively to the passage than subjects for whom the more conservative family reference group had been primed.

In sum, then, the grist for a deliberative processing mill may stem from automatic processes. Whether the grist concerns attitudinal or normative dimensions, the specific information that is to be considered may be determined in part by its accessibility in memory. Furthermore, if previously analyzed and refined summary information is available in memory, such as an attitude toward the specific behavior in question, this information may be considered, rather than the raw material from which the summary was constructed.

B. CONTROLLED COMPONENTS WITHIN A SPONTANEOUS PROCESS

Just as deliberate, planned behaviors sometimes may involve a process that includes automatic components, spontaneous behavior that typically follows from an automatic attitude activation occasionally may involve a controlled component. The spontaneous attitude–behavior process that has been discussed centers on the likelihood of automatic activation of the attitude from memory when the individual encounters the attitude object. Essentially, the focus had been on the chronic accessibility of attitudes from memory. Yet, the activation of an attitude also may be induced in an acute manner. A contextual cue may define attitudes as relevant to the immediate situation. For example, in a recent experiment, Snyder and Kendzierski (1982) exposed individuals with favorable attitudes toward psychological research to a sign posted on a wall of a waiting room that requested volunteers to participate in a particular experiment. The subject overheard two confederates discuss the request. When one indicated that he was trying to decide whether to volunteer, the other replied in a way that either promoted attitude activation or did not. In the experimental condition, the reply defined the situation as attitudinally relevant. The confederate said that the decision is "really a question of how worthwhile you think experiments are." In the control condition, the second confederate's reply was "beats me—it's up to you." Although all the subjects felt positive about psychological research, significantly more volunteered in the experimental condition than in the control condition. Apparently, the confederate's cue was sufficient to prompt subjects to consider their own attitudes toward volunteering.

The implication of this and similar research findings (Borgida & Campbell, 1982) is that situations sometimes provide cues that prompt individuals to access their attitudes from memory and thus momentarily affect the acute accessibility of the attitude. Such activation as a result of a cue may occur regardless of whether the individual's attitude is one that involves a strong object-evaluation association. Yet, once it is activated, the attitude may color individuals' definitions of the event and affect their subsequent behavior in a fairly automatic manner. Thus, the automatic attitude-to-behavior sequence that has been proposed may be initiated by a controlled activation of the relevant attitude in a situation that provides a cue regarding such attitude relevance.

Yet another manner in which a controlled subprocess may be relevant to the spontaneous sequence concerns cases in which the individual does not possess an affective linkage to the specific object that is encountered. Some relevant affect may be activated following some preliminary cognitive work on the part of the individual. The necessary cognitive work consists of identifying the object as a member of some category for which an evaluative association does exist. The process of categorization has received considerable empirical and theoretical attention (e.g., Cantor & Mischel, 1977; Smith & Medin, 1981). Generally speaking, the degree to which the features of the specific object match the features of the category seems to determine whether the object will be categorized as an instance of the category. This process of categorization may itself be accomplished in either an automatic or a controlled fashion. Such categorization may precede the various steps involved in the spontaneous attitude-to-behavior sequence.

This sort of two-stage processing—one involving categorization and the other involving both the activation of the evaluation associated with the category and the consequences of such activation for subsequent processing—is most applicable to cases in which the individual holds a general attitude toward a category of objects, but no attitude toward the novel, specific object. For example, in considering the roles of general and specific attitudes, Lord, Lepper, and Mackie (1984) suggested that general attitudes will promote consistent behavior only to the extent that the specific instance matches the prototype of the general attitude object. These researchers examined the consistency between subjects' attitudes toward a typical member of a given Princeton University eating club and the extent to which the subjects would like to work with a specific member of the club on a joint task. Greater consistency was observed when this ostensible club member was described in a way that embodied subjects' prototypes of members of the eating club than when the target was described as possessing characteristics that were atypical. Thus, categorization of the target individual as a typical club member and application of the evaluation associated with the club were more likely in the former than in the latter case.

Such categorization may proceed in an automatic fashion. That is, exposure to a number of prototypical features may automatically activate the relevant category. Alternatively, the individual may consciously and actively attempt to identify the object as an instance of a particular class in a controlled fashion. Given successful categorization, the evaluation associated with the category may then be activated from memory (Fiske, 1982; Fiske & Pavelchak, 1986; see Fiske & Neuberg, in this volume) and the spontaneous attitude-to-behavior sequence then may proceed.

Once again, the focus has been upon the step of the process involving attitude. However, as with the discussion of the theory of reasoned action, it should be kept in mind that other steps in the spontaneous attitude-to-behavior sequence also may involve controlled components. A particularly striking instance concerns a situation in which the activation of knowledge regarding normative requirements induces an individual to define the event as one in which he or she needs to control and monitor carefully impulsive behavior. We have all experienced situations in which we feel the need to "bite our tongue." Such active control over the behavioral responses that one emits seems particularly likely when normative constraints intervene and prevent one from behaving in accordance with perceptions of the attitude object in the immediate situation.

VII. Conclusions

This discussion of "mixed models" illustrates the complexity of the role of spontaneous and deliberative processing in attempts to understand the manner in which attitudes influence behavior. Multiple processes clearly exist. Nevertheless, these processes can be divided roughly into two basic classes. A spontaneous sequence centers on individuals' spontaneous behavior as it flows from their constructions of the event that is occurring and links attitudes to behavior via the influence that attitudes can have on individuals' definitions of the event. Such a process appears to be quite common in individuals' daily lives and enables smooth, relatively effortless functioning. In contrast, the deliberative sequence is effortful and motivated; it requires reflection and the active retrieval or construction and consideration of attitudes. As a result, relative to the spontaneous process, this mechanism occurs less frequently. When it does occur, it stems from the individual's motivation and opportunity to reach an appropriate behavioral intention in a highly consequential action setting.

In concluding, it is useful to return to the earlier summary of the current state of the literature on attitude–behavior consistency. Recall that empirical efforts have produced a rather lengthy catalog of variables known to determine attitude–behavior consistency with little in the way of theoretical development to explain how attitudes guide behavior or why the identified variables moderate attitude–behavior consistency. The present attempt to delineate possible attitude–behavior processes may provide a theoretical integration of this catalog and suggest why these moderators have their effect.

The potential role of various personality variables is evident in both the spontaneous and the deliberative processing modes. The personality variables that are known to moderate the attitude–behavior relation may do so because they identify individuals who are not particularly sensitive to normative concerns. Within a deliberative mode, some individuals may consider the expectations of others more heavily than do other types of individuals. Recent research suggests that this possibility may operate with respect to the personality construct of self-monitoring. Low self-monitors display less sensitivity to subjective normative expectations than do high self-monitors (Ajzen, Timko, & White, 1982). Within a spontaneous mode, some kinds of individuals may be more likely than others to have guidelines regarding normative behavior in a given situation activated from memory. Jamieson and Zanna (1989) have suggested that the accessibility of norms may be less for low self-monitors than for high self-monitors. Finally, within a spontaneous process, personality moderators also may exert an influence because they serve to identify people who tend to form attitudes involving strong object-evaluation associations. Again, recent research confirms this notion with respect to the self-monitoring construct; low self-monitors generally hold attitudes that are more accessible from memory (Kardes *et al.*, 1986).

In a similar manner, situational variables that are known to moderate attitude–behavior consistency are relevant to the process models that have been discussed. Obviously, norms are involved in the attitude–behavior process. Likewise, the importance of situational cues that imply that one's attitude is relevant to a behavioral decision has been discussed. Finally, Sivacek and Crano's (1982) finding that individuals who hold a vested interest in the behavioral issue are more likely than low-interest individuals to behave consistently with those attitudes is explicable by both the automatic and the controlled mechanisms. Such individuals would appear to be far more likely to develop a highly accessible attitude that is capable of automatic activation. Furthermore, the vested interest may provide the motivation necessary for individuals to reflect on the implications of their attitudes in a deliberative fashion.

The various attitudinal qualities that have been identified as moderators of the attitude–behavior relation also can be considered within the context of spontaneous and deliberative processing. Fazio (1986) has suggested that these attitudinal qualities may exert their impact within a spontaneous process because they relate to the strength of the object-evaluation association and hence to attitude accessibility. Thus far, research has supported this conjecture for one such attitude quality, the manner of attitude formation. Attitudes based on direct behavioral experience with the attitude object are both more accessible from memory (Fazio et al., 1982) and more predictive of later behavior (Fazio & Zanna, 1981) than are attitudes formed through indirect, nonbehavioral experience with the attitude object.

In discussions of the theory of reasoned action, Ajzen and Fishbein (1980) have speculated that the various attitudinal qualities that moderate the attitude–behavior relation may do so because they affect the stability of attitudes and intentions over time. To the extent that attitudes fluctuate over time, the deliberative analysis underlying the actual behavior may not coincide with the information collected at the time of attitudinal assessment. Recall that this appeared to be the case with the role of attitude accessibility in the Fazio and Williams (1986) investigation of voting behavior.

The importance of assessing attitudes and behavior at equivalent levels of specificity also can be considered in terms of the general notions that have been discussed. More specifically, such assessments can be considered in terms of the information that is either actively retrieved or automatically activated from memory. Regardless of whether the behavioral decision is arrived at spontaneously or deliberatively, an attitude measure that is as specific as the behavioral action in question increases the likelihood that an individual will consider the same attitudinal information when the attitude measure is completed as when the behavioral opportunity is encountered (Borgida, Swann, & Campbell, 1977). Attitude and behavior measures that are not equivalent may lead to the activation and consideration of different information from memory and hence to less apparent attitude–behavior consistency.

Such is the value of considering the issue of process within the attitude–behavior relation. To the extent that an understanding of the processes by which attitudes guide behavior can be achieved, it becomes much easier to understand why attitudes affect behavior only sometimes and to identify when that might be. Hopefully, the present attempt to compare and contrast a spontaneous and a deliberative attitude–behavior process and the attempt to integrate the two into the more comprehensive MODE model can serve as a first step toward understanding the multiple processes by which attitudes influence behavior.

Acknowledgments

Preparation of this chapter was supported by Grant MH38832 and by Research Scientist Development Award MHOO452 from the National Institute of Mental Health. I thank Mark Zanna for his helpful comments on an earlier version.

References

Abelson, R. P. (1982). Three modes of attitude–behavior consistency. In M. P. Zanna, E. T. Higgins, & C. P. Herman (Eds.), *Consistency in social behavior: The Ontario Symposium* (Vol. 2, pp. 131–146). Hillsdale, NJ: Erlbaum.

Ajzen, I. (1982). On behaving in accordance with one's attitude. In M. P. Zanna, E. T. Higgins, & C. P. Herman (Eds.), *Consistency in social behavior: The Ontario Symposium* (Vol. 2, pp. 3–15). Hillsdale, NJ: Erlbaum.

Ajzen, I. (1985). From intentions to actions: A theory of planned behavior. In J. Kuhl & J. Beckmann (Eds.), *Action-control: From cognition to behavior* (pp. 11–39). Heidelberg: Springer.

Ajzen, I. (1987). Attitudes, traits, and actions: Dispositional prediction of behavior in personality and social psychology. In L. Berkowitz (Ed.), *Advances in experimental social psychology* (Vol. 20, pp. 1–63). New York: Academic Press.

Ajzen, I., & Fishbein, M. (1973). Attitudinal and normative variables as predictors of specific behaviors. *Journal of Personality and Social Psychology, 27,* 41–57.

Ajzen, I., & Fishbein, M. (1977). Attitude–behavior relations: A theoretical analysis and review of empirical research. *Psychological Bulletin, 84,* 888–918.

Ajzen, I., & Fishbein, M. (1980). *Understanding attitudes and predicting social behavior.* Englewood Cliffs, NJ: Prentice-Hall.

Ajzen, I., Timko, C., & White, J.B. (1982). Self-monitoring and the attitude–behavior relation. *Journal of Personality and Social Psychology, 42,* 426–435.

Allport, G. W. (1935). Attitudes. In C. Murchison (Eds.), *Handbook of social psychology.* Worcester, MA: Clark University Press.

Anderson, L. R., & Fishbein, M. (1965). Prediction of attitude from the number, strength, and evaluative aspects of beliefs about the attitude object: A comparison of summation and congruity theories. *Journal of Personality and Social Psychology, 2,* 437–443.

Baldwin, M. W., & Holmes, J. G. (1987). Salient private audiences and awareness of the self. *Journal of Personality and Social Psychology, 52,* 1087–1098.

Bargh, J. A., & Pietromoñaco, P. (1982). Automatic information processing and social perception: The influence of trait information presented outside of conscious awareness on impression formation. *Journal of Personality and Social Psychology, 43,* 437–449.

Bechtold, A., Naccarato, M. E., & Zanna, M. P. (1986, June). *Need for structure and the prejudice-*

–discrimination link. Paper presented at the annual meeting of the Canadian Psychological Association, Toronto.

Bentler, P. M., & Speckart, G. (1979). Models of attitude–behavior relations. *Psychological Review,* **86,** 452–464.

Borgida, E., & Campbell, B. (1982). Belief relevance and attitude–behavior consistency: The mediating role of personal experience. *Journal of Personality and Social Psychology,* **42,** 239–247.

Borgida, E., Swann, W. B., & Campbell, B. (1977, August). *Attitudes and behavior: The specificity hypothesis revisited.* Paper presented at the annual meeting of the American Psychological Association, San Francisco.

Bruner, J. S. (1957). On perceptual readiness. *Psychological Review,* **64,** 123–152.

Cantor, N., & Mischel, W. (1977). Traits as prototypes: Effects on recognition memory. *Journal of Personality and Social Psychology,* **35,** 38–48.

Chaiken, S. (1980). Heuristic versus systematic information processing and the use of source versus message cues in persuasion. *Journal of Personality and Social Psychology,* **39,** 752–766.

Chaiken, S., & Stangor, C. (1987). Attitudes and attitude change. *Annual Review of Psychology,* **38,** 575–630.

Cialdini, R. B., Petty, R. E., & Cacioppo, J. T. (1981). Attitude and attitude change. *Annual Review of Psychology,* **32,** 357–404.

Conway, M., & Ross, M. (1984). Getting what you want by revising what you had. *Journal of Personality and Social Psychology,* **47,** 738–748.

Cooper, J., & Croyle, R. T. (1984). Attitudes and attitude change. *Annual Review of Psychology,* **35.**

Corey, S. M. (1937). Professed attitudes and actual behavior. *Journal of Educational Psychology,* **28,** 271–280.

Eagly, A. H., & Himmelfarb, S. (1978). Attitudes and opinions. *Annual Review of Psychology,* **29.**

Fazio, R. H. (1986). How do attitudes guide behavior? In R. M. Sorrentino & E. T. Higgins (Eds.), *The handbook of motivation and cognition: Foundations of social behavior* (pp. 204–243). New York: Guilford Press.

Fazio, R. H. (1989). On the power and functionality of attitudes: The role of attitude accessibility. In A. R. Pratkanis, S. J. Breckler, & A. G. Greenwald (Eds.), *Attitude structure and function* (pp. 153–179). Hillsdale, NJ: Erlbaum.

Fazio, R. H., Chen, J., McDonel, E. C., & Sherman, S. J. (1982). Attitude accessibility, attitude–behavior consistency, and the strength of the object-evaluation association. *Journal of Experimental Social Psychology,* **18,** 339–357.

Fazio, R. H., Powell, M. C., & Herr, P. M. (1983). Toward a process model of the attitude–behavior relation: Accessing one's attitude upon mere observation of the attitude object. *Journal of Personality and Social Psychology,* **44,** 723–735.

Fazio, R. H., Powell, M. C., & Williams, C. J. (in press). The role of attitude accessibility in the attitude-to-behavior process. *Journal of Consumer Research.*

Fazio, R. H., Sanbonmatsu, D. M., Powell, M. C., & Kardes, F. R. (1986). On the automatic activation of attitudes. *Journal of Personality and Social Psychology,* **50,** 229–238.

Fazio, R. H., & Williams, C. J. (1986). Attitude accessibility as a moderator of the attitude–perception and attitude–behavior relations: An investigation of the 1984 presidential election. *Journal of Personality and Social Psychology,* **51,** 505–514.

Fazio, R. H., & Zanna, M. P. (1978a). On the predictive validity of attitudes: The role of direct experience and confidence. *Journal of Personality,* **46,** 228–243.

Fazio, R. H., & Zanna, M. P. (1978b). Attitudinal qualities relating to the strength of the attitude–behavior relationship. *Journal of Experimental Social Psychology,* **14,** 398–408.

Fazio, R. H., & Zanna, M. P. (1981). Direct experience and attitude–behavior consistency. In L.

Berkowitz (Ed.), *Advances in experimental social psychology* (Vol. 14, pp. 162–202). New York: Academic Press.

Fishbein, M. (1963). An investigation of the relationship between beliefs about an object and attitude toward that object. *Human Relations,* **16,** 233–240.

Fishbein, M. (1967). Attitude and the prediction of behavior. In M. Fishbein (Ed.), *Readings in attitude theory and measurement* (pp. 477–492). New York: Wiley.

Fishbein, M., & Ajzen, I. (1974). Attitudes toward objects as predictors of a single and multiple behavioral criteria. *Psychology Review,* **81,** 59–74.

Fiske, S. T. (1982). Schema-triggered affect: Applications to social perception. In M. S. Clark & S. T. Fiske (Eds.), *Affect and cognition: The 17th annual Carnegie symposium on cognition* (pp. 55–78). Hillsdale, NJ: Erlbaum.

Fiske, S. T., & Pavelchak, M. A. (1986). Category-based versus piecemeal-based affective responses: Developments in schema-triggered affect. In R. M. Sorrentino & E. T. Higgins (Eds.), *The handbook of motivation and cognition: Foundations of social behavior* (pp. 167–203). New York: Guilford.

Goodmonson, C., & Glaudin, V. (1971). The relationship of commentment-free behavior and commitment behavior: A study of attitude toward organ transplantation. *Journal of Social Issues,* **27,** 171–183.

Hastorf, A. H., & Cantril, H. (1954). They saw a game: A case study. *Journal of Abnormal and Social Psychology,* **49,** 129–134.

Higgins, E. T., Rholes, W. S., & Jones, C. R. (1977). Category accessibility and impression formation. *Journal of Experimental Social Psychology,* **13,** 141–154.

Houston, D. A., & Fazio, R. H. (1989). Biased processing as a function of attitude accessibility: Making objective judgments subjectively. *Social Cognition,* **7,** 51–66.

Jamieson, D. W., & Zanna, M. P. (1985, June). *Moderating the attitude–behavior relation: The joint effects of arousal and self-monitoring.* Paper presented at the annual convention of the Canadian Psychological Association, Halifax, Nova Scotia.

Jamieson, D. W., & Zanna, M. P. (1989). Need for structure in attitude formation and expression. In A. R. Pratkanis, S. J. Breckler, & A. G. Greenwald (Eds.), *Attitude structure and function* (pp. 383–406). Hillsdale, NJ: Erlbaum.

Kardes, F. R., Sanbonmatsu, D. M., Voss, R., & Fazio, R. H. (1986). Self-monitoring and attitude accessibility. *Personality and Social Psychology Bulletin,* **12,** 468–474.

Katz, D. (1960). The functional approach to the study of attitudes. *Public Opinion Quarterly,* **24,** 163–204.

Kelley, S., & Mirer, T. W. (1974). The simple act of voting *American Political Science Review,* **68,** 572–591.

Kruglanski, A. W. (in press). *Basic processes in social cognition: A theory of lay epistemology.* New York: Plenum Press.

Kruglanski, A. W., & Freund, T. (1983). The freezing and unfreezing of lay-inferences: Effects of impressional primacy, ethnic stereotyping, and numerical anchoring. *Journal of Experimental Social Psychology,* **19,** 448–468.

Langer, E. J. (1978). Rethinking the role of thought in social interaction. In J. H. Harvey, W. Ickes, & R. F. Kidd (Eds.), *New directions in attribution research* (Vol. 2, pp. 35–58). Hillsdale, NJ: Erlbaum.

LaPiere, R. T. (1934). Attitudes vs. actions. *Social Forces,* **13,** 230–237.

Latane, B., & Darley, J. M. (1970). *The unresponsive bystander: Why doesn't he help?* New York: Appleton-Century-Crofts.

Lord, C. G., Lepper, M. R., & Mackie, D. (1984). Attitude prototypes as determinants of attitude–behavior consistency. *Journal of Personality and Social Psychology,* **46,** 1254–1266.

Lord, C. G., Ross, L., & Lepper, M. R. (1979). Biased assimilation and attitude polarization: The effects of prior theories on subsequently considered evidence. *Journal of Personality and Social Psychology, 37,* 2098–2109.

Lydon, J., Zanna, M. P., & Ross, M. (1988). Bolstering attitudes by autobiographical recall: Attitude persistence and selective memory. *Personality and Social Psychology Bulletin,* **14,** 78–86.

Norman, R. (1975). Affective-cognitive consistency, attitudes, conformity, and behavior. *Journal of Personality and Social Psychology,* **32,** 83–91.

Petty, R. E., & Cacioppo, J. T. (1986). The Elaboration Likelihood Model of persuasion. In L. Berkowitz (Ed.), *Advances in experimental social psychology* (Vol. 19, pp. 123–205). New York: Academic Press.

Powell, M. C., & Fazio, R. H. (1984). Attitude accessibility as a function of repeated attitudinal expression. *Personality and Social Psychology Bulletin,* **10,** 139–148.

Proshansky, H. M. (1943). A projective method for the study of attitudes. *Journal of Abnormal and Social Psychology,* **38,** 393–395.

Regan, D. T., Straus, E., & Fazio, R. H. (1974). Liking and the attribution process. *Journal of Experimental Social Psychology,* **10,** 385–397.

Rholes, W. S., & Bailey, S. (1983). The effects of level of moral reasoning on consistency between moral attitudes and related behaviors. *Social Cognition,* **2,** 32–48.

Ross, M., McFarland, C., Conway, M., & Zanna, M. P. (1983). Reciprocal relation between attitudes and behavior recall: Committing people to newly formed attitudes. *Journal of Personality and Social Psychology,* **45,** 257–267.

Ross, M., McFarland, C., & Fletcher, G. J. O. (1981). The effect of attitude on the recall of personal histories. *Journal of Personality and Social Psychology,* **40,** 627–634.

Sample, J., & Warland, R. (1973). Attitude and prediction of behavior. *Social Forces,* **51,** 292–304.

Sanbonmatsu, D. M,. & Fazio, R. H. (1988). *The role of attitudes in memory-based decision making.* Unpublished manuscript, University of Utah, Salt Lake City.

Scheier, M. F., Buss, A. H., & Buss, D. M. (1978). Self-consciousness, self-report of aggressiveness, and aggression. *Journal of Research in Personality,* **12,** 133–140.

Schneider, W., & Shiffrin, R. M. (1977). Controlled and automatic human information processing: I. Detection, search, and attention. *Psychological Review,* **84,** 1–66.

Schofield, J. W. (1975). Effects of norms, public disclosure, and need for approval on volunteering behavior consistent with attitudes. *Journal of Personality and Social Psychology,* **31,** 1126–1133.

Schuman, H., & Johnson, M. P. (1976). Attitudes and behavior. *Annual Review of Sociology,* **2,** 161–207.

Schwartz, S. H. (1978). Temporal instability as a moderator of the attitude–behavior relationship. *Journal of Personality and Social Psychology,* **36,** 715–724.

Seeleman, V. (1940). The influence of attitudes upon the remembering of pictorial material. *Archives of Psychology,* No. 258.

Seligman, C., Kriss, M., Darley, J. M., Fazio, R. H., Becker, L. J., & Pryor, J. B. (1979). Predicting summer energy consumption from homeowners' attitudes. *Journal of Applied Social Psychology,* **9,** 70–90.

Sherman, S. J. (1980). On the self-erasing nature of errors of prediction. *Journal of Personality and Social Psychology,* **39,** 211–221.

Sherman, S. J. (1987). Cognitive processes in the formation, change, and expression of attitudes. In M. P. Zanna, J. M. Olson, & C. P. Herman (Eds.), *Social influence: The Ontario Symposium* (Vol. 5, pp. 75–106). Hillsdale, NJ: Erlbaum.

Sherman, S. J., & Fazio, R. H. (1983). Parallels between attitudes and traits as predictors of behavior. *Journal of Personality,* **51,** 308–345.

Sherman, S. J., Presson, C. C., Chassin, L., Bensenberg, M., Corty, E., & Olshavsky, R. W. (1982). Smoking intentions in adolescents: Direct experience and predictability. *Personality and Social Psychology Bulletin, 8,* 376–383.

Shiffrin, R. M. (1988). Attention. In R. C. Atkinson, R. J. Herrnstein, G. Lindzey, & R. D. Luce (Eds.), *Stevens' handbook of experimental psychology* (2nd ed., pp. 739–811). New York: Wiley.

Shiffrin, R. M., & Dumais, S. T. (1981). The development of automatism. In J. R. Anderson (Ed.), *Cognitive skills and their acquisition.* Hillsdale, NJ: Erlbaum.

Shiffrin, R. M., & Schneider, W. (1977). Controlled and automatic human information processing: II. Perceptual learning, automatic attending, and a general theory. *Psychological Review, 84,* 127–190.

Sivacek, J., & Crano, W. D. (1982). Vested interest as a moderator of attitude–behavior consistency. *Journal of Personality and Social Psychology, 43,* 210–221.

Smith, E. E., & Medin, D. L. (1981). *Categories and concepts.* Cambridge, MA: Harvard University Press.

Smith, M. B., Bruner, J. S., & White, R. W. (1956). *Opinions and personality.* New York: Wiley.

Snyder, M., & Kendzierski, D. (1982). Acting on one's attitude: Procedures for linking attitude and behavior. *Journal of Experimental Social Psychology, 18,* 165–183.

Snyder, M., & Swann, W. B. (1976). When actions reflect attitudes: The politics of impression management. *Journal of Personality and Social Psychology, 34,* 1034–1042.

Songer-Nocks, E. (1976). Situational factors affecting the weighting of predictor components in the Fishbein model. *Journal of Experimental Social Psychology, 12,* 56–59.

Srull, T. K., & Wyer, R. S., Jr. (1979). The role of category accessibility in the interpretation of information about persons: Some determinants and implications. *Journal of Personality and Social Psychology, 37,* 1660–1672.

Warner, L. G., & DeFleur, M. L. (1969). Attitudes as an interactional concept: Social constraint and social distance as intervening variables between attitudes and action. *American Sociological Review, 34,* 153–169.

Wicker, A. W. (1969). Attitudes versus actions: The relationship of verbal and overt behavioral responses to attitude objects. *Journal of Social Issues, 25,* 41–78.

Wood, W. (1982). Retrieval of attitude-relevant information from memory: Effects on susceptibility to persuasion and on intrinsic motivation. *Journal of Personality and Social Psychology, 42,* 798–810.

Zanna, M. P., & Fazio, R. H. (1982). The attitude–behavior relation: Moving toward a third generation of research. In M. P. Zanna, E. T. Higgins, & C. P. Herman (Eds.), *Consistency in social behavior: The Ontario Symposium* (Vol. 2, pp. 283–301). Hillsdale, NJ: Erlbaum.

Zanna, M. P., Olson, J. M., & Fazio, R. H. (1980). Attitude–behavior consistency: An individual difference perspective. *Journal of Personality and Social Psychology, 38,* 432–440.

PEAT: AN INTEGRATIVE MODEL OF ATTRIBUTION PROCESSES

John W. Medcof

I. Introduction

Attribution theory (for recent reviews, see Harvey & Weary, 1984; Kelley & Michela, 1980) is a body of ideas in psychology that attempts to describe how observers interpret the events they see in everyday life. In the past 20 or so years attribution theory has enjoyed considerable attention in the literature, has generated a great deal of research, and has been shown capable of explaining a wide range of empirical phenomena.

Despite this success (or perhaps because of it), attribution theory has remained a rather loose federation of theories and research. Recently the three most influential theorists have been Jones and Davis (1965) and Kelley (1973), but a great many attribution phenomena fall outside the bounds of their theories. The grouping of theories and phenomena under the title "attribution theory" is widely accepted but is based as much on a rather vague intuition that they belong together as on any systematic demonstration that there is a common, elegant core of ideas underlying them all.

Although attribution research has enjoyed considerable success in its vague form, the development of an elegant conceptual core for attribution theory and other theories of causal judgment is a desirable aim (Einhorn & Hogarth, 1986; Harvey & Weary, 1984). The primary reason for this is that such a core is one of the signs of a mature science. Physics, for example, is characterized by the ability to describe and explain a wide variety of empirical phenomena, and by the ability to conceptually relate most of those explanations to a single elegant statement, $E = MC^2$. Furthermore, the relationship between the conceptual core and the other concepts and theories is clearly and explicitly drawn; it is not left to vague intuition. As psychology matures as a science it must develop in both of these ways as well, explaining and predicting a wider and wider range of empirical phenomena and refining its conceptual core. At this point in time psychology does not have a single conceptual core but it does have theories. It is these theories that must be refined.

There can be little doubt that the aim of establishing a clear and elegant core for attribution research is viewed as desirable and attainable by a number of researchers. It is generally accepted that most of what we call attribution research and theory springs ultimately from the work of Heider (1958). But although Heider is accepted as the intellectual forefather of this field of study, his work, in its richness and suggestiveness, is not necessarily drawn with much clarity. Consequently, a number of writers, including Ajzen and Fishbein (1975), Jones and McGillis (1976), and Kruglanski (1980), have attempted to show more clearly the links between various parts of attribution theory.

In keeping with this spirit of conceptual clarification, this article presents a single elegant core for Kelley (1973), Jones and Davis (1965), and several other more recent theoretical developments in attribution theory. The idea that these theories are all connected is not new. What has not yet been done is a thorough demonstration of this linkage, showing in detail the interchangeability of concepts and terminology. This analysis will make clear that these theories need not be described separately, as has been done in the past, but can be treated as a single theoretical entity.

The core model that integrates these theories uses some old terminology in some new ways, which may tempt the reader to object that this is not what was intended by the original theorist. This may be true in some cases, but the ultimate test of such reinterpretations is whether the empirical support for the old definition is also consistent with the new. This will be found to be the case.

But this integration is not primarily an invalidation of former theories. It is primarily a demonstration that, with a modified interpretation of some terms and the addition of some linking concepts, the older theories are valid and consistent with each other and are much more intimately interrelated than has previously been suspected or demonstrated. The core model does, however, provide some insights of its own and points to some possibly fruitful areas of research.

II. PEAT

The first step in the integration of these theories will be the presentation of the core model. This model will be called PEAT for reasons explained below. PEAT is a relatively brief set of propositions about how observers store and use information about their environments, propositions that underlie both causal and disposition attributions.

The name of this model, PEAT, comes from a fundamental assumption that expectations play an important role in attribution processes and that a useful way to express those expectations is as probability statements. This will be argued in more detail below. For now, suffice it to say that this model is a *p*robability, *e*xpectancy, *a*ttribution *t*heory and its name is derived from these three fundamental concepts.

PEAT will borrow some terminology from Kelley (1973). As in his system, causal agents can be actors or entities. Actors are, of course, people. The term *entity* can refer to just about anything in the attribution situation besides the focal actor. The entity is usually nonhuman, but it can be human as well. An entity can be a specific thing, such as an automobile, a person, or an animal, or it can be a complex configuration of specific entities, persons, or both. For example, a cocktail party is a situation that consists of a number of actors (host, hostess, friends, acquaintances, etc.) and entities (drinks, food, chairs, etc.). Such complex entities will be called *situations*. So the term entity will refer to both specific, individual entities and to situations. Also, the word *agent* will be used to refer generically to any possible or actual causal agent, whether actor, specific entity, or situation.

A. PROPOSITION 1

People observe the world and store their observations about agents and events as probability statements. For most events of which they are aware, people develop some expectations about how likely those events are across a variety of circumstances. For example, people have an impression of how likely snowstorms are, and they will remark if, in a particular year, snowstorms are more frequent than usual. This will occur without any conscious attempt to systematically record and compare the frequencies of snowstorms. These impressions of likelihood are not always accurate but they are there and people spontaneously make statements about them. PEAT assumes that these beliefs about the general probabilities of events are stored as unconditional probabilities of the form p (event) $= X$. PEAT assumes further that observers note that the probabilities of some events are higher in the presence of some agents than they are in the presence of others. For example, snowstorms are more probable given the presence of clouds than they are in the presence of sunshine. These kinds of observations are stored as conditional probabilities, $p(\text{event}/A) = X$. Observers are capable of storing probabilities involving multiple conditions as well. For example, they may have some impression of $p(\text{accident}/\text{rain} \cap \text{night} \cap \text{narrow road})$.

This assumption that observers store and use probabilities may engender some controversy. One criticism is that there are ample demonstrations in the literature showing that people deviate from ''correct'' probability thinking (e.g., Kahneman & Tversky, 1973; Slovic, Fischhoff, & Lichtenstein, 1979; Tversky &

Kahneman, 1980). It can be argued from there that since people are poor users of probabilities, it is not wise to attempt to model their thinking processes with probabilities. There are two replies to this argument. The first reply is that, even if people are poor users of probability information, the statement of probabilistic models of human function provides ideal cases to which actual human processes can be compared. The work of Kahneman and Tversky (e.g., 1973) is an example of a very fruitful line of research that has taken this approach. Another argument against this criticism is that as we improve our understanding of people's use of probabilities, we find that they do use them "correctly" in many ways (e.g., Budesur & Wollsten, 1985; Einhorn & Hogarth, 1985; Fischhoff & Bar-Hillel, 1984; Hinsz, Tindale, Nagao, Davis, & Robertson, 1988; Kruglanski, Friedland, & Farkash, 1984; Solomon, Ariyo, & Tomassini, 1985; Wagenaar & Keren, 1985). For example, Hinsz *et al.* (1988) showed that base rate information is ignored only under certain circumstances. The argument here states that people can use correct probability thinking, but that we need research to determine why they apparently do not under some circumstances (Ajzen & Fishbein, 1983). Einhorn and Hogarth, (1986) argue further that all causal reasoning in the real world must go beyond the information given, since nothing is known with certainty. Therefore, all causal reasoning is a matter of judging probable cause.

Another advantage of the use of probabilities in PEAT is that it strips away some excess conceptual baggage to show the core logic of the theorist. It is because of this that PEAT is able to show the common logic of a number of attribution theories. It must be borne in mind, though, that stripping away the excess conceptual baggage also strips away some of the useful conceptual baggage. Some of the value of the original theorists is lost. Because of this it is important to think of PEAT as complementary to the other theories rather than as a replacement for them. For the foreseeable future, all the theories will have a role to play. In summary, PEAT is based on probabilities because I believe that it is highly likely people do use probabilities effectively, and that we need research to show how this happens. If I am wrong and people do not use probabilities correctly, it is still very likely that the research used to demonstrate this will tell us a great deal about human reasoning. Furthermore, the present article will show that probabilities are a very useful way to show clearly the logical connections between different attribution theories. This can be done without losing the rich insights provided by the original theorists.

B. PROPOSITION 2

Observers use probability statements as the basis for assigning characteristics to agents. When those agents are people, the characteristics assigned are called dispositions; when the agents are entities, the characteristics assigned are called constraints. The assignment of dispositions to actors begins when observers perceive reliable associations between specific individuals and certain events or behaviors. These associations are stored as probabilities. Observers notice that Jack Smith, for instance, often gets into arguments. This can be stored as p(argument/Jack Smith) $= .75$. On the other hand, Jack's brother Bill seldom gets into arguments, p(argument/Bill Smith) $= .05$. In addition, observers can compare probabilities and notice whether the probability of an event, given the presence of a particular actor, is greater or less than the unconditional probability of the event. If p(argument) $= .45$, then Jack Smith is above this norm and Bill Smith is below it.

When observers perceive that the probability of an event, given a particular actor, is greater or less than the unconditional probability, they tend to say that that person has a certain trait or disposition. They label Jack Smith as "argumentative" and Bill Smith as "nice." Such assertions seem to provide some observers with the feeling that they "understand" Jack and Bill Smith. The actions of the Smith brothers are "explained" by the fact that they have certain traits or dispositions. But these are pseudo-explanations. They are really just labels that reflect observers' beliefs about the past and future behaviors of the individuals observed.

A general definition of disposition will now be given. So far, the only events discussed here have been human behaviors. However, other kinds of events might also be associated with an individual, for example, car accidents. For this reason, this general definition is stated in terms of events rather than in terms of the particular kind of event of most interest here, human behavior. An actor is said to have a *disposition* if:

$$p(\text{event/actor}) \neq p(\text{event}).$$

The assignment of constraints to entities follows the same general principles as the assignment of dispositions to actors. Observers notice that actors tend to act in predictable ways when in the presence of certain entities. For example, there may be a great deal of audience laughter at a particular movie. The movie is therefore likely to be labeled a comedy. This constraint label indicates a certain probability of laughter associated with this particular movie. Such constraint labels are used when the probability of the event, given the presence of the entity, is different from the unconditional probability. The definition for constraint labeling is therefore analogous to that for disposition labeling. An entity is said to have a *constraint* if

$$p(\text{event/entity}) \neq p(\text{event}).$$

Later in this paper there will be some theoretical discussions in which it will be cumbersome to identify agents as either actors or entities and to refer to dispositions and constraints. To facilitate these discussions the following general definition of how characteristics are assigned to agents will be used. An agent is said to have a *characteristic* if

$$p(\text{event}/\text{agent}) \neq p(\text{event}).$$

People can come to believe that an agent has a particular characteristic by means other than direct observation. These cases can also be represented as probabilities. For instance, one may hear from associates that Jack Smith is argumentative. This statement can be stored by the hearer as $p(\text{argument}/\text{Jack Smith}) = x$. But the x value assigned by the hearer in response to the word "argumentative" may be different from the x value intended by the speaker who said that Jack is argumentative. Regardless of the source, direct observation or hearing from other people, PEAT suggests that characteristics can be represented as probabilities.

C. PROPOSITION 3

Observers will perceive the strength or potency of a characteristic assigned to an agent to be a positive function of the difference between the probability of the event given the presence of the agent and the unconditional probability of the event. For example, if the $p(\text{argument}/\text{Jack Smith}) = .75$, the $p(\text{argument}/\text{Bill Bailey}) = .95$, and the unconditional probability of argument is .45, then observers will say that Bill Bailey is more argumentative than Jack Smith. In probabilities, this proposition has the following form. The perceived *strength of an agent's characteristic* is directly proportional to

$$|p(\text{event}/\text{agent}) - p(\text{event})|.$$

D. PROPOSITION 4

When asked about the characteristics of an agent, observers will base their answers upon the stored probability statements associated with that agent. This stored information allows the observer to determine whether or not an agent has a particular kind of characteristic and, if the agent does, the strength of that characteristic. Different observers may report different characteristics for the same agent. Those differences may come from a number of sources. For example, when reporting on the disposition of an actor, if different observers have different beliefs about $p(\text{event}/\text{actor})$, they are likely to name different dispositions. But differences in perceived $p(\text{event})$ could also lead to different disposition labels, even when there is agreement on $p(\text{event}/\text{actor})$. This is because perceived dispositions depend on variations around $p(\text{event})$. Differences in the nature of disposition labels themselves could also influence the labeling process.

Sometimes disposition labels designate quite obviously the particular behaviors being associated with an actor (e.g., talkative). Very often though, the disposition term refers to a class of behaviors that is not clearly designated (e.g., careless). When such general terms are used, observers will have to do more interpreting to determine if a particular behavior fits into a class of behaviors. This may lead to some variation between observers in what is stored and therefore in statements about what is stored.

The phenomenon of stereotyping can be understood in this framework. Stereotypes usually include statements about the physical characteristics of the individual involved (e.g., female, black) and statements about their typical or most probable behaviors (e.g., nondominant, musical). In this model, a stereotype is a collection of probability statements about the kinds of behaviors likely to be emitted by certain classes of people. Once a person is identified as belonging to a certain stereotyped group, a whole host of assumptions about behavior probabilities is made. These behaviors are sometimes explained by stating that the person is a member of the stereotyped group, for example, "She acts that way because she is a woman." This kind of explanation operates on the same basis as explaining behavior in terms of dispositions. To the user it seems to explain, but it is really just a statement about the user's belief about the probability that some behavior will occur. Treatments of stereotypes as probabilities are already available in the literature. Rasinski, Crocker, and Hastie (1985), for instance, used probabilities as measures of observers' stereotypes and went on to compare the strength of these values with the strength of new information in determining observers' predictions of the probabilities of future behaviors. Entities can be treated in a stereotypical way as well. For example, the stereotypical haunted mansion has a whole host of human behaviors and other events associated with it. The concept of script (Schank & Abelson, 1977) posits that certain entities and situations have certain sets of behaviors strongly associated with them. It is not a great step to suggest that those associations can be expressed as probabilities. Schutte, Kenrick, and Sadalla (1985) specifically investigated the effects of situation prototypicality (stereotypicality) on both memory and predicted behavior.

It is now seen that these stored probabilities are multipurpose tools that can arise from more than one source. Each probability expression is a statement of belief about the past or future behaviors of an agent. It is a generalization about an agent. That belief may come from personal observation of the agents. Alternatively, an observer who has never seen the agent in question before may have a probability statement for that agent based upon hearsay, written records, or other sources. Once the probability statement is in place, it becomes very much an expectancy about what that person will do in the future. It is a predictor of the probable behaviors of that agent. It is also used as an information base for supplying labels for the agent in order to communicate the beliefs about the agent to others.

E. PROPOSITION 5

When asked about their expectations regarding future events, observers will base their answers upon the stored probabilities they have about past events. This assumption suggests that observers perceive characteristics to be relatively enduring things, stable aspects of the agents involved. The probability statements represent the best predictors available about the likelihood of future events. For that reason they are very useful for observers. This assumption ties PEAT to Heider's (1958) proposition that a prime objective of human cognitive activity is to predict future events.

F. PROPOSITION 6

Observers will perceive an agent to be a facilitator of an event when the presence of that agent is a predictor that there is a higher than normal probability that the event will occur. The strength of that facilitative effect is determined by the difference between the probability of the event given the agent and the unconditional probability of the event. In probabilities this proposition has the following form: *An agent will be perceived to be a facilitator of an event when*

$$p(\text{event}/\text{agent}) > p(\text{event}).$$

The strength of the facilitative force of the agent, FF (agent), on the event is

$$FF\ (\text{agent}) = p(\text{event}/\text{agent}) - p(\text{event}).$$

This proposition is based upon lay people's tendency to base perceptions of causality on predictability. For example, if Bill Smith is constantly getting into arguments with a variety of people in a variety of circumstances so that p(argument/Bill Smith) $> p$(argument), observers begin to believe that Bill Smith causes the arguments; "He brings it on himself." Although he does not get into an argument on every encounter, he certainly facilitates arguments. Further, when asked about Bill Smith's characteristics, observers, in accord with Proposition 4, will probably label him "argumentative."

G. PROPOSITION 7

Observers will perceive an agent to be an inhibitor of an event when the presence of that agent is a predictor that there is a less than normal probability that the event will occur. The strength of the inhibitory effect is determined by the difference between the probability of the event given the agent and the uncondi-

tional probability of the event. In probability terms, this proposition is as follows: *An agent will be perceived to be an inhibitor of an event when*

$$p(\text{event}/\text{agent}) < p(\text{event}).$$

The strength of the inhibitory force of the agent, IF (agent), on the event is

$$IF \text{ (agent)} = p(\text{event}/\text{agent}) - p(\text{event}).$$

This proposition is an analogue of Proposition 6. An example of inhibition is seen when the audience ceases to talk as the presence of the conductor is noticed. The probability statements that define facilitative and inhibitive agents are similar to those that define characteristics (dispositions and constraints) of agents. It follows that the assignment of a disposition to an actor represents the assignment of a facilitative or inhibitive effect to that actor. In addition, to perceive an actor as a facilitator or an inhibitor of an event is to assign a disposition to that actor. The analogous logic applies to the assignment of constraints to entities.

H. PROPOSITION 8

When asked to give causal or characteristic attributions after observing an event, observers, because they prefer conservative explanations, will give their attributions using one of four explanation modes: (1) *unknown cause,* (2) *known characteristics,* (3) *new characteristics, and* (4) *revised characteristics.* The distinction between causal and characteristic attributions should be clarified. When an observer is asked to make a causal attribution the observer is being asked what caused the event in question. Usually, the intent is to have the observer name one of the agents present when the event occurred. In contrast, characteristic attribution asks the observer to name what particular characteristic of an agent was responsible for the event. These two kinds of attribution are intricately interrelated. One cannot ask what characteristic of the agent was responsible for the event unless one assumes that that agent was the cause of the event. Alternatively, one cannot reasonably say that agent X caused the event without also assuming that agent X has some characteristic capable of causing the event. Although causal and characteristic attributions are intimately connected they are discernibly different. This will be seen below as the probabilities of PEAT are applied to attribution processes.

The statement in Proposition 8 that observers are conservative springs from Heider's (1958) point that human beings are constantly striving to construct cognitive models of the world that provide a stable interpretation of the world and allow events to be predicted. Hence observers will prefer explanations of events, or descriptions of agents, that are consistent with the stable, already known characteristics of agents. Only when an explanation is not possible in these terms will they move to some other mode of explanation. Other modes of explanation include the belief that the event is unexplainable, the inference of a new characteristic of an agent, and the revision of a belief about an agent.

In the unknown cause mode of explanation, the first of the four modes listed above, the event in question was not predictable given the observers' prior beliefs about the agents available for the explanation of the event. This mode will be discussed first, even though it is not the preferred mode, because some of the ideas associated with it are necessary in order to explain the preferred mode, that is, the known characteristics mode. In the unknown cause mode, when observers are asked for the cause of the event, they will name "luck," "fate," or some other poorly defined and/or poorly understood factor. They will not name any of the available agents alone or in combination. Observers' beliefs about the characteristics of available agents will not be altered much, if at all, by the occurrence of the event. This mode is more fully explained in Proposition 9.

In the known characteristics mode of explanation, the event was predictable given the observers' prior beliefs about the available agents. In this mode, when asked for the cause of the event, observers will name one or a combination of the available agents. Observers prefer this mode over the others because an explanation is possible in terms of their already held beliefs. Observers' beliefs about the characteristics of the available agents will not be altered much, if at all, by the occurrence of the event. This mode is more fully explained in Proposition 10.

In the new characteristics mode of explanation, the event was not predictable given the observers' prior beliefs about the available agents. However, when asked for the cause of the event, observers will name one, or a combination of, the available agents. But this explanation is made possible by observers inferring new characteristic(s) of the agent(s) expressly for the purpose of explaining the event. This explanation is therefore not based upon prior beliefs about the available agents. Observers' characteristic attributions for the agent(s) named as cause could therefore show considerable change as a result of the occurrence of the event. The amount of change will be determined by the nature of the characteristics that must be inferred in order to explain the event. The newly inferred characteristics do not contradict any of the prior beliefs of observers. For agents not implicated as causal, the occurrence of the event will have little, if any, impact on their perceived characteristics. This mode is more fully explained in Proposition 11.

In the revised characteristics mode, the event was not predictable given the observers' prior beliefs about the available agents. However, when asked for the cause of the event, observers will name one, or a combination of, available agents. But this is made possible by observers revising prior beliefs about the characteristic(s) of agent(s) expressly for the purpose of explaining the event. Observers' characteristic attributions to causally implicated agents could therefore change considerably as a result of the occurrence of the event. This mode is more fully explained in Proposition 12.

I. PROPOSITION 9: UNKNOWN CAUSE

Observers will attribute an event to unknown cause unless they believe that

$$p(\text{event}/\text{AGENT}) > p(\text{event}),$$

where AGENT represents the single agent or the congregation of agents available at the time of the event. This proposition is based on Heider's (1958) idea that the cognitive activities of observers can be understood as attempts to predict the future. Hence when observers provide a causal explanation for an event, they prefer to do so in terms of unchanging characteristics of the agents involved. However, such explanations, in terms of stable characteristics, are viable only if observers believe that if these same agents came together in the past or were to come together again in the future, the same event occurred or would occur. The interaction of the stable characteristics of available agents should produce the same result, regardless of time. In other words, the congregation of available agents must be a facilitator of the event. If observers believe that the congregation of agents is a facilitator of the event, they can proceed to explain the event in terms of stable characteristics of one or more of the available agents. In this case, they would be operating under Proposition 10, described below.

If observers believe that this congregation is not a facilitator of the event, they cannot explain the event in terms of stable characteristics, so they will plead "unknown explanation." In this case, observers may refer to "chance," "luck," "fate," "circumstances," or some other ill-defined force as the cause.

Although observers may initially believe that the event is not predictable given this congregation of events, they may change their minds in order to provide an explanation for the event. They may begin to believe that this event was predictable, that this congregation of agents is a facilitator of the event. If this is done, observers will then be operating under either Proposition 11 or 12, described below.

If observers are operating under Proposition 9, the observation of the event will have little or no impact upon their beliefs about agent characteristics. Since the event is believed to be owing to some unknown cause, it is irrelevant to the stable characteristics of the available agents. Observers maintain their prior beliefs about the agents and perceive the event as an unexplainable anomaly.

J. PROPOSITION 10: KNOWN CHARACTERISTICS

When asked to explain the cause of an event that has occurred with a particular congregation of agents, observers, if they believe that the congregation is a facilitator of the event (Proposition 9), will scan their probability statements and will name as the cause of the event an agent, or combination of agents, that fulfills the following conditions: (1) p(event)/AGENT) > p(event) and (2)

$|p(event/AGENT) - p(event)| > |p(event/AGENT_n) - p(event)|$, where AGENT represents either a single agent or a combination of agents and $AGENT_n$ represents any other single agent or combination of agents. The first of these conditions means that the agent named as the cause must be a facilitator of the event. As discussed above, an agent cannot be a cause unless it is a facilitator.

The second of the conditions captures two requirements. The first of those requirements is that the focal agent must have a facilitative effect stronger than that of any other agent. In other words, when observers name the cause of an event, they name the strongest available facilitator. For example, suppose a teacher writing on the blackboard with his or her back to the class is hit on the back of the head with a piece of chalk. The teacher must decide which of several students is the cause of the thrown chalk. Several possibilities exist based on the teacher's beliefs about the past behaviors associated with each student. Little Willie Frolic has never done anything bad in his life (at least in the mind of the teacher), so p(chalk missile/Willy) = .00. Mary Smith is a more likely suspect, p(chalk missile/Mary) = .05. But she is not nearly as bad as her brother, Jack, p(chalk missile/Jack) = .10. Jack Smith has the highest probability and is therefore the most likely cause. The teacher will probably blame him for the chalk missile. This vignette shows that the agent chosen as the cause must be a facilitator of the event and must also be the strongest available facilitator.

The second requirement captured by the second probability statement is that the agent named as the cause must be of sufficient facilitative strength to overcome the available inhibitors. For example, the event in question might be a large catch of fish today, by Bill, in a particular creek. If the creek is known to be a poor fishing place, and Bill is believed to be a very good fisherman, observers could attribute the large catch to Bill's great fishing ability. If, however, the fishing place were very bad and Bill were a middling fisherman, Bill's skill would not be perceived as sufficient to overcome the inhibitive effect of the creek. In this case observers would probably attribute the large catch to luck. Stating this in probability terms, let us suppose that the observers have the impression from their past experiences that the probability, across all fishermen and all fishing places, of getting a large catch is .40; that Bill is an excellent fisherman, p(large catch/Bill) = .65; and that this creek is not as good as most as a place to fish, p(large catch/creek) = .20. Bill's disposition, fishing ability, is a facilitative force for the event in this example. The strength of this facilitative force is, according to Proposition 6,

$$FF \text{ (agent)} = p(event/agent) - p(event)$$
$$FF \text{ (Bill)} = p(\text{large catch/Bill}) - p(\text{large catch})$$
$$= .65 - .40 = .25.$$

The strength of the creek's inhibitory force on the event of getting a large catch can be derived from Proposition 7:

$$IF \text{ (agent)} = p(\text{event/agent}) - p(\text{event})$$
$$IF \text{ (creek)} = p(\text{large catch/creek}) - p(\text{large catch})$$
$$= .20 - .40 = -.20.$$

Since the magnitude of Bill's facilitory effect is greater than the magnitude of the inhibitory effect of the creek (.25 > .20), observers will name Bill as the cause of the large catch. If, however, the inhibitive effect of the creek were much stronger, this explanation would not be viable. Suppose the observers' beliefs about $p(\text{large catch})$ and $p(\text{large catch/Bill})$ remained the same as they are above, but the creek involved was a very bad fishing hole, $p(\text{large catch/creek}) = .05)$. In this case, the inhibitive effect of the creek is

$$.05 - .40 = -.35.$$

The magnitude of this inhibitive effect is greater than the magnitude of Bill's facilitative effect (.35 > .25). So although Bill is a facilitator of the event, observers will not name him as the cause because his facilitation is not seen as strong enough to overcome the available inhibitors. Observers therefore cannot explain the event in terms of their currently held probability statements. They will have to attribute the event to luck or change their probability statements to provide an explanation. In other words, they would have to switch to one of the less preferred explanatory modes, which are described in Propositions 9, 11, and 12.

The above examples show why Proposition 10 is the preferred mode of causal explanation for observers. If observers scan their probability statements and find an agent that fulfills the two conditions of Proposition 10, they have found an explanation for the event in terms of their prior beliefs. They can thus explain the event in terms of stable, predictable characteristics of the available agents, and no revision of their prior beliefs is necessary.

If asked about the characteristics of the available agents, observers could answer easily by consulting their probability statements. In addition, the answers they would have given before the event would be about the same as those given after the event, since no change in prior beliefs was necessary in order to explain the event. The event might have an incremental effect upon the beliefs of observers because the event represents one more observation to be added to their storehouse of knowledge. However, this increment, which might be predicted using Bayes's theorem (see the discussion of Ajzen & Fishbein, 1975, below), will be small when compared to changes in beliefs that are described in Propositions 11 and 12.

The illustrative examples discussed here are simple but that should not be allowed to obscure the possibility of dealing with more complex cases. In both of the examples cited here, an explanation was possible using only a single agent. In many real-life situations multiple agents are causal. How do observers deal with these more complex situations? Further refinement of theory is needed here.

For example, it seems likely that observers will prefer an explanation that involves as few agents as possible. It also seems likely that when observers are combining facilitative agents in order to have a facilitative effect sufficient to overcome some available inhibitor(s), they will combine only as many as are necessary to meet the inhibitory force.

K. PROPOSITION 11: NEW CHARACTERISTICS

When asked to explain the cause of an event that has occurred with a particular congregation of agents, observers, if they believe that the congregation is a facilitator of the event (Proposition 9) but are unable to explain it in terms of known characteristics of the available agents (as described in Proposition 10), may provide an explanation by fulfilling the conditions of Proposition 10 by inferring completely new characteristic(s) for one or more of the available agents. An example of this process is seen when Jack, a fisherman of unknown ability, gets a large catch in a poor fishing creek. There are no agents available that are known to be facilitators of the event, therefore the conditions of Proposition 10 are not fulfilled. However, if observers allow themselves to believe that Jack is a good fisherman of sufficient ability to overcome the inhibitive effects of the creek, they will be able to fulfill the conditions of Proposition 10 and provide an explanation for the event. But this causal attribution is possible only by making a characteristic attribution to Jack. In probabilities, assume that observers believe that

$$p(\text{large catch}) = .40,$$
$$p(\text{large catch}/\text{creek}) = .20,$$
$$p(\text{large catch}/\text{Jack}) = ?$$

From Proposition 7 we know that the inhibitory effect of the creek is given by

$$IF(\text{agent}) = p(\text{event}/\text{agent}) - p(\text{event})$$
$$IF(\text{creek}) = p(\text{large catch}/\text{creek}) - p(\text{large catch})$$
$$= .20 - .40 = -.20.$$

To overcome this inhibitory force, which has a magnitude of .20, Jack must provide a facilitory force with a magnitude of at least .20. This value of .20 can be substituted into the equation for facilitory forces given in Proposition 6:

$$FF(\text{agent}) = p(\text{event}/\text{agent}) - p(\text{event})$$
$$FF(\text{Jack}) = p(\text{large catch}/\text{Jack}) - p(\text{large catch})$$
$$.20 = (\text{large catch}/\text{Jack}) - .40$$
$$p(\text{large catch}/\text{Jack}) = .20 + .40 = .60.$$

So, if observers allow themselves to believe that $p(\text{event}/\text{Jack}) \geq .60$, they have a causal explanation for the event that fulfills the conditions of Proposition 10.

This avenue of explanation will be attractive to observers because it does not require them to alter any of their prior beliefs. It also is compatible with the requirement of Proposition 9 that if Jack and that creek were to "meet" again, the outcome would probably be the same.

If observers had been asked about Jack's disposition, fishing ability, rather than about the cause of the event, they would have been able to answer. Although their prior knowledge of Jack contained no information about this characteristic, taking the event into account would allow observers to give an answer. By assuming that Jack caused the event, they can infer his disposition. In this case a characteristic attribution is possible only by making a causal explanation.

The processes described in Propositions 10 and 11 make it very clear how intimately causal and characteristic attributions can be related. In Proposition 11, neither attribution can be done unless the conditions of Proposition 10 are brought into place. But that bringing into place simultaneously sets the information for both causal and characteristic attributions.

The explanatory process involved here in Proposition 11 involves a major, but narrowly focused, change in a belief about an agent. From having no belief, observers come to believe that an agent has a particular characteristic of sufficient facilitative force to overcome the available inhibitors. This may not be an incremental change and it is a change essential to providing attributions. In Proposition 10, the change was incremental and it was incidental to the provision of attributions. But the processes in Proposition 11 do not change all of the observers' prior beliefs. Agents that are not causally implicated directly, such as the fishing creek in the examples, undergo no change. Observers maintain their prior beliefs about the creek throughout. Even characteristics of the causally implicated agent that are not directly relevant to this event, for example, Jack's singing ability, should go unchanged.

In this proposition, as in earlier ones, simple examples are used, but this should not distract readers from considering more complex cases. What additional principles are necessary in order to explain complex cases with many causes? This issue will be addressed later when Kelley's covariation theory and concept of discounting are discussed.

L. PROPOSITION 12: REVISED CHARACTERISTICS

When asked to explain the cause of an event that has occurred with a particular congregation of agents, observers, if they believe that the congregation is a facilitator of the event (Proposition 9) but are unable to explain it in terms of known characteristics of available agents (as in Proposition 10), may provide an explanation by fulfilling the conditions of Proposition 10 by changing one of their currently available probability statements for an agent. The proverbial fishing creek can also be used to illustrate the operation of Proposition 12. If Jack gets a large catch in a poor fishing creek, and Jack is known prior to the event to be a poor fisherman, observers have an unexplainable event. Jack is a facilitator but not strong enough to overcome the inhibitory creek. One explanation is luck (Proposition 9). Another is to revise beliefs about Jack's fishing ability. Observers may conclude that Jack is a better fisherman than they originally believed. Alternately they may decide the creek is not as bad as their prior expectations. They could make adjustments in their beliefs about both Jack and the creek. Presumably observers will revise their probability statements only to the degree necessary to explain the event.

The explanatory process involved in Proposition 12 can involve major but narrowly focused changes in beliefs about the characteristics of agents. By making the assumption that the agent caused the event, the event is explained, but the cost for the observer is a change in beliefs. In some cases a small revision will do. In other cases the change necessary for the explanation may be major. Observers will presumably try to avoid the latter type. As in Proposition 11, changes in characteristics will be confined to those that are directly causally implicated

M. PROPOSITION 13: SELECTION OF EXPLANATION MODE

When asked to explain an event, observers will choose among the explanation modes given in Propositions 9–12 on the basis of conservatism, parsimony, and the relative strengths of the available pieces of information. The principle of conservatism suggests that observers will prefer to provide explanations that allow them to maintain a belief that the world is orderly, that they understand it, and that they can predict and explain events. For the most part, this means that observers will try to explain events using beliefs held before the event occurred and will resist changing any of those beliefs. If they can, they will explain the event entirely with beliefs held before the event occurred, in which case they would be operating under Proposition 10. If that fails, they will move to Proposition 11, which allows an explanation by attributing new characteristics to an agent. In this mode, no previously held beliefs are changed, just new beliefs added.

Bell, Wicklund, Manko, and Larkin (1976) found that attributions tend to flow to that part of the environment about which least is known. The more unknown an agent is, the less likely it is that a characteristic inferred in order to explain an event will contradict a prior belief about the agent. This mechanism suggests that some vaguely understood agents could become repositories of explanations for unexplainable events. The attribution of events to the Olympian gods comes to mind as an example. Failing an explanation via Proposition 11, observers will move to Proposition 12. Here, they provide an explanation by altering belief(s) they held prior to the event. This is not as desirable as Proposition 11 because in Proposition 11 no previous belief had to be changed, something new was just added. Under Proposition 12 there is a contradiction of a prior belief, which can be a major threat to observers' sense of being able to understand and predict the world. Failing an explanation under Proposition 12, observers would use Proposition 9. In Proposition 9, no explanation is possible using known agents, so attribution is to chance or to luck. This is the least preferred explanation mode because it suggests that the world is unpredictable, that the observer does not know or understand why things happen.

The principle of parsimony suggests that observers will prefer to make a small change over a big one. For example, a slight modification in beliefs about Jack's fishing ability is preferable to a large change in beliefs about the creek. In addition, observers will prefer to attribute an event to one agent rather than to two or three.

The principle of relative strength of information suggests that different beliefs are held with different degrees of strength and that observers will prefer to modify weaker ones. For example, an event that contradicts a person's expectations about a particular agent may occur. If the originally held beliefs about the agent's characteristics are strongly held, and the event observed is unclear or not very salient, the preferred interpretation will be to maintain the old beliefs and attribute the event to luck. If the originally held probability statement is vague and weak, and the observed event represents very strong evidence, the observer will be very likely to change the probability statement to accommodate the new information. Kassin (1979) has a very good discussion of the roles of expectations and new information upon consensus information, which is very relevant here. The principles described there will also apply to distinctiveness information.

These principles can produce effects that are consonant, opposite, or neutral with respect to each other. One observer may readily add a new belief about an actor named Mary Smith rather than attribute an event to luck. In this case the force of conservation prevailed. Another observer may have very strong beliefs about Mary Smith, refuse to change them, and attribute the event to luck. In this case, the force of the relative strength of beliefs will have prevailed.

This completes the description of PEAT. It assumes that observers base their attributions of causes and characteristics upon stored probability statements. Those probability statements are the basis for observers' beliefs and expectancies about the enduring characteristics of agents. Attribution processing is seen as a relatively conservative activity in which observers prefer to explain events in terms of presently held beliefs about stable characteristics of agents. Only when this is not possible will new characteristics be assigned to agents or present beliefs be changed in order to provide an explanation. In these processes there is an intimate interaction of causal and characteristic attribution. It is now time to show that PEAT provides a single basis for the theoretical ideas of Kelley (1973), Jones and Davis (1965), and some other theorists.

III. Kelley's Theories

Kelley's (1973) ideas about attributions are typically presented in two separate models called covariation theory and configuration theory. These will each be explained in terms of PEAT, which will show that they are intimately connected. They should not be treated as separate models even though they tend to focus on different aspects of attribution processes. PEAT will also allow a better understanding of the role of causal and characteristic attributions in Kelley's models. Traditionally, Kelley has been thought of as a theorist concerned with causal attribution. Although this is true for the most part, he discusses many aspects of characteristic attribution.

A. COVARIATION THEORY

Covariation theory (Kelley, 1973) reduces the attribution situation to one in which only a single actor and a single entity are available when an event occurs. The observer is asked to decide if the event is caused by the actor, by the entity, by some combination of the two, or by the circumstances of the interaction. The theory states that observers base their attributions upon three kinds of covariation information: consensus, distinctiveness, and consistency. Empirical studies (e.g., Jaspars, 1983; McArthur, 1972) give general support to this theory.

The relationship between PEAT and covariation theory will be demonstrated by showing that each of the three kinds of covariation information can be defined in terms of probabilities. Observers can then scan these probabilities and arrive at causal attributions. Kelley's theory will be seen as an expression of and an elaboration on PEAT.

1. Consensus

In covariation theory, consensus is defined in the following way. The observer knows that some actor has made some response in the presence of some entity. Consensus information states whether or not other people usually produce that response in the presence of that same entity. If they do, consensus is high; if they do not, consensus is low. In an example used by McArthur (1972), the event is Paul being enthralled by a particular painting at the art museum. High consensus means that most other people are also enthralled by the painting; low consensus, that most other people are not enthralled. According to Kelley, high consensus tends to induce attribution to the entity and low consensus tends to induce attribution to the actor.

In PEAT, consensus has to do with the probability of the event given the presence of the entity. With high consensus practically everyone makes the same response in the presence of the entity, so the entity is a good predictor that the event (the actors' response) will occur. In other words, high consensus means p(event/entity) = high. With low consensus, however, practically no one makes the response in the presence of the entity, or p(event/entity) = low. But stating consensus information in probabilities in this way is only a first approximation. This kind of statement leaves ambiguity about the meaning of the terms high and low. What is high for one entity/event combination may be low for another. If p(food poisoning/restaurant X) = .25, that is, one quarter of all customers get food poisoning, most people would say that this is a high rate. On the other hand, if p(landing safely/airline Y) = .25, that is, only one quarter of all passengers arrive without serious mishap, most people would say that this is a low rate. PEAT provides a basis for removing this ambiguity. The unconditional probability of the event in question provides a standard of comparison that determines whether a probability value is high or low. Most of us have an impression that p(food poisoning) across all eating places is very much lower than .25, so restaurant X's value of .25 seems large. Likewise, most of us feel that p(landing safely), taken across all airlines and all passengers, is considerably higher than .25, so .25 represents low consensus in that case. This leads to the following, more refined definitions: HIGH CONSENSUS occurs when p(event/entity) > p(event); LOW CONSENSUS occurs when p(event/entity) < p(event).

Stating consensus in this way does not violate Kelley's (1973) predictions about how consensus information affects attributions. Kelley said that high consensus tends to induce attributions to the entity and low consensus tends to induce attribution to the actor. PEAT agrees. With high consensus, p(event/entity) > p (event), which means the entity is a facilitator of the event and therefore likely to be named as the cause of the event (taking into account the requirements of Propositions 9–12). With low consensus, p(event/entity) < p (event), so the entity is an inhibitor of the event. As such, it is unlikely to be named as the cause, so observers will look for other causal agents. Since in covariation theory the only other available agent is the actor, by default the probability of the actor being named the cause is high when consensus is low.

Although PEAT agrees with Kelley's (1973) predictions about the effects of consensus information on attributions, it differs with the interpretation of how the information in consensus data brings this about. This difference represents a subtle but very important shift in interpretation that has not heretofore been dealt with in the literature, even though other theorists have expressed consensus in probabilistic terms. It will be helpful in discussing this difference to refer to the interpretation of Kelley as the *contrast interpretation* and that of PEAT as the *prediction interpretation*.

Kelley's (1973) explanation of how consensus plays its role is called the contrast interpretation because it is based upon a contrast between the focal actor and other actors. In this widely accepted interpretation, the attention is on whether or not the focal actor is like other actors. In the example of the painting at the art museum, the low-consensus information that Paul is enthralled (while nobody else is) can be taken to mean that Paul is different from other actors. From there it can be said that since Paul is different from other actors and is therefore in some sense unique, it is Paul who is the cause of the event. Alternately, when consensus is high, it suggests that Paul acts like everyone else with this painting, is therefore not unique, and is therefore not a viable source of explanation for this event.

This interpretation depends on the assumption that consensus information allows observers to decide if the actor is unique or not, but that assumption may not be correct. Stripped of all assumptions, low-consensus information shows that on this particular occasion the actor acted in a certain way in the presence of the entity, and that other people do not usually react that way in the presence of the entity. If an observer is to use this information to conclude that the actor is unique (i.e., has the enduring characteristic of being unlike other people), the observer must assume that on other occasions, not just on this particular occasion, the actor would act in the same unique way in the presence of the entity. But this assumption goes beyond the information given in the consensus information, which reports only the actors behavior on this particular occasion. Observers may be willing to make this large assumption on some occasions, but it is likely that they will avoid it when they can.

The PEAT interpretation of the role of consensus information is called the prediction interpretation because it stresses how consensus information can be used to predict events. The prediction interpretation highlights the fact that, whether high or low, consensus always allows the observer to predict how most people act or do not act in the presence of the entity. The usual reaction to the entity is given fully, with no assumptions necessary from the observer. With high consensus, it is a given that other people usually react the way the actor did; with low consensus, it is a given that other people usually do not react the way the actor did. Consensus information is therefore a statement about an enduring characteristic of the entity as a predictor of events.

This shift in interpretation also leads to a subtle but important shift in what both high and low consensus refer to. In Kelley's contrast interpretation, high consensus means that this actor is like other actors and low consensus means that this actor is unlike other actors. In the prediction interpretation of PEAT, high consensus means that the presence of the entity is a good predictor that the event will occur and low consensus means that the presence of the entity is a good predictor that the event will not occur.

This shift in interpretation has important theoretical consequences. It is the foundation that allows PEAT to integrate the theories of Kelley, Jones and Davis, and others. Failure to make the shift has been a stumbling block that has hindered the success of some other attempts to apply probability to attributions and to integrate attribution theories. These issues will be discussed more extensively later in this article.

2. Distinctiveness

In covariation theory, the second kind of covariation information is distinctiveness, which is defined in the following way (Kelley, 1973). Given that the actor has made a response in the presence of the entity, distinctiveness information states whether or not the actor usually makes the same response in the presence of other entities. For the example used earlier, low distinctiveness occurs if Paul is enthralled by paintings in general as well as by the focal painting. High distinctiveness occurs if Paul is seldom enthralled by paintings.

The PEAT analysis of distinctiveness is analogous to its analysis of consensus and so is based on a prediction interpretation rather than a contrast interpretation. In Kelley's contrast version, distinctiveness information tells observers something about the entity because the event on this occasion is contrasted to what usually happens when the actor is present. If the event does not usually occur with this actor (high distinctiveness), the entity has caused a unique reaction from the actor and is therefore the cause of the event. With low distinctiveness, the actor behaves the same with this as with all entities, the entity is not unique, and therefore the actor is the cause. As with the contrast interpretation of consensus, an assumption about an enduring characteristic of an agent is necessary to make this work. In the prediction interpretation of PEAT, low distinctiveness means that the actor usually makes this response across all entities, so the actor is a facilitator of the event and a likely cause. With high distinctiveness, the actor is not a good predictor of the event, is an inhibitor, and is unlikely to be named as the cause. These ideas can be stated in probabilities in a way analogous to that for consensus: HIGH DISTINCTIVENESS occurs when $p(\text{event}/\text{actor}) < p(\text{event})$; LOW DISTINCTIVENESS occurs when $p(\text{event}/\text{actor}) > p(\text{event})$.

3. Consistency

According to covariation theory, this third kind of covariation information tells whether or not the event (response) has occurred on past occasions when the entity and actor have come together (Kelley, 1973). In the example, high consistency means that on past occasions, when Paul has viewed this particular painting, he has been enthralled. Low consistency means that on past occasions Paul has not been enthralled by this particular painting.

The prediction interpretation of consistency is analogous to the prediction interpretation of consensus and distinctiveness. High consistency means that in the past, when this actor and entity have come together, the event has usually occurred, so the actor and entity are joint facilitators of the event. Low consistency means that the actor and entity are joint inhibitors of the event. In probabilities, this is as follows. HIGH CONSISTENCY occurs when p(event/actor $\cap$ entity) $> p$(event); LOW CONSISTENCY occurs when p(event/actor $\cap$ entity) $< p$(event).

The fundamental role that consistency information plays in PEAT is described above in Proposition 9. Observers must believe that the available congregation of agents is a facilitator of the event before they will make attributions to the agents, alone or in combination. Otherwise they will plead no explanation, luck, or chance. In Kelley's covariation theory, which is confined to one actor and one entity, consistency information represents the facilitory or inhibitive effect of the congregation of those two agents.

4. Combinations of Information

Now that the three kinds of covariation information have been stated as probabilities, the attributions that result from various combinations of these three kinds of information can be predicted and discussed. Given that the three kinds of information can each be in one of two states, high or low, eight combinations of information are possible. These eight combinations are shown in Table I. These are the same eight that have been discussed by Hilton and Slugoski (1986), Jaspars (1983), and McArthur (1972). The relationship between covariation theory and PEAT can be seen by examining the cells in Table I, one by one.

a. Cell 1. In this cell consensus is low, distinctiveness is low, and consistency is high. For example, suppose that the event to be explained is Jim winning a race today while riding a horse named Speedy. In this case the actor is Jim and the entity is Speedy. Low consensus would be present if Speedy were a poorer than average race horse who seldom won. In probabilities, this is

$$p(\text{win}) > p(\text{win/Speedy}).$$

In other words, Speedy is an inhibitor of the event of winning. Low distinctiveness would be present if Jim were an above average rider who usually won. In probabilities, this is

$$p(\text{win/Jim}) > p(\text{win}).$$

In other words, Jim is a facilitator of the event of winning. High consistency would occur if in the past, when Jim had ridden Speedy, they had usually won. In probabilities, this is

$$p(\text{win}/\text{Jim} \cap \text{Speedy}) > p(\text{win}).$$

All three of these probability statements contain the term $p(\text{win})$. They can be aligned in the following way:

$$p(\text{win}) > p(\text{win}/\text{Speedy})$$
$$p(\text{win}/\text{Jim}) > p(\text{win})$$
$$p(\text{win}/\text{Jim} \cap \text{Speedy}) > p(\text{win}).$$

It can be seen in this layout, because of the presence of $p(\text{win})$ in all three statements, that the relationships of all of the probability terms to each other can be specified, except the relationship between $p(\text{win}/\text{Jim})$ and $p(\text{win}/\text{Jim} \cap \text{Speedy})$. These two can be equal to each other or one can be larger than the other. The exact nature of the relationship between these two probabilities is not specified in the verbal statement of covariation theory. If the three separate probability statements just shown are combined into a single expression, three versions are possible, depending on the relationship between $p(\text{win}/\text{Jim})$ and $p(\text{win}/\text{Jim} \cap \text{Speedy})$ that is used. The three possible combined expressions for this example follow, each coupled with the corresponding general expression from Table I.

Expression 1:

$$p(\text{win}/\text{Jim}) > p(\text{win}/\text{Jim} \cap \text{Speedy}) > p(\text{win}) > p(\text{win}/\text{Speedy})$$
$$p(\text{event}/\text{actor}) > p(\text{event}/\text{actor} \cap \text{entity}) > p(\text{event}) > p(\text{event}/\text{entity})$$

Expression 2:

$$p(\text{win}/\text{Jim}) = p(\text{win}/\text{Jim} \cap \text{Speedy}) > p(\text{win}) > p(\text{win}/\text{Speedy})$$
$$p(\text{event}/\text{actor}) = p(\text{event}/\text{actor} \cap \text{entity}) > p(\text{event}) > p(\text{event}/\text{entity})$$

Expression 3:

$$p(\text{win}/\text{Jim} \cap \text{Speedy}) > p(\text{win}/\text{Jim}) > p(\text{win}) > p(\text{win}/\text{Speedy})$$
$$p(\text{event}/\text{actor} \cap \text{entity}) > p(\text{event}/\text{actor}) > p(\text{event}) > p(\text{event}/\text{entity})$$

It is thus seen that in Cell 1, PEAT specifies three patterns of information while covariation theory specifies only one. This is because covariation theory specifies the information rather vaguely in English, while PEAT specifies its information patterns more precisely as probabilities. All three of the probability patterns given by PEAT are consistent with the covariation theory statement. Here PEAT provides a refinement of covariation theory.

TABLE I
PATTERNS OF COVARIATION INFORMATION[a]

Cell 1

Defining characteristics:

Covariation information	PEAT probabilities
low consensus	$p(\text{event/entity}) < p(\text{event})$
low distinctiveness	$p(\text{event/actor}) > p(\text{event})$
high consistency	$p(\text{event/actor} \cap \text{entity}) > p(\text{event})$

Predicted attributions (from covariation theory): actor

Summary expressions and predicted attributions (from PEAT):

Summary expressions	Attributions
1. $p(\text{event/actor}) > p(\text{event/actor} \cap \text{entity}) > p(\text{event}) > p(\text{event/entity})$	actor
2. $p(\text{event/actor}) = p(\text{event/actor} \cap \text{entity}) > p(\text{event}) > p(\text{event/entity})$	actor
3. $p(\text{event/actor} \cap \text{entity}) > p(\text{event/actor}) > p(\text{event}) > p(\text{event/entity})$	actor and entity

Cell 2

Defining characteristics:

Covariation information	PEAT probabilities
high consensus	$p(\text{event/entity}) > p(\text{event})$
high distinctiveness	$p(\text{event/actor}) < p(\text{event})$
high consistency	$p(\text{event/actor} \cap \text{entity}) > p(\text{event})$

Predicted attributions (from covariation theory): entity

Summary expressions and predicted attributions (from PEAT):

Summary expressions	Attributions
4. $p(\text{event/entity}) > p(\text{event/actor} \cap \text{entity}) > p(\text{event}) > p(\text{event/actor})$	entity
5. $p(\text{event/entity}) = p(\text{event/actor} \cap \text{entity}) > p(\text{event}) > p(\text{event/actor})$	entity
6. $p(\text{event/actor} \cap \text{entity}) > p(\text{event/entity}) > p(\text{event}) > p(\text{event/actor})$	actor and entity

TABLE I (*Continued*)

Cell 3

Defining characteristics:

Covariation information	*PEAT probabilities*
low consensus	$p(\text{event/entity}) < p(\text{event})$
high distinctiveness	$p(\text{event/actor}) < p(\text{event})$
high consistency	$p(\text{event/actor} \cap \text{entity}) > p(\text{event})$

Predicted attributions (from covariation theory): actor and entity

Summary expressions and predicted attributions (from PEAT):

Summary expressions	*Attributions*
7. $p(\text{event/actor} \cap \text{entity}) > p(\text{event}) > p(\text{event/entity}) = p(\text{event/actor})$	actor and entity
8. $p(\text{event/actor} \cap \text{entity}) > p(\text{event}) > p(\text{event/entity}) > p(\text{event/actor})$	actor and entity
9. $p(\text{event/actor} \cap \text{entity}) > p(\text{event}) > p(\text{event/actor}) > p(\text{event/entity})$	actor and entity

Cell 4

Defining characteristics:

Covariation information	*PEAT probabilities*
high consensus	$p(\text{event/entity}) > p(\text{event})$
low distinctiveness	$p(\text{event/actor}) > p(\text{event})$
high consistency	$p(\text{event/actor} \cap \text{entity}) > p(\text{event})$

Predicted attributions (from covariation theory): actor, entity, actor and entity

Summary expressions and predicted attributions (from PEAT):

Summary expressions	*Attributions*
10. $p(\text{event/actor}) > p(\text{event/entity}) > p(\text{event/actor} \cap \text{entity}) > p(\text{event})$	actor
11. $p(\text{event/actor}) > p(\text{event/actor} \cap \text{entity}) > p(\text{event/entity}) > p(\text{event})$	actor
12. $p(\text{event/actor}) > p(\text{event/actor} \cap \text{entity}) = p(\text{event/entity}) > p(\text{event})$	actor
13. $p(\text{event/entity}) > p(\text{event/actor}) > p(\text{event/actor} \cap \text{entity}) > p(\text{event})$	entity
14. $p(\text{event/entity}) > p(\text{event/actor} \cap \text{entity}) > p(\text{event/actor}) > p(\text{event})$	entity
15. $p(\text{event/entity}) > p(\text{event/actor} \cap \text{entity}) = p(\text{event/actor}) > p(\text{event})$	entity
16. $p(\text{event/actor} \cap \text{entity}) > p(\text{event/entity}) > p(\text{event/actor}) > p(\text{event})$	actor and entity
17. $p(\text{event/actor} \cap \text{entity}) > p(\text{event/entity}) = p(\text{event/actor}) > p(\text{event})$	actor and entity
18. $p(\text{event/actor} \cap \text{entity}) > p(\text{event/actor}) > p(\text{event/entity}) > p(\text{event})$	actor and entity
19. $p(\text{event/actor}) = p(\text{event/actor} \cap \text{entity}) > p(\text{event/entity}) > p(\text{event})$	actor
20. $p(\text{event/entity}) = p(\text{event/actor} \cap \text{entity}) > p(\text{event/actor}) > p(\text{event})$	entity
21. $p(\text{event/actor}) = p(\text{event/entity}) > p(\text{event/actor} \cap \text{entity}) > p(\text{event})$	actor, entity
22. $p(\text{event/actor}) = p(\text{event/entity}) = p(\text{event/actor} \cap \text{entity}) > p(\text{event})$	actor, entity

(*continued*)

TABLE I (*Continued*)

Cell 5

Defining characteristics:

Covariation information	*PEAT probabilities*
low consensus	$p(\text{event/entity}) < p(\text{event})$
low distinctiveness	$p(\text{event/actor}) > p(\text{event})$
low consistency	$p(\text{event/actor} \cap \text{entity}) < p(\text{event})$

Predicted attributions (from covariation theory): luck

Summary expressions and predicted attributions (from PEAT):

Summary expressions	*Attributions*
$p(\text{event/actor} \cap \text{entity}) < p(\text{event})$	luck

Cell 6

Defining characteristics:

Covariation information	*PEAT probabilities*
high consensus	$p(\text{event/entity}) > p(\text{event})$
high distinctiveness	$p(\text{event/actor}) < p(\text{event})$
low consistency	$p(\text{event/actor} \cap \text{entity}) < p(\text{event})$

Predicted attributions (from covariation theory): luck

Summary expressions and predicted attributions (from PEAT):

Summary expressions	*Attributions*
$p(\text{event/actor} \cap \text{entity}) < p(\text{event})$	luck

Cell 7

Defining characteristics:

Covariation information	*PEAT probabilities*
low consensus	$p(\text{event/entity}) < p(\text{event})$
high distinctiveness	$p(\text{event/actor}) < p(\text{event})$
low consistency	$p(\text{event/actor} \cap \text{entity}) < p(\text{event})$

Predicted attributions (from covariation theory): luck

Summary expressions and predicted attributions (from PEAT):

Summary expressions	*Attributions*
$p(\text{event/actor} \cap \text{entity}) < p(\text{event})$	luck

TABLE I (Continued)

Cell 8

Defining characteristics:

Covariation information	PEAT probabilities
high consensus	$p(\text{event}/\text{entity}) > p(\text{event})$
low distinctiveness	$p(\text{event}/\text{actor}) > p(\text{event})$
low consistency	$p(\text{event}/\text{actor} \cap \text{entity}) < p(\text{event})$

Predicted attributions (from covariation theory): luck

Summary expressions and predicted attributions (from PEAT):

Summary expressions	Attributions
$p(\text{event}/\text{actor} \cap \text{entity}) < p(\text{event})$	luck

^aIn Cells 5–8 only one summary expression is given because, owing to the nature of that expression, all attributions are to luck. The relationships of other probabilities to each other are irrelevant in those cells.

The attributions predicted to arise from the three patterns of information specified by PEAT for Cell 1 are as follows. According to Proposition 9, observers will ascertain if the available congregation of agents is a facilitator of the event to be explained. In this example, the congregation of agents consists of Jim and Speedy. When they scan their probabilities, observers will find for all three expressions that

$$p(\text{win}/\text{Jim} \cap \text{Speedy}) > p(\text{win}).$$

This congregation of agents is thus a facilitator of wins, and a causal explanation in terms of that congregation (or some subset of it) is possible. Observers will therefore scan their probabilities to discern which agent, or combination of agents, is the strongest facilitator of the event, as described in Proposition 10. If the information stored by observers is as shown in Expression 1, Jim is the available agent with the strongest facilitative force and so will be named as the cause of the win (Proposition 10). If the information available to observers is as shown in Expression 2, observers find two equally viable causal agents because, in Expression 2,

$$p(\text{win}/\text{Jim}) = p(\text{win}/\text{Jim} \cap \text{Speedy}).$$

PEAT predicts that when observers have two sets of agents that are equally strong facilitators of an event, they will name as the cause the set with fewer members (principle of parsimony, Proposition 13). They will thus name Jim alone as the cause of the win. If the information available to observers is as shown in Expression 3, observers will find that (Jim ∩ Speedy) is the best predictor of the win and will name them jointly as the cause of the win. For example, observers might say that Jim is a pretty good rider, but when he gets on Speedy he is a real star. That is why they won today.

These predictions of covariation theory and PEAT can be compared. Covariation theory specifies only one version of Cell 1 and predicts for that one version that attributions will be to the actor. PEAT specifies three patterns of information. Two of those patterns predict attribution to the actor, the third predicts attribution to (actor ∩ entity). Hilton and Slugoski (1986), Jaspars (1983), and McArthur (1972) all did empirical studies that involved measuring observers' attributions when they were given information representing Cell 1, as specified by covariation theory. All three studies found that the predominant attribution made by observers for Cell 1 was to the actor. This is consistent with both covariation theory and PEAT. In all three studies the second most favored attribution is to (actor ∩ entity). This is predicted by PEAT but not by covariation theory.

These refinements suggested by PEAT should be subjected to further empirical test. Covariation theory specifies only one pattern of information for Cell 1 and one attribution to go with it. PEAT predicts two different kinds of attribution for Cell 1 on the basis of relative magnitudes of p(win/Jim) and p(win/Jim ∩ Speedy). This could be empirically tested with a methodology similar to those of Hilton and Slugoski (1986), Jaspars (1983), and McArthur (1972). One group of observers could be given the somewhat ambiguous covariation information that is common in studies of this kind:

1. The event to be explained is Jim and Speedy winning the race today.
2. Speedy usually does not win races, as seen in his record over the last several years (LOW CONSENSUS).
3. Jim usually wins his races, as seen in his record over the past several years (LOW DISTINCTIVENESS).
4. Jim and Speedy have usually won the races in which they have been together in the past (HIGH CONSISTENCY).

In the actual study, the state of the covariation information given in brackets would not be included. It is given here to facilitate discussion. Given this pattern of information, covariation theory would predict that observers will attribute the win to Jim, the actor. PEAT would say that any of Expressions 1, 2, and 3 is consistent with this information so that although most observers will attribute the event to Jim, some will also attribute it to (Jim ∩ Speedy). A second group of observers could be given information that is more clearly consistent only with Expression 3. For example:

1. The event to be explained is Jim and Speedy winning the race today.
2. Speedy usually does not win races, as seen in his record over the last several years (LOW CONSENSUS).

3. Jim usually wins his races, as seen in his record over the last several years (LOW DISTINCTIVENESS).
4. Jim and Speedy have always won the races in which they have been together in the past (HIGH CONSISTENCY).

Since this information consists of low consensus, low distinctiveness, and high consistency, as did the information in the previous example, covariation theory would predict that observers would make the same attributions to Jim, the actor. PEAT, on the other hand, would note that, in this second example, the covariation information is *more* consistent with Expression 3 than with Expressions 1 and 2. This is because the statement for distinctiveness notes that "Jim *usually* wins his races," whereas the statement for consistency notes that "Jim and Speedy have *always* won." This suggests that

$$p(\text{win}/\text{Jim} \cap \text{Speedy}) > p(\text{win}/\text{Jim}).$$

Since this latter information set is consistent only with Expression 3, PEAT would predict that, for it, most attributions would be to (Jim ∩ Speedy).

Another empirical test of PEAT could be done by moving away from this traditional methodology. Instead of presenting covariation information in English, experimenters could present it as probabilities. An example for Expression 1 might be presented in the following way:

1. The event to be explained is Jim and Speedy winning the race today. The probability of any horse and rider combination winning a race is .15: $p(\text{win}) = .15$.
2. The probability of Speedy winning a race, as shown in his record over the last several years, is .10: $p(\text{win}/\text{Speedy}) = .10$.
   [LOW CONSENSUS: $p(\text{win}) = .15 > p(\text{win}/\text{Speedy}) = .10$]
3. The probability of Jim winning a race, as shown in his record over the last several years, is .50: $p(\text{win}/\text{Jim}) = .50$.
   [LOW DISTINCTIVENESS: $p(\text{win}/\text{Jim}) = .50 > p(\text{win}) = .15$]
4. The probability of Jim and Speedy together winning a race is .25, as shown in the records: $p(\text{win}/\text{Jim} \cap \text{Speedy}) = .25$.
   [HIGH CONSISTENCY: $p(\text{win}/\text{Jim} \cap \text{Speedy}) = .25 > p(\text{win}) = .15$]

The information given in square brackets after each verbal statement would not be given to observers. It is provided here for clarification. Since this information is consistent with Expression 1, but not with Expressions 2 and 3, PEAT would predict that virtually all observers would attribute the win to Jim. Other observers could be given probabilities consistent with Expression 3:

1. The event to be explained is Jim and Speedy winning the race today. The probability of any horse and rider combination winning a race is .15: $p(\text{win}) = .15$.

2. The probability of Speedy winning a race, as shown in his record over the past several years, is .10: $p(\text{win}/\text{Speedy}) = .10$
   [LOW CONSENSUS: $p(\text{win}) = .15 > p(\text{win}/\text{Speedy}) = .10$]
3. The probability of Jim winning a race, as shown in his record over the past several years, is .25: $p(\text{win}/\text{Jim}) = .25$.
   [LOW DISTINCTIVENESS: $p(\text{win}/\text{Jim}) = .25 > p(\text{win}) = .10$]
4. The probability of Jim and Speedy together winning a race is .50, as shown in the records: $p(\text{win}/\text{Jim} \cap \text{Speedy}) = .50$.
   [HIGH CONSISTENCY: $p(\text{win}/\text{Jim} \cap \text{Speedy}) = .50 > p(\text{win}) = .10$]

This pattern of information is consistent with Expression 3 but not with Expressions 1 and 2 since

$$p(\text{win}/\text{Jim} \cap \text{Speedy}) = .50 > p(\text{win}/\text{Jim}) = .25.$$

As a consequence, PEAT would predict that observers would attribute the win to Jim and Speedy.

Another approach to empirically testing PEAT would be to measure observers' reactions to covariation information. In the two empirical studies suggested above, it was proposed that the covariation information be more precisely manipulated than in past studies. An alternative approach is to present observers with the rather vague kind of information they have been given in the past and to collect their interpretations of it. PEAT would predict that the interpretations would correspond to the expressions given in Table I. Further, if observers' attributions were also collected, PEAT would have predictions for them as well, expression by expression, as shown in Table I. For example, in the case of Cell 1, it would be possible to determine if an observer were perceiving the information in accordance with Expression 1, 2, or 3. The attributions reported by observers should correspond to those expressions. This might be done in either of two ways. The first would be to ask observers to report their interpretations just before they make their attributions. With this procedure it could be argued that the statement of the interpretation acts as a primer to give the "appropriate" attributions. This argument would weaken the impact of such a study. A second way to measure the interpretations before attributions are made is to obtain a sample for which it is reasonable to expect that the perceptions and interpretations are quite homogenous across observers. Half of the observers could be asked to report only their interpretations, the other half could be asked to report only their attributions. This procedure would reduce the problem of priming that was found in the previous procedure. However, this latter method is a between-observers test of what is a within-observers hypothesis of PEAT.

This completes the discussion of Cell 1 of Table I. It has been seen that PEAT presents a refinement on the basic principles articulated in covariation theory and holds the promise of more refined predictions. Methods for testing those refined predictions have been suggested.

b. Cell 2. Moving on to Cell 2 of Table I, it is found that consensus is high, distinctiveness is high, and consistency is high. If the event to be explained is Jim winning the race today, while riding Speedy, high consensus would be present if Speedy was a horse with an above-average win record, high distinctiveness would be present if Jim had a below-average win record, and high consistency would be present if Jim and Speedy usually win when they are together. In this cell, Speedy is normally a winner and thus a facilitator of wins, unlike Cell 1 in which Speedy was an inhibitor of wins. In this cell, Jim is normally not a winner and is therefore an inhibitor of wins, unlike Cell 1 in which Jim was a facilitator of wins. Cells 1 and 2 have identical underlying logic. The difference between the two is that Jim and Speedy play reversed facilitatory and inhibitory roles. Akin to Cell 1, then, there are three probability expressions for Cell 2. Each of these can be given in a version for the Jim and Speedy example, and each can be given in the general version shown in Table I.

Expression 4:

$p(\text{win}/\text{Speedy}) > p(\text{win}/\text{Jim} \cap \text{Speedy}) > p(\text{win}) > p(\text{win}/\text{Jim})$
$p(\text{event}/\text{entity}) > p(\text{event}/\text{actor} \cap \text{entity}) > p(\text{event}) > p(\text{event}/\text{actor})$

Expression 5:

$p(\text{win}/\text{Speedy}) = p(\text{win}/\text{Jim} \cap \text{Speedy}) > p(\text{win}) > p(\text{win}/\text{Jim})$
$p(\text{event}/\text{entity}) = p(\text{event}/\text{actor} \cap \text{entity}) > p(\text{event}) > p(\text{event}/\text{actor})$

Expression 6:

$p(\text{win}/\text{Jim} \cap \text{Speedy}) > p(\text{win}/\text{Speedy}) > p(\text{win}) > p(\text{win}/\text{Jim})$
$p(\text{event}/\text{actor} \cap \text{entity}) > p(\text{event}/\text{entity}) > p(\text{event}) > p(\text{event}/\text{actor})$

Given that the attributional logic of Cells 1 and 2 is identical, except for the actor and entity role reversals, it is not surprising that the empirical evidence for Cell 2 is similar to that for Cell 1. Both covariation theory and PEAT predict that the predominant attribution for Cell 2 is to the entity, and all three empirical studies bear this out (Hilton & Slugoski, 1986; Jaspars, 1983; McArthur, 1972). PEAT goes on to predict that the second most likely attribution for Cell 2 is to (actor $\cap$ entity), and all three empirical studies bear this out. Notice that the second most likely attribution is the same for Cells 1 and 2. Methods for further empirical tests of the PEAT predictions for Cell 2 would be analogous to those suggested for Cell 1 above.

c. Cell 3. In this cell of Table I, consensus is low, distinctiveness is high, and consistency is high. The event to be explained is Jim winning the race today, on Speedy. Low consensus is present if Speedy usually does not win:

$p(\text{win}) > p(\text{win}/\text{Speedy}).$

High distinctiveness is present if Jim usually does not win:

$$p(\text{win}) > p(\text{win}/\text{Jim}).$$

High consistency is present if, when Jim rides Speedy, they usually win:

$$p(\text{win}/\text{Jim} \cap \text{Speedy}) > p(\text{win}).$$

In this cell Speedy is normally an inhibitor of wins and Jim is normally an inhibitor of wins too. The only time they win is when they are together. These probability statements can be arranged as follows:

$$p(\text{win}) > p(\text{win}/\text{Speedy})$$
$$p(\text{win}) > p(\text{win}/\text{Jim})$$
$$p(\text{win}/\text{Jim} \cap \text{Speedy}) > p(\text{win}).$$

When these probabilities are laid out in this way, it can be seen that all of the relationships between them are specified except the relationship between $p(\text{win}/\text{Speedy})$ and $p(\text{win}/\text{Jim})$. These two can be equal or one can be larger than the other. Therefore, as in Cells 1 and 2, there are three overall expressions possible for Cell 3, depending on how the relationship between $p(\text{win}/\text{Speedy})$ and $p(\text{win}/\text{Jim})$ is specified. These can be given in a version for this example and for the general case, as shown in Table I.

Expression 7:

$$p(\text{win}/\text{Jim} \cap \text{Speedy}) > p(\text{win}) > p(\text{win}/\text{Speedy}) = p(\text{win}/\text{Jim})$$
$$p(\text{event}/\text{actor} \cap \text{entity}) > p(\text{event}) > p(\text{event}/\text{entity}) = p(\text{event}/\text{actor})$$

Expression 8:

$$p(\text{win}/\text{Jim} \cap \text{Speedy}) > p(\text{win}) > p(\text{win}/\text{Speedy}) > p(\text{win}/\text{Jim})$$
$$p(\text{event}/\text{actor} \cap \text{entity}) > p(\text{event}) > p(\text{event}/\text{entity}) > p(\text{event}/\text{actor})$$

Expression 9:

$$p(\text{win}/\text{Jim} \cap \text{Speedy}) > p(\text{win}) > p(\text{win}/\text{Jim}) > p(\text{win}/\text{Speedy})$$
$$p(\text{event}/\text{actor} \cap \text{entity}) > p(\text{event}) > p(\text{win}/\text{actor}) > p(\text{win}/\text{entity})$$

The predictions of covariation theory and PEAT can be compared for Cell 3. Covariation theory predicts attribution to the joint presence of the actor and the entity. In the example used here, observers might by saying that although neither Jim nor Speedy is much good at racing normally, when they get together there is some kind of "chemistry." The two are dynamite. That is why they won today. They cannot win without each other. PEAT begins with the fact that in all three expressions, the congregation of the agents, Jim and Speedy, is a facilitator of the event, since consistency is high:

$$p(\text{event}/\text{Jim} \cap \text{Speedy}) > p(\text{event}).$$

A causal explanation in terms of this congregation, or some part of it, is therefore possible. In all three expressions, the strongest and only facilitator available is (Jim ∩ Speedy). Therefore, for Cell 3, the only attribution predicted is to (Jim ∩ Speedy). The data from the three empirical studies (Hilton & Slugoski, 1986; Jaspars, 1983; McArthur, 1972) show that this is the most common attribution for this cell. So, for Cell 3, the predictions for PEAT and for covariation theory are the same and they therefore receive equal empirical support.

d. Cell 4. In this cell, consensus is high, distinctiveness is low, and consistency is high. For example, let the event be Jim and Speedy winning the race today. High consensus means that Speedy usually wins:

$$p(\text{win}/\text{Speedy}) > p(\text{win}).$$

So Speedy is a facilitator of wins. Low distinctiveness means that Jim usually wins:

$$p(\text{win}/\text{Jim}) > p(\text{win}).$$

So Jim is also a facilitator of wins. High consistency means that Jim and Speedy have usually won in the past when they were together:

$$p(\text{win}/\text{Jim} \cap \text{Speedy}) > p(\text{win}).$$

So Speedy and Jim together are a facilitator of wins. When one attempts to make a single long expression of these terms, one finds that the relationships between $p(\text{win}/\text{Speedy})$, $p(\text{win}/\text{Jim})$, and $p(\text{win}/\text{Jim} \cap \text{Speedy})$ are not specified by the verbal descriptions of covariation theory. What is specified is that each of these probabilities is greater than $p(\text{win})$. Using all possible combinations of the three terms, 13 expressions can be derived. These are shown in Table I. They are not repeated here in the text with the versions from the example because it is too large a body of material to conveniently present in two places. Both covariation theory and PEAT predict that in this cell attributions will be to the actor, to the entity, or to the combination of the two. Empirical studies (Hilton & Slugoski, 1986; Jaspars, 1983; McArthur, 1972) found these to be the most frequent attributions given by subjects presented with Cell 4 information.

However, PEAT is much more specific than covariation theory about the conditions under which each of these attributions can occur. Covariation theory states only that with high consensus, low distinctiveness, and high consistency, attributions can be to actor, entity, or their combination. Covariation theory does not go on to describe what the specific antecedents are to each of the three specific attributions. In contrast, PEAT specifies information patterns for each of the three. Again, PEAT is seen to be a considerable refinement of covariation theory. In Table I, Expressions 10–22 are all consistent with the covariation theory specification for Cell 4. They can be grouped according to the attributions they predict. According to PEAT, in all of Expressions 10–22, observers will scan their probabilities and find that

$$p(\text{win}/\text{Jim} \cap \text{Speedy}) > p(\text{win}).$$

This probability statement shows high consistency, so this congregation of agents, or some subpart of it, is viable as a causal explanation for the win. In Expressions 10, 11, and 12, Jim is the strongest available facilitator, so he will be named as the cause. In Expressions 13, 14, and 15, Speedy is the strongest available facilitator, so he will be named as the cause. In Expressions 16, 17, and 18, (Jim ∩ Speedy) is the strongest available facilitator, so they will be named as the cause. In Expression 19, Jim and (Jim ∩ Speedy) are equally strong facilitators of the event, but Jim will be named as the cause for reasons of parsimony. In Expression 20, Speedy and (Jim ∩ Speedy) are equally strong facilitators, but Speedy will be named as the cause for reasons of parsimony. In Expressions 21 and 22, Jim and Speedy are, separately, equally strong facilitators of the event, so either could be named as the cause. If observers are presented with covariation information stated vaguely, as it has been in the covariation theory operationalizations to date, they are free to interpret it in any of the ways represented by Expressions 10–22. Attributions in empirical studies have reflected this freedom. If the information presented to observers is prepared to be specific to one of Expressions 10–22, the attributions that follow should also be specific. For example, for Expression 10, observers must be told that both Jim and Speedy are normally winners but that Jim is more of a winner than is Speedy. If this were to be conveyed in words, Speedy might be described as a regular but not spectacular winner, while Jim might be described as a superstar who has not lost a race in his last three seasons. Alternately, the information might be presented to observers in purely probabilistic form, for example $p(\text{win}/\text{Jim}) = .87$ and $p(\text{win}/\text{Speedy}) = .43$. For some observers this probabilistic information might be more palatable if the information statement said something like, ''Jim has won 87 of his last 100 races. Speedy has won 43 of his last 100 races.''

This discussion of Cell 4 has shown that the statement of the covariation information for it, by covariation theory, is somewhat ambiguous. It was shown that PEAT provides 13 different expressions for it. No wonder this cell has caused so much conceptual difficulty for other theorists such as Hilton and Slugoski (1986) and Jaspars (1983). This refinement by PEAT should permit more precise manipulations of information in future empirical studies and therefore more precise predictions.

e. Cells 5–8. These cells can be considered as a group because they have one very important characteristic in common. In all four consistency is low, according to covariation theory. In terms of PEAT, this means that

$$p(\text{event}/\text{actor} \cap \text{entity}) < p(\text{event}).$$

In other words, this congregation of agents is an inhibitor of the event in question. As such, according to Proposition 9, observers will not attribute the event to this congregation of agents or to some subset of it. They will prefer to attribute the event to luck, chance, or some ill-defined cause. Jaspars (1983) and McArthur (1972) both found that the predominant attributions in these cells are to luck or to circumstances. In Table I, the summary expression for each of Cells 5–8 is given as

$$p(\text{event}/\text{actor} \cap \text{entity}) < p(\text{event}).$$

This expression does not include the other terms usually contained in the covariation information, $p(\text{event}/\text{actor})$ and $p(\text{event}/\text{entity})$. These latter terms are left out because they are irrelevant once it established that $p(\text{event}/\text{actor} \cap \text{entity}) < p(\text{event})$.

This discussion of covariation theory makes it clear why past empirical tests of it have been plagued by a good many unexpected attributions in each cell, despite the fact that the predominant attribution for each cell is as predicted. In these empirical tests, high and low consensus, distinctiveness, and consistency have been operationalized into vignettes presented verbally. It has been seen that these verbal statements leave some ambiguity about the state of the covariation information, when they are compared to the probability statements of PEAT. Observers in the experiments are, therefore, given some latitude in how they interpret the vignettes and in the attributions they make. Observers presumably bring their own differing past experiences to bear when resolving those ambiguities. As a result, there is some variation in the attributions they report. PEAT suggests that greater care in the wording of the vignettes should be exercised so that they will unambiguously correspond to the expressions for each covariation cell given by PEAT. This procedure should lessen the opportunity for varied interpretation that is given to observers and therefore increase the precision of predictions.

Another characteristic of covariation theory that can be derived from this analysis is that it presents the observer as being in either one of two very different circumstances. The first circumstance is seen in Cells 1–4. There, observers are given all of the information they need in order to make an attribution. In every case there is at least one facilitator of the event available to which the event can be attributed. Observers do not have to attribute new characteristics to any agent, or modify their beliefs about any agent, in order to provide a causal explanation. The already known characteristics of the available agents, as given in the covariation information, are capable of explaining the event. Hence observers can operate under Proposition 10, their preferred mode of operation. Proposition 10 describes circumstances in which observers start with all the information they need in order to explain the focal event.

The second type of circumstance seen in covariation theory is found in Cells 5–8. For these cells consistency is low, so

$$p(\text{event}/\text{actor} \cap \text{entity}) < p(\text{event}).$$

This probability statement means that the event is unlikely to happen, given the congregation of agents available. Observers will be reluctant to attribute the event to any of the available agents and will attribute it to luck or some other vaguely known agent. This circumstance is described under Proposition 9. So observers confronted with information as specified by covariation theory find themselves in either the best or the worst of possible information circumstances. In Cells 1–4, they are confronted with an event that can be explained, given what they already know. In Cells 5–8, they are confronted with an event that should never have happened, given what they already know.

This concludes the analysis of covariation theory, which has shown that it is a subset of the logic of PEAT. Each kind of covariation information, consensus, distinctiveness, and consistency, was expressed as a probability. Each gives the probability that the event will occur given the presence of the actor and/or entity. Each is, therefore, a kind of prediction or expectation. This prediction interpretation of covariation information is different from the contrast interpretation of Kelley and others. The contrast interpretation suggests that consensus and distinctiveness indicate whether or not a given agent is like or unlike other agents and is therefore a likely cause of the event. This move to the prediction interpretation constitutes a fundamental change in our understanding of covariation information. When combinations of covariation information were considered by examining the eight cells of Table I, it was found that PEAT gives more precision than covariation theory. Empirical support was found for PEAT since PEAT was able to account for attributions given by observers that were unpredicted and unexplainable using covariation and other theories. These previously unexpected attributions are owing to observers applying their own interpretations to the rather vague vignettes given to them, according to PEAT. The shift from the contrast to the prediction interpretation of covariation information suggested by PEAT could be further tested with more empirical work. An important part of this should be to provide observers with less ambiguous vignettes, which correspond closely to the probabilities of PEAT and which should, therefore, yield more accurate predictions. Next it will be shown that expressing covariation theory in probabilities with the prediction interpretation of PEAT will allow it to be integrated with configuration theory and correspondent inference theory.

B. CONFIGURATION THEORY

According to Kelley (1973), configuration theory applies when observers must make attributions after only a single observation of an event. But Kelley points out that in such circumstances observers are seldom completely ignorant. They have observed similar events before and have some knowledge of the causal processes involved. It is by using this stored knowledge that observers are able to make attributions.

PEAT makes the assumption that this knowledge that is relevant to the interpretation of events is stored by observers as probabilities. In configuration theory these probability statements are used to derive attributions in the same way as they are used in covariation theory.

An important concept in configuration theory is that of the schema. According to Kelley (1973), schemas are cognitive frameworks into which observers put information in order to organize it into meaningful patterns from which attributions can be made. PEAT represents schemas as patterns of probabilities.

1. Multiple Necessary Causes Schema

In this schema, "both causes *must* be present or favorable if the event is to occur" (Kelley, 1973). As Kelley explains, the presence of both causes is also sufficient for the occurrence of the event. Since both causes must be present if the event is to occur, it means that their joint presence is necessary for the event. That is, if either agent appears alone the event will not occur. If two agents are labeled A and B, in probabilities this is

$$p(\text{event}/A) = p(\text{event}/B) = 0.$$

However, when both agents are present, they are sufficient for the event to occur. That means that whenever they are together the event occurs. In probabilities this is

$$p(\text{event}/A \cap B) = 1.$$

The laws of mathematics require that the unconditional probability that the focal event occurs is between 0 and 1. This can be expressed as

$$1 > p(\text{event}) > 0.$$

All three of these expressions involved in Kelley's definition of multiple necessary causes can be combined into a single expression, which gives the following definition:

Agents A and B are MULTIPLE NECESSARY CAUSES
of an event when:
$$p(\text{event}/A \cap B) = 1 > p(\text{event}) > p(\text{event}/A) = p(\text{event}/B) = 0.$$

Stating the multiple necessary causes schema in this way shows that it is an extreme case of Expression 7 in Cell 3 of Table I, which summarizes covariation theory. Expression 7 is

$$p(\text{event}/\text{actor} \cap \text{entity}) > p(\text{event}) > p(\text{event}/\text{actor}) = p(\text{event}/\text{entity}).$$

The schema, as formally stated, is extreme in its requirements that the event *always* happens in some circumstances and *never* happens in others. This extreme pattern is very unlikely in real life. PEAT's Expression 7 gives a statement for this kind of information pattern without the unrealistically extreme requirements.

McArthur (1972) originally pointed out the connection between multiple necessary causes and Cell 3. She worked out causal predictions for them, with which PEAT agrees. This pattern of data leads observers to believe that the event is caused by the *joint* presence of the agents. For example, parents of small children sometimes find themselves faced with the following kind of situation. Little Billy is a model child:

$$p(\text{trouble}/\text{Billy}) < p(\text{trouble}).$$

Little Mary is also an angel:

$$p(\text{trouble}/\text{Mary}) < p(\text{trouble}).$$

But when Billy and Mary play together there is no end to the mischief they get into:

$$p(\text{trouble}/\text{Billy} \cap \text{Mary}) > p(\text{trouble}).$$

Putting these together gives

$$p(\text{trouble}/\text{Billy} \cap \text{Mary}) > p(\text{trouble}) > p(\text{trouble}/\text{Billy}) \text{ or } p(\text{trouble}/\text{Mary}).$$

The parents' explanation is that Billy and Mary are not bad children (neither has an enduring characteristic called bad); rather, they are bad influences on each other (their joint presence is necessary for trouble). The explanation is extracted from the stored probability statements.

2. Multiple Sufficient Causes Schema

According to Kelley (1973), this schema occurs when more than one cause is present and each is alone sufficient to cause the event. If A and B are the causes, and each alone is sufficient to cause the event, then the event always occurs when either is present. In probabilities this is

$$p(\text{event}/A) = p(\text{event}/B) = 1.$$

Further, because the event always occurs when either is present, it will also always occur when both are present:

$$p(\text{event}/A \cap B) = 1.$$

As in the previous schema, the unconditional probability of the event is between 0 and 1, or:

$$1 > p(\text{event}) > 0.$$

Combining these three gives the following definition.

Agents A and B are MULTIPLE SUFFICIENT CAUSES of an event when:
$$p(\text{event}/A) = p(\text{event}/B) = p(\text{event}/A \cap B) = 1 > p(\text{event}).$$

Examination of Table I shows that this is an example of Expression 22 in Cell 4. Expression 22 is

$$p(\text{event}/\text{actor}) = p(\text{event}/\text{entity}) = p(\text{event}/\text{actor} \cap \text{entity}) > p(\text{event}).$$

Thus, a second schema is shown to correspond to an expression from the PEAT interpretation of covariation theory.

3. Compensatory Causes Schema

Kelley (1973) uses an example of task success to demonstrate the idea of compensatory causes. Using an actor and a task as the agents, and success on the task as the event, his model shows that characteristics of the actor and task can trade off with each other to produce the event. Table II is adapted from Kelley's (1973, p. 114) diagram representing this schema. Kelley's diagram and values will be used for illustrative purposes, as he used them. However, whether these particular values are actually used by subjects is an empirical question.

The event (represented by E in Table II) is the occurrence of a successful outcome when a person of either high, medium, or low ability works on a task that is difficult, moderate, or easy to do. Table II shows that when a person of

TABLE II
COMPENSATORY CAUSES SCHEMA[a]

Ability	Task[b]		
	Difficult	Moderate	Easy
High	E	E	E
Medium	—	E	E
Low	—	—	E

[a]Adapted from Kelley (1973).
[b]The E indicates that the event (success on the task) occurs with the indicated combination of task and ability. See text for full explanation.

medium ability tackles a moderate task, E occurs. The person is successful. When a person of medium ability takes on a difficult task, the event does not occur; the actor is unsuccessful.

In PEAT, Kelley's diagram serves the purpose of showing the probabilities of events associated with various disposition and constraint labels. Since the person here is an actor, the terms high, medium, and low ability are disposition labels. Since the task here is an entity, the terms difficult, moderate, and easy are constraint labels. Dispositions and constraints are kinds of characteristics, according to PEAT. In Table II the following probabilities are represented. In the column for the difficult task, only one of the three cells has an E in it, or:

$$p(\text{event/difficult task}) = .3\dot{3}.$$

Analogous logic applies to the other two columns:

$$p(\text{event/moderate task}) = .6\dot{6}$$
$$p(\text{event/easy task}) = 1.$$

This kind of representation allows observers to do at least two things. First, if they notice that a particular task has a certain probability of success associated with it, they can label it as difficult, moderate, or easy, thus applying a constraint label. Second, if someone else informs observers that a task is moderate, for example, they can easily attach a probability of success value to it to be used later to make attributions and predictions.

The rows in Table II represent the dispositions of actors. For example, the bottom row represents the disposition "low ability." Only one of the three cells in that row contains an E, so

$$p(\text{event/difficult task}) = .3\dot{3}.$$

Analogous logic applies to the other two rows, as follows:

$$p(\text{event/medium ability}) = .6\dot{6}$$
$$p(\text{event/high ability}) \;\;\;= 1.$$

The individual cells in Table II can also be represented as probabilities. Each cell represents the joint occurrence of a particular level of ability with a particular level of task difficulty.

$$p(\text{event/difficult task} \cap \text{high ability}) = 1.$$
$$p(\text{event/difficult task} \cap \text{medium ability}) = 0.$$
$$p(\text{event/difficult task} \cap \text{low ability}) = 0.$$
$$p(\text{event/moderate task} \cap \text{high ability}) = 1.$$
$$p(\text{event/moderate task} \cap \text{medium ability}) = 1.$$
$$p(\text{event/moderate task} \cap \text{low ability}) = 0.$$

p(event/easy task ∩ high ability) = 1.
p(event/easy task ∩ medium ability) = 1.
p(event/easy task ∩ low ability) = 1.

Finally, looking at all nine cells and their E's:

$$p(\text{event}) = .6\dot{6}.$$

PEAT assumes that all of these probabilities are stored by observers and can be used to make attributions. For example, if observers see a person who is labeled as having high ability succeed on a task that is labeled high difficulty, the following probabilities will be consulted:

p(event/high ability) = 1
p(event/difficult task) = .3$\dot{3}$
p(event/difficult task ∩ high ability) = 1
p(event) = .6$\dot{6}$.

If the event is represented by E, high ability by HA, and difficult task by DT, and these four expressions are combined into a single expression, the result is

$$p(E/HA) = p(E/DT \cap HA) > p(E) > p(E/DT).$$

This expression is a special case of Expression 2 of Table I, so observers will use the processes described in Proposition 10 to conclude that the person's high ability (strongest available single facilitator) is the cause of the event.

Kelley (1973) also shows that the compensatory causes schema can be used by observers to infer the characteristics of an unknown agent when the nature of another agent and of the event are known. This process of inferring characteristics goes beyond the purely causal attributions that are the main focus of Kelley's theories. PEAT uses the processes described in Proposition 11 to explain how these characteristics would be inferred in the compensatory causes schema. For example, suppose an agent of unknown ability succeeds at a difficult task. Observers must attribute to the actor sufficient ability to explain the event, despite the fact that the task is difficult. It is assumed that observers have the contents of Table II in their heads. They therefore know that

$$p(\text{event/difficult task}) = .3\dot{3}.$$

They also know that

$$p(\text{event}) = .6\dot{6}.$$

Earlier, under Proposition 11, it was shown that the inhibitory force of an entity is given by

$$IF = p(\text{event/entity}) - p(\text{event}).$$

In the case at hand, the difficult task is the entity, so

$$\text{IF} = p(\text{event/difficult task}) - p(\text{event})$$
$$= .3\dot{3} - .6\dot{6}$$
$$= -.3\dot{3}.$$

For the event to occur, a facilitative force equal to or greater than this inhibitory force must be attributed to the actor. The facilitative force must therefore be equal to at least $.3\dot{3}$. Going back to the definition of facilitative force of an actor,

$$\text{FF} = p(\text{event/actor}) - p(\text{event}).$$

The appropriate values can be substituted:

$$.3\dot{3} = p(\text{event/actor}) - .6\dot{6}.$$

Transposing the values gives

$$p(\text{event/actor}) = 1.$$

So, in order to explain the event, observers had to assume this probability value of 1. When observers consult Table II (in their heads), they will find that only one of the rows that represent actors' dispositions has a probability of 1 specified. That row is the top row, which represents the disposition high ability. Observers will then say that the event occurred, despite the presence of the difficult task, because of the actor's high ability. In this example of using the compensatory causes schema both a causal and characteristic attribution had to be assigned simultaneously in order to provide an explanation. The facile interaction of causal and characteristic attributions is seen in operation here, again, just as it was seen above in Proposition 11.

It is also important to notice how the processes described here under compensatory causes can be further integrated into the framework of covariation theory, as analysed by PEAT. In this example, observers started with Table II in their heads and with the knowledge that the unknown actor succeeded at the difficult task. The difficult task is an entity, the success is an event. Observers know that

$$p(\text{event/difficult task}) = .3\dot{3},$$

and that

$$p(\text{event}) = .6\dot{6}.$$

These two can be combined to yield

$$p(\text{event/difficult task}) = .3\dot{3} < p(\text{event}) = .6\dot{6}.$$

Since the difficult task is the entity, this becomes

$$p(\text{event/entity}) < p(\text{event}).$$

This is the definition of low consensus, from PEAT, given earlier. So the observers started with a situation involving low consensus. With low consensus the entity is an inhibitor of the event and unlikely to be named as the cause. After doing their facilitory–inhibitory calculations, observers found that they could explain the event if they attributed high ability to the actor:

$$p(\text{event}/\text{actor}) = 1.$$

This can be combined with the knowledge that $p(\text{event}) = .66$, to yield

$$p(\text{event}/\text{actor}) = 1 > p(\text{event}) = .66,$$

which is

$$p(\text{event}/\text{actor}) > p(\text{event}).$$

This is the PEAT definition of low distinctiveness, given earlier. So in order to explain this event that involved low consensus, observers had to assume low distinctiveness. Further, as they were doing this, they were also completing the logic that constitutes high consistency. They knew from the beginning that the task had high difficulty. They inferred that the actor had high ability. From Table II, they then know that

$$p(\text{event}/\text{high difficulty} \cap \text{high ability}) = 1.$$

This can be combined with their knowledge that $p(\text{event}) = .66$, to yield

$$p(\text{event}/\text{high difficulty} \cap \text{high ability}) = 1 > p(\text{event}) = .66.$$

Given that high difficulty pertains to the entity and high ability pertains to the actor, this expression becomes

$$p(\text{event}/\text{entity} \cap \text{actor}) > p(\text{event}).$$

This is the PEAT definition of high consistency. So observers started with a situation of low consensus and through inference built it into a case of low consensus, low distinctiveness, and high consistency. This set of covariation information is what defines Cell 1 of covariation theory in Table I.

This example shows that when the compensatory causes schema is used to attribute causes and characteristics in order to explain an event, observers are inferring enough information to put themselves into one of Cells 1–4 of covariation theory. As stated earlier, Cells 1–4 of covariation theory represent situations in which observers have all the information they need in order to explain events. Therefore, observers who lack information for an explanation must infer information sufficient to complete the specifications of one of Cells 1–4. This does not apply to Cells 5–8 of covariation theory. In those cells, observers do not have information that enables a causal explanation in terms of the enduring characteristics of known, available agents.

This discussion of three kinds of schemas has shown that they are all closely related in their logic to covariation theory as analysed by PEAT. Multiple necessary causes correspond to Cell 3 of covariation theory. Multiple sufficient causes correspond to Cell 4. Compensatory causes can be related to any of cells 1–4, depending on the kind of information that must be inferred to explain an event.

4. Augmentation and Discounting

There are two other important concepts in Kelley's (1973) configuration theory, discounting and augmentation. These are not schemas but rather phenomena that occur because of the way in which attribution processes work. PEAT permits a clear analysis of these phenomena and gives some insight into recent research on them.

a. Augmentation. An example will be used to illustrate this concept. Suppose the event to be explained is an argument between a woman and her brother. Suppose the woman is known to be a calm person with very good social skills who seldom gets into arguments. She has been known to prevent or to avert arguments on a number of occasions by dent of her own calm state of mind and demeanor and her adroit handling of the situations. Given this information, observers might be asked to make attributions about who caused the argument and about the characteristics of the brother. These two attributions are very much interdependent so that one cannot really be done without the other.

If observers are to answer either of these attribution questions, they will first assume that the forces facilitating the argument are stronger than the forces inhibiting it. Since the woman is known to be an inhibitor of arguments, a facilitory force must have been provided from somewhere in order for the argument to have occurred. This very fundamental requirement will be called the *principle of facilitory force predominance*. This can be put into the following abbreviated form, which will be useful later when integrating the principle with other ideas. The principle of facilitory force predominance states that if an event is to be explained, it must be assumed that

$$FF(t) > IF(t).$$

Here, $FF(t)$ is the total of the facilitory forces that make the event more likely. These forces may be provided by a single agent or a congregation of agents. And $IF(t)$ is the total of the inhibitory forces that make the event less likely. These forces may be provided by a single agent or a congregation of agents.

Augmentation follows as a necessary consequence of the principle of facilitory force predominance. Argumentation concerns the amount of facilitory force that is assigned to an *individual* agent in order to explain an event. In the simplest case there is only one agent available to provide the facilitory force necessary to have the event occur. In our example that one agent was the brother. When there is only one such agent, a special case of the principle of facilitory force predominance occurs. That special case can be put into symbols like those used to express the basic principle:

$$FF(a) > IF(t).$$

Here $FF(a)$ is the facilitory force attributed to the single available facilitory agent, and $IF(t)$ is the total of the inhibitory forces that must be overcome if the event is to occur. These forces may be provided by a single agent or a congregation of agents.

It clearly follows from this expression that the greater the inhibitory forces to be overcome, the greater will be the facilitory force attributed to the single available facilitory agent. This is the *principle of argumentation*. For illustrative purposes an example with only one facilitory agent (the brother) has been used. This may not always be the case. For some events there may be several agents available so that the simple expression just used would not be appropriate. The definition of argumentation will now be given in a more general form that can be applied when there are multiple facilitory agents available. However, although there may be multiple facilitory agents available, the argumentation principle is stated as applying to the attributions made to one particular individual agent. The principle of argumentation refers to the fact that when observers make facilitory attributions to a single agent, they will follow the rule

$$FF(a) = f[IF(t)].$$

Here, $FF(a)$ is the facilitory force attributed to a single facilitory agent, $IF(t)$ is the total of the inhibitory forces that had to be overcome for the event to occur, and f[ ] represents the idea that $FF(a)$ is a positive function of $IF(t)$.

The operation of augmentation can be demonstrated numerically in our example by considering the facilitory force necessary to overcome the woman's inhibition. As discussed earlier in Proposition 11, the inhibitory effect of the woman is given by the difference between the unconditional probability of an argument and the probability of an argument given the presence of the woman. This can be expressed as

$$IF(w) = p(\text{argument/woman}) - p(\text{argument}).$$

Here, $IF(w)$ is the inhibitory force provided by the woman. Illustrative, hypothetical probability values can be provided. For instance, if observers believed that $p(\text{argument}) = .10$ and $p(\text{argument/woman}) = .05$, then put these into the above equation, the result is

$$IF(w) = .05 - .10 = -.05.$$

This is the total inhibitory force that must be overcome by the brother if an argument is to occur. Earlier, the following expression was developed to represent the special case of the principle of facilitory force predominance which occurs when there is only one facilitative agent available:

$$FF(a) > IF(t).$$

In the current example, the facilitory agent is the brother and the total inhibitory force is provided by the women, so

$$FF(\text{brother}) > IF(w).$$

We already know that, $IF(w) = -.05$, so

$$FF(\text{brother}) > .05.$$

According to the augmentation principle, if the woman were a stronger inhibitor of arguments, an even stronger facilitory force would have to be attributed to the brother in order to explain the event. If the woman were a stronger inhibitor of arguments, it would mean that the probability of an argument, given her presence, was smaller than the number just used to illustrate. If it were believed, for example, that $p(\text{argument}/\text{woman}) = .01$, then

$$IF(w) = .01 - .10 = -.09.$$

If this value is put into the expression just used, then

$$FF(\text{brother}) > IF(\text{woman}), \text{ and}$$
$$FF(\text{brother}) > .09.$$

In this case the facilitory force of the brother is greater than .09, whereas in the previous version it was greater than .05. Thus augmentation is demonstrated using probabilities.

The definition of augmentation used here is consistent with Kelley's (1973, p. 114) statement of the principle: "When there are known to be constraints, costs, sacrifices or risks involved in taking an action, the action once taken is attributed more to the actor than it would otherwise." In this definition, constraints, costs, sacrifices, and risks are inhibitors of the action.

b. Discounting. This concept can also be explained using the example of the woman who inhibits arguments. Kelley (1973, p. 113) defined discounting, very elegantly, as "the role of a given cause in producing a given effect is discounted if other plausible causes are also present." This can be seen by considering what would happen if the woman had more than one brother and they were all involved in the argument. In one of the examples used earlier, the woman was said to have an inhibitory force of .05. In this case the facilitory force provided by the brothers must be greater than .05. Suppose, for example, that it is .06. If the woman had only one brother, named Harry, and she got into an argument with him, all of the facilitory force would have to be assigned to him alone, so $p(\text{argument}/\text{Harry}) = .06$. However, if Harry were one of two brothers, the facilitory force would be divided between the two, so $p(\text{argument}/\text{Harry}) = .03$. If Harry were one of three brothers, $p(\text{argument}/\text{Harry}) = .02$.

PEAT thus suggests, as did Kelley's (1973) definition, that the total facilitative force necessary for the event to occur is divided among the available facilitators. Hence the more such facilitators there are, the less the facilitative effect assigned to any one of them. This can be expressed using symbols in the following way. *Discounting* refers to the fact that when observers make facilitory attributions to an individual agent, they follow the rule

$$FF(a) = \frac{FF(t)}{n}.$$

Here, $FF(a)$ is the amount of facilitory force assigned to the individual agent, n is the number of available facilitators, and $FF(t)$ is the total facilitory force operating during the event.

Expressing discounting in this way allows it to be neatly integrated into a single expression with the earlier definition of augmentation. Earlier, the principle of facilitory force predominance stated that

$$FF(t) > IF(t).$$

This can be reexpressed as

$$FF(t) = f[IF(t)].$$

This expression shows that the total facilitory force will be a positive function of the total inhibitory force, all other things being equal.

Above, discounting was defined as

$$FF(a) = \frac{FF(t)}{n}.$$

Substitute into this expression the expression for $FF(t)$ just derived, and

$$FF(a) = \frac{f[IF(t)]}{n}.$$

This expression is, then, an alternate way to express discounting. But notice that the symbol to the left of the equal sign, the equal sign, and the numerator of the symbol to the right of the equal sign are, together, the expression derived above for augmentation. So both augmentation and discounting are captured in this single expression. This can be altered slightly, without changing its meaning, to be more elegant visually:

$$FF(a) = f\left[\frac{IF(t)}{n}\right].$$

This expression captures two very basic attributional principles and so will be given a formal title and definition. The *law of facilitory attributions* states that when observers make facilitory attributions to an individual agent in order to explain an event, they will do so according to the following rule:

$$FF(a) = f\left[\frac{IF(t)}{n}\right].$$

Here, $FF(a)$ is the total facilitory force attributed to the individual agent, $IF(t)$ is the total inhibitory force that had to be overcome when the event in question occurred, n is the number of available facilitory agents, and f[ ] shows that the dependent variable is a positive function of the expression in squared brackets.

This law can be stated verbally as well. In connection with the numerator of the expression to the right of the equal sign, it states that when a characteristic is assigned to an agent in order to explain an event, the strength of that characteristic will be stronger the greater the inhibitory force that had to be overcome in order for the event to occur. This is augmentation. In connection with the denominator of the term to the right of the equal sign, the law states that when a characteristic is assigned to an agent in order to explain an event, the strength of that characteristic will be weaker the greater the number of other facilitory agents there are available to explain the event. This is discounting.

The law of facilitory attributions has been developed and defined using characteristic attributions, but assumptions about causal attributions were being made throughout the process. The law of facilitory attributions operates when observers are making assumptions about what caused the event in question. In the example used here, a characteristic was assigned to the brother by assuming that the brother caused the argument. The characteristic attribution was not possible without the causal one. Alternately, if observers were asked about causes, they would have to attribute a characteristic to the brother in order to name him as a cause. So in augmentation and in discounting, the intimate interaction of causal and characteristic attributions is again seen.

The processes of augmentation and discounting, as described here, are the same as the processes described earlier in this article under other names. Propositions 11 and 12 describe the processes whereby observers assign new characteristics to agents or modify current characteristics. The processes described there were essentially the same as those in discounting and augmentation. Kelley's (1973) compensatory causes schema also involved these same processes. Because the principle of facilitory force predominance and the law of facilitory attributions apply in all of these places, they are fundamental to attribution theory.

Although the law of facilitory attributions gives a very elegant definition of discounting, it may not be universally applicable. This definition of discounting, which might be called pure discounting, assumes that the necessary facilitative force is distributed equally across the available agents. In one of the above examples, it was assumed that the total facilitative force was .06. When only one brother was available, the full .06 was assigned to him. When three brothers were available, it was proposed that each brother would get .02. This provides a neat formula but will observers do it this way? They could, for example, assign all of the facilitative force do the first brother and perceive the other two as neutral. If this were to happen, discounting would not be demonstrated when the facilitative force attributed to the brother (when he was the only available agent) was compared to the facilitative force attributed to the same brother (when he was only one of the three available agents).

Pure discounting is most likely to occur when observers must attribute new characteristics to agents in order to provide an explanation for an event. The processes involved here are described in Proposition 11. If observers know nothing of the three brothers mentioned in our example above and are asked about the facilitative force of any one of them, they will assign one-third of the facilitative force to him for want of a better strategy. In experimental studies of discounting, observers are often given virtually no information about the available agents, and so discounting is very cleanly and purely demonstrated. For example, Hansen and Hull (1985) carried out a very elegant demonstration of pure discounting in their Experiment 1.

Discounting will not occur at all if observers are not in a position to infer new or revised characteristics about available agents. For example, suppose that the event in question is an airplane crash. Observers know that just before the crash one of the airplane's engines blew up. Most observers have impressions of p(air crash/engine explosion). An engine explosion is a strong facilitator of the crash and would undoubtedly be named as the cause. Here observers do not have to infer any new characteristics about engine explosions in order to explain the event. Neither would they have to change their current beliefs about p(crash/ engine explosion) in order to explain the event. In an alternate scenario, observers could be told that the plane crashed during a light rain and that before the crash one of its engines blew up. A light rain is a facilitator of plane crashes, but it is a relatively weak one. On the face of it, with pure discounting, it would be expected that, in this latter scenario, the crash would be equally attributed to the engine explosion and the light rain. In other words, the attribution to the engine explosion in this case, with two facilitators, would be less than in the previous case in which it was the only facilitator. But this will not occur because observers do not have to infer any new or revised characteristics in order to explain the event of the crash. They have relatively well-defined, preconceived notions about light rain, engine explosions, and aircrashes. These are all stored as probabilities. Proposition 10 states that when asked to name the cause of an event, observers will scan their probabilities and name as the cause the strongest available facilitator. In this case the engine explosion will be named as the sole cause because it is a stronger facilitator than is light rain. The observers' probability statements about engine explosions will go unchanged and there will be no discounting.

Wells and Ronis (1982) have done an empirical study that supports this point that discounting does not occur when observers do not need to infer new characteristics about agents. In the Wells and Ronis study, observers were told that certain actors had to make choices between different packages of prizes. On the basis of information about the actors' choices, observers were asked to make attributions about the actors and the prizes. In some conditions the packages chosen by the actors contained two prizes, in other conditions the chosen packages contained four prizes. Observers were asked how much they believed the actors liked one of the prizes in the chosen package (a characteristic attribution) and how much they believed that prize caused the actor to choose that package (a causal attribution). If discounting occurred, the attributions to the named prize would be greater when it was one of two prizes in a package than when it was one of four prizes in a package. Discounting did not occur. Number of prizes in the chosen package had no effect upon attributions. PEAT would explain this finding in terms of the method that Wells and Ronis used to manipulate another variable in their study, which they called valence. In order to manipulate valence, Wells and Ronis gave dollar values to each of the prizes in each package. For example, one package was worth $24 and consisted of a $12 prize and three $4 prizes. So every prize about which observers were asked to make attributions had a dollar value assigned to it by the experimenter, and the observers were clearly told what those dollar values were. However, assigning a dollar value to a prize constitutes the assignment of a facilitative characteristic to that prize. When it comes to being chosen, a $12 prize has a stronger facilitative effect than a $4 prize. Thus, Wells and Ronis clearly assigned characteristics to all of the available agents (prizes). There was no need for observers to assign characteristics to them in order to explain the event. As a result, discounting did not occur. This is in contrast to Hansen and Hull's (1985) study, mentioned earlier, in which observers made attributions to unknown agents and clearly demonstrated pure discounting.

This completes the discussion of augmentation and discounting. It has been shown that both phenomena can be related to two basic ideas. The first is the principle of facilitory force predominance, which states that in order for an event to be explained it must be assumed that the forces facilitating the event are greater than the forces inhibiting the event. From this, the law of facilitory attributions was developed. It states that the amount of facilitory force assigned to an agent in order to explain an event is a positive function of the inhibitory forces that had to be overcome in order for the event to occur (augmentation), and an inverse function of the number of potential facilitators available during the event (discounting). However, discounting does not occur in all circumstances. When observers are free to attribute new or revised characteristics to agents in order to explain an event, pure discounting occurs, as demonstrated by Hansen and Hull (1985). When observers do not attribute new or revised characteristics to agents in order to explain an event, discounting does not occur, as demonstrated by Wells and Ronis (1982).

C. CONCLUSIONS CONCERNING KELLEY'S THEORIES

Both of Kelley's (1973) theories have now been explained in terms of PEAT, and the following general conclusions can be drawn from that explanation. The basic concepts of Kelley's two theories can be expressed in the relatively elegant and precise probabilities of PEAT. Since PEAT shows the facile interaction of cause and characteristic attributions, while keeping their separate integrities intact, the roles of the two kinds of attribution in Kelley's theories were clarified. In the discussion of covariation theory, it was shown that consensus, distinctiveness, and consistency could each be expressed in probabilities. This was done by using a prediction interpretation of the covariation information. This is different from the contrast interpretation used by most other theorists. The combinations of the three kinds of covariation information were considered using the eight cells shown in Table I. It was shown that these probabilities give a much more precise analysis of these cells than does Kelley's original covariation theory. PEAT was thus able to explain the presence of some of the unexpected attributions that have appeared in the cells in past empirical studies. Suggestions were made for empirically testing some of the predictions of this PEAT analysis by making more precise predictions. It was also shown that in Cells 1–4 observers have all of the information they need to make attributions. In Cells 5–8 observers have information that suggests that attributions to stable characteristics of available entities are not possible.

The concepts of configuration theory were also expressed as probabilities. When this was done, it was shown that the multiple necessary causes schema and the multiple sufficient causes schema are special cases of Cells 3 and 4, respectively, of covariation theory, as shown in Table I. It was also shown that the compensatory causes schema uses the logic of covariation theory. When observers infer characteristics about agents in order to explain events, they are essentially moving from a situation of information deficit to one of the cells in Table I, in which complete covariation information is available. PEAT thus shows that all three of these schemata can be integrated into covariation theory. The discussion of augmentation and discounting, and their translation into the terms of PEAT, led to the statement of two very fundamental attribution principles. The first, the principle of facilitory force predominance, states that in order for an explanation of an event to be provided, observers must assume that the total facilitory forces available at the time of the event were greater than the total inhibitory forces. This idea had appeared earlier in the discussion of the compensatory causes schema and in the discussions of Propositions 11 and 12. This principle underlies Kelley's concept of augmentation. The second fundamental principle, called the law of facilitory attributions, states that the amount of facilitory force attributed to an agent in order to explain an event is directly proportional to the inhibitory forces that must be overcome, and inversely proportional to the total number of facilitory agents available. This law is the basis for augmentation and discounting. But this law applies only when observers have to infer new or revised characteristics about agents in order to explain an event. It does not apply when observers can explain the event using the known characteristics of available agents. This is why discounting occurs in some studies (e.g., Hansen & Hull, 1985) but not in others (e.g., Wells & Ronis, 1982).

IV. Correspondent Inference Theory

The purpose of this section is to show that correspondent inference theory (CIT) can be reformulated in terms of PEAT and that it has a great deal of overlap with Kelley's (1973) attribution theories. CIT (Jones & Davis, 1965; Jones & McGillis, 1976), like Kelley's theories, has had a tremendous impact upon attribution theory and research (Harvey & Weary, 1984). Although the theories (CIT and Kelley's) are based on the work of Heider (1958), they are superficially quite dissimilar. At no time has a clear and intimate connection between them been shown. Jones and McGillis (1976) drew many parallels between them and demonstrated a number of correspondences, but their analysis also demonstrated a number of problems (including some apparent contradictions). These will have to be overcome if the theories are to be truly integrated. Howard (1985) has given an excellent critique of the Jones and McGillis (1976) paper. The analysis presented here, based on PEAT, will overcome the problems described by Jones and McGillis (1976) and by Howard (1985) and will show that the two theories are based on the same fundamental logic. They are so intimately interrelated that they need not be treated as separate theories. Some aspects of the theories are complementary and represent different developments on the core logic, but there are no contradictions.

CIT has to do with the processes whereby observers come to believe that a particular individual has a particular disposition, given that the individual has chosen to act in a particular way when faced with a particular set of options (Jones & Davis, 1965). If the individual chooses a desirable option (i.e., the one that most people would choose), it tells observers little except that the individual is like other people. If the individual chooses an undesirable option, observers infer that the individual is different from other people and has a strong disposition to choose that particular option. For example, suppose an actor is choosing a new automobile to buy. The actor has gone to several dealerships and has decided on the desired make and model. Two of the dealers, A and B, will sell the car for the same price. The car available at dealer A is a rather pleasing color that is currently very much in vogue. The car available at dealer B is a revolting, shocking pink. To most observers, buying the car from dealer A is the more desirable option. If the actor chooses it, observers will not have much to say about the actor. He or she would be choosing the car that almost anyone else would have chosen, the more desirable one. If the actor chooses the car from dealer B, observers would be more likely to develop and articulate beliefs about the dispositions of the actor. Observers might be tempted to say that the actor either must like pink or else has no taste when it comes to color. Observers can further diagnose the actor by considering the number of effects (consequences) of the chosen and foregone actions. If only one effect differed as a function of which action was chosen, observers could feel quite confident that it was that single effect that swayed the individual, and that the individual has a disposition associated with the effect. If, however, there are several effects that differ as a result of choosing one act over the other, observers cannot be sure which effect swayed the actor and so will be less confident about what disposition to assign the individual. For example, if the car at dealer A not only differs in color from the car at dealer B but also is lower in price, observers will be less clear about the dispositions of the actor. When only color differs between the cars, it is possible to assign to the actor, with confidence, a disposition having to do with taste in color. When both price and color differ, both effects suggest dispositions of the actor, and observers will be much less confident in making statements about the actor's taste. In summary, observers more confidently assign a disposition to an actor when the actor chooses an undesirable act that has few differential (noncommon) effects.

The first step in showing the relationships between CIT, Kelley's theory, and PEAT is to show that certain basic terms can be applied in all of them. Although the shades of meaning attached to these terms by Kelley's theory and by CIT may be different, the meaning given by PEAT will be broad enough to encompass both of the others and is consistent with available empirical data.

The terms actor, event, and dispositions are used in about the same way by the different theories. The actor is the person observed and about whom attributions may be made. In Kelley's theory and in CIT, the term event refers to some human behavior that will be explained by observers. In PEAT, the event can be a human action, but it can be other kinds of occurrences as well. In order to show the connection between the different theories, the focus here will be on human activities as events. A disposition is a characteristic that observers may infer about an individual in order to explain the occurrence of events. Observers may also have beliefs about actors' dispositions before observing the event.

CIT, as stated by Jones and Davis (1965) and Jones and McGillis (1976), does not give an official theoretical role to the concept entity, but it can be found embedded in their logic. It is essential to show this if the connection of CIT to Kelley and PEAT is to be demonstrated. In Kelley's (1973) theory, an entity is usually some specific, nonhuman object such as a dog or a painting, or perhaps a human other than the actor, for example, a comedian. In PEAT, the term entity can be used in this way but can also include a combination of such single entities, for example, a cocktail party. In PEAT, then, an entity can be a situation that the actor faces, but the focus may be on some particular aspect of it, such as a painting. In CIT, the actor is depicted as facing a choice situation, as having to choose one of two or more actions. It is this choice situation that represents the entity in CIT. For example, in the case of the car purchase, the entity is the car purchase choice situation. The actor faces this choice (entity) and makes a decision. The actual decision made or action taken by the actor is the event that is to be explained. This concept of entity is entirely consistent with the expanded meaning of the term used in PEAT. Kelley used a less enriched meaning that focuses on discreet things because he was primarily interested in how people assign causes to agents, and it is easier to develop this logic if the agents in question are discreet. Jones and Davis were interested in explaining how people assign dispositions to actors, given actors' fairly complex choices, so their concept needed to be more enriched to include many discreet things. PEAT shows that these two concepts are not incompatible. They are just complementary articulations of the same reality.

A. FUNDAMENTAL CONCEPTS: JONES AND DAVIS

Now that the basic terms of the various theories have been shown to be parallel, it is possible to explain the important concepts of CIT in terms of PEAT and Kelley. The two most fundamental concepts of CIT are desirability and number of noncommon effects (Jones & Davis, 1965).

1. Desirability

It will be shown here that the role of desirability in attributions, as articulated by Jones and Davis (1965), can be explained using the concepts of consensus and of Propositions 10 and 11 of PEAT. Since the PEAT concept of consensus is closely related to Kelley's (1973) definition of that term, this demonstration will also link desirability to Kelley's concept of consensus. As a result, it will be seen that desirability, and some other concepts discussed in CIT, can be subsumed under the more general concept of consensus. This discussion will show a clear logical connection between these very fundamental concepts from the different theories.

The basic phenomenon involving desirability, as it is articulated in CIT, and as it must be explained here, is as follows. An actor is given a choice between a desirable act and an undesirable act. If the actor chooses the desirable act, observers are unlikely to attribute dispositions (characteristics) to the actor. If the actor chooses the undesirable act, observers more readily attribute dispositions to the actor.

The terms desirable act and undesirable act need to be clarified for the discussion that follows. Although these terms are widely used, it should be made clear that it is not the acts themselves that are desirable or undesirable. It is the consequences of the acts that have these characteristics. Desirable acts are those that lead to desirable consequences. Undesirable acts are those that lead to undesirable consequences.

Desirability can be expressed in probabilities. Although it is convenient to speak of desirability as if it were a dichotomy with two categories, desirable and undesirable, it is actually a continuum. Acts and their consequences can be placed along the continuum in a way that represents their relative desirability. The relative desirability of two consequences can be determined by ascertaining which of the two is chosen when people are given a choice between them. The one that is more chosen is the more desirable. This can be stated as a formal definition. The consequence A is *more desirable* than another consequence, B, when

$$p(\text{choose A}/\text{choice of A or B}) > p(\text{choose B}/\text{choice of A or B}).$$

For example, suppose the choice is between a car with a relatively smooth, comfortable ride (desirable consequence) and a car with a more bumpy, uncomfortable ride (undesirable consequence). The more comfortable car will be labeled Car A, the less comfortable, Car B. In accordance with our definition of desirability, it would follow that

$$p(\text{choose A}/\text{choice of A or B}) > p(\text{choose B}/\text{choice of A or B}).$$

Now that it has been shown that the concept of desirability can be represented with probabilities, it is possible to go on and show the connection between desirability and consensus. First it will be shown that when the more desirable of two options is chosen, it is an example of high consensus. To do this it will be necessary to show that the probabilities involved in the above definition of desirability fit the PEAT definition of high consensus. The PEAT definition of high consensus is

$$p(\text{event}/\text{entity}) > p(\text{event}).$$

It will be shown that certain of the probabilities in the desirability choice situation fit the two probabilities, p(event/entity) and p(event), in this expression, and that they have the appropriate relationship to each other.

With respect to which part of the definition corresponds to p(event/entity), it was shown earlier that, in the choice situation, the expression that represents the act of choosing the more desirable choice is

$$p(\text{choose A/choice of A or B}).$$

A concept from PEAT can be substituted for this. As explained earlier, any choice situation, including the one here with options A and B, is an entity. Further, it was stated that the act of choosing is an event. When these are substituted into the expression just given, we have p(event/entity). In the car example used earlier, in which the more comfortable car is the more desirable, this is seen as

$$p(\text{choose car A/choice of car A or car B}).$$

Next it will be shown which part of the definition corresponds to p(event). In the case in which the more desirable A is chosen, the choice of A is the event. The unconditional probability of the event is, therefore, p(choose A). In the car example used earlier, this would be p(choose car A).

Now the relationship between the two expressions will be derived. The unconditional probabilities just given, p(choose A) and p(choose car A), represent the probabilities that people will choose these particular consequences across all possible choice situations. Although car A is the more comfortable (and, therefore, more desirable) option when offered as an alternative to car B, it will probably not be the more desirable in *all* choice situations. In some situations the alternative might be even more comfortable than car A. In other choices the alternative may be of equal comfort with car A but have a significantly lower price. In which case car A might not be chosen. In other cases, of course, the alternatives are less desirable. In short, across all situations, there will be many situations in which car A will not be chosen. Contrast that to the present choice in which car A is pitted against a clearly less desirable option, car B. Here, A will be the predominant choice, much more so than when A is pitted against all other choices. The result is

$$p(\text{choose A/A or B}) > p(\text{choose A}).$$

When the corresponding terms from PEAT are substituted here, it gives

$$p(\text{event/entity}) > p(\text{event}).$$

This is the PEAT definition of high consensus. In summary, when an actor has a choice between a desirable and an undesirable action, if the actor chooses the more desirable action, this event is an example of high consensus, as defined by PEAT.

Given that the choice of the desirable act constitutes high consensus, several implications for attributions follow. As discussed under the topic of consensus, high consensus means that the entity is a facilitator of the event. If observers are asked what caused the event (the purchase of the comfortable car), they would have a ready explanation. It was the choice itself: "Given that choice, what would you do?" Alternately they might say that the actor "had no choice, there was only one thing he or she could do. Take the better car." Here the situation (entity) is perceived to constrain the behavior of the actor. The observers here are operating under Proposition 10. Proposition 10 applies to situations in which the already held beliefs of observers are able to provide an explanation for the event. If observers are asked about the cause of the event, they will scan their available probability statements looking for an available agent that is a facilitator of the event. In this case the entity, the choice situation, is a readily available facilitator. Observers do not have to infer any new characteristics about any of the available agents in order to explain the event. This is observers' preferred method of explanation since it explains the event in terms of their already held beliefs.

PEAT also explains why observers do not make dispositional attributions to the actor on the basis of the selection of the desirable act. In earlier discussion, it was noted that causal and characteristic attributions are intimately linked. For instance, observers will infer that Jim has the characteristic of being a good fisherman only if they can simultaneously attribute today's good catch in the creek to Jim. And, alternately, they will not say that Jim's characteristic, substantial fishing ability, was the cause of today's good catch unless they can attribute to Jim the characteristic of high fishing ability. In the case in which an actor has chosen a desirable act, there is no basis for attributing a causal role to the actor. A causal agent is already available, the entity. In order to assign a characteristic to the actor, the observers would also have to assign some causal role to the actor. But that would violate the observers' preference for giving causal explanations on the basis of information already held. There is nothing about the event and the agents, of which observers are aware, that would lead them to attribute cause or characteristics to the available actor.

It will now be shown that when an actor has a choice between a desirable and an undesirable consequence and chooses the undesirable one, this constitutes a case of low consensus. The expression from our definition of desirability that corresponds to the less desirable of the two options is

$$p(\text{choose B}/\text{choice of A or B}).$$

And the version of it given by our car example is

$$p(\text{choose car B}/\text{choice of car A or car B}).$$

These can be compared to their corresponding unconditional probabilities, which are, respectively, $p(\text{choose B})$ and $p(\text{choose car B})$. These unconditional probabilities represent the probabilities that people will chose those consequences across all possible choices. In the car example, the alternative could be a car that is even less comfortable than car B. In other cases it could be a car of equal discomfort but higher price. In short, across all situations, there will be some instances in which car B is chosen. In contrast, in the choice being considered here, car B is pitted against a clearly more desirable option, car A. In this circumstance, car B is very unlikely to be chosen. It therefore follows that

$$p(\text{choose car B/choice of car A or car B}) < p(\text{choose car B}).$$

This corresponds to the PEAT definition of low consensus, which is

$$p(\text{event/entity}) < p(\text{event}).$$

In short, when an actor has a choice between a desirable and an undesirable act, if the action chosen is the undesirable, this event is an example of low consensus, as defined by PEAT.

Given that the choice of the undesirable act constitutes low consensus, several implications for attributions follow. Low consensus means that the entity is an inhibitor of the event. If observers were asked what caused the event, they would have no ready explanation. They would perceive that, given that choice, it would be very unlikely for any actor to chose the uncomfortable car. The entity cannot be named as the cause of the event without violating the already held beliefs of the observers about the constraints offered by the choice between car A and car B. Observers, therefore, cannot explain the event while operating under Proposition 10, their preferred mode, in which they explain an event using their already held beliefs. But they can explain the event and make attributions while operating under Proposition 11. That is what they will do. Under Proposition 11, observers explain an event by attributing new characteristics to one of the available agents. They thus provide an explanation without contradicting or changing any beliefs held prior to the occurrence of the event.

In the event of the undesirable car choice, observers have few, if any, preconceived notions about the nature of the actor, so dispositions can be assigned to him or her in order to explain the event. Observers might say that the actor is stupid for not picking the more comfortable car, or perhaps that the actor is the "rugged" type, oblivious to things such as riding comfort. By attributing a disposition to the actor, the observers simultaneously provide a causal explanation for the event. That disposition must, therefore, be a facilitator of the event. The law of facilitory attributions will play a role here as augmentation. As discussed earlier, the facilitative characteristic assigned to an agent, in order to explain an event, must be strong enough to overcome the available inhibitors of the event. In this case the entity, the choice offered to the actor, was the inhibitor. If the actor is described as a rugged individual, in order to explain the event the degree of ruggedness attributed would have to be great enough to compensate for the degree of discomfort provided by the car. The more uncomfortable the car, the greater the degree of ruggedness that would have to be attributed.

It has now been shown that the concept of desirability, as articulated in CIT, can be subsumed under consensus, Proposition 10, and Proposition 11 in PEAT. When given a choice between a desirable act and an undesirable act, if the actor chooses the desirable act, this constitutes high consensus and observers will operate under Proposition 10. They will attribute the event to the entity (the choice situation) and will be reluctant to make attributions to the actor. If the actor chooses the undesirable act, this constitutes low consensus, observers will operate under Proposition 10 and will attribute both cause and dispositions to the actor in order to explain the event. They will do this in accordance with the law of facilitory attributions.

Jones and Davis (1965) and Jones and McGillis (1976) have pointed out several other factors that influence attributions, and these, because of their logical similarity to desirability, can also be linked to consensus. Jones and McGillis refined the concept of desirability and renamed it valence. They stated that desirable acts have positive valence and undesirable acts have negative valence. Their conceptual refinements do not damage the logic used here to link desirability to consensus. It follows that valence is related to consensus in the same way that desirability is. So, when actors choose an act of positive valence, consensus is high; when actors choose an act of negative valence, consensus is low. Jones and Davis also pointed out that in-role behaviors and out-of-role behavior have different effects on attributions. They state that in-role behaviors are explained by the presence of role demands, so in-role behaviors are not used as a basis for attributing dispositions to actors. PEAT would agree and add that this is another case of high consensus. Role demands represent constraints upon the behavior of people. Most people, when in the role, adhere to the prescribed behaviors. They act as the situation demands. So the role is a situation (entity) in the frame of reference provided by PEAT. The presence of the role is a facilitator of certain behaviors and an inhibitor of others. So in-role behaviors have high probabilities given the entity. They thus have high consensus. Out-of-role behaviors have low probability given the entity. They have low consensus. So the logic that applied to desirability, under the general concept of consensus, also applies to the concept of role behavior.

Jones and Davis and Jones and McGillis state that observers will not attribute dispositions to actors unless they perceive the actors to have freedom to make action choices. This is also related to consensus. A person without freedom is a person strongly constrained by the situation (entity). Given the presence of this entity, the behaviors of people are quite predictable. Almost everyone does what the warden says when they are in prison. Since the behavior is highly predictable given the entity, consensus is high and we attribute actions to the freedom-constraining situation, not to the actor. No dispositions are assigned to the actor.

But this applies only to those behaviors that are consistent with the constraints on freedom. If behaviors are performed contrary to the situational constraints, they will not be attributed to the situation (entity) but to the person. A person who serves his prison sentence without noticeable deviations from prison rules is not assigned any particular disposition. A prisoner who repeatedly attempts to break out, despite repeated punishment, is assigned all sorts of dispositions, running the gamut from incorrigible to freedom fighter.

This discussion of desirability, valence, role behavior, and freedom has shown that all are related to the concept of consensus from PEAT. However, this linkage did not refute the insights provided by Jones and Davis (1965), Jones and McGillis (1976), and others. It merely showed a way to include those insights as part of the broader, and more precisely articulated, theoretical framework provided by PEAT. This linkage also showed that the CIT concepts are related to Kelley's (1973) concept of consensus from covariance theory. However, the linkage is possible because of the prediction interpretation of consensus used by PEAT. Propositions 10 and 11 were also important in understanding how desirability and the other CIT concepts relate to PEAT. It is now time to consider the second fundamental idea in CIT, number of noncommon effects.

2. Number of Noncommon Effects

The number of noncommon effects is the second basic factor that influences the strength of dispositions attributed, according to Jones and Davis (1965). Noncommon effects are consequences of actions that follow from some actions but not from others. For instance, in the marriage example used by Jones and Davis, a woman has a choice among three suitors, all of whom are physically attractive. So, no matter which one she chooses, she will have an attractive husband. This is an effect common to all of her options. On the other hand, only one of her suitors is intellectually stimulating. This effect is, therefore, not common to them all. It is a noncommon effect. The more noncommon effects there are, the more difficult it is for observers to decide why the actor made a particular choice and to assign a disposition to that actor. Suppose the woman in question, named Adams, has a choice between two men, one of whom is wealthy and one of whom is not. This is one noncommon effect and observers can conclude quite clearly from the choice what her disposition is with respect to wealth. If, however, Adams has a choice between a man who is wealthy and healthy and a man who is neither, there are two noncommon effects. Observers will have some difficulty deciding if her choice was due to her disposition with respect to wealth or her disposition with respect to health. Their attributions will, therefore, not be as strong as in the case of a single noncommon effect. It is this theory about noncommon effects that will now be integrated into PEAT.

If PEAT is to include an explanation of noncommon effects, the concept of constraint must be elaborated. The unidimensional concept of constraint that has been used until this point must be embellished so that there is a way for a number of factors to affect a constraint.

In PEAT, as so far developed in the discussions of Kelley and CIT, entities have all been treated as unidimensional agents that are not broken down into component parts. An example of such unidimensionality can be seen in the vignette just used, in which Adams is the actor, the choice between suitors is the entity, and her act of choosing is the event. Suppose that the suitors are named Smith and Wells, and that Smith is generally more desirable than Wells. Given a choice of Smith and Wells then, the probability of choosing Smith is above .5. Suppose it is .6. The situation is represented in probabilities as

$$p(\text{choose Smith/Choice of Smith or Wells}) = .6$$

This can be abbreviated and given the title *overall constraint:*

$$p(\text{Smith/Smith, Wells}) = .6.$$

This expression has been titled overall constraint because it shows what can be predicted knowing that the choice is present, but it does not reveal any details about Smith and Wells that might explain why the probability is .6. Only the overall impact of the choice is given. In this sense it is unidimensional.

This unidimensional concept of constraint can be elaborated. Suppose it is known that Smith is wealthier than Wells. In CIT, it would be said that wealth is a noncommon effect and that Smith is the more desirable choice. In PEAT, the choice between Smith and Wells is an entity that has a constraint such that the probability of choosing Smith is greater than the probability of choosing Wells. The force of that constraint comes from the difference in the wealth of Smith and Wells. If there is a large difference in their wealth, the constraint to choose Smith will be very strong, for example, $p(\text{Smith/Smith, Wells}) = .9$. If there is only a small difference in wealth, the constraint to choose Smith will be weaker and might be $p(\text{Smith/Smith, Wells}) = .55$. This kind of choice is represented in Table III. There, a number of choices are listed and described in the column called entities (in PEAT a choice situation is an entity). Choice 1 is between Smith and Wells, with Smith wealthier than Wells, so $p(\text{Smith/Choice 1}) = .6$. To the right of this description is a graphic representation of the choice. Table III shows that on the dimension wealth, there is a force constraining the actor to choose Smith. Wealth, which would be called a noncommon effect in CIT, is called a dimension here. This is to emphasize that wealth is not a dichotomy. Jones and Davis treat noncommon effects as dichotomies in their examples, stating that people are wealthy or not, physically attractive or not, and so on. Although Jones and Davis dichotomize only for illustrative purposes, it detracts from their model. PEAT treats noncommon effects as dimensions. This is not only true to life, it also permits an elegant theoretical analysis.

TABLE III
ANALYSIS OF NONCOMMON EFFECTS

Entities	Force analyses		
	Dimensions	Smith	Wells
Choice 1			
Between Smith and Wells; Smith wealthier than Wells p(Smith/Choice 1) = .6	Wealth	←	
Choice 2			
Between Smith and Wells; Smith wealthier and healthier than Wells; wealth, health, equal force p(Smith/Choice 2) = .7	Wealth Health	← ←	
Choice 3			
Between Smith and Wells; Smith wealthier and healthier than Wells; wealth much stronger force than health p(Smith/Choice 3) = .61	Wealth Health	← ←	
Choice 4			
Between Smith and Wells; Smith wealthier than Wells; Wells healthier than Smith; wealth stronger than health p(Smith/Choice 4) = .55	Wealth Health	←	→

In the example shown in Choice 1 of Table III, observers' attributions will be as follows. If the actor were to choose Smith, it would be an instance of choosing the more desirable suitor and would constitute high consensus. As discussed earlier, high consensus means that the presence of the entity (which in this case is the choice between Smith and Wells) is a good predictor that the event in question (choose Smith) will occur. Most people would do it. In other words, the entity is a facilitator of the event. Observers will, therefore, attribute the choice to something about the entity. For example, when asked why Adams married Smith, observers might say, "She married him because of his money." Here is a reference to one aspect of the entity. Alternately observes might say that she married Smith because Wells was penniless. Again, this is a reference to one aspect of the entity. Notice that the noncommon effect (wealth) here is used as a basis for labeling the entity, for saying what constraint of the entity caused the event. Jones and Davis discussed noncommon effects only with respect to the role of helping observers assign dispositions to actors. Here we see that they can also play a role in attributing constraints to entities.

Continuing with the case in which Smith is chosen, it is unlikely that observers will attribute the event to the actor. For example, it is unlikely that observers would say that Adams married Smith because she is a gold digger or was after his money. There is no evidence available to them that suggests she is any more interested in money than anyone else. Consider now the other possible choice. If Adams had chosen Wells, she would have chosen the less desirable option and consensus would have been low. As discussed earlier, this means that the entity is an inhibitor of the event. The event cannot, therefore, be attributed to the entity unless observers change their beliefs about the entity. Observers will prefer to attribute the event to the only other available agent, Adams. When asked why she married Wells, observers might say that she has no interest in money or, perhaps, that she does not know the value of money. Since Smith and Wells differ on only one dimension, observers have little problem deciding which aspect of Adams and her suitors to focus on in their causal explanations. Notice that in this example, when she chooses Wells, conditions are present that Jones and Davis (1965) said yield the strongest attributions. There is only one noncommon effect (wealth) and the option chosen (Wells) is the less desirable of the two available.

The example shown in Choice 1 has shown that the concept of constraint can be tied to a particular dimension of the choice situation. In this case it was the difference in wealth of the suitors. The concept of constraint is still unidimensional in this example, but it is richer in its explanatory possibilities than the overall expression given earlier because a specific dimension, wealth, is named. It is possible now to elaborate further by adding more dimensions.

A slightly more complicated situation, involving two dimensions, can be tied to the concept of constraint. Suppose that Smith is different from Wells in two ways: he is wealthier and healthier. Assume that the strength of the wealth dimension is the same as in Choice 1 and that the difference on the health dimension is about equal in force to the wealth difference. This situation is shown as Choice 2 in Table III. Because there are two forces contributing to Smith's desirability, it is greater than it was in Choice 1. This is reflected in the fact that in Choice 1 the probability of selecting Smith is .6, whereas here is .7. If Smith, the more desirable, were chosen, there would be high consensus and observers would deliberate among and within themselves about the degree to which Smith's wealth and health influenced Adams. If Wells were chosen, it would constitute low consensus and attributions would be to Adams. There would be some question about her insensitivity to wealth and health and the degree to which each played a role. As a consequence, attributions to her will not be as clearly focused on wealth-related issues as they were in Choice 1, in which the only dimension in effect was wealth. The greater number of dimensions in Choice 2 is thus seen to weaken attributions of dispositions to actors *and* attributions of constraints to entities. Thus the comparison of Choices 1 and 2 shows the effect of number of noncommon effects as originally hypothesized by Jones and Davis.

But this demonstration of the role of number of noncommon effects depends on a particular circumstance that might not always be present. In Choice 2, the effects of health and wealth are equal so that observers may have trouble deciding which of the two, or both, to use in explaining the event. This ambiguity accounts for the effect of number of noncommon effects. This can be contrasted to Choice 3 in Table III in which there are also two dimensions, but one is much stronger than the other. In Choice 3, wealth will be the predominant explanation, as it was in Choice 1, and health will play no attributional role since its force is so much smaller than that of wealth. An example will make this clearer. In Choice 1, wealth is the only dimension differentiating the suitors. If Smith is a millionaire and Wells makes only an average salary, this difference in wealth will be important in the explanation of Adams's choice, whatever it might be. In Choice 2, Smith is also a millionaire and Wells an average wage earner, but in addition Smith is considerably healthier than Wells. Suppose Wells has a chronic illness that greatly restricts his activities and requires considerable medical attention while Smith is a laudable example of the fit, amateur athlete. Since health and wealth are strong and approximately equal forces, they will both get credit in the explanation of Adams's choice. Sharing the credit, wealth will not play as predominant a role as it did in Choice 1. In Choice 3, wealth is as strong a force as it was in Choice 2. Suppose again Smith is a millionaire and Wells an average wage earner. In Choice 3, however, health is a weaker force than it was in Choice 2. Suppose Wells has bunions while Smith does not. In this case, although there are two noncommon effects present, observers will give virtually all of their attributional attention to wealth and ignore health.

This comparison of Choices 1, 2, and 3 shows a boundary condition to Jones and Davis's hypothesis that number of noncommon effects influences the strength of attributions. It shows that the relative strengths of those noncommon effects also play a role. Jones and Davis's hypothesis about the effects of number of noncommon effects will be most clearly supported when the strengths of the noncommon effects involved are approximately equal. The greater the differences in the strengths, the less clearly will Jones and Davis's hypothesis be supported. The exact differences necessary to get support or lack of support will have to be determined by empirical studies.

Another example that shows a boundary condition to Jones and Davis's (1965) hypothesis about the effects of number of noncommon effects is seen in Choice 4 in Table III. It also involves two dimensions, but in this case they work in opposite directions. Smith and Wells differ on both wealth and health: Smith is wealthier than Wells, but Wells is healthier than Smith. In this choice, Smith is still more desirable than Wells but is less desirable than in Choices 1, 2, or 3. In Choice 1, Smith was more desirable and there was only one force in his favor, wealth. In Choices 2 and 3, Smith was more desirable owing to two forces, wealth and health. In the present choice, because wealth and health are acting in opposite directions, the force of one must be subtracted from the other. If Smith were chosen by Adams, the more desirable choice would have been taken, and consensus would be high. As a result, attribution would be to the entity. Observers would say that Adams married him because of his money and despite his poorer health. If Wells were chosen, there would be low consensus and attribution would be to the actor, Adams. Observers might say she values health more than wealth. They might say she undervalues wealth. This example shows another limiting condition to Jones and Davis's statement that the greater the number of noncommon effects the weaker the attribution. In Choice 2, there are two noncommon effects and they work in the same direction. Because the two forces work in the same direction and are of approximately equal force, when observers explain events using those two forces, they will invoke both to some degree. The attributions to wealth, then, will be less in Choice 2 than in Choice 1, in which wealth is the only available force. In Choice 1, all of the explanatory power will be focused solely on wealth. In Choice 4, there are also two dimensions (noncommon effects) but they operate in opposite directions. Because they operate in opposite directions, there is no ambiguity when it comes to explaining events. When Smith is chosen, observers do not have to consider health and wealth as alternative explanations. Wealth will be the dimension named as the cause and health will not be considered since it is operating in the wrong direction. So, although there are two noncommon effects present, only one is viable as an explanation. For this reason, attributions in Choice 4, with two noncommon effects, will be just as strong as those in Choice 1, which has only one noncommon effect. The Jones and Davis rule about noncommon effects should, therefore, be changed to say that the strength of the attribution depends not only on the total number of noncommon effects but also on the direction of the forces of those noncommon effects.

This suggestion, that the direction of noncommon effects as well as their number affects strength of attributions, can be tested empirically. Observers could be given vignettes in which number and direction of noncommon effects (dimensions) are manipulated independently. Such a study could be done with four basic vignettes. The first would have a low number of dimensions, all unidirectional. For example, an actor could be depicted as choosing to purchase a home that was both less expensive and roomier than another home available for purchase. The second vignette would have low number of dimensions and opposite directions. The actor could be depicted as choosing a home that is less expensive and less roomy than the other one available. The third vignette would have a high number of dimensions, all unidirectional. The actor would be depicted as choosing a home that was less expensive, roomier, in a better neighborhood, and having more modern conveniences. In the fourth vignette, the number of dimensions would be high but opposite in direction. The actor would be depicted as choosing a home that was less expensive and roomier but also in a less prestigious neighborhood and with fewer modern conveniences. Four more vignettes could be given but they would depict the actor as choosing the other house in each of the vignettes just described. Attributions to the actor and entity could be elicited from observers. If an ANOVA were done with attributions as the dependent variable, and number of dimensions and direction of dimensions as independent variables, the propositions of PEAT could be tested. PEAT would predict significant main effects of both number and direction of dimensions. Given the earlier discussion of another boundary condition to Jones and Davis's (1965) original hypothesis, that the forces of the dimensions be of approximately equal strength, it would be necessary in this study to pretest the vignettes used to ensure that the forces were equal.

This analysis of noncommon effects has accomplished a number of things. It has shown that noncommon effects can be represented as dimensions with force that make some events more likely than others. Thus, noncommon effects are linked to the probabilities of PEAT. These dimensions are seen as contributing to the constraints exerted by entities. Earlier it was shown that desirability, another concept from CIT, can also be tied to the probabilities of PEAT. As a result, the present analysis showed an intimate connection between desirability and noncommon effects, as they are used in CIT. Desirability is the net effect of the noncommon effects. Because of this logical connection, it was possible to show that noncommon effects are related to consensus. Now the two most fundamental concepts of CIT, desirability and noncommon effects, have been integrated into PEAT under the concept of consensus. They are thus linked to Kelley's (1973) concept of consensus. This analysis of noncommon effects has required an elaboration on the idea of constraint. All of Kelley's theory, and the part of CIT that deals with desirability, could be included in PEAT using a unidimensional concept of constraint. That was not possible with number of noncommon effects. This analysis also showed two boundary conditions to Jones and Davis's hypothesis that the greater the number of noncommon effects the weaker the attributions. Those noncommon effects must be of equal force and operate in the same direction.

This completes the discussion of the two basic concepts of CIT, desirability and number of noncommon effects. It has been shown that both of these concepts can be integrated into PEAT because they are analogous to consensus. In addition, an elegant connection between desirability and noncommon effects was demonstrated using probabilities.

B. LATER DEVELOPMENTS: JONES AND MCGILLIS

The primary purpose of this section is to show additional elegant correspondences between CIT and Kelley's theory using PEAT. Jones and Davis (1965), the founders of CIT, made no attempt to integrate their theory with Kelley's. They introduced the basic concepts, desirability and noncommon effects, and demonstrated how they operate to produce attributions. The discussion above has shown that these two concepts can be tied to the probabilities of PEAT, and from there to the concept of consensus in Kelley's theory. But other fundamental concepts from Kelley's theory have not been discussed in relation to CIT, most notably, distinctiveness and consistency. In addition, CIT has been developed beyond the statement of it by Jones and Davis. Jones and McGillis (1976) have presented a number of insightful improvements to CIT and have showed some weaknesses. It will now be shown that by using Jones and McGillis's improvements, further correspondences between CIT, Kelley, and PEAT can be demonstrated.

Jones and McGillis (1976) produced a major theoretical paper in which they made a number of improvements to attribution theory. They refined Jones and Davis's (1965) concept of desirability and renamed it valence. They developed new concepts that they called category-based expectancies and target-based expectancies. Armed with these refinements, they attempted an integration of CIT with Kelley's covariation theory. In addition, they explored a number of apparent problem areas in attribution theory. Their insightful article has improved attribution theory in a number of ways. Unfortunately, they were unable to provide an elegant integration of CIT and Kelley, and they even found some apparent contradictions between the theories.

It will be shown here, however, that important ideas from Jones and McGillis can be elegantly related to theoretical ideas from Kelley's covariation and configuration theories, and that there are no contradictions among the theories. The fundamental concepts of covariation theory are consensus, distinctiveness, and consistency. It will be shown that these concepts correspond to certain concepts of CIT. These correspondences are shown in Table IV. Jones and McGillis also stated that consensus, distinctiveness, and consistency correspond to certain terms in CIT. However, as shown in Table IV, there is some disagreement between the present article and Jones and McGillis' about what corresponds to what. A resolution of these disagreements will be offered.

1. Target-Based and Category-Based Expectancies

It will be shown here that two concepts from CIT, target-based expectancies and category-based expectancies, correspond to the concept of disposition from PEAT and, because of that, have some correspondence to distinctiveness information in Kelley's covariation theory. This will be done by taking Jones and McGillis's definitions of the terms, translating them into probabilities, and comparing these to the appropriate probability definitions of PEAT and covariation theory.

TABLE IV
CORRESPONDENCES BETWEEN KELLEY'S COVARIATION THEORY
AND CORRESPONDENT INFERENCE THEORY (CIT)

Concepts from Kelley's theory	Corresponding CIT concepts	
	From Jones & McGillis	From PEAT
Distinctiveness	Target-based expectancies	Target-based expectancies Category-based expectancies Contrast effect (actor based)
Consensus	Category-based expectancies	Desirability–valence Noncommon effects Contrast effect (entity based)
Consistency	Target-based expectancies	No explicit concept Must be assumed

Jones and McGillis's (1976) definition of target-based expectancies can be translated into the concept of disposition from PEAT. According to Jones and McGillis, target-based expectancies are observers' beliefs about how a particular target actor will behave, based upon the observers' knowledge of the past behaviors of that actor. For example, since observers have seen Jill get A's on all of her past tests, observers expect that on future tests she will also get A's. It is also possible for observers to have expectations about this actor's future behavior based on information other than direct knowledge of this individual's past behavior. For instance, they might expect certain behaviors because they know that the person is a member of some stereotyped group. These alternate sources of expectations will be discussed below. Jones and McGillis (1976) also state that target-based expectancies are probabilistic in nature. Presumably, they mean that the expectation that Jill is very likely to get an A could be expressed as

$$p(A/Jill) = \text{high}.$$

An implication of this is that the probability of getting A's, given the presence of Jill, is higher than the probability of getting A's in general. This can be expressed as

$$p(A/Jill) \neq p(A).$$

Since getting an A is an event, and Jill is an actor, this expression can be restated as

$$p(\text{event}/\text{actor}) \neq p(\text{event}).$$

This statement is identical to that given in Proposition 2 of PEAT as the definition of disposition. Thus, target-based expectancies as defined by CIT are analogous to dispositions as defined by PEAT. However, the two are not synonymous, as will be seen below.

Jones and McGillis's (1976) definition of category-based expectancies can also be translated into the concept of disposition. According to Jones and McGillis (1976, p. 393), "A category-based expectancy derives from the perceiver's knowledge that the target person is a member of a particular class, category or reference group." In other words, given that the actor is a member of some group, the observer expects the actor to emit a particular kind of behavior, to choose a particular act, and to produce some particular event. The stereotype is the classic example of this. Although category-based expectancies are derived from the group membership of the actor, the expectation is clearly tied to the actor. It is true that all group members are expected to behave in this way, but the Jones and McGillis definition makes it clear that it is the target actor's behavior that is being predicted. Jones and McGillis also state that category-based expectancies tend to be probabilistic. PEAT agrees. Suppose the observer in question has a stereotype that people of Asian extraction are very good in math. Suppose the same observer knows nothing of Jill's past math marks but does know that Jill is Asian. On the basis of this, the observer may hold a category-based expectancy about Jill, that

$$p(A/Jill) = \text{high}$$

and, therefore, that

$$p(A/Jill) \neq p(A).$$

Here we see again an expression that is an example of the PEAT definition of disposition.

Although target-based expectancies, category-based expectancies, and dispositions are analogous terms, they are not synonymous. A target-based expectancy is a belief about the probability of an event given only the observers' knowledge about the target actor's past behavior. A category-based expectancy is a belief about the probability of an event given only the observer's knowledge of the actor's group membership. These two types of information, target-based and category-based, probably do not work independently. Observers will, presumably, combine the two kinds of expectancies, perhaps with information from other sources as well, to derive an overall expectancy about the probability of an event given the actor. A disposition, as defined by PEAT, represents this overall expectancy. In short, target-based and category-based expectancies are separate kinds of information that might be combined by observers in order to perceive dispositions and make attributions.

Now that target-based and category based expectancies have been shown to contribute to dispositions, their relationship to distinctiveness can be shown. Strictly speaking, only target-based expectancies contribute to distinctiveness as

Kelley (1973) defines distinctiveness in covariation theory. However, as PEAT defines distinctiveness, both target-based and category-based expectancies contribute to it.

The close relationship between target-based expectancies and distinctiveness, as Kelley (1973) defines it, can be seen with an example. In Kelley's definition, distinctiveness is based on a comparison of what the actor did on this occasion with what the actor has normally done in the past. Suppose the event in question is Jill getting an A on yesterday's math exam. If Jill has always gotten A's in the past, yesterday's A is not unusual for her and distinctiveness is low. So yesterday's A will be attributed to something about Jill, perhaps that she is highly intelligent. If, however, Jill has never gotten an A in her life, yesterday's A is quite distinct. Given this high distinctiveness, the A is unlikely to be attributed to Jill. It might be attributed to luck, or perhaps to the exam being easy. In this example, distinctiveness is based on knowledge of Jill's individual behavior in the past. It is not based on stereotypes or other categorical information. Kelley clearly defined distinctiveness as based on knowledge of the past behavior of the target actor. This knowledge clearly involves an expectation that Jill will get certain marks on tests. For this reason, the knowledge of past behavior used to establish distinctiveness information is a target-based expectancy. Jones and McGillis (1976) concluded that target-based expectancies correspond to distinctiveness but that category-based expectancies do not.

However, distinctiveness, as PEAT defines it, draws upon both category-based and target-based expectancies. High and low distinctiveness were defined by PEAT above, in the section on Kelley's (1973) covariation theory. These definitions are as follows. High distinctiveness occurs when

$$p(\text{event}/\text{actor}) < p(\text{event}).$$

Low distinctiveness occurs when

$$p(\text{event}/\text{actor}) > p(\text{event}).$$

Suppose the event in question is Jill getting an A on yesterday's math exam. If observers believe that Jill is an excellent student, knowing that Jill was writing the exam would be a good predictor that she would get an A. She is much more likely to get an A than people in general. In probabilities, this is

$$p(A/\text{Jill}) > p(A).$$

This expression is an example of the general expression for low distinctiveness, from PEAT, just given. Given that Jill is a predictor of the event, observers are likely to attribute the event to her. They will say she got an A because she is smart. On the other hand, if Jill got an A yesterday but is believed to be a poor student, knowing that she was writing the exam would have been a predictor that she would not get an A. In probabilities this would be

$p(A/\text{Jill}) < p(A)$.

This expression is an example of the general expression for high distinctiveness, from PEAT, just given. Since Jill is a predictor that the event will not occur (she is an inhibitor of the event), observers will not attribute the event to her. They will attribute it to such things as luck and an easy exam. It is seen that, in PEAT, distinctiveness depends on a probability statement that captures observers' expectancies about the probability of an event given the presence of the actor. That probability statement does not distinguish between different kinds of information that contribute to that expectancy. It summarizes an expectation that is based on whatever sources of information happen to be available to the observer, target-based, category-based, and, perhaps, others.

It is thus seen that the PEAT definition of distinctiveness is more general than Kelley's (1973) definition of distinctiveness given in covariation theory. Because Kelley's definition is narrower, it only includes target-based expectancies, as Jones and McGillis (1976) suggested. Because the PEAT definition is broader, it can take into account both category-based and target-based expectancies. Because the PEAT definition is more general, it provides more theory-integrating power.

This does not mean, however, that the distinction between category-based and target-based expectancies, made by Jones and McGillis (1976), is not an important one. On the contrary, it is a possibly rich source of ideas for future research. By making this distinction and exploring its implications in the context of attribution theory, they have shown a connection between attribution theory and another important line of research. For some time now, there has been an active literature on the dynamics of the combination of stereotyped beliefs with actor-specific information (see, e.g., Fiske, Neuberg, Beattie, & Milberg, 1987; Weber & Crocker, 1983). An examination of this literature might yield interesting implications for attribution theory now that its relationship to attribution theory has been more clearly drawn. Furthermore, Kassin (1979) presents a thorough discussion of the same type of issue as it applies to expectations based not on the actor but on the entity. These parallel areas of research might benefit from cross-fertilization.

Jones and McGillis (1976) argue that category-based expectancies correspond to consensus in Kelley's covariation theory. This is contrary to the PEAT position just explained, which says that category-based expectancies contribute to distinctiveness. Jones and McGillis point out that category-based expectancies are based on a reference group, a population of people of which the actor is perceived to be a member. The actor's behavior during the event in question either confirms or disconfirms this belief based on group membership. Jones and McGillis point out that this is analogous to Kelley's (1973) concept of consensus. Consensus, they say, is based on whether the actor behaves, on this occasion, like other people. If the actor behaves the way the observer expects most people to behave, then consensus is high and the event will be attributed to the entity. So when category-based expectancies are confirmed, there is high consensus. If the actor behaves in a way unlike most people, consensus is low. Attribution is thus to the actor.

It will now be shown that PEAT and CIT disagree on the role of category-based expectancies because PEAT uses the prediction-based interpretation of consensus while CIT uses the contrast-based interpretation of consensus. The distinction between prediction-based and contrast-based interpretations was made earlier in the discussion of Kelley's covariation theory.

The contrast-based interpretation of consensus states that the essential information given in consensus information is that the actor is or is not like other people. If, on this occasion, the actor behaves unlike other people, there is a contrast. The actor is unique or unusual. Since the actor is unique, the event will be attributed to this uniqueness, hence to the actor. For example, because Jack is enthralled by this painting, and nobody else is (high contrast, low consensus), there must be something about Jack that causes the enthrallment. If, on the other hand, there is high consensus, there is low contrast between the actor and other people. Suppose Jack is enthralled by this painting and so is everyone else. There is nothing special or unique about Jack, so the event to be explained (his enthrallment) is not attributed to him. It is important to notice a particular aspect of the logic involved in this interpretation of consensus. In the case of low consensus, observers have observed the actor on this one occasion and on this basis conclude that since the actor's behavior contrasts with other people's, the actor is unique. This means that the actor has the enduring characteristic of being unlike other people. So the contrast-based interpretation assumes that observers will make an attribution about an enduring characteristic of the actor based on only one observation. Observers will undoubtedly do this on some occasions but how readily will they do it?

Given this contrast-based interpretation of consensus, it makes sense to say that category-based expectancies contribute to consensus. Category-based expectancies are beliefs about how people in certain categories behave. If an actor behaves unlike other people in his or her category, there is high contrast and low consensus.

The prediction-based interpretation of consensus, favored by PEAT, says that consensus has to do with whether or not the focal event could be predicted given the presence of the entity. High consensus means that $p(\text{event}/\text{entity}) > p(\text{event})$. In the example, this means that since everyone else was enthralled by this particular painting, it is very likely that Jack will be enthralled as well. Since Jack was enthralled, the painting correctly predicted Jack's behavior. The painting is, therefore, very likely to be named as the cause. If there is low consensus, Jack did not conform to expectations based on the presence of the painting. The painting was an inhibitor of Jack's behavior because, in low consensus, the presence of the entity is a predictor that the focal event (behavior) would not occur. Given that the picture is an inhibitor of the event, it is very unlikely to be named as the cause of the event. Observers will scan their probabilities looking for available facilitators of the event. Note that in this interpretation low consensus is not seen to be the direct cause of the attribution to the actor. It merely makes attribution to the actor more likely because low consensus makes attribution to the entity very unlikely.

Given this prediction-based interpretation of consensus, it is not reasonable to say that category-based expectancies contribute to consensus. It is reasonable to say that they contribute to distinctiveness. In the prediction-based interpretation, consensus has to do with p(event/entity). But category-based expectancies have nothing to do with the entity, they have to do with the expected behaviors of the target actor, given that actor's group membership. In PEAT, expectations about the actor, whatever their source, are subsumed under distinctiveness.

One reason why the PEAT interpretation is to be favored over the Jones and McGillis (1976) interpretation has to do with the logic assumed to be used by the observer. As noted above, in the case of low consensus, the contrast-based interpretation of Jones and McGillis required observers to assume that the actor was unique on the basis of one observation. This inference about an enduring characteristic, on the basis of one observation, is a major assumptive leap. The prediction-based interpretation of PEAT requires no such leap. In that interpretation, low consensus means that the entity is not a good predictor of the event and is, therefore, unlikely to be named as the cause. Given this, the actor is more likely to be named as the cause, particularly if distinctiveness information suggests that the behavioral event is characteristic of the actor.

A second reason why the PEAT interpretation is to be favored is that the empirical evidence supports it more strongly. PEAT states that both category-based and target-based expectancies contribute to distinctiveness and that distinctiveness will affect attributions in a particular way, regardless of the source of the information on which distinctiveness is based. If this is so, the manipulation of the two types of expectancies, in empirical studies, should lead to essentially the same effects. Jones and McGillis (1976), however, say that target-based expectancies correspond to distinctiveness, while category-based expectancies correspond to consensus. If this is so, the effects of category-based and target-based expectancies on attributions should be quite different. If target-based expectancies correspond to distinctiveness, when these expectancies are violated, distinctiveness is high, and so attribution should be to the entity. If category-based expectancies correspond to consensus, when these expectancies are violated, consensus is low, and so attribution should be to the actor. The effects of expectancy violation on attributions are seen to be opposite for target-based and category-based expectancies. It follows that the effects of expectancy confirmation should also be opposite. If the empirical literature is examined and it is found that the two types of expectancies have essentially the same effect on attributions, this would be support for the PEAT interpretation. If the results show that the two types of expectancies have different effects on attributions, this would be support for the Jones and McGillis interpretation.

Jones and McGillis (1976, p. 394) posed the question of whether or not the two kinds of expectancies affect attributions in the same way and proceeded to examine the empirical literature. Jones and Harris (1967) manipulated only category-based expectancies. They did this by telling observers that the target actors were either rural southerners or urban northerners. Jones, Worchel, Goethals, and Grumet (1971), on the other hand, manipulated only target-based expectancies. They did this by telling observers that the target actor had given answers of a particular type when filling out an opinion questionnaire on individual rights and related topics. Jones and McGillis examined the results of these two studies and concluded that the effects of the two kinds of expectancies were essentially the same. Jones and McGillis also cited a paper by Jones and Berglas (1976) in which the two kinds of expectancies were manipulated in the same study. Category-based expectancies were manipulated by saying that the actor was either a female judge or a North Carolina deputy sheriff. Target-based expectancies were manipulated by stating that the actor either had made a speech against employment discrimination against homosexuals or had made a speech stating that any method, including violence, should be used to prevent busing. Jones and McGillis examined the results and concluded that the effects of the two kinds of expectancies were virtually identical. This empirical literature therefore supports the PEAT interpretation that both target-based and category-based expectancies contribute to distinctiveness.

The correspondences between dispositions and distinctiveness, as defined by PEAT, and category-based expectancies and target-based expectancies, as defined by Jones and McGillis (1976), have now been demonstrated. It has also been shown that distinctiveness, as defined by Kelley (1973), corresponds only to target-based expectancies. It has also been shown, on logical and empirical grounds, that Jones and McGillis's contention that category-based expectancies correspond to consensus is not as well supported as the PEAT position that category-based expectancies contribute to distinctiveness.

2. Consistency in CIT

This section will show that CIT, as articulated by Jones and Davis (1965) and Jones and McGillis (1976), has no theoretical role for consistency and that it should have been included. First it will be shown why an attempt by Jones and McGillis to link consistency to target-based expectancies did not work. Then an improved model of how consistency fits into CIT will be presented.

Consistency is defined in very similar ways by Kelley (1973) and PEAT. According to Kelley (1973), consistency has to do with whether or not the event has occurred on past occasions when the target actor and the target entity have come together. For example, if Paul is enthralled by this painting today, and on past occasions when he has seen this painting he has also been enthralled, consistency is high. If on past occasions Paul has not been enthralled, consistency is low. PEAT defines consistency with probabilities. High consistency occurs when

$$p(\text{event}/\text{actor} \cap \text{entity}) > p(\text{event}).$$

Low consistency occurs when

$$p(\text{event}/\text{actor} \cap \text{entity}) < p(\text{event}).$$

When consistency is high, the joint presence of the actor and the entity is a facilitator of the event. When consistency is low, the joint presence of the actor and the entity is an inhibitor of the event.

Jones and McGillis (1976) attempted to show that consistency is a particular kind of target-based expectancy. Since consistency has to do with what has happened in the past in certain circumstances when the actor was present, they reasoned that it represents an expectancy of what will happen when the actor is present. Because of this, consistency is something like distinctiveness and they reasoned that it should be included as a kind of target-based expectancy. Although they maintained this position in one part of their article (Jones and McGillis, 1976, p. 413), in another part a close analysis showed that this correspondence has some problems (Jones and McGillis, 1976, pp. 410–411).

PEAT helps us to understand why Jones and McGillis's (1976) attempt to link consistency to target-based expectancies was ill fated. In PEAT, consistency has to do with the probability of the event given the presence of both actor and entity. Target based expectancies have to do with the probability of the event given the presence of the actor, with no other conditions. It is true that cases in which the actor and entity are present are a subset of all cases in which the actor is present, but the two are certainly not equivalent. The difference concerns the necessary presence of the entity. The presence of the entity is a very important piece of information when it comes to making attributions. As a consequence, it is essential that a theory give separate status to probabilities that are conditional on just the actor versus those that are conditional on the actor and the entity.

Although CIT does not have a concept analogous to consistency, PEAT suggests that observers will use such information when it is available or make assumptions about it when it is not. Proposition 9 states that observers will not attribute events to actors or entities unless they believe that the event in question is predictable. If the event is not predictable, they will attribute it to luck. One precondition for the event to be predictable is that on past occasions in which this actor and entity have come together the event has occurred. In other words, observers must believe that there is high consistency before they will make attributions to actors or to entities. Hence if observers are not given consistency information but are asked to make disposition attributions about the actor, as they are in CIT, the observers will assume consistency information about the situation in order to make their attributions. CIT does not explicitly make this prediction. An empirical test of it could be carried out by replicating the classic astronaut and submariner experiment (Jones, Davis, & Gergen, 1961), asking observers to report their impressions of how the actors would behave on future occasions if put into the same situations.

3. Consensus in CIT

Consensus, as defined by PEAT, has already been shown to correspond to the CIT concepts of desirability, valence, and number of noncommon effects. Above, it was shown that noncommon effects constitute forces that draw actors to one action option or another. The net effect of all of those forces represents the desirability of each of the options. If actors choose the less desirable option when faced by a choice, this constitutes low consensus. If actors choose the more desirable option, this constitutes high consensus. The concept of valence is a refinement of the concept of desirability that was developed by Jones and McGillis (1976). Valence has the same relationship to consensus as does desirability.

4. Kelley, CIT, and PEAT

Before going on to discuss a somewhat unrelated topic, it is worthwhile to summarize briefly the correspondences between Kelley, CIT, and PEAT that have so far been described. These correspondences are shown in Table IV. The concept of consensus, as articulated by Kelley and PEAT, corresponds to the CIT concepts of desirability, valence, and noncommon effects. The concept of distinctiveness, as articulated in PEAT, corresponds to the concept of distinctiveness from Kelley's theory and the concepts of target-based expectancies and category-based expectancies from CIT. Kelley's concept of distinctiveness is equivalent to only target-based expectancies in CIT. Consistency means much the same thing in Kelley and PEAT, but the concept is not used in CIT. PEAT suggests that CIT needs the concept of consistency.

5. The Contrast Effect

The contrast effect was originally defined by Jones and McGillis (1976), but PEAT gives considerable insight into its nature and its relationship to other theoretical ideas, including Kelley's (1973). The concept of contrast effect makes a lot of sense, intuitively, in the frame of reference provided by CIT. In addition, a number of phenomena observed in empirical tests of CIT could apparently be brought together under this theoretical idea. However, when experiments were conducted with the explicit purpose of demonstrating the contrast effect, the results were disappointing. Jones and McGillis did not attempt to show a link between the contrast effect and any of Kelley's concepts. The analysis of the contrast effect using PEAT, which follows, will show that the concept is fundamentally valid. However, attempts to demonstrate it empirically were based upon a misinterpretation of its nature. When those misinterpretations are clarified, the appropriate way to demonstrate it will be clear. Further, it will be shown that the contrast effect is analogous to Kelley's concept of consensus and, by inference, related to the concept of distinctiveness.

According to Jones and McGillis (1976, p. 396), "A contrast effect is defined by comparing an expectancy confirmation case to an expectancy disconfirmation case. There is contrast when the disconfirming behavior leads to a more extreme inference than the confirming behavior." Jones and McGillis give an example involving a self-made financier and a postal clerk. If the self-made financier makes a pro-union statement, this is quite unexpected. There is contrast between what is expected and what is observed. If the postal clerk makes the same pro-union statement, this is not unexpected. There is no disconfirmation of expectations and there is no contrast. By Jones and McGillis's definition of contrast, then, more liberal attitudes will be attributed to the self-made financier (for whom there is contrast) than to the postal clerk (for whom there is no contrast).

Jones and McGillis (1976) stated that they derived the idea of the contrast effect from earlier work described in Jones and Davis (1965). As described there, the contrast effect has to do with the desirability of a chosen act. Choice of an undesirable act (unexpected, high contrast) leads to stronger attributions to the actor than does the choice of a desirable act (expected, low contrast). The contrast effect, as defined in this context, using desirability to create the contrast, has been demonstrated empirically many times (Jones & Davis, 1965) and there can be little doubt about its validity.

However, later attempts to demonstrate the contrast effect, which Jones and McGillis (1976) describe, gave very disappointing results. In one such study, Jones and Harris (1967) had actors deliver speeches favoring desegregation. The actors had previously been identified to observers as either northerners or southerners. The prodesegregation speech would be unexpected from the southerner (high contrast) and not so unexpected from the northerner (low contrast). The prediction was, using the concept of contrast effect, that the southerner would be judged more liberal than the northerner. However, observers consistently rated the northerner as more liberal on the race issue. A similar experiment by McGillis (1974) had equally disappointing results. Black or white actors were depicted as voting for candidates who advocated more minority employment. It was assumed that observers would expect that black people would be more likely to vote for this candidate than would white people. It was therefore predicted that the white actor (who voted contrary to expectations, high contrast) would be seen as more in favor of minority employment than the black actor (who voted in accordance with expectations, low contrast). The results were opposite to this prediction. According to Jones and McGillis, Jones and Berglas (1976) also found no evidence for the contrast effect.

PEAT suggests that these attempts failed to demonstrate the contrast effect because they involve a misinterpretation of its nature. The original studies that demonstrated contrast using desirability, which were reported in Jones and Davis (1965), are based on a valid concept of contrast. However, Jones and McGillis's (1976) definition of the contrast effect has an important flaw in it. The failed attempts to demonstrate contrast used the flawed definition of Jones and McGillis.

In the studies involving desirability, on which the idea of contrast was originally based, the contrast effect is equivalent to consensus as defined by PEAT. The basic proposition in these studies was that when actors choose the more desirable of two options, there is no contrast between expectations and the action; but when actors choose the less desirable of two options, there is contrast because this choice is unexpected. As a result, attributions to the actor making the desirable choice are not as strong as attributions to the actor making the undesirable choice. Earlier, in the discussion of desirability in CIT, it was shown how this relates to PEAT. Suppose the event in question is the choice, by the actor, of car A. Suppose the actor had a choice between car A and car B and that car A was clearly more desirable. The entity in this case is the choice situation. Since car A is the more desirable, observers expect that it will be the one chosen. And since car A is matched here with a clearly less desirable car, the probability of choosing A here is greater than the probability of choosing A in general, across all possible choices. In the probabilities of PEAT, this yields

$$p(\text{choose A/choice of A or B}) > p(\text{choose A}).$$

Given that "choose A" constitutes the event, and "choice of A or B" is the entity, this above probability can also be expressed as

$$p(\text{event/entity}) > p(\text{event}).$$

This is the PEAT definition of high consensus. As discussed earlier, high consensus fosters attribution to the entity. So, in this example involving desirability, when the actor chooses the more desirable outcome, the choice is expected, there is low contrast, there is high consensus, and attributions to the entity are more likely than attributions to the actor. If, however, the actor were to choose car B, the less desirable car, this would be unexpected. The probability of choosing B here, given that it was clearly the less desirable car, is less than the probability of choosing B across all choice situations. In probabilities, this is

$$p(\text{choose B}/\text{choice of A or B}) < p(\text{choose B}).$$

Given that "choose B" constitutes the event here, and that "choice of A or B" is the entity, this above probability translates into the following expression:

$$p(\text{event}/\text{entity}) < p(\text{event}).$$

This is the definition of low consensus in PEAT. Low consensus indicates that the entity is an inhibitor of the event and therefore is unlikely to be named as the cause. As a consequence, attributions to the actor are favored. In short, when the undesirable option is chosen, the choice is unexpected, there is high contrast, there is low consensus, and attributions to the actor are more likely than attributions to the entity. Thus it is seen that, in the desirability examples from which Jones and McGillis originally got the idea of contrast, contrast comes from expectancies based on the presence of the entity and is equivalent to consensus. Low contrast constitutes high consensus and fosters attributions to the entity, and high contrast constitutes low consensus and fosters attributions to the actor. So the original phenomena on which Jones and McGillis based the idea of the contrast effect are very well supported, theoretically and empirically. It should be emphasized that, in this example, the expectancies about which car would be chosen were based on knowledge of the cars. These expectancies were therefore based on knowledge of the entity. They were not based on information about the actor. Further, in their discussion, Jones and McGillis emphasized the effects that contrast has on attributions to the actor. Attributions to the actor are strengthened by the contrast. So, the contrast effect, as originally observed in the example of desirability, is equivalent to consensus and involves a contrast with expectations based on knowledge of the entity (not of the actor); in their discussion, Jones and McGillis emphasized the effects of contrast on attributions to the actor.

Despite this good beginning, Jones and McGillis (1976) made a subtle change when they formally defined the contrast effect. This change can best be seen by considering the example they used. In their example, they suggest that if a self-made financier makes a pro-union statement (high contrast), that person will be seen as more liberal than a postal clerk who makes a pro-union statement (low contrast). Note that in this example the contrast effect is expected to manifest itself in the attributions made to the actor, just as it was in the original examples involving desirability. However, unlike the desirability examples, the source of the contrast is in knowledge about the actor, not about the entity. Because one actor is a member of the group (category) self-made financiers, the pro-union statement is unexpected. The pro-union statement violates a category-based expectancy. The pro-union statement from the person who is a member of the category postal clerk confirms a category-based expectancy. So Jones and McGillis are assuming that the contrast phenomenon, whether it comes from expectations based on knowledge of the entity or knowledge of the actor, will have equivalent effects on attributions to the actor. In both cases, high contrast leads to greater attributions to the actor.

Jones and McGillis (1976) did not notice that when contrast is based on knowledge of the entity, it is equivalent to consensus; but when contrast is based on knowledge of the actor, it is equivalent to distinctiveness. Above, it was shown that in the desirability examples, on which the idea of contrast was originally based, contrast results from knowledge of the entity. In that case, contrast is equivalent to consensus and has the effects on actor attributions that Jones and McGillis suggest. It will now be shown that when contrast is based on knowledge of the actor, which is how Jones and McGillis defined it with their self-made financier versus postal clerk example, contrast is equivalent to distinctiveness. In the Jones and McGillis example, it is presumed that most observers believe that a self-made financier is less likely to make a pro-union statement than the average person. In probabilities, this is

$$p(\text{pro-union statement/self-made financier}) < p(\text{pro-union statement}).$$

Given that the event here is the pro-union statement, and that the self-made financier is the actor, this expression can be translated to

$$p(\text{event/actor}) < p(\text{event}).$$

This is the definition of high distinctiveness given in PEAT. High distinctiveness fosters attributions to the entity. The idea that category-based expectancies contribute to distinctiveness information was discussed earlier in the section on expectancies. So the following are seen in the financier versus postal clerk example: When contrast is high, category-based expectancies are violated, distinctiveness is high, and attributions to the entity are favored. With the postal clerk, it is presumed that observers believe that such people are more likely than average to make a pro-union statement. This can be expressed as

$$p(\text{pro-union statement/postal clerk}) > p(\text{pro-union statement}).$$

Given that the postal clerk is the actor and the pro-union statement is the event, this translates into

$$p(\text{event/actor}) > p(\text{event}).$$

This is the PEAT definition of low distinctiveness. Low distinctiveness enhances attributions to the actor. So the following are seen in Jones and McGillis' illustrative example: When contrast is low, category-based expectancies are confirmed, distinctiveness is low, and attributions to the actor are favored.

The major problem with the Jones and McGillis (1976) example is that when contrast is equivalent to consensus, it affects attributions to the actor in one way; but when contrast is equivalent to distinctiveness, it affects attributions in the opposite way. As shown above in the desirability example, where contrast is equivalent to consensus, high contrast constitutes low consensus and facilitates attribution to the actor. But in the postal clerk example, where contrast is equivalent to distinctiveness, high contrast constitutes high distinctiveness and this facilitates attribution to the entity. The effects of high contrast are opposite in the two cases. It follows that in the desirability example in which contrast is equivalent to consensus, low contrast constitutes high consensus and facilitates attribution to the entity. In the postal clerk example, low contrast constitutes low distinctiveness and facilitates attribution to the actor. So, when contrast is based on knowledge of the entity, it is equivalent to consensus and affects attributions to the actor in the way that Jones and McGillis say contrast affects actor attributions. However, when contrast is based on knowledge of the actor, it is equivalent to distinctiveness and affects attributions to the actor in a way opposite to that proposed by Jones and McGillis.

The empirical evidence reviewed by Jones and McGillis (1976) supports the interpretation of the contrast effect presented here. For example, Jones and Harris (1967) had antisegregation speeches delivered by northerners and southerners. The prediction, based on Jones and McGillis's logic, was that the southerners would be judged more liberal than the northerners because of the contrast effect. Their logic was that southerners would not be expected to make an antisegregation speech, and so when they did, there would be contrast and this would lead to strong attributions of liberal views to the southerners. On the other hand, an antisegregation speech is less unexpected from northerners, there is less contrast, and so less liberal views would be attributed to the northerners. PEAT makes the opposite prediction. If it is unlikely that a southerner would make an antisegregation speech, it means that

$$p(\text{antisegregation speech/southerner}) < p(\text{antisegregation speech}).$$

Given that the speech is the event and the southerner is the actor, this can be expressed as

$$p(\text{event/actor}) < p(\text{event}).$$

This is the definition of high distinctiveness. With high distinctiveness, the actor is an inhibitor of the event and is unlikely to be named as the cause. Attributions to the entity are, therefore, favored.

When the antisegregation speech is given by the northerner, this is expected, so

$$p(\text{antisegregation speech/northerner}) > p(\text{antisegregation speech}).$$

This is equivalent to

$$p(\text{event}/\text{actor}) > p(\text{event}).$$

This is low distinctiveness in PEAT. With low distinctiveness, the actor is a facilitator of the event and very likely to be named as the cause, and, therefore, appropriate liberal views attributed. So PEAT predicts more liberal views will be attributed to the northerner than to the southerner, whereas Jones and McGillis predicted more liberal views attributed to the southerner. The empirical data showed that the northerners were judged uniformly more liberal than the southerners. PEAT is supported. Similar logic can be applied to the McGillis (1974) and Jones and Berglas (1976) attempts to demonstrate the contrast effect. In both cases the data support PEAT.

A further test of these two approaches could be done by replicating the Jones and Berglas (1976), Jones and Harris (1967), and McGillis (1974) studies, with only slight modification. As these studies were discussed by Jones and McGillis, attention was given only to attributions to the actor because that is what CIT focuses on. But PEAT also makes predictions about attributions to the entity. If these three studies were replicated, but with observers having the opportunity to make attributions to the entity, the predictions of PEAT could be tested for that kind of attribution as well.

The basic and very valid principle conveyed by the contrast effect is that when an event is unexpected given observer's beliefs about one agent, it tends to enhance attributions of causes and characteristics to other available agents. If the agent about which something is known is the actor, and an unexpected event occurs (high contrast), this is high distinctiveness, so attributions to the entity are favored. If the agent about which something is known is the entity, and an unexpected event occurs (high contrast), this is low consensus, so attributions to the actor are favored.

Table IV summarizes the connections between Kelley's (1973) theories and CIT that have just been explored. The CIT concept of desirability was translated into probabilities and shown to be analogous to the concept of consensus as defined by PEAT and, from there, to Kelley's concept of consensus. When an actor chooses the more desirable of two options, consensus is high and attributions to the actor are weak. When the less desirable option is chosen, consensus is low and attributions to the actor are strong. In addition, dispositions will be attributed to the actor. Given this, certain ideas discussed earlier, including augmentation, discounting, the principle of facilitory force predominance, and the law of facilitory attributions, can all play a role. It was also shown that the CIT concepts of role behavior, freedom, and valence are also special cases of consensus. Noncommon effects were also translated into the terms of PEAT and found to be closely related to desirability and hence to consensus. Noncommon effects were treated as dimensions of force that constrain actors' behaviors in one direction or the other. The analysis of noncommon effects led to a considerable embellishment of the idea of constraint. It was also noted that the directions and strengths of noncommon effects are important in the formulation of attributions, just as is the number of noncommon effects. An empirical test of this was suggested.

Although the fundamental logic of desirability, valence, freedom, and role behavior can be related back to consensus, the CIT discussion of these concepts represents an enrichment of our understanding of that logic. It was shown that both target-based and category-based expectancies contribute to distinctiveness, as PEAT defines it, but only target-based expectancies contribute to distinctiveness as Kelley defines it. When these actor-centered expectancies are confirmed, there is low distinctiveness; and when they are disconfirmed, there is high distinctiveness. The CIT proposition that category-based expectancies correspond to consensus information is not supported by empirical evidence. CIT does not have a concept that corresponds to consistency but PEAT suggests that the concept is necessary in attribution theory. An empirical test of this, which involves having subjects predict future behaviors of actors, was suggested. An analysis of the contrast effect using PEAT showed that the basic phenomenon that it identifies is valid but that Jones and McGillis misinterpreted its functioning in certain circumstances. When this was sorted out, it became clear that the contrast effect involves situations in which observers expectancies are disconfirmed (there is a contrast between what is expected and what is observed). When contrast is based on knowledge of the actor, it constitutes high distinctiveness and enhances attributions to the entity. When contrast is based on knowledge of the entity, it constitutes low consensus and enhances attributions to the actor. The empirical data in several studies cited by Jones and McGillis support this interpretation. Overall, this interpretation of CIT in terms of PEAT depended on two basic points. The first is that the entity in PEAT and in Kelley corresponds to the choice situation in CIT. The second is that the prediction interpretation of covariation information is favored over the contrast interpretation.

V. PEAT, Kelley, and CIT

Now that Kelley's (1973) theories and those of CIT (Jones and Davis, 1965; Jones & McGillis, 1976) have both been explained in terms of PEAT, it is appropriate to summarize the connections between all of them. Proposition 9 of PEAT describes the observers' requirement that the focal event be predictable, given the available congregation of agents, if enduring characteristics of the agents are to be used to provide a causal explanation of the event. Observers must believe that other meetings of these same agents have the same outcomes or events. This idea appears in Kelley's covariation theory as consistency. In Cells 1–4 of Table I, consistency is high (on past occasions when this actor and entity came together, the same event occurred), so observers can make attributions to actor, entity, or both. In Cells 5–8 of Table I, consistency is low. In those cells observers attribute events to chance or to luck rather than to enduring characteristics of available agents. CIT has no concept that corresponds to consistency even though, for its other concepts to be viable, observers must be making assumptions about consistency. An empirical test of this proposition has been suggested.

Proposition 10 of PEAT involves situations in which observers are able to explain an event using beliefs that they held prior to the event. This is the observers' favored mode of attribution because it enables them to explain the event with what they already know. They do not have to change any of their prior beliefs or to infer any new beliefs about agents. The first four cells of Kelley's covariation theory, shown in Table I, give the fullest description of observers' mental processes under these circumstances. Observers, after observing the event, scan their available probability statements, looking for the strongest available facilitator of the event. That strongest facilitator will be named as the cause. The probability statement associated with the agent also designates a characteristic of that agent. The information already in place allows the observer to make both causal and characteristic attributions. Information that tells about the probability of the event, given the presence of the entity, is called consensus. According to PEAT, high consensus indicates the event was expected given the presence of the entity. According to Kelley and PEAT, high consensus enhances attribution to the entity. According to PEAT, low consensus means that the event is unexpected given the presence of the entity. According to Kelley and PEAT, low consensus enhances attributions to the actor.

CIT discusses these same ideas but under different names. When the act chosen by an actor is the more desirable one, constitutes in-role behavior, is made under conditions with little freedom, involves outcomes with the more positive valence, and/or is in the same direction as the noncommon effects with the strongest forces, CIT says that attributions to the actor will be weak. All of these conditions constitute high consensus in the framework provided by PEAT. The behaviors in all of those cases are expected by observers, given their knowledge of the entity (choice situation). When the act chosen is the less desirable one, constitutes out-of-role behaviors, is made under conditions of freedom, involves outcomes with the less positive valence, and/or is in the direction opposite to the noncommon effects with the strongest forces, CIT says that attributions to the actor will be strong. All of these conditions constitute low consensus in the framework provided by PEAT. The behaviors are unexpected given observers' knowledge of the entity, and so the entity is not likely to be named as the cause. The only other available agent is the actor, so the actor is quite likely to be named as the cause. These examples of low consensus also constitute what CIT calls high contrast.

Information that tells about the probability of an event, given the presence of the actor, is called distinctiveness. According to PEAT, high distinctiveness indicates that the event was unexpected given the presence of the actor. According to Kelley and PEAT, high distinctiveness facilitates attribution to the entity. According to PEAT, low distinctiveness indicates that the event was expected given the presence of the actor. According to Kelley and PEAT, low distinctiveness enhances attributions to the actor. Category-based and target based expectancies are two concepts from CIT that correspond to distinctiveness. If the event confirms these actor-centered expectancies, there is low distinctiveness. This enhances attribution to the actor. If the event disconfirms these expectancies, there is high distinctiveness and attributions to the entity are enhanced. High distinctiveness involves what CIT calls high contrast.

The third basic kind of covariation information is consistency, the probability that the event will occur given both actor and entity are present. The role of consistency has just been discussed in connection with Proposition 9. CIT does not have a concept that corresponds to consistency.

The concepts of multiple necessary causes and multiple sufficient causes from Kelley's configuration theory are special cases of Cells 3 and 4 of covariation theory; thus they also fall under Proposition 10.

Propositions 11 and 12 of PEAT involve situations in which observers do not initially have information that allows them to explain the observed event. As a consequence, they must either attribute new characteristics to agents (Proposition 11) or modify their already held beliefs about agents (Proposition 12) in order to provide an explanation. The logical principles are the same under these two propositions. Observers prefer, however, to attribute new characteristics to agents rather than to modify old beliefs. In order to provide explanations, under the conditions of Propositions 11 and 12 observers will first assume the principle of facilitory force predominance. They will assume that the force of the available facilitators is greater than the force of the available inhibitors. Then, using the law of facilitory attributions, they will attribute the necessary facilitative force(s) to the available agent(s). In accordance with that law, the greater the inhibitory force that had to be overcome, the greater the facilitory force they will attribute (augmentation); and the greater the number of facilitory agents available, the less the facilitory force that will be assigned to any one of them (discounting).

This attribution of a facilitory characteristic to an agent is equivalent to assigning a probability that reflects the probability that the focal event will occur given the presence of that agent. If the agent is an entity, this is called a constraint. If the agent is an actor, this is called a disposition. In this process, the acts of causal and characteristic attribution are simultaneous. As the characteristic is assigned, a causal explanation is provided, and vice versa. This process of assigning characteristics, in accord with principle of facilitory force predominance and the law of facilitory attributions, is also found in Kelley's description of how the compensatory causes schema is used to assign ability dispositions to actors of unknown characteristics, given that the actor has had success, or lack of it, in an encounter with a task that is of low, medium, or high difficulty. The same logic is applied in CIT when it discusses the assignment of dispositions to actors. Given that an actor has chosen an undesirable act (or done one of the other things from CIT that constitute low consensus), observers will attempt to explain the event by attributing an appropriate disposition to the actor. They will follow the law of facilitory attributions and thus commit augmentation and discounting. To be logically consistent, PEAT argues, these observers must also be assuming high consistency. It also follows that in these inferential processes observers are moving into one of the Cells 1–4 from covariation theory, shown in Table I. Before making their attributions, observers do not have beliefs about the available agents that enable them to explain the event. After attributions they do. Cells 1–4 represent conditions in which observers have all the information they need in order to explain the event. Thus, by attributing, observers are putting into place one of the information patterns shown in Cells 1–4 of Table I.

Two characteristics of PEAT are primarily responsible for its ability to elegantly integrate all of these important concepts from Kelley and CIT. The first is the use of the prediction-based, as opposed to the contrast-based, interpretation of covariation information. This comes directly from the use of probabilities to describe the information. Without the prediction interpretation, the errors of some past attempts to integrate the theories would have been repeated. The second characteristic of PEAT of great importance is the articulation of its propositions and a statement of how the propositions are related to each other in Proposition 13. This framework provides a coherent overview of when and how these various processes will be used. Although many of these processes were identified years ago, there has hitherto been no elegant way to organize so many of them.

VI. Other Theories

Now that the two most influential theories have been analysed using PEAT, some others will be examined as well. It would be impossible to deal with all of the available theories, so some selection has been necessary. Several that are either current or deal with attributions as probabilities will be discussed.

A. JASPARS

Jaspars and his colleagues have recently provided useful insights into the issues raised by Kelley's (1973) covariation theory of attribution (Hewstone & Jaspars, 1983, 1984, 1987; Hilton & Jaspars, 1987; Jaspars, 1983; Jaspars, Hewstone, & Fincham, 1983). The general framework of these ideas can be brought into PEAT so that the relationship of these insights to other aspects of attribution theory can be shown.

1. Logical Model of Attributions

Jaspars and his colleagues developed what they called the logical model of attributions (Jaspars et al., 1983), which was based on a restatement of Kelley's (1973) covariation theory. The three kinds of covariation information were treated as logical propositions that showed whether or not a particular agent (person, stimulus, or circumstance) is a necessary or sufficient condition for the occurrence of the event in question. For example, Jaspars and his colleagues proposed that low consensus (the event does not occur in the presence of other actors) indicates that the event does not generalize over actors and the focal actor is therefore a necessary (and sufficient) condition for the occurrence of the event. The focal actor is therefore likely to be named as the cause of the event. This kind of logic was developed for each of the eight cells shown in Table I of the present article, and predictions of attributions were made. This approach, based on a very clear analysis of Kelley's (1973) ideas, has considerable empirical support (Hewstone & Jaspars, 1983; Hilton & Jaspars, 1987; Jaspars, 1983). Jaspars (1983) noted, however, that there are two important weaknesses. The first is that, although the model usually predicts the most frequent attribution made for each of the eight cells, observers make many attributions besides the modal ones. But this criticism also applies to most of the other theories that attempt to make predictions for the eight cells in Table I, so it cannot be held specifically against the logical model. It was shown earlier, however, that PEAT provides some improvement on this problem. A second weakness is that for the cell with high consensus, low distinctiveness and high consistency (Cell 4 in Table I), the logical model predicts that no attributions will occur. Yet observers make attributions in predictable patterns for this cell. Hilton and Slugoski (1986) also had problems dealing with this cell theoretically.

PEAT gives some insight into the problem with Cell 4. The logical model used a dichotomous interpretation of covariation information and this seriously restricted its predictive accuracy. For instance, the terms necessary and sufficient were used in the strict sense that the event always occurs in the presence of the agent and never occurs in its absence. This tendency to dichotomize is shared by other theorists as well. Kelley (1973) and McArthur (1972) treat covariation information as either high or low. Although it can be argued that this artificiality is used for illustrative purposes only, and that the principles thus described also apply to the intermediate cases, it can happen that the dichotomous conceptualization of variables truly restricts a theory. This is seen in the case of the high-consensus, low-distinctiveness, and high-consistency cell (cell 4), which Jaspars (1983) cites as a particularly difficult one for logical theory. Because the logical model does not allow any deviations from the strict logic of necessary and sufficient causes and the clear categorizations that go with them, the logical model predicts no attributions in this cell. This is because all agents and combinations of agents are, logically speaking, sufficient causes of the event. This prediction of no attributions was not borne out empirically. PEAT attempts to deal with this problem by using probabilities that allow for all degrees of intermediate cases. It thus predicts a variety of attributions for Cell 4 that are supported by the data in Hilton and Slugoski (1986), Jaspars (1983), and McArthur (1972).

A second weakness of the logical model is its use of a contrast-based interpretation of covariation information. For example, the logical model states that low consensus means that the event does not generalize over actors and that the focal actor is therefore a necessary and sufficient cause of the event. But this interpretation is not possible unless one assumes that the event never occurs in the absence of the focal actor and always occurs in his or her presence. But this is an assumption about enduring characteristics of the actor that is not given directly in low-consensus information. Low consensus says only that *on this occasion* the event occurred in the presence of the actor and that the event does not usually occur in the presence of other actors. The general problems of the contrast-based interpretation are more fully discussed above. Again, this is a weakness that the logical model shares with several other theories.

2. *Probabilities in Attribution*

Jaspars and his colleagues (Jaspars *et al.*, 1983) twice raised the possibility of using probabilities to express covariation information, but in both cases they did not take the idea very far. One reason for this may be that they translated covariation information into probabilities in a way different from that of PEAT. For instance, in PEAT, consensus has to do with p(event/entity), while in Jaspars' version, it is p(event/entity *and* circumstances). The implications of these alternate expressions of covariation information might bear theoretical fruit if they were carefully explored.

3. *Subjective Scaling Model*

In addition to the logical model of attributions, Jaspars (1983) proposed what he called a subjective scaling model. As an explanatory example, Jaspars (1983) said that when a person succeeds at a task, it shows that the person's ability is at least equal to the ability required for successful completion of the task. Thus the person dominates the task. Coupled with this explanation, high consensus would mean that all people dominate the task, and low consensus would mean that only the focal person dominates the task. All three kinds of covariation information could be expressed as dominance relationships, and those dominance relationships can be used to make attributions. Jaspars (1983) uses a graph to show the dominance relationships.

This idea that dominance relationships between agents plays a role in the attribution process has a parallel in PEAT. In Proposition 11, the relative strength of inhibitors and facilitators are discussed. For example, the disposition of fishing ability must be of sufficient facilitative force to overcome the inhibitory effects of the poor fishing creek. In PEAT, the relative dominance of these agents is expressed with probabilities. Thus, Jaspars (1983) independently developed an idea found in PEAT.

4. Social Dimensions of Attribution

Hewstone and Jaspars (1984) have developed some ideas on the social dimensions of attribution. They decry the neglect of the role that social factors play in attributions and present theory and data in an attempt to mount a general understanding of these factors. They point out four important social dimensions of attributions: Observers categorize others and are members of social categories themselves; the social context in which an attribution is made influences that attribution; social cognitions are systems of beliefs shared by, and jointly constructed by, groups of people; and most of the acts about which observers in the natural world must make attributions are social acts.

Although these are certainly important issues, pursuing them does not make irrelevant the insights provided by Kelley (1973), Jones and Davis (1965), Jones and McGillis (1976), Hilton and Slugoski (1986), the subjective scaling model (Jaspars, 1983), and PEAT. The activities whereby individuals process information inside their own heads in order to develop attributions are something worth understanding in their own right, as are the social processes that influence these individual cognitive processes.

Overall, it seems that PEAT is quite compatible with the work of Jaspars and his colleagues. In addition, PEAT helps us understand some of the weaknesses of Jaspars's (1983) logical model and of the attempts by Jaspars and his colleagues (Jaspars *et al.*, 1983) to use probabilities to understand attributions. PEAT is very compatible with Jaspars's (1983) ideas about how dominance relationships play a role in attributions. Finally, PEAT, like many other attribution theories, is complementary to Hewstone and Jaspars's (1984) ideas about the social dimensions of attributions.

B. REEDER AND BREWER

Reeder and Brewer (1979) have developed a theory that is also compatible with PEAT. The primary focus of Reeder and Brewer (1979) is situations in which attributions act in asymmetrical ways. For example, people of high ability are seen as capable of behaviors that require high ability or low ability, while people of low ability are seen as capable of low-ability behaviors but not of high-ability behaviors. Reeder and Brewer (1979) explain this kind of phenomenon by proposing that observers apply particular kinds of schemas when making attributions. They suggest that these schemas are based on observers' tendency to organize behaviors and dispositions along parallel continua so that for each point on the behavior continuum, there is a corresponding point on the disposition continuum. When behaviors are seen, observers will place them on their behavior continua, and the dispositions that occur at the corresponding points on their disposition continua will be inferred to apply to the actor. For any given point on a disposition continuum, however, there will usually be several points on the behavior continuum that correspond to it. So a range of behaviors can be indicative any given disposition. Further, a single behavior might not be unambiguously diagnostic. For example, the behavior of being very friendly might indicate either the disposition "friendly" or the disposition "manipulative." Reeder and Brewer (1979) represent these continua in a figure and use straight lines to represent the range of behaviors associated with a disposition.

These ranges of behavior discussed by Reeder and Brewer can also be represented as probabilities, and thus PEAT can be applied. Observers can be assumed to believe that if a given disposition is present, the probabilities of certain behaviors are at certain values. For example, if someone has the disposition honest, the probability of that person stealing a car is very low, while the probability of that person returning a found wallet is very high. The correspondence between these statements and the PEAT definition of a disposition, that is, p(event/actor), is clear. One might even go so far as to suggest that the range of behavior probabilities for a given disposition can be represented by a normal curve. If this step is taken, it becomes possible to represent the process of inferring dispositions by using signal detection theory (Swets, 1974). Given that a behavioral event has occurred, what is the probability that it represents disposition A, disposition B, or whatever disposition?

Reeder and Brewer (1979) developed a concept of schema that can also be represented using probabilities. These schemas are refinements of their ideas about disposition and behavior continua. For example, their partially restrictive schema is symmetrical about some modal behavior. This might be represented by the symmetrical normal distribution. Their hierarchically restrictive schema, which is used to explain those cases in which attributions are made in an asymmetrical way, could be represented by a skewed distribution. Such probability distributions would fit very nicely with the earlier proposal to apply signal detection theory in this theoretical framework.

This brief description has shown that the essential ideas in Reeder and Brewer's (1979) study can be linked to the probabilities of PEAT. Some speculations for further theoretical development were also proposed.

C. BAYES' THEOREM AND ATTRIBUTION

Ajzen and Fishbein (1975, 1983) have developed a probability model of the attribution process that uses Bayes' theorem and, when compared to PEAT, brings to the fore some interesting theoretical issues. It is beyond the scope of the present paper to develop in detail any of the issues that can be raised by looking strictly at the mathematical nature of probabilities. However, the role of belief revision in attribution will be discussed.

A fundamental assumption of Ajzen and Fishbein (1983) is that the process of making attributions is equivalent to the process of revising beliefs given that new information has been obtained. Bayes' theorem is a mathematical expression for describing how people's beliefs *should* change once that they have been given some new information. Since all of the components of Bayes' theorem are stated as probabilities, the process of making attributions is a process of using probabilities. This idea is quite powerful as is shown by their application of it to Kelley's (1973) theory, Jones and Davis's (1965) theory, and a number of other attribution phenomena.

Without using probabilities, PEAT does give some insight into Ajzen and Fishbein's (1975, 1983) basic assumption that causal attribution corresponds to a revision in belief about the actor. PEAT shows that in some circumstances this is true, and in others it is not, but, interestingly, Bayes' theorem only applies in those cases in which attribution is not equivalent to revision.

Ajzen and Fishbein's (1975, 1983) statement that attribution equals revision is based on an elegant fusion of their own analysis and some statements made by Jones and Davis (1965). In their own analysis, Ajzen and Fishbein show in a very convincing fashion that Kelley's (1973) concepts of consensus, distinctiveness, and consistency can be expressed as likelihood ratios and that attributions can be predicted using likelihood ratios. They go on to show that there is a mathematical relationship between the likelihood ratio and the amount of belief revision that occurs when Bayes' theorem is applied. This ties in neatly with Jones and Davis's (1965) statements that belief revision occurs during the process of attribution.

PEAT states that belief revision is a necessary part of attribution only under certain conditions, namely, when observers are operating under Propositions 11 and 12. Under these conditions, observers are unable to explain an event using the information they had at the time of the event. In order to provide an explanation, they must either attribute a new characteristic to an agent (Proposition 11) or alter a previously held belief about an agent (Proposition 12). However, Propositions 11 and 12 also showed that the characteristics inferred during these processes are quite different from those originally believed by the observers. The type and magnitude of the newly inferred characteristics are determined by the type and magnitude of available inhibitors. By contrast, in the Ajzen and Fishbein (1975, 1983) model the size of the changes are incremental, as dictated by Bayes' theorem. The Ajzen and Fishbein model does not easily allow the strength of the available inhibitors to play a role. So, in PEAT, Ajzen and Fishbein's idea that belief revisions are necessary for attributions applies only under certain circumstances, but the magnitudes of those revisions, as predicted by Bayes' theorem, will usually be underestimates.

Contrary to Ajzen and Fishbein (1975, 1983), PEAT proposes that under some circumstances belief revision is not essential to causal attribution. Under Proposition 10, observers' prior beliefs are fully capable of explaining the event and so no revisions of beliefs are necessary. Observers scan their available probabilities and find an agent whose known characteristics are capable of causing the event in question. No revision in belief about the characteristics of that agent are necessary in order to provide a causal explanation. But, although a revision is not necessary in order to provide a causal explanation, a revision will probably occur. The event has just occurred in the presence of the available agents and so the probabilities of the event, given each of the agents, will be revised upward in order to reflect this new bit of information. This one bit of information will usually make a small revision in probabilities, and it is not unreasonable to suggest that this revision will follow the predictions of Bayes' theorem. PEAT therefore suggests an interesting state of affairs. In some cases, belief revision is necessary for causal attributions to occur. For such cases, the belief revisions will not be of the magnitude predicted by Bayes' theorem. In other cases, belief revisions are unnecessary for causal attributions. For such cases, the revisions that do occur probably can be predicted by Bayes' theorem.

In Summary, the relationship between PEAT and Ajzen and Fishbein's (1975, 1983) model is as follows: PEAT is capable of explaining the phenomena that Ajzen and Fishbein explain. PEAT also helps us understand some of the boundary conditions of Ajzen and Fishbein's fundamental assumption that attribution requires belief revision. Very careful analysis using probabilities will be necessary to work out the detailed correspondences between the two models. The detailed work may further our understanding of attributions but is beyond the scope of the present article.

D. ABNORMAL CONDITIONS FOCUS MODEL

Hilton and his colleagues (Hilton, 1989; Hilton & Jaspars, 1987; Hilton & Knibbs, 1988; Hilton & Slugoski, 1986) have been exploring and testing a number of alternatives to covariation theory as models for attribution. This exploration has been rich in the generation of ideas and in the discussion of attributions in real world settings. Among the alternatives explored is Hilton and Slugoski's (1986) abnormal conditions focus model. This provides an insightful theoretical analysis that can be usefully linked to PEAT. PEAT and the abnormal conditions focus model agree on a number of points, but PEAT suggests some boundary conditions for the Hilton and Slugoski model.

Hilton and Slugoski's (1986) greatest contribution is their convincing argument that the general knowledge and beliefs about the world, which observers bring to the attribution process, should be seriously studied. They focus primarily on the idea that scripted behaviors (Schank & Abelson, 1977) will elicit different kinds of attributions than nonscripted behaviors. The idea that observers' own knowledge influences attributions is not new, but Hilton and Slugoski do make an original and convincing advocacy. There are two related points here. The first is that this world knowledge of observers can contaminate attribution experiments. In a great many attribution studies, particularly those concerned with theory, experimenters present observers with information that they believe manipulates variables of interest. If the experiment does not turn out as predicted, experimenters cannot tell if these unexpected results are owing to a fault in the theory or to observers ignoring or modifying the information provided. Attribution studies should have some sort of pretesting to determine observers' original beliefs. The second point is that observers use their world knowledge when they make attributions in the real world (as opposed to the psychology lab). This world knowledge is therefore a valid object of study in its own right and Hilton and Slugoski's (1986) work therefore addresses an important issue.

Another issue that Hilton and Slugoski (1986) bring to the fore is that of multiple plausible causes. Their theory attempts to explain how observers choose one cause as *the* cause among the many plausible ones available in real-life situations. Although PEAT provides a parsimonious explanation (choose the strongest available facilitator, see Proposition 10), the Hilton and Slugoski (1986) discussion of this is a rich and insightful contribution that should lead to future research.

Hilton and Slugoski (1986) make a strong case for, and attempt to provide, improved response formats for collecting data in attribution research. As will be seen below, their particular version has problems of its own, but it is very definitely a step in the right direction primarily because it provides observers with more flexibility in how they can respond.

Hilton and Slugoski (1986) use some ideas from the prediction-based model of covariation, but they never completely abandon the contrast-based model. For example, their adherence to the contrast-based explanation is clearly shown in their discussion of consensus: "Specifically, it is suggested that low consensus information (hardly anyone else does it), throws the target person into focus as abnormal" (Hilton & Slugoski, 1986, p. 77). But the target person is abnormal only if the abnormal behavior shown on this occasion is characteristic of the target persons' enduring behavioral repertoire. As explained above, this kind of information is not given directly by consensus. But Hilton and Slugoski (1986, p. 78) say that low-consensus information provides information about the target person and also about the entity. Their discussion shows that they are aware of the point made by PEAT that consensus gives information about the entity but have not been able to integrate it with the old idea that consensus information tells the observer something important about enduring characteristics of the actor. Given this, their theoretical ideas (Hilton & Slugoski, 1986, p. 78) are quite cumbersome, with special cases for low and high consensus and for low and high distinctiveness. PEAT, by developing the prediction-based model, provides a more elegant analysis.

Hilton and Slugoski (1986) show a bias toward the consideration of unusual events. This bias is, perhaps, owing to the fact that they were strongly influenced by the work of Hart and Honore (1959), who were primarily interested in causal attributions in legal situations. Given that for most people events receiving legal attention (robberies, fraud, murder, etc.) are unusual, this bias is understandable. But it does bias Hilton and Slugoski (1986) to base their analysis upon abnormal events such as railway crashes and script-deviant behaviors. As a consequence, they are moved to conclude that "a scripted action such as, 'Mary bought something on her visit to the supermarket' should produce no contrastive attention at all, because there is no abnormal condition to focus on" (Hilton & Slugoski, 1986, p. 85). This suggestion that observers cannot or will not make attributions about scripted events is rather strong when one considers how many everyday behaviors, which we explain to ourselves, are scripted. This exclusion of so much everyday behavior from consideration by Hilton and Slugoski (1986) is surprising given that they also emphasize the virtue of considering the everyday knowledge of observers in attribution theory.

This bias toward abnormal cases weakens Hilton and Slugoski's (1986) proposed response format for subjects in attribution studies. Their primary contribution in this respect is that they have increased the number of response categories. But they include the word "special" in every category. Observers are asked if it was something special about the stimulus, the person, or the circumstances that caused the event. However, excluding causal agents that are not special is unwise given the number of daily events caused by nonspecial agents. This weakness is exacerbated by Hilton and Slugoski's (1986) failure to make a distinction between causal attributions and characteristic attributions. When an observer is asked if the event was caused by something special about the agent, the observer must decide two things. First, "Was the event caused by the agent?" Second, "Was the characteristic of the agent, which led to the action, special, or was it nonspecial?" In their second empirical study (data are in Hilton & Slugoski, 1986, in Table 5, p. 87), the results of having to answer these two questions simultaneously can be seen. In the script-deviation case, not tipping, observers conclude that something special is going on. (Why else would there be the script deviation?) They are thus able to attribute cause to something special about the agent. In the case of the scripted action, however, there is a problem. The actor has gone to the supermarket and bought something. Observers, seeing nothing special here, will shy away from indicating that an agent caused the act and that the responsible characteristic of that agent is special (as the response wording requires). Observers will prefer to use what Hilton and Slugoski (1986) call the null option here because they want to avoid saying that it was a special characteristic of the agent that caused the event. Hilton and Slugoski (1986) are saying that observers choose the null option because they want to avoid making a causal attribution to any of the agents. This conflict could be resolved with an empirical study. PEAT would predict that given the supermarket vignette—but response categories without the word "special"—observers will provide causal attributions very similar to those found in the tipping vignette. I find nothing surprising about a person going to the supermarket and buying something, but I would be surprised to find that observers are unable to make causal attributions about it.

In summary, Hilton and Slugoski (1986) provide some valuable insights, but, within the context of PEAT, some of their limitations become apparent. Their advocacy of the study of observers' real-world knowledge, and of situations involving multiple plausible causes that use improved response formats, is timely and well mounted. However, their partial retention of the contrast-based interpretation of covariation information and their emphasis on unusual events put limitations on their studies.

VII. Conclusions

This paper has described a core model of attribution processes, PEAT, stated in probabilities. This model provides a vehicle for integrating other attribution theories, for clarifying many of the concepts of attribution theory, and for generating empirical research.

Two mechanisms are primarily responsible for the ability of PEAT to integrate so much of attribution theory. First, the demonstration that most of the basic concepts of attribution theory can be stated in probabilities allowed disparate vocabularies to be placed on a common basis. It became clear that, in many cases, the different theories, which superficially seemed to be discussing different things, were actually discussing the same things. Second, PEAT provides an overall conceptual scheme that links the various individual concepts. For example, the idea that observers prefer to explain in terms of prior beliefs gives a rationale for the relationship between Propositions 10 and 11, and therefore between Kelley's theories and CIT. This integration has shown that the traditionally separate theories need no longer be treated as separate. It also showed that there are virtually no contradictions between the theories. Past attempts at integration typically showed apparent contradictions. Further, PEAT, by its integration, does not invalidate the ideas contained in the other theories. It links and clarifies them but also acknowledges their validity.

PEAT has been able to provide some improvement in the clarity of the concepts used in attribution theory because it has reduced those concepts to the precise vocabulary of probabilities. The most important such clarification was the distinction between contrast-based and prediction-based definitions of covariation information. This insight oiled the integration of the theories and was very useful for clarifying why some past attempts at integration were not taken very far. It also showed limitations of past attempts to express attribution theory as probabilities. A second clarification was the distinction, expressed in probabilities, between causal and characteristic attributions. The precise language of probabilities allowed the development of clearer ideas about such things as augmentation and how causal and characteristic attributions interact intimately, but with discernible independence.

PEAT is also promising as a generator of empirical research. Some of that research may arise from its comments on other theories. For example, PEAT states that when observers are operating under CIT, they will spontaneously make assumptions about consistency even though CIT has no theoretical role for consistency. This suggestion could be empirically checked. Some of the research can arise from the propositions of PEAT by itself, without reference to other theories. For example, PEAT, by expressing its propositions in terms of agents rather than in terms of actors or entities, suggests that attributions to the two kinds of agents follow the same rules. Therefore, if there is a contrast effect in attributions made to actors, there should also be a contrast effect in attributions made to entities. This possibility is empirically testable.

Further theoretical work needs to be done to extend the basics of PEAT described here into new areas. This could include the analysis of other theories, the development of completely new concepts, or further refinement of what is presented here. PEAT promises to generate both theoretical and empirical work.

Acknowledgments

I thank Mark Zanna, John Arrowood, Martin Evans, and anonymous reviewers for their comments on earlier versions of this article.

References

Ajzen, I., & Fishbein, M. (1975). A Bayesian analysis of attribution processes. *Psychological Bulletin,* **82,** 261–277.
Ajzen, I., & Fishbein, M. (1983). Relevance and availability in the attribution process. In J. Jaspars, F. D. Fincham, & M. Hewstone (Eds.), *Attribution theory and research: Conceptual, developmental and social dimensions.* Orlando, FL: Academic Press.
Bell, L. G., Wicklund, R. A., Manko, G., & Larkin, C. (1976). When unexpected behaviour is attributed to the environment. *Journal of Research in Personality,* **10,** 316–327.
Budesur, D. V., & Wollsten, T. S. (1985). Consistency in interpretation of probabilistic phrases. *Organizational Behavior and Human Decision Processes,* **36,** 391–405.
Einhorn, H. J., & Hogarth, R. M. (1985). Ambiguity and uncertainty in probabilistic inference. *Psychological Review,* **92,** 433–461.
Einhorn, H. J., & Hogarth, R. M. (1986). Judging probable cause. *Psychological Bulletin,* **99,** 3–19.
Fischoff, B., & Bar-Hillel, M. (1984). Focusing techniques: A shortcut to improving probability judgments. *Organizational Behavior and Human Performance,* **34,** 175–194.
Fiske, S. T., Neuberg, S. L., Beattie, A. E., & Milberg, S. J. (1987). Category-based and attribute-based reactions to others: Some informational conditions of stereotyping and individual processes. *Journal of Experimental Social Psychology,* **23,** 399–427.
Hansen, R. D., & Hull, C. A. (1985). Discounting and augmenting facilitative and inhibitory forces: The winner takes almost all. *Journal of Personality and Social Psychology,* **49,** 1482–1493.
Hart, H. L. H., & Honore, A. M. (1959). *Causation and the law.* Oxford: Clarendon Press.
Harvey, J. H., & Weary, G. (1984). Current issues in attribution theory and research. *Annual Review of Psychology,* **35,** 427–459.
Heider, F. (1958). *The psychology of interpersonal relations.* New York: Wiley.
Hewstone, M., & Jaspars, J. (1983). A re-examination of the roles of consensus, consistency, and distinctiveness: Kelley's cube revisited. *British Journal of Social Psychology,* **22,** 41–50.
Hewstone, M., & Jaspars, J. M. F. (1984). Social dimensions of attribution. In H. Tajfel (Ed.), *The social dimension: European developments in social psychology* (Vol. 2.). London: Cambridge University Press.
Hewstone, M., & Jaspars, J. M. F. (1987). Covariation and causal attribution: A logical model of the intuitive analysis of variance. *Journal of Personality and Social Psychology,* **53,** 663–672.
Hilton, D. J. (1989). Logic and causal attribution. In D. J. Hilton (Ed.), *Contemporary science and natural explanation: Commonsense conceptions of causality.* Brighton, England: Harvester Press, in press.
Hilton, D. J., & Jaspars, J. M. F. (1987). The explanation of occurrences and non-occurrences: A test of the inductive logic model of causal attribution. *British Journal of Social Psychology,* **26,** 189–201.

Hilton, D. J., & Knibbs, C. S. (1988). The knowledge-structure and inductivist strategies in causal attribution: A direct comparison. *European Journal of Social Psychology*, **18**, 79–92.

Hilton, D. J., & Slugoski, B. R. (1986). Knowledge-based causal attribution: The abnormal conditions focus model. *Psychological Review*, **93**, 75–88.

Hinsz, V. B., Tindale, R. S., Nagao, D. H., Davis, J. H., & Robertson, B. A. (1988). The influence of the accuracy of individuating information on the use of base rate information in probability judgment. *Journal of Experimental Social Psychology*, **24**, 127–145.

Howard, J. A. (1985). Further appraisal of correspondent inference theory. *Personality and Social Psychology Bulletin*, **11**, 467–477.

Jaspars, J. M. F. (1983). The process of causal attribution in common sense. In M. Hewstone (Ed.), *Attribution theory*. Oxford: Blackwell.

Jaspars, J. M. F., Hewstone, M., & Fincham, F. D. (1983). Attribution theory and research: The state of the art. In J. M. F. Jaspars, F. D. Fincham, & M. Hewstone (Eds.), *Attribution theory and research: Conceptual, developmental and social dimensions*. New York: Academic Press.

Jones, E. E., & Berglas, S. (1976). A recency effect in attitude attributions. *Journal of Personality*, **44**, 433–448.

Jones, E. E., & Davis, K. E. (1965). From acts to dispositions. The attribution process in person perception. In L. Berkowitz (Ed.), *Advances in experimental social psychology* (Vol. 2). New York: Academic Press.

Jones, E. E., Davis, K. E., & Gergen, K. J. (1961). Role playing variations and their information value for person perception. *Journal of Abnormal and Social Psychology*, **63**, 302–310.

Jones, E. E., & Harris, V. A. (1967). The attribution of attitudes. *Journal of Experimental Social Psychology*, **3**, 1–24.

Jones, E. E., & McGillis, D. (1976). Correspondent inferences and the attribution cube: A comparative reappraisal. In J. H. Harvey, W. Ickes, and R. F. Kidd (Eds.), *New directions in attribution research* (Vol. 1). Hillsdale, NJ: Erlbaum.

Jones, E. E., Worchel, S., Goethals, G. R., & Grumet, J. F. (1971). Prior expectancy and behavioral extremity as determinants of attitude attribution. *Journal of Experimental Social Psychology*, **7**, 59–80.

Kahneman, D., & Tversky, A. (1973). On the psychology of prediction. *Psychological Review*, **80**, 237–251.

Kassin, S. M. (1979). Consensus information, prediction, and causal attribution: A review of the literature and issues: *Journal of Personality and Social Psychology*, **37**, 1966–1981.

Kelley, H. H. (1973). The process of causal attribution. *American Psychologist*, **28**, 107–128.

Kelley, H. H., & Michela, J. L. (1980). Attribution theory and research. *Annual Review of Psychology*, **31**, 457–501.

Kruglanski, A. W. (1980). Lay epistemologic process and contents. *Psychological Review*, **87**, 70–87.

Kruglanski, A. W., Friedland, N., & Farkash, E. (1984). Lay persons' sensitivity to statistical information: The case of high perceived applicability. *Journal of Personality and Social Psychology*, **46**, 503–518.

McArthur, L. A. (1972). The how and what of why: Some determinants and consequences of causal attributions. *Journal of Personality and Social Psychology*, **22**, 171–193.

McGillis, D. A. (1974). *A correspondent inference theory analysis of attitude attribution*. Unpublished doctoral dissertation, Duke University, Durham, NC.

Rasinski, K. A., Crocker, J., & Hastie, R. (1985). Another look at sex stereo-types and social judgments: An analysis of the social perceiver's use of subjective probabilities. *Journal of Personality and Social Psychology*, **49**, 317–326.

Reeder, G. D., & Brewer, M. B. (1979). A schematic model of dispositional attribution in interpersonal perception. *Psychological Review*, **86**, 61–79.

Schank, R. C., & Abelson, R. P. (1977). *Scripts, plans, goals and understanding: An enquiry into human knowledge structures.* Hillsdale, NJ: Erlbaum.

Schutte, N. S., Kenrick, D. T., & Sadalla, E. K. (1985). The search for predictable settings: Situational prototypes, constraint, and behavioral variation. *Journal of Personality and Social Psychology,* **49,** 121–128.

Slovic, P., Fischhoff, B., & Lichtenstein, S. (1977). Behavioral decision theory. *Annual Review of Psychology,* **28,** 1–39.

Solomon, I., Ariyo, A., & Tomassini, L. A. (1985). Contextual effects on the calibration of probabilistic judgments. *Journal of Applied Psychology,* **70,** 528–532.

Swets, J. A. (1974). *Signal detection theory and psychophysics.* Huntington, NY: R.E. Krieger.

Tversky, A., & Kahneman, D. (1980). Causal schemas in judgments under uncertainty. In M. Fishbein (Ed.), *Progress in social psychology* (Vol. 1). Hillsdale, NJ: Erlbaum.

Wagenaar, W. A., & Keren, G. B. (1985). Calibration of probability assessments by professional blackjack dealers, statistical experts, and lay people. *Organizational Behavior and Human Decision Processes,* **36,** 406–416.

Weber, R., & Crocker, J. (1983). Cognitive processes in the revision of stereotypic beliefs. *Journal of Personality and Social Psychology,* **45,** 961–977.

Wells, G. L., & Ronis, D. L. (1982). Discounting and augmentation: Is there something special about the number of causes? *Personality and Social Psychology Bulletin,* **8,** 566–572.

READING PEOPLE'S MINDS: A TRANSFORMATION RULE MODEL FOR PREDICTING OTHERS' THOUGHTS AND FEELINGS

Rachel Karniol

> It hurts Jack
> to think
> that Jill thinks he is hurting her
> by (him) being hurt
> to think
> that she thinks he is hurting her . . .
>   (R.D. Laing, *Knots*)

I. Predicting Others' Psychological Experiences

A. INTRODUCTION

As the above excerpt from Laing illustrates, we often try to read other people's minds to understand their thoughts and feelings. Although such attempts may be relatively common in close relationships, they are not unique to them and may occur in contexts as varied as job interviews, reading novels, and blind dates. To give a somewhat mundane example, two male friends are waiting at a bar for a female whom one of them knows well and the other is about to meet for the first time. The former is curious about how his friend will react to meeting her. How can he predict what his friend might think? The following are some possible predictions about his friend's likely reactions in this context: "He'll probably think she's just another bleached blond," "He'll think she looks just like his former girlfriend," "He'll think about how his girlfriend ditched him," and "He'll fall for her blue eyes." How do people make such predictions about others' likely thoughts and feelings? Current approaches to social cognition do not address such issues.

Although social cognition encompasses both the way we characterize or make attributions about other people's stable dispositions and the way we draw inferences about their covert, inner psychological experiences, it is the former process that has dominated the field of social cognition (e.g., Cantor & Mischel, 1979; Fiske & Taylor, 1984; Hastie et al., 1981; Schneider, 1973; Tagiuri & Petrullo, 1958). Much less attention has been given to the second aspect of social cognition, which is the focus of the current article—the drawing of inferences regarding the covert experiences of others—probably because such experiences are transitory or episodic (Warr & Knapper, 1968) and are therefore accorded less importance than dispositional characteristics.

There are two types of inferences individuals can draw about the episodic experiences of others, *postdictive* and *predictive*.[1] Postdictive inferences arise after a given behavior is observed. They are concerned with the processes that may have motivated or caused that behavior and constitute explanations for past events (e.g., "Why did he do that?"). Because of the interest in explanations that reflect the stable dispositions of targets, social psychology in general, and attribution theory (Kelley, 1967, 1972) in particular, have focused almost exclusively on postdictive inferences regarding the possible dispositional reasons for others' prior actions.

The predictive inference process that is the focus of this article concerns the episodic experiences that individuals are likely to have in a given setting; such inferences have the status of predictions about ongoing or future events (e.g., "What will he think or feel when he meets her?"). Making predictions about such episodic psychological experiences is important since, as Heider (1958) noted, "a person reacts to what he thinks the other person is perceiving, feeling, and thinking, in addition to what the other person may be doing" (p. 1). Yet predictive inferences regarding others' likely affective reactions or cognitions have rarely been examined empirically, nor have they been the focus of much theoretical attention in social psychology (for an exception, see Sarbin, 1954).

In the area of developmental psychology, predictive inferences have been extensively examined both theoretically and empirically (for reviews see Shantz, 1975, 1983). Attention to this issue was stimulated by Piaget's (1965) contention that predictive ability undergoes a transition with the child's entry into the peer group. Within this context, three types of predictive inferences about others' episodic experiences have been discussed under the rubric of role taking: the prediction of others' visual experiences, the prediction of their affective experiences, and the prediction of their cognitions in a given setting. In all three domains, development is presumed to proceed from egocentric to nonegocentric functioning, where egocentrism is the Piagetian term for children's inability to differentiate their perspective from that of others. The major focus of attention in this realm has been the relation between these three types of predictive ability

---

[1] For a similar distinction in artificial intelligence, see Charniak and McDermott (1985) who call these two types of inferences abductive projection and projection, respectively.

and the age at which each matures (see Chandler, 1976; Shantz, 1975, 1983, for reviews). There has been little attempt within developmental psychology to integrate this body of research formally within a theoretical framework that builds on cognitive psychological principles (for an exception see Higgins, 1981, to be discussed later). In this article, we present a model that builds on current theorizing in cognitive psychology and we demonstrate its relevance for both social and developmental psychology.

To overview the model, we distinguish between procedural and declarative knowledge, where the former represents general rules for making predictions about others' thoughts and feelings, and the latter represents the content with which specific predictions are made. First, we identify the rules that are used for making predictions about others' likely thoughts and feelings. Next, we specify the types of declarative knowledge that are employed for making specific predictions. In the context of declarative knowledge, we differentiate between prototypical or general knowledge structures and structures that reflect deviations from prototypical knowledge. We then turn to the implications of this differentiation for the use of self-knowledge, which in our model is not ordinarily used for making predictions about others, and we discuss false consensus effects from this perspective. Last, we discuss situational influences and individual differences in relation to the model. Before doing so, we summarize extant approaches to how such predictive inferences are made.

B. EXTANT APPROACHES

In this section, we outline the various approaches that have specified how we predict what another person's psychological experiences might be. The most common view of how we make predictions about others' thoughts and feelings is that we do so by putting ourselves analogically into the other's place. For instance, Adam Smith (1759) contended that we only know about others' inner experiences by conceiving what we ourselves would feel in similar situations. More recently, Schutz (1964) posited that "I am able to understand other people's acts only if I can imagine that I myself would perform analogous acts if I were in the same situation directed by the same *because motives* or oriented by the same *in order to motives*" (p. 13). Similar statements about the importance of one's own phenomenological experience in the understanding of other persons have been made by many others (e.g., Adams, 1928; Halpern, 1955; Stewart, 1956; Stotland & Canon, 1972; Wolf & Murray, 1937).

The most elaborate version of this analogical viewpoint has been presented by Abel (1948, 1970) in his discussion of the operation of Verstehn. Abel suggests that when Verstehn is applied to make predictions about reactions to events, we imagine what emotion or reaction would have been aroused in us by the same situation. That is, I predict some reaction "which I recall having felt—or imagine that I might feel—under similar circumstances" (Abel, 1948, p. 215). Abel contends that to engage in this process, we depend on our ability to describe a situation by categorizing it and evoking a personal experience that fits into that category. Predictions are therefore generalizations of direct personal experience that are derived from introspection and self-observation. Franz Alexander (1935) similarly contended that such generalizations appear to be self-evident because they are derived from daily introspective experiences as we witness the emotional sequence in ourselves. From this point of view, role taking is an analogical or "as if" activity (Sarbin, 1954) in which the individual engages in the hypothetical act of imagining the self in the other's place and attempts to predict what thoughts and feelings the self would experience in the other's place.

The status of analogical role taking as a means of predicting other's episodic psychological experiences has by no means gone unchallenged. According to Chandler (1976), if individuals make predictions about others by determining what they (or anyone else) might feel in the same situation, this constitutes projection. But Chandler argues that projection is the exact opposite of legitimate empathic understanding. Such understanding requires that individuals "through a kind of conceptual boot strapping operation, clear the boundaries of their own egocentric perspective and successfully transport themselves into the vantage of someone else" (Chandler, 1976, p. 110). Although the precise nature of this bootstrapping operation has not been made explicit, from this point of view, mature role taking cannot involve introspection about one's own likely experiences.

Higgins (1981) has similarly questioned the legitimacy of analogical role taking as a means of making predictions about others' thoughts and feelings. He differentiates between situational role taking (i.e., "What would I feel or think if I were in that situation?") and individual role taking (i.e., "What would I feel or think if I were that individual?"). Situational role taking is comparable to analogical role taking in that it requires only self-based introspective processes. In individual role taking, individuals have knowledge both about self and about the target, can distinguish between them, and must suppress self-knowledge (Higgins, 1981; Higgins & Bargh, 1987). Higgins suggests that while situational role taking represents egocentric or immature functioning, individual role taking represents mature social skills.

As important as the differentiation between situational and individual role taking may be, it appears to beg the question of how one predicts reactions to being in the other's situation (i.e., situational role taking) versus being in the other's skin (i.e., individual role taking). Is there a different search process for predicting how one would feel in any given setting than for predicting how one would feel if one were someone else in that setting? As long as the knowledge structures employed for individual versus situational role taking have not been elaborated, this question cannot be answered.

A third view of how individuals make predictions about others' psychological experiences has been presented by Flavell (1974). According to Flavell, predictions about other people's psychological experiences are not based on one's own recollected or imagined experiences but rather on knowledge structures of a general nature, that is, about how various sorts of people are likely to react internally and externally in various situations. In this view, predictions about others' psychological experiences require a synthesis of information from two sources: (1) the individual's knowledge of people and their behavior in various situations, including previous knowledge of the particular target and (2) perceptual input from the target's behavior and from cues in the immediate situation. Although they are not explicitly discussed, there actually seem to be three knowledge structures implicated in Flavell's model: knowledge about situations, knowledge about people, and knowledge about specific others. Making predictions requires the integration of information from these knowledge structures.

If, as Flavell suggests, role taking requires the individual to integrate information from these three knowledge sources, the role of self-knowledge seems problematic. Specifically, given that development is assumed to proceed from being egocentric to being nonegocentric, a knowledge structure that contains self-information must exist for making egocentric predictions. But why would there be a transition from relying on self-knowledge in making predictions about others' psychological experiences to suppressing self-knowledge when making such predictions? Why does self-knowledge prevent access to other knowledge structures about situations, about people, and about specific others? Flavell does not provide answers to these questions and there is no obvious explanation from current cognitive theorizing for the shift from self-knowledge to more general knowledge structures for making predictions about others' thoughts and feelings. Nonetheless, from this perspective as well, use of self-knowledge is considered an immature or egocentric mode of predicting others' thoughts and feelings.

C. CRITIQUE

We have presented the three major views of how predictions regarding others' thoughts and feelings are made.[2] The analogical role-taking view specifies that individuals need only recollect their own experiences in similar settings and

---

[2]Selman (1971, 1980) has outlined a model of perspective taking in which knowledge about people's intrinsic psychological characteristics and knowledge of how different individuals' points of view are related and coordinated undergo a stagelike progression. In this model, however, there is no explicit discussion of how predictions are made and the emphasis is on what Flavell (1977) has called the existence, rather than the inference, stage. Flavell's (1974) model of role taking involves four stages, in which the inference stage is analogous to the predictive process we are discussing. Flavell acknowledges that little is known about how this is done.

generalize from these recollections to the current situation of the target. The second view states that individuals must transport themselves in some unspecified manner out of their own skin into the perspective of the other and concomitantly suppress their own viewpoints. The third view states that general rather than self-based knowledge structures are used by mature role takers and that use of these general structures similarly requires suppression of structures relating to the self. Not only would there seem to be disagreement as to which of these processes is used to make predictions about others' psychological experiences but the disagreement extends to which of these processes represents an advance over the others. Moreover, while there is agreement that predictive ability develops, the nature of its development and the end point of development is contentious (cf. Higgins, 1981).

We think the debate in this area has not been resolved owing to conceptual confusion. Although role taking is occasionally discussed as only a method of gathering information (e.g., Turiel, 1978), in most contexts both the method of gathering information and the product of this method of gathering information are confounded and discussed as role taking (e.g., Flavell, 1977; Higgins, 1981; Selman, 1980). Such isomorphism between the process and its product precludes the possibility that the process may be present, but for various reasons its application yields inappropriate predictions. That is, it is implicitly assumed that once the ability to role take has developed, it *necessarily* yields only correct predictions (according to some experimenter-defined criterion).

Related to this confusion is the failure to draw the distinction between declarative and procedural knowledge (Ryle, 1949), which cognitive psychology has recently embraced (e.g., J. R. Anderson, 1983; Cantor & Kihlstrom, 1985). Declarative knowledge is "knowing that" and procedural knowledge is "knowing how." To illustrate this distinction, personality prototypes (Cantor & Mischel, 1979) represent declarative knowledge whereas the availability heuristic (Tversky & Kahneman, 1973) represents procedural knowledge. In our view, making predictions about other people's thoughts and feelings must involve procedural knowledge in the form of heuristics.[3] But procedural knowledge must be differentiated from the declarative knowledge structures that determine the content of specific predictions. Any model of role taking not only must explain the kind of procedural knowledge involved in making predictions about others' thoughts and feelings but also must specify the types of declarative knowledge that are used once the procedural knowledge required for making predictions is applied.

From this perspective, role taking involves knowing general procedures or rules for making predictions, applying these procedures appropriately, and, fi-

---

[3]Heuristics here mean principles or rules that contribute to a reduction of search time in problem solving (Newell, Shaw, & Simon, 1963).

nally, accessing declarative knowledge structures in order to make specific predictions. Failures in role taking may reflect inadequate procedural knowledge, inappropriate application of this procedural knowledge, or inappropriate use of the various types of declarative knowledge that determine the content of specific predictions. If in the assessment of role-taking ability accuracy of predictions is used as a criterion, it is not possible to identify the source of the problem. Moreover, from this point of view, role-taking tasks differ in which of these various functions they involve, and, consequently, one would expect little correlation in performance across role-taking tasks (cf. Rubin, 1973; Shantz, 1975). The model we present below elaborates how procedural and declarative knowledge are used to make predictions about others' thoughts and feelings.

Before presenting the model, we first turn to the issue of others' visual experiences, which is not explicitly part of our model although it has played a major role in developmental research (e.g., Flavell, Botkin, & Fry, 1968) and, as we elaborate below, must be assumed a priori in any model of role taking.

D. PREDICTING OTHERS' VISUAL EXPERIENCES

In most discussions of how predictions about others' episodic psychological experiences are made (e.g., Flavell, 1977; Hoffman, 1978; Selman, 1971, 1980), there has been an implicit, if not explicit, assumption that to predict what another person is feeling or thinking, the individual must be able to infer the other's visual perspective when it is different from one's own. This assumption regarding the divergent visual perspectives of the target and the observer would seem to be highly questionable.

In fact, it would seem that a necessary assumption guiding most human interaction and communication is that others' visual experiences match one's own. In this vein, Schutz (1962) argued that all communicative acts and interaction build on "the idealization of reciprocity of perspectives" (p. 315). In this idealization, we assume both that "I and my fellow man would have typically the same experience of the common world if we changed places" (p. 316) and that we both interpret the shared experience in the same way. Mead (1934) similarly argued for the "irrelevance of the difference of the different perspectives" (p. 89). A rose is a rose when viewed by each participant of an interaction, irrespective of his or her particular view of the rose. Individuals need to assume the matching of visual experiences. Only if individuals accept the assumption of the reciprocity of their own perspective and the perspective of the target of the prediction can they attempt to make predictions regarding the affective reactions or cognitions that the target might experience in any given setting. The reciprocity of perspectives, then, is viewed as the basis of successful communication and interaction.

What is the relevance of the assumed reciprocity of visual perspectives for the study of social cognition? The assumption of reciprocity is implicit in every study in which subjects who are exposed to a pictorial, televised, or verbally presented context are asked to infer the target's psychological experiences in that context. Subjects are clearly being asked to assume that they are exposed to the same relevant stimuli and events as the target and to make predictions on that basis. Hence, there is no a priori reason to assume that the ability to infer another's visual perspective when it is different from one's own would be a prerequisite for predicting others' cognitive or affective episodic experiences. For purposes of our model, we assume that the idealization of the reciprocity of perspectives holds, since otherwise predictions about others' likely affective reactions or cognitions cannot be made.

II. Procedural Knowledge

In a recent paper (Karniol, 1986), we described a model of how procedural knowledge is used to make predictions about other people's thoughts and feelings. The basis of this model is a heuristic that consists of a hierarchically ordered system of rules. These rules govern predictions about the psychological reactions that other people are likely to experience when certain stimulus conditions arise. The model is based on several postulates, which we briefly present below.

A. POSTULATES

Postulate 1: Observers assume that the target's psychological reactions are rule governed. To explain this postulate, we must first explain the notion of directed thinking (Berlyne, 1965). Directed thinking is characterized by a chain in which transformation rules are employed to link input to output. The transformation rules specify the way successive links in the thought chain are connected to each other. Irrespective of whether the target engages in directed thinking, the observer who attempts to predict the target person's psychological experiences must assume that such experiences are rule governed (cf. Pylyshyn, 1984). Unless reactions to stimuli and events are assumed to be rule governed, observers cannot attempt to predict others' psychological experiences. The above implies that there are transformation rules that are assumed by observers to connect the target's psychological reactions to his or her prior perceptions. The problem is that the transformation rules that account for the target's reactions are unknown to observers. Observers nonetheless assume that such transformation rules exist, in the same manner that a computer user assumes that a computer has transformation rules that allow it to perform calculations by which it provides an output given the user's input.

Postulate 2: Observers know a finite number of transformation rules and assume that these rules account for the target's psychological reactions. Because observers have no direct knowledge of the target's transformation rules, observers assume that the transformation rules they themselves know account for the link between the target's perceptions and psychological reactions. To present a mathematical analogy, if I only know the rules of addition and multiplication and I am asked to predict how someone would respond to the following query "2 (?) = 4," it is impossible for me to predict his or her use of the power function since for me this rule does not exist as a possibility. Similarly, observers can only use the transformation rules they know for making predictions about others' likely psychological reactions. Making predictions then requires observers to select a transformation rule from the finite number of transformation rules that they know. This selection process is independent of the target's own manner of relating perceptions to psychological experiences and depends only on the set of transformation rules that observers themselves know.

Postulate 3: The transformation rules exist and are independent of input stimuli. This postulate specifies that rules are not dependent on declarative knowledge structures, although in the application of any given rule the observer uses declarative knowledge. To give an analogy, the rules of addition and subtraction are independent of any particular problem that needs to be solved in mathematics. That is, transformation rules represent procedural knowledge that is independent of any declarative knowledge to which they must be applied. The specific situation to which the rules are applied will determine only the selection of the transformation rule that is deemed most appropriate for making a prediction in that particular setting.

The independent existence of transformation rules implies that it is possible for more than one transformation rule to be applicable in any given instance and there must therefore be a means of selecting one of several available rules in order to make a prediction. The way this is done is the topic of the next section.

B. THE MODEL

The transformation rules are heuristic devices that serve to channel the memory search required for making predictions about others' thoughts and feelings in any given context. These rules specify the possible directions into which others' psychological experiences can be channeled in response to stimuli and events. The stimuli that can induce psychological experiences in others are infinite, and the number of possible psychological reactions to stimuli is incredibly large. The observer needs a means of reducing the potential number of possible predictions in any given instance. Transformation rules serve this function; the selection of a given transformation rule channels the observer toward a specific prediction out of the more limited number of possibilities within that transformation rule. The transformation rule limits the number of possible predictions that can be made in any context (for a similar argument regarding the need to constrain the search in autobiographical memory, see Reiser, 1986).

In this model (Karniol, 1986), the transformation rules that an individual know are arranged in a fixed-order hierarchy that can be viewed as a metarule. To predict others' thoughts and feelings, individuals access the entire hierarchy of transformation rules and attempt to make predictions by trying the rules in the hierarchy sequentially. Observers are assumed to be cognitive economizers (Hansen, 1985; Taylor, 1981) who terminate the search as soon as they find the first transformation rule that appears adequate given the stimulus that constitutes the target's input.[4] Though accessing is conducted in sequential order, the order of the items in the hierarchy does not change as a function of use. For instance, BOMDAS, the acronym for brackets, multiplication, division, addition, and subtraction, represents the metarule that governs the solution of algebra problems. Within this metarule, each procedural rule must be applied to any given problem prior to the application of the next rule in the system. Moreover, the order of application of the rules does not change as a function of their previous use. This is in contrast to models of storage for declarative knowledge in which it is assumed that accessing any item changes its position and hence the likelihood that it will be accessed in the future (e.g., Wyer & Srull's [1983] storage-bin model).

One difference between BOMDAS and the hierarchy of transformation rules used to predict others' thoughts and feelings is that in the latter case there is no "correct" order in which the rules must be applied, and, consequently, different observers may be expected to develop different and unique hierarchies. Moreover, because observers are assumed to be cognitive economizers who terminate the search as soon as they find an adequate transformation rule for making a prediction, the existence of unique hierarchies implies that individuals have preferred ways of making predictions about others. Such preferences may well account for the finding that there is greater variability in the social perceptions of different individuals viewing the same target than in the social perceptions of the same individual viewing different targets (cf. Dornbusch, Hastorf, Richardson, Muzzy, & Vreeland, 1965).

If observers have unique transformation-rule hierarchies, how do similarities

---

[4]In heuristic models, it is assumed that individuals search for quick, "likely to be correct" solutions to problems rather than for slow, optimal solutions and that heuristic devices serve this goal (Feigenbaum & Feldman, 1963).

between different observers arise? First, similarities may arise because the similar experiences of individuals within a social group may lead to similar ways of construing the world (Kelley, 1955) and to similar transformation-rule hierarchies. Second, similarities may occur because of common implicit beliefs that guide judgments regarding the adequacy of any given transformation rule for making predictions in any given context. Such implicit beliefs build on knowledge of human goals, situations, and stereotypes—declarative knowledge that tends to be culturally determined and more or less common within a culture. That is, within any culture there are shared implicit beliefs about why people undertake actions, beliefs about situations and their antecedents and outcomes, as well as beliefs about how specific types of people behave, think, and feel. Consistencies across observers, then, are owing in part to such shared beliefs and do not necessarily occur because targets themselves evidence consistencies. From our perspective, though, it is the nature of transformation rules that is of interest rather than the content or accuracy of observers' specific predictions.

As we indicated previously, the transformation rules serve to direct the search process by providing possible directions in which others' thoughts and feelings may be channeled. Each transformation rule represents knowledge about one possible relation between contexts and psychological reactions to them. Although the actual taxonomy of rules was derived on an empirical basis (see Karniol, 1986, Table 1 for the rules and examples of them), we were guided by models of directed thinking that have specified the types of transformations that allow individuals to link perceptions with stored knowledge.

First, in discussing thought associations, Whorf (1956) distinguished associations from social connections. Associations are cognitions that relate to an individual's personal experiences and cannot be understood without knowing these personal experiences. In the associative mode, then, the way any A is transformed into B can only be understood via an associative chain that may be unique to the individual in question. Connections, on the other, are intelligible without reference to the target person's experience and are part of the social domain of knowledge, embodied in the common linguistic stock of concepts (F. Schwartz & Rouse, 1961). Anyone within a given culture would be expected to share this knowledge and hence to understand the way the transformation of A into B occurred. Based on this distinction, we expected that some transformation rules would involve the personal associations of the target while others would reflect social connections.[5]

In line with Whorf's distinction between associations and social connections, Schank (1982) has argued that while knowledge is first represented in personal episodes (i.e., the associative mode), over time the nature of what is represented

---

[5]Although we have drawn this distinction here, because of space limitations we do not deal with it in presenting the results of our research, which have been discussed elsewhere (Karniol, 1986).

changes so that culturally shared representations of episodes (i.e., social connections in Whorf's terms) become dominant (cf. Nelson, 1981, 1986). In discussing how reminding occurs, he outlines several types of transformations that are intelligible without reference to the individual's unique personal experiences. For instance, any stimulus may lead to dictionary-based reminding. Such a transformation may occur because concepts exist in a "mental dictionary" that includes standard dictionary-type entries (e.g., intension and extension of concepts) that are culturally shared. Visually based reminding differs in that it represents a transformation that uses perceptual similarity between external stimuli and internal representations. But similarity may be idiosyncratically perceived in that one can see similarity between stimuli that are unique to one's past experiences and would not be shared by others (e.g., "That sculpture looks like my mother's hat").

Given these types of reminding, we would expect a transformation rule that provides dictionary-type information. In this transformation rule, which we call category instantiation, stimuli are assumed to lead to psychological experiences focusing on other members of the category or its superordinates. We would also expect two transformation rules involving perceptual analogues: First, a transformation rule we call category-based similarity shift assumes that others have psychological experiences that focus on comparable stimuli. These stimuli are members of the same category and therefore represent culturally shared perceptual analogues. Second, a transformation rule we call target-relevant similarity shift accounts for idiosyncratically determined perceptual analogues.

Other types of transformation rules were derived from Schank and Abelson's (1977) discussions of the types of representations that allow understanding to occur. One type of such knowledge is the script, which Abelson (1981) defines as a coherent sequence of events expected by the individual, involving him or her either as participant or as an observer. That is, stimuli may be expected to evoke culturally shared scripts that are connected to them, where such scripts are not unique to the individual in whose memory they are stored. This would give rise to a transformation rule we call scripted connections. Also, individuals' understanding of human goal systems (Schank & Wilensky, 1978) enable them to generate desires, plans, and expectations that targets may have in response to stimuli. Thus, observers would be expected to have a transformation rule we call stimulus-directed desires–plans–expectations in which common knowledge about others' plans and goals is used to predict their likely psychological experiences. Both of these types of transformation rules would be classified as social connections in Whorf's terminology since they are intelligible without reference to any given target's personal history or experience.

But we would also expect analogous transformation rules that build on episodic knowledge that is unique to the target in question. For instance, if the stimulus is known to have featured in some episode in the target's past and is expected to elicit recall of this episode, this would give rise to a transformation rule we call stimulus-containing reminiscences. Similarly, if the stimulus is related conceptually to another stimulus that is known to have featured in some episode in the target's past, and this related episode is expected to be recalled, this would give rise to a transformation rule we call stimulus-associated reminiscences.

Building on the notion of recursive thought (Laing, Phillipson, & Lee, 1966; Miller, Kessel, & Flavell, 1970), we would also expect transformation rules that allow targets to think about themselves, both in direct relation to the stimulus (stimulus-contingent state of target) and as a consequence of being reminded of some aspect of self by the stimulus (stimulus-reminded state of target). These two rules differ from each other. In the first, the stimulus is assumed to produce some direct consequence for the state of the target, who is then assumed to focus on this state of self. In the latter, the stimulus is assumed to remind the target of some state of the self, though it is not a cause of that state.

And finally, there must be a transformation rule wherein the target is assumed to have a psychological experience that is a direct response to the stimulus itself and in which features of the stimulus may be assumed to be the focus of the target's psychological experience. This would give rise to a transformation rule we call state or characteristic of stimulus.

To illustrate, let us take an example given by Salaman (1970/1981) of a target person who looks up and sees a cloud. There are several transformation rules that would seem intuitively possible for an observer to use in attempting to predict the target's reactions to seeing the cloud. For instance, the observer may assume that the target will focus on the shape of the cloud (the rule we call state or characteristic of stimulus) and predict that the target would think the cloud is lovely, threatening, or white. The observer may assume that the target will only categorize the cloud (the rule we call category instantiation) and think that it is a cumulus cloud. Or the observer may think, just as Salaman (1970/1981) reports her experience, that the target will be reminded of a similar cloud seen on a certain occasion in the past (the rule we call stimulus-associated reminiscence) and try to predict what that past experience might be. As this example illustrates, selecting a given transformation rule serves to constrain the number of predictions that are possible for the observer to make with respect to a given stimulus. But it is clear that several transformation rules can be used to make a prediction in any given instance.

How then does the observer decide which particular rule to use? He or she does so by accessing the entire hierarchy of rules and trying them sequentially. To illustrate how the hierarchy works at the individual subject level, let us continue with the above example and ask an observer to predict a particular target's psychological experiences on seeing a cloud. If the observer has the following three rules sequentially ordered in his or her hierarchy: stimulus-directed desires–plans–expectations, stimulus-containing reminiscences, and state or characteristic of stimulus, then the observer would first try to link the stimulus with possible desires and goals. If the search in this direction does not prove fruitful (i.e., in contrast to most stimuli, possessing or planning does not seem likely in the case of clouds), the next rule in the hierarchy would be invoked for making a prediction. If recalling an occasion on which similar clouds played some special role does seem likely, the observer tries to search for some event in the target's past that matches this specification. If such an event is found, a prediction is made. Otherwise, the next rule is attempted until all the rules are exhausted. Only when none of the rules seems to yield a likely prediction is an "I don't know" response given. Since observers tend to have many rules in their hierarchy, there are only rare instances when no prediction can be made.[6]

C. THE STUDIES

Two studies (Karniol, 1986, Studies 1 and 2) were conducted to derive the taxonomy of transformation rules employed to predict other people's thoughts and feelings. To do this, subjects were asked to make predictions regarding the psychological experiences (i.e., thoughts or feelings) that target persons would have when a subject-provided stimulus was either seen or ideated about (e.g., "When he saw/thought about_____he felt/thought/was reminded of_____because_____"). In the two studies, 150 subjects provided four such predictions, two for visual versus ideational stimuli and two for cognitive versus affective reactions.

To derive the transformation rules, we examined each response and identified a transformation that could account for the relationship between the stimulus cited, the cognitions or affects evoked, and the explanations for these reactions. Ten transformation rules were derived in both studies, and agreement between two independent raters on the classification of all the data into mutually exclusive rules was .84 and .87 in the two studies, respectively. The taxonomy of transformation rules and examples of how they would be used are shown in Table I.

These two studies were used to test whether the data were consistent with a fixed-order hierarchy of transformation rules and whether there were consistencies in rule use across subjects. Since there is no direct test for fixed hierarchical order, to examine the possibility that the rules form a fixed-order hierarchy

---

[6]In our research, we have found that subjects generate an average of 4.3 different rules for making predictions (Karniol & Bresler, 1989; Karniol & Sabo, 1989) and have about 6 independent rules when they assess rule adequacy (Karniol, 1986, Study 3).

TABLE I
Transformation Rules and Exemplars

Link the stimulus via transformation rule number to cognitions or affects	E.g., "When he saw/thought about the new waitress, _____."
1. State or characteristic of stimulus	"He thought how nice she looked in her uniform"; "he felt excited because she was so attractive."
2. Stimulus-directed desires–plans–expectations	"He thought about asking her out"; "he felt excited because he was thinking about what they would do on their first date."
3. Category-based similarity shift	"He thought how much she looked like the previous waitress"; "he felt happy because she reminded him of Jane Fonda when she was younger."
4. Category instantiation	"He thought she was just another bleached blond."
5. Scripted connections	"He thought about the meal"; "he felt that the bar scene was changing."
6. Stimulus-containing reminiscences	"He remembered that he had seen her at the laundromat"; "he felt upset because he remembered when he saw her being attacked."
7. Stimulus-associated reminiscences	"He remembered the time her boss married one of his waitresses"; "he felt sad because he remembered how her boss treated the previous waitress."
8. Target-relevant similarity shift	"He thought about his former girlfriend because they looked alike"; "he felt happy because she looked like his younger sister."
9. Stimulus-contingent state of target	"He thought he needed someone like her"; "he felt that he was falling for her."
10. Stimulus-reminded state of target	"He thought about how much older he was getting"; "he felt that his youth was slipping away from him."

several types of analyses were conducted. First, the proportion of use of each transformation rule in each study was determined. These proportions ranged from a high of .29 to a low of .01.

Fixed hierarchical order requires that the proportion of rule use across the 10 rules differ from chance, where chance is .10. The observed distribution of proportions was found to be significantly different than expected by chance, with 2 rules being employed significantly more frequently than chance and 2 employed less frequently than chance. Moreover, since fixed hierarchical order implies that the order in which the rules as accessed is constant, it requires that rule repetition occur more frequently than expected by chance. Since each subject provided four predictions, each rule could be repeated from zero to three times. In both studies, the occurrence of rule repetition was significantly greater than expected by chance.

Although the above two analyses are consistent with a fixed hierarchical order, they are also consistent with another type of storage system, the storage bin. In a storage-bin system, both input and output are made at one end. Removing any item results in its replacement at the top of the bin and increases the likelihood that the item will be accessed again, leading to recency effects. Models of social cognition for declarative knowledge (e.g., Higgins & King, 1981; Wyer & Srull, 1983) generally assume that storage occurs in this manner. Consequently, additional analyses were conducted to contrast predictions from a storage-bin model with predictions based on a fixed-order hierarchy.

The first of these contrasting predictions relates to whether rule repetitions occur more frequently for sequential versus nonsequential predictions (i.e., a given rule could be repeated as AA, ABA, or ABCA). A storage-bin model would suggest that sequential repetitions would be more frequent than nonsequential ones, whereas the fixed-hierarchy model suggests that since selections are independent, rule repetition may be equally likely in nonsequential predictions. In keeping with the fixed-order hierarchy model, in both studies nonsequential and sequential repetitions were found to be equally likely to occur. An additional, contrasting prediction concerned which specific rules were repeated. The storage-bin model predicts that the probability of repetition of all the rules should be greater than chance, whereas the fixed-hierarchy model predicts that repetition should occur only for the rules at the top of the hierarchy. In both studies, we found that only the two most frequently employed rules were repeated more often than expected by chance. These analyses, then, provide strong evidence that the transformation rules represent procedural knowledge that is not subject to the same laws of frequency and accessibility as declarative knowledge.

To examine for consistencies in rule use across subjects, we examined whether any rules were consistently employed in conjunction with either affective versus cognitive experiences or with visual versus ideational stimuli. To the extent that judgments about the adequacy of transformation rules are guided by implicit beliefs about others' psychological experiences, we would expect some commonalities in the manner that subjects use the transformation rules. In both studies, consistencies across subjects were found only in the use of certain transformation rules for affective versus cognitive experiences. One rule was used primarily for predicting affective reactions (Rule 1), and five rules were used primarily for predicting cognitions (Rules 3, 4, 5, 7, and 8). No consistencies were found in the use of the transformation rules for visual versus ideational stimuli. Subjects appeared to have more similar beliefs about others' cognitive and affective experiences than about the nature of the stimuli that precipitate such psychological experiences.

Although the separation between affective and cognitive predictions was made for heuristic purposes, it is possible to examine the pattern of association of the rules with affective and cognitive predictions in order to draw some conclusions about how affective material is represented in memory. The fact that most of the rules could be employed for predicting both cognitive and affective experiences strongly suggests that the process of making predictions in both realms draws on the same declarative knowledge structures (cf. Bower & Cohen, 1982; Clark & Isen, 1982). This is consistent with recent evidence (Cantor, Mischel, & Schwartz, 1982; Reiser, Black, & Abelson, 1985; Zuroff, 1982) indicating that prototypical knowledge about personality types and situational contexts ordinarily has affective information associated with it. On the other hand, several rules did not readily yield affective material. It is possible, therefore, that certain types of associative memory networks do not have affective information directly related to them or else that such affective information is not readily accessible. This would suggest that the formulation of affective predictions depends on the observer's use of the transformation rules to find an associative network that does contain affective information (cf. Johnson, 1985). A second possibility is that affective information is not directly encoded but is reconstructed with reference to possible goal states that the target is assumed to have (cf. Dyer, 1983a, 1983b, 1987; Lehnert & Vine, 1987). This would imply that to the extent that the transformation rule selected does not lead to a context relevant to such goal states, no affective predictions will be made. It would seem therefore, that the content of the specific prediction depends on the nature of declarative knowledge that is accessed once a given transformation rule is selected. We now turn to the declarative knowledge that is used in such contexts.

III. Declarative Knowledge

After selecting a given transformation rule, the specific prediction the observer makes in any given context depends on the use of declarative knowledge. Within our model, there are several types of declarative knowledge structures from which information must be culled to make predictions about others' thoughts and feelings. These knowledge structures determine the content of the specific predictions the observer makes about others' psychological experiences. Specifically, we assume that since there are several knowledge structures, there are pathways interconnecting them, and often information from two or more sources must be integrated to make a prediction. Consequently, individual differences in predictive ability may reflect differences in the knowledge base of different individuals as well as differential abilities to integrate information from diverse knowledge structures. Developmentally, this model implies that children must acquire these declarative knowledge structures as well as the ability to integrate information (Wilkening, Becker, & Trabasso, 1980).

A. TYPES OF DECLARATIVE KNOWLEDGE

In our view, declarative knowledge is organized around generalized knowledge about situations or episodes (Schank, 1982; Schank & Abelson, 1977). That is, repeated sequences of events and actions experienced by the individual are used to generate representations that abstract the similarities between these events, and these representations are labeled so as to maximize the likelihood of easy retrieval. The representations include information regarding typical characters, settings, events, temporal sequences, and causal relations, and, consequently, they provide a means of making sense of other people's behavior and their reactions to events. *Memory organization procedes by noting differences or deviations* from these generalized knowledge representations (cf. Kolodner, 1984; Schank, 1982). This method of organization, which will be elaborated later, reduces redundancy and maximizes economy. It has parallels to Jones and Davis's (1965) notion of noncommon effects and to Kelley's (1967) principle of covariation in that it uses unique features of events.

In this model of declarative knowledge, inferences are generated automatically whenever an episodic representation is activated. The generation of inferences about situations is to a large extent dependent on an understanding of human goal systems (Foss & Bower, 1986; Pervin, 1983; Schank & Wilensky, 1978) and the plans they generate to accomplish these goals. All stimuli are processed with reference to the goal systems that individuals believe motivate their own and others' behavior. The implication of a given stimulus for a goal system will determine the particular ideational and affective content that the target would be expected to have (Dyer, 1983a, 1983b, 1987).

Schank and Wilensky (1978) have outlined several types of these goals: satisfaction, enjoyment, achievement, preservation, and instrumental. While these may not constitute an exhaustive list of human goal systems, we believe that such goals determine how classes of stimuli are assumed to affect ideational content and induce affective reactions. There is evidence (Cantor *et al.*, 1982; Conway & Bekerian, 1987a) that generalized representations of situations contain knowledge about specific psychological processes such as affective reactions and cognitions that people are likely to have in situations. Knowledge about goals specifies why actions are performed, what states cause what actions and satisfy what desires, and so forth. The system of goals can be ranked according to their relative importance to a prototypical member of a given culture, and predictions can be made about which goals will supersede others (cf. Maslow, 1954).

When no information about the target is supplied or known, default values are assigned and the target is assumed not only to function in accordance with the prototypical goal system but also to think or feel like a prototypical individual (Rieger, 1979). Target and category knowledge express the deviations between the normative goal system and the ordering of goals by the particular target individual or category (cf. Carbonell, 1980, 1981), where such deviations include knowledge not only about differences between the target's goal system and the goal system of a prototypical individual but also differences between the target and prototypical individuals in reactions and behavior (cf. Bond & Brockett, 1987; Bond & Sedikides, 1988; Kolodner, 1984). Predictions about others' thoughts and feelings can then be modified by using knowledge about the target.

There are two types of target knowledge. The first of these relates to historical knowledge about the specific target of the prediction (e.g., "Bob participated in the sit-in protest in 1971"). One can modify predictions by using historical information about the specific target. For instance, my knowledge of a given individual's past history and personality may lead me to assume that he or she would be more likely to employ self-relevant similarity shifts (e.g., "He'll probably think about his girlfriend when he sees the new waitress") than stimulus-directed desires/plans–expectations (e.g., "When he sees the new waitress, he'll want to ask her out"). Alternatively, such historical knowledge may determine the content of the specific prediction made (e.g., "Most guys would be thrilled to meet her, but she is so much like his former girlfriend that he'll probably be too scared to approach her"). The second source of knowledge, category-specific knowledge (Higgins, 1981), includes representations of categories of individuals. For instance, one can adduce knowledge about roles that the target may have in order to modify the more general prediction (e.g., "Most people would think that kid is cute, but if I were that kid's parent I would be embarrassed"). One can also modify the prediction by using stereotypes. If we know that a given individual is Machiavellian, black, or Republican, we may make a different prediction than if this knowledge were not available about the target (e.g., "Being a Republican, he'll probably be elated by the outcome of the elections"). In general, then, stereotypes set up expectations for how members of that category will differ from prototypical others in their behavior in goal-oriented settings and in their responses to both the achievement and nonachievement of their goals.

B. FINDING INTERSECTIONS FOR DECLARATIVE KNOWLEDGE

The studies we conducted examined predictions for targets unfamiliar to the subject and about whom no information was provided. What do individuals do when target information is available to them? In such cases, they need to find the intersection between what is known about the target and the relevant episodic representation. Observers ask themselves whether the information known about the target carries any implications for the generalized representation of the situation. For instance, when one is asked how someone would feel at a birthday party, the generalized representation for such events is employed. When one is asked how introverted Johnny would feel, one examines the generalized representation to see if the fact that Johnny is introverted has any relevant implications for how he might feel. Since the generalized representation for birthdays yields the information that extroverted and gregarious individuals are typical of such settings (Cantor *et al.*, 1982), the individual would predict that Johnny would not enjoy himself in that setting. Young children should have difficulty in finding such intersections because their knowledge structures on which these intersections are based are not well developed. Knowledge about the types of people best suited for different settings as well as the implications of given traits for affective experiences must be acquired. In general, though, when target information is provided, predictions based on two knowledge structures must be made and an intersection between them must be found.

The finding of intersections of two knowledge structures is not only a problem for target knowledge. Studies on incongruent affect (e.g., Borke, 1971; Feshbach & Roe, 1968; Greenspan, Barenboim, & Chandler, 1976) can be viewed in the same light. In such studies, children are shown a scene that is known to elicit a given affect (e.g., birthdays), but the scene includes a child whose facial affect is incongruent with the setting (i.e., sad). From the point of view of these researchers, younger children err because they tend to ignore the facial cues and state that the experienced affect is scene congruent. Older children tend to state possible reasons for the incongruent affect.

From our point of view, correct responses require accessing the generalized representation for birthdays and finding that it is positively coded for happy affect. Working from the facial affect backwards, one would attempt to find generalized representations of situations that produce sadness and that can be activated at birthday parties. At birthday parties one receives gifts and this leads to happiness, but sadness is known to be elicited by not getting desired objects (Karniol & Koren, 1987). Hence, a child that did not get a desired object would be expected to feel sad at a birthday party (e.g., "He's sad because he didn't get the electric train he wanted for his birthday"). Since young children are able to provide antecedents for affective states (e.g., Brody & Harrison, 1987; Trabasso, Stein, & Johnson, 1981; R. M. Schwartz & Trabasso, 1984), their difficulty would seem to lie in finding intersections between representational structures.

A similar example of the need to find intersections is evident in Selman's research (Selman & Byrne, 1974), a sample story of which tells of two boys trying to decide what gift to buy a mutual friend whose puppy has just died. The question subjects must answer is how the gift recipient will feel if he receives a new puppy. The problem is that there are two relevant generalized representations. The one for gift getting predicts happiness, but the representation for losing loved objects predicts sadness. Selman assumes that mature perspective takers would access both relevant representations and would therefore predict that the affects would be coexperienced in the gift recipient.[7] From our perspective, the task requires the child to make a prediction by finding the intersection of the two generalized representations. The inability to do so most likely reflects both the child's lack of well-developed representational structures as well as the inability to find such intersections.

C. USING THE HIERARCHY WITH TARGET KNOWLEDGE

We indicated that similarities between observers may occur because of similarities in both procedural and declarative knowledge. Similarities in procedural knowledge may occur because different social experiences may lead to different ways of construing the world. This may result in similar transformation-rule hierarchies within a social category and different hierarchies between social categories. Consequently, the transformation-rule hierarchies of subjects in different social categories need to be compared when they make predictions regarding other people's likely thoughts and feelings in various contexts. If membership in that social category leads to different ways of construing the world, this should manifest itself in different hierarchies of transformation rules between groups.

Second, similarities between subjects may occur because of similarities in the declarative knowledge structures that are used to make specific predictions. But such similarities in declarative knowledge cannot be examined by having subjects make predictions about others' thoughts and feelings because each subject's application of the hierarchy and selection of a given transformation rule may lead to the use of different declarative knowledge structures. The operation of common declarative knowledge can be examined by having subjects judge the adequacy of predictions using each of the transformion rules for targets in different social categories. To the extent that such implicit beliefs are part of the common

---

[7]Selman assumes that the two affects will be coexperienced, but of course it is possible that each serves to dampen the effect of the other. This possibility cannot be examined unless subjects are asked to indicate the level of each affect and their scaled responses are compared to control subjects who are asked to indicate the level of affect in response to each event independently of the other event. Since this has not been done, it is difficult to draw any conclusions about young children's ability to integrate information about two affect-eliciting events that differ in valence.

culture and are not unique to the social category in which the observer is a member, social category membership may not be a relevant factor in determining such judgments.

For instance, one might expect females to have a hierarchy of transformation rules more similar to other females than to males. But to the extent that stereotypes of male and female behavior are culturally accepted, adequacy judgments regarding transformation-rule use for predictions about female targets might be expected to differ from their use for male targets. Since most research has found that both sexes have the same stereotypes of males and females (Ashmore, 1981; Broverman, Vogel, Broverman, Clarkson, & Rosenkrantz, 1972), one would expect no interaction between the observer's sex and the target's sex in judging the adequacy of predictions.

We examined these hypotheses in a study (Karniol & Bresler, 1989) in which males and females were first required to generate predictions about male and female targets' likely thoughts and affective reactions in different situations (prediction task). Subjects then rated the adequacy of exemplars of all 10 transformation rules for making predictions about male and female targets' cognitive versus affective reactions in eight different situations (ratings task). Significant effects for sex of subject were found only on the prediction task, with males and females evidencing somewhat different hierarchies of transformation rules. Significant differences in the frequencies of rules in the hierarchy were found for only 2 of the 10 rules. Females were more likely than males to make predictions using transformation Rules 1 (state or characteristic of the stimulus) and 10 (stimulus-reminded state of target). But there were no significant differences in the hierarchy of transformation rules used for making predictions about male versus female targets.

On the ratings task, on the other hand, sex of the observer had a negligible effect (in general, females tended to have higher adequacy ratings than males) and sex of the target had a significant effect on the judged adequacy of specific rules. Four rules were judged as more adequate for making predictions about male targets (Rules 1, 3, 4, and 8), and 2 rules were judged as more adequate for making predictions about female targets (Rules 6 and 9). Moreover, collapsing across the 10 transformation rules, lower adequacy ratings were assigned by both sexes to transformation rules associated with cognitive as opposed to affective experiences in female targets. Adequacy ratings for male targets were not differentiated by the type of psychological experience involved.

These data indicate that individuals who have similar social experiences tend to have similar ways of construing the world and, consequently, have similar hierarchies of transformation rules. But their declarative knowledge builds on shared implicit beliefs about the nature of goal systems, situations, and cultural stereotypes. Such implicit beliefs tend to be culturally determined and are largely responsible for the similar content of specific predictions as well as the judged adequacy of transformation rules for making such predictions.

IV. Role of Self-Knowledge

As we saw in the Introduction, the most controversial knowledge structure in making predictions about others' thoughts and feelings is self-knowledge. The question of how self-knowledge is represented is critical for any model of role taking that attempts to explain the transition from immature to mature patterns of predictions. There are at least two possibilities for representing self-knowledge, with each leading to somewhat different expectations about how predictions are made.

A. MARKUS'S MODEL

The first view of how self-knowledge is represented builds on the notion of self-schemas (Markus, 1977). Self-schemas are generalizations about the self that are drawn on the basis of one's behavioral experience across settings. Schematic self-representations include schema-relevant generic labels as well as comparative knowledge in the schematic domain (e.g., "I'm chubby and I eat more than my friends").

Within such a representational structure, in order to make any prediction about oneself, one has to find a self-schema in the domain in which the predictions are to be made. After accessing the self-schema, the individual can make predictions about how the self would react in that setting (Markus & Smith, 1981). When there is no self-schema in the domain in which predictions are to be made, predictions about oneself are made either by searching other associated nodes in the memory system or by creating temporary intersections of the self with the domain of predictive interest.

The more important issue from our perspective is how self-schematic knowledge might determine the content of predictions about others' thoughts and feelings. From the self-schematic view, the self is automatically activated in processing information about others. If the individual has a self-schema in the relevant domain, he or she will use this self-schema to make predictions about others. In fact, Markus contends that *not* using a relevant self-schema requires concentrated attempts at suppressing the self-schema and that such efforts are likely to meet with limited success (Markus & Smith, 1981). In areas where no relevant self-schema exists, one would presumably make predictions by searching associated nodes and inferring what people in general would experience.

B. SELF-AS-DISTINCT VIEW

An alternate view of making self-based predictions—the "self-as-distinct" view (Karniol & Koren, 1987)—builds on the notion of memory as organized around deviations from generalized representations. In the self-as-distinct view, we differentiate between the generalized representations of situations, the labels attached to these representations, and deviant tags (cf. Graesser, 1981). Once the transformation-rule hierarchy is accessed and a given rule is selected, declarative knowledge must be searched for making specific context-appropriate predictions. Situations activate a memory search within declarative knowledge for a representation that matches the situation. The search is conducted by looking through the representation labels that are summary codes, akin to file names. The individual searches through the generalized representation labels to find a label that seems most appropriate in the specific context. If the individual decides that a given label is highly likely to include representations of the required situation, then he or she examines the representation itself and can use it to make predictions specific to that context. These episodic representations include knowledge about prototypical affective reactions and cognitions that are experienced in these situations.

Attached to the generalized representation labels there are tags, similar to cross-references, to indicate that self-experience or generalizations about the self deviate from the experiences that prototypical individuals have in these situations. When there is a self-is-distinct tag attached to the label of a given generalized representation, the individual searches for self-information in the relevant self-node, and deviant information about the self that is related to the relevant generalized representation becomes available. When there is no tag attached to the label, the generalized representation itself is used to make a prediction. But information about the self that matches the generalized representation is assimilated to it and becomes undifferentiable from other content within this representation. Consequently, in the absence of a self-is-distinct tag, the default value for predicting self's thoughts and feelings is the same as the generalized representation, and predictions about the self are based on the generalized representation.

To illustrate, when I am asked how I would feel at a birthday party, if I have no memorable deviant experiences, then on reaching the label I would find no tag and I would have to examine the generalized representation for birthday parties. This representation is likely to contain the information that people find birthday parties enjoyable, so I answer that I would feel good. If, on the other hand, I am an introvert and in my memory store are encoded three occasions during which I felt miserable in such settings, there would be a tag attached to the label of the generalized representation and I would examine the relevant self-node rather than the generalized representation in order to generate a prediction. This model is consistent with the finding (McGuire & McGuire, 1986) that the self is described in negative terms of what one is not rather than in positive terms of what one is. Moreover, this model can account for the difficulty of finding evidence for the self as an independent cognitive structure (Higgins, Van Hook, & Dorfman, 1988; Klein & Kihlstom, 1986; McDaniel, Lapsley, & Milstead, 1987).

The major issue, though, is how this model allows for predictions about others' thoughts and feelings to be made in any given setting. When there is no self-is-distinct tag attached to the representation label, making predictions about others' thoughts and feelings requires the individual to access the representation itself and to make a prediction based on the information contained therein.

When there is a self-is-distinct tag attached to label of the generalized representation, if the task requires a prediction about another person, then the individual ignores this tag and accesses the generalized representation. To give an analogy, when searching through a subject index, one often finds labels to which are attached "See also_____" instructions. Such instructions are ignored until a content search in the original file is exhausted and does not yield the sought-after information. In the same way, the self-as-distinct view (Karniol & Koren, 1987) suggests that tags that indicate one's distinctive standing in a given domain are ignored in making predictions about others. Thus, self-information is not used for making predictions about others' thoughts and feelings precisely because it is atypical and indicates that the self deviates from the generalized representation of that situation. The exception is when one knows something about the target that leads one to believe that the target deviates from prototypical others in the same way. In such instances, one may base predictions about the target on oneself. As discussed previously, if the target deviates in a different manner, the individual must find intersections between the relevant generalized representation and the information known about the target.

Within this analysis, tagging as well as generalized representations of situations are assumed to be a developmental process. Specifically, we assume that children originally have personal scripts (Schank, 1982) that represent private expectations about the situations they encounter. As development proceeds, children realize the cultural nature of many of these expectations. They discover that others have the same expectations for behavior and reactions in the same settings. Once the shared nature of these expectations about situations is understood, memory organization can proceed in a different manner (Nelson, 1981, 1986). Specifically, information is organized in terms of cultural norms with certain personal markings that store one's own distinct or idiosyncratic points of view.

To realize that any specific experience is atypical, one must have a well-developed concept of what is typical. Consequently, for young children, very few experiences are tagged and their reactions for both the self and the target are based on the content of the situation prototype. As they develop, children become aware of their own unique or atypical response patterns and develop a self-structure that stores these unique characteristics (cf. McGuire & McGuire, 1986, 1988; McGuire & Padawer-Singer, 1976). There is evidence that children below the age of 7 seldom make psychological or dispositional generalizations about themselves (Flapan, 1968; Livesely & Bromley, 1973). Once such self-generalizations do develop, they become linked to generalized representations of situations with the deviant tag that is attached to the representation label. In this view, the self consists of knowledge that contrasts with prototypical knowledge about others. The view of self as consisting primarily of distinct information implies that all nondeviant information about the self becomes available through accessing generalized representations of situations. Unless distinct self-knowledge is available, such generalized representational structures will determine the content of predictions about both the self and others.

In one test of this model (Karniol & Koren, 1987), 32 sentence-long stories about positive and negative affect-eliciting events were presented to kindergarten children who were asked about either their own or the target's likely affective reactions to these events. If the same generalized episodic representations are used for responding about both the self and the other, or if self-knowledge is used for responding about both the self and the other, there should be no difference between these two conditions. If, as we contend, self-knowledge is used for responding about the self when there is a self-is-distinct tag only and generalized episodic representations are used in other cases, there should be some differences between these two conditions. We would argue that for young children, self-is-distinct knowledge is more prevalent for negative situations than for positive ones and, therefore, would expect children to give different responses primarily for the negative affect-eliciting events.

The data indicated that subjects in the self-affect condition made fewer negative affective inferences, offered more coping responses for transforming negative situations to more positive ones, and used different justifications for the cited affective reactions than did subjects in the target-affect condition. These data are consistent with the view that individuals do not predict others' thoughts and feelings by using self-knowledge. Rather they are highly likely to know their own, but not others', means of coping with aversive situations and to assume that they are unique in this regard. In a more recent test of the self-as-distinct view (Karniol, Liberman, & Ovad, 1989), adult subjects high and low in self-monitoring were required to generate predictions about the likely affective reactions and thoughts that either they (e.g., "When I saw the boy___") or another person (e.g., "When he saw the boy___") would experience when exposed to 9 different stimulus contexts. Irrespective of their self-monitoring score, subjects who made predictions about self used different transformation rules than did subjects who made predictions about others. Specifically, even though the number of different rules invoked by subjects in both conditions was the same, significantly more predictions using associations (i.e., Rules 6–10) were generated by subjects responding in the third person than those responding in the first person. But the only transformation rule on which this difference was statistically significant was Rule 6, stimulus-containing reminiscences. That is, subjects assumed that stimuli perceived by others would remind them of past experiences that included these stimuli, but they did not assume that such reminders would occur when they themselves perceived these same stimuli.

Other research, not within the transformation-rule model framework, has also found evidence consistent with the view that people do not use self-information when making judgments about others. For instance, Spence and her colleagues (Spence & Helmreich, 1978; Spence & Sawin, 1985) found a zero correlation between the traits males and females assigned to themselves and those they assigned to males and females in general. McGuire and McGuire (1986) found that the self, more than others, is thought of as having affective rather than cognitive reactions. These findings are consistent with the view that self-knowledge is knowledge about how one is distinct, and, consequently, such self-knowledge is not employed to make predictions about other people.

These findings are bolstered by the data of another study (Karniol, 1989), which examined the effect of priming on transformation-rule use. A storage-bin model would suggest that if individuals are primed with autobiographical memories or thoughts about their likely future, this should increase the likelihood of their making predictions that focus on thoughts about the past or about the future. The fixed-hierarchy model suggests that irrespective of previous priming, the hierarchy of transformation rules is accessed in the same way each time, and thinking about ones' past or likely future should have no impact on subsequent transformation-rule use for making predictions about others' likely psychological experiences.

To test these predictions, subjects were asked to describe their family life 10 years ago, to describe their family life 10 years hence, or to do neither of these tasks. They were subsequently required either to generate predictions (Karniol, 1989, Study 1) or to rate the adequacy of predictions (Karniol, 1989, Study 2) about the affective reactions and cognitions that other people would have in different contexts (e.g., ''When he saw his father,_____''). Since the priming related directly to the content of predictions involving use of transformation Rule 2 (stimulus-directed desires–plans–expectations) and Rule 6 (stimulus-containing reminiscences), one would expect experimental subjects to generate more predictions using these transformation rules and to evaluate predictions using these two transformation rules more highly. Even though subjects in the two priming conditions generated extremely elaborate scenarios about their past or their expected future, such priming had no effect on their use of the relevant transformation rules, either for generating predictions about others or for rating the adequacy of rules in accounting for others' psychological reactions. Though null effects need to be interpreted with caution, these findings are in marked contrast to research on declarative memory structures in which priming with "lifetime periods" has been found to lead to remarkably robust effects in recalling autobiographical memories (Conway & Bekerian, 1987b). Moreover, C. A. Anderson and Godfrey (1987) found that imagining oneself in a behavioral script influences expectations about oneself but not about others and that imagining other people in a behavioral script influenced expectations about these others but not about oneself. Again, it seems that subjects do not use self-information to make predictions about other people.

C. FALSE CONSENSUS AND SELF-KNOWLEDGE

If, as we have claimed, the self represents knowledge about how one is distinct from others, why is false consensus with the self so prevalent (e.g., Ross, Greene, & House, 1977; Sherman, Presson, & Chassin, 1984)? We contend that false consensus will occur whenever there is no self-is-distinct tag attached to the relevant generalized representation of the situation. Specifically, when one is asked how others will behave or the likelihood that a trait description or attitude will reflect their standing, the declarative knowledge structure that is relevant to the specific issue is activated. If there is no self-is-distinct tag, the prediction for others and for the self will be the same since it will be based on the generalized representation. If there is a tag, predictions about others will not be the same as those for the self since the former will be based on the generalized representation whereas the latter will be based on the relevant self-node.

Evidence consistent with the above analysis comes from several sources. First, a metanalysis of false-consensus research (Mullen *et al.*, 1985) indicates that the effect is least robust when subjects first indicate their own behavioral choices and then estimate others' likely behavioral choices. Second, individuals high in need for uniqueness, low in self-esteem, and self-schematic on the relevant dimension exhibit smaller false-consensus effects (Campbell, 1986; Kernis, 1984). Also, individuals who are extreme on a given dimension (e.g., introverts and extroverts) exhibit less false consensus when judging behavior that is consistent with their self-concept (Kulik, Sledge, & Mahler, 1986). Since all these variables would be conceptualized as equivalent to having a self-is-distinct tag, the above findings are consistent with our analysis. Also consistent with this analysis, Goldings (1954) found that subjects who were in the average range of happiness tended to attribute to others similar degrees of happiness, but those at the two extremes of the happiness scale displayed a contrast effect and attributed to others opposite ratings.

Finally, the way self-schemas have been operationalized, being self-schematic means that one is extreme on the relevant dimension (Markus, 1977). In the self-as-distinct view, being self-schematic means that one has a deviant tag attached to the trait and hence "me–not me" decisions can be made very quickly by noting the presence of a tag. The finding that being self-schematic leads to shorter processing latencies for schematic information (Markus, 1977) is fully consistent with our model since self-schematics need only examine the information stored with the deviant tag and aschematics must search within the generalized representation until they find some information that may be self-relevant in the context. In general, then, false consensus would seem to be an epiphenomenon of the way inferences are drawn from declarative knowledge structures.

V. Situational Influences on Transformation Rule Use

We have described the way individuals use the transformation-rule hierarchy to make predictions about other people's thoughts and feelings under ideal circumstances. Such ideal circumstances are rarely present in most situations in which predictions need to be made. There is usually a temporal constraint as well as other factors that serve to put some stress on the observer. In a recent study (Karniol & Sabo, 1989), we examined the effects of stress on the way individuals use the transformation-rule hierarchy to make predictions about others' thoughts and feelings. Subjects were asked to make cognitive or affective predictions about 10 TAT pictures using sentence stems similar to those used in our previous research. Two groups of subjects were required to perform the task while exposed to medium-level or high-level white noise, whereas a third group was not exposed to noise. Stress reduced the number of different rules used for making predictions and, in comparison to the control group, led to less verbose predictions and to a greater tendency to select those rules that rely on the portrayed context in making the predictions. It seems from these data that stress both alters the way the hierarchy of rules is examined prior to making a selection and restricts the search of declarative knowledge that is conducted for making a specific prediction (cf. Easterbrook, 1959). Thus, when people make predictions about others' thoughts and feelings under stress, the information search in both procedural and declarative knowledge structures appears to be affected. The impact of other situational variables on such predictions will have to be examined in future research.

VI. Individual Differences

We indicated above that because of the way the transformation-rule hierarchy is used, individuals have preferred modes of making predictions. Such preferences become evident when individuals repeatedly use the same rules to make predictions. Rule repetition necessarily reduces the number of different rules that individuals employ. In our research, we have found a wide range in the number of different rules used for making predictions about others' thoughts and feelings. The lowest number of different rules used by any one subject was two, and the highest number was six, across the 8 (Karniol & Bresler, 1989) and 9 (Karniol & Sabo, 1989) contexts for which predictions about others' thoughts and feelings were made. Hence, rule repetition is quite prevalent. Moreover, individuals appear to have idiosyncratic ways of assuming how others will respond. When given a choice between predicting affective versus cognitive experiences in others, some subjects consistently tend to predict that others will have primarily affective rather than cognitive experiences. Future research will have to examine the personality correlates of such idiosyncracies in the way individuals use the transformation-rule hierarchy to generate predictions about others' thoughts and feelings.

The way individuals use the transformation-rule hierarchy for making predictions about others' psychological experiences may be important for more than theoretical reasons. Clinical populations have generally been discussed (e.g., Cameron, 1947; Cameron & Magaret, 1951; Lidz, 1978; Little & Kendall, 1979) both as being unable to engage in such predictive processes and as being particularly unlikely to try to predict what others may be feeling or thinking. Research that has examined this issue (e.g., Chandler, 1972; Simeonsson, 1973) seems to indicate that emotionally disturbed children, for instance, are less adept in role-taking skills than are normal children. But it is unclear whether such differences reflect problems in procedural knowledge, in declarative knowledge, or in information integration.

There is some evidence, though, that at least part of the problem may lie in idiosyncratic assumptions on the part of some observers about how others will react. For instance, in disturbed families, particularly those with schizophrenic offspring, mothers tend to assume that others are responding to ideational as opposed to visual stimuli and engage in predictive processes much more than in nondisturbed families (Hassan, 1974; Laing & Esterson, 1970; Lennard & Bernstein, 1969). In several studies, Lennard and colleagues (Lennard, Beaulieu, & Embrey, 1965; Lennard & Bernstein, 1969) found that mothers of schizophrenics devote more than twice the proportion of their communication to their offsprings' episodic psychological experiences as compared to control mothers. The relation between such tendencies of the schizophrenogenic mother and her offspring's symptoms has not yet been examined, although there is some evidence that the children of schizophrenics do not differ from normals in their responses to standard visual role-taking tasks (e.g., Worland, Edenhart-Pepe, Weeks, & Konen, 1984). We expect that the transformation rule model will prove to have heuristic value when such predictive processes are examined in clinical populations.

VII. Conclusions

In this article, we have outlined a transformation-rule model for predicting others' thoughts and feelings and presented several studies to support it. We have not elaborated on the implications of the model for the myriad of studies conducted under the title of role taking since doing so is beyond the scope of this article. From the current perspective, in addition to suffering from a confusion between procedural and declarative knowledge, the majority of studies of role taking have failed to consider the possibility that taking the role of the other is a figure of speech. We think that taking the role of the other is only a figure of speech. This figure of speech is used by individuals in a shorthand way to describe the predictive process we have described in our model. In our view, it is unfortunate that this figure of speech has been treated in psychology as if it was a model of what actually happens in the process. As discussed above, individual differences in role taking refer to differences in the tendency to undertake this predictive process, differences in the hierarchies of transformation rules, differences in the knowledge base that is used to make specific predictions, and differences in the ability (or tendency) to integrate information from declarative knowledge structures.

From this point of view, there is nothing inherent to either children's or adults' cognitive capacities to prevent them from using all modes of making predictions about others' thoughts and feelings. Speaking of egocentrism or of the inability to engage in role taking leads to a circularity that is avoided by the transformation-rule model. Moreover, this model allows us to assess where failures in predictive ability may lie since the model yields explicit hypotheses about the way individuals make predictions about others' episodic psychological experiences. Such hypotheses are not derivable from other models, and, as we demonstrated with respect to the integration of declarative knowledge, the model can be used to account parsimoniously for previous data and to interpret our own research in a way that is not possible from other formulations. Finally, the problem that children and many adults have is that the process of making such predictions about others' likely thoughts and feelings is complex and requires much effort. We have yet to understand the circumstances that lead observers to engage in it. It remains for future research to examine this issue.

References

Abel, T. (1948). The operation called "Verstehn." *American Journal of Sociology*, **54**, 211–218.
Abel, T. (1970). *The foundation of sociological theory*. New York: Random House.

Abelson, R. P. (1981). Psychological status of the script concept. *American Psychologist*, **36**, 715–729.
Adams, D. K. (1928). The inference of mind. *Psychological Review*, **35**, 235–252.
Alexander, F. (1935). The logic of emotions and its dynamic background. *International Journal of Psychoanalysis*, **16**, 399–413.
Anderson, C. A., & Godfrey, S. S. (1987). Thoughts about actions: The effect of specificity and availability of imagined behavioral scripts on expectations about oneself and others. *Social Cognition*, **5**, 238–258.
Anderson, J. R. (1983). *The architecture of cognition*. Cambridge, MA: Harvard University Press.
Ashmore, R. D. (1981). Sex stereotypes and implicit personality theory. In D. L. Hamilton (Ed.), *Cognitive processes in stereotyping and intergroup behavior*. Hillsdale, NJ: Erlbaum.
Berlyne, D. E. (1965). *Structure and direction in thinking*. New York: Wiley.
Bond, C. F., Jr., & Brockett, D. R. (1987). A social context–personality index theory of memory for acquaintances. *Journal of Personality and Social Psychology*, **52**, 1110–1121.
Bond, C. F., Jr., & Sedikides, C. (1988). The recapituation hypothesis in person retrieval. *Journal of Experimental Social Psychology*, **24**, 195–221.
Borke, H. (1971). Interpersonal perception of young children: Egocentrism or empathy? *Developmental Psychology*, **5**, 263–269.
Bower, G. H., & Cohen, P. R. (1982). Emotional influences in memory and thinking: Data and theory. In M. S. Clark & S. T. Fiske (Eds.), *Affect and cognition* (pp. 291–331). Hillsdale, NJ: Erlbaum.
Brody, L. R., & Harrison, R. H. (1987). Developmental changes in children's abilities to match and label emotionally laden situations. *Motivation and Emotion*, **11**, 347–366.
Broverman, I. K., Vogel, S. R., Broverman, D. N., Clarkson, F. E., & Rosenkrantz, P. S. (1972). Sex role stereotypes: A current appraisal. *Journal of Social Issues*, **28**, 59–78.
Cameron, N. (1947). *The psychology of behavior disorders*. Cambridge, MA: Houghton Mifflin.
Cameron, N., & Magaret, A. (1951). *Behavior pathology*. Cambridge, MA: Houghton Mifflin.
Campbell, J. D. (1986). Similarity and uniqueness: The effects of attribute type, relevance, and individual differences in self-esteem and depression. *Journal of Personality and Social Psychology*, **50**, 281–294.
Cantor, N., & Kihlstrom, J. (1985). Social intelligence: The cognitive basis of personality. In P. Shaver (Ed.), *Review of personality and social psychology* (Vol. 6, pp. 15–34). Beverly Hills, CA: Sage.
Cantor, N., & Mischel, W. (1979). Prototypes in person perception. In L. Berkowitz (Ed.), *Advances in experimental social psychology* (Vol. 12, pp. 3–52). New York: Academic Press.
Cantor, N., Mischel, W., & Schwartz, J. C. (1982). A prototypic analysis of psychological situations. *Cognitive Psychology*, **19**, 45–77.
Carbonell, J. G. (1980). Towards a process model of human personality traits. *Artificial Intelligence*, **15**, 49–74.
Carbonell, J. G. (1981). *Subjective understanding: Computer models of belief systems*. Ann Arbor: University of Michigan Research Press.
Chandler, M. J. (1972). Egocentricity in normal and pathological child development. In F. Monks, W. Hartup, & J. De Witt (Eds.), *Determinants of behavioral development*. New York: Academic Press.
Chandler, M. (1976). Social cognition: A selective review of current research. In W. F. Overton & J. M. Gallagher (Eds.), *Knowledge and development* (Vol. 1). New York: Plenum Press.
Charniak, E., & McDermott, D. (1985). *Introduction to artificial intelligence*. Reading, MA: Addison-Wesley.
Clark, M. S., & Isen, A. M. (1982). Toward understanding the relationship between feeling states and social behavior. In A. Hastorf & A. N. Isen (Eds.), *Cognitive social psychology* (pp. 73–108). New York: Elsevier.

Conway, M. A., & Bekerian, D. A. (1987a). The role of situations in knowledge of emotions. *Cognition and Emotion,* **1,** 145–181.
Conway, M. A., & Bekerian, D. A. (1987b). Organization in autobiographical memory. *Memory & Cognition,* **15,** 119–132.
Dornbusch, S. M., Hastorf, A. H., Richardson, S. A., Muzzy, R. E., & Vreeland, R. S. (1965). The perceiver and the perceived: Their relative influence on categories of interpersonal perception. *Journal of Personality and Social Psychology,* **1,** 434–440.
Dyer, M. G. (1983a). *In-depth understanding: A computer model of integrated processing for narrative comprehension.* Cambridge, MA: MIT Press.
Dyer, M. G. (1983b). The role of affect in narratives. *Cognitive Science,* **7,** 211–242.
Dyer, M. G. (1987). Emotions and their computations: Three computer models. *Cognition and Emotion,* **1,** 323–347.
Easterbrook, J. A. (1959). The effect of emotion on cue utilization and the organization of behavior. *Psychological Review,* **66,** 183–201.
Feigenbaum, E. A., & Feldman, J. (1963). *Computers and thought.* New York: McGraw Hill.
Feshbach, N. D., & Roe, K. (1968). Empathy in 6 and 7 year olds. *Child Development,* **39,** 133–145.
Fiske, S. T., & Taylor, S. E. (1984). *Social cognition.* Reading, MA: Addison-Wesley.
Flapan, D. (1968). *Children's understanding of social interaction.* New York: Teacher's College Press.
Flavell, J. H. (1974). The development of inferences about others. In T. Mischel (Ed.)., *Understanding other persons.* Oxford: Blackwell, Basil & Mott.
Flavell, J. H. (1977). *Cognitive development.* Englewood Cliffs, NJ: Prentice-Hall.
Flavell, J. H., Botkin, P. T., & Fry, C. L. (1968). *The development of role taking and communication skills in children.* New York: Wiley.
Foss, C. C., & Bower, G. H. (1986). Understanding actions in relation to goals. In N. E. Sharkey (Ed.), *Advances in cognitive science, 1.* New York: Halsted Press.
Goldings, H. J. (1954). On the avowal and projection of happiness. *Journal of Personality,* **23,** 30–47.
Graesser, A. C. (1981). *Prose comprehension beyond the word.* New York: Springer-Verlag.
Greenspan, S., Barenboim, C., & Chandler, M. (1976). Empathy and pseudoempathy: The affective judgments of first and third graders. *Journal of Genetic Psychology,* **129,** 77–88.
Halpern, H. M. (1955) Empathy, similarity and self-satisfaction. *Journal of Consulting Psychology,* **19,** 449–452.
Hansen, R. D. (1985). Cognitive economy and commonsense attribution processing. In J. H. Harvey & G. Weary (Eds.), *Attribution: Basic issues and applications* (pp. 65–85). New York: Academic Press.
Hassan, S. A. (1974). Transaction and contextual invalidation between the parents of disturbed families: A comparative study. *Family Process,* **13,** 53–76.
Hastie, R., Ostrom, T. M., Ebbesen, E. B., Wyer, R. S., Jr., Hamilton, D. L., & Carlston, D. E. (Eds.). (1981). *Person memory: The cognitive basis of social perception.* Hillsdale, NJ: Erlbaum.
Heider, F. (1958). *The psychology of interpersonal relations.* New York: Wiley.
Higgins, E. T. (1981). Role taking and social judgment: Alternative developmental perspectives and processes. In J. H. Flavell & L. Ross (Eds.), *Social cognitive development.* New York: Cambridge University Press.
Higgins, E. T., & Bargh, J. A. (1987). Social cognition and social perception. *Annual Review of Psychology,* **38,** 369–425.
Higgins, E. T., & King, G. (1981) Accessibility of social constructs: Information processing consequences of individual and contextual variability. In N. Cantor & J. F. Kihlstrom (Eds.), *Personality, cognition and social interaction.* Hillsdale, NJ: Erlbaum.

Higgins, E. T., Van Hook, E., & Dorfman, P. (1988). Do self-attributes form a cognitive structure? *Social Cognition, 6*, 177–207.

Hoffman, M. L. (1978). Empathy, its development and prosocial implications. In C. B. Keasey (Ed.), *Nebraska Symposium on Motivation, 1977*. Lincoln: University of Nebraska Press.

Johnson, M. K. (1985). The origins of memories. In P. C. Kendall (Ed.), *Advances in cognitive and behavioral research and therapy* (pp. 1 27). Hillsdale, NJ: Erlbaum.

Jones, E. E., & Davis, K. E. (1965). From acts to dispositions: The attribution process in person perception. In L. Berkowitz (Ed.), *Advances in experimental social psychology* (Vol. 2). New York: Academic Press.

Karniol, R. (1986). What will they think of next? Transformation rules used to predict other people's thoughts and feelings. *Journal of Personality and Social Psychology, 51*, 932–944.

Karniol, R. (1989). *The effects of priming on transformation rule use*. In preparation.

Karniol, R., & Bresler, O. (1989). *Transformation rule use for making predictions about same and opposite sex targets*. In preparation.

Karniol, R., & Koren, L. (1987). How would you feel? Children's inferences regarding their own and other's affective experiences. *Cognitive Development, 2*, 269–276.

Karniol, R., Liberman, G. M., & Ovad, T. (1989). *Self-monitoring and transformation rule use in generating predictions regarding self and others*. In preparation.

Karniol, R., & Sabo, N. (1989). *The effects of stress on transformation rule use with projective stimuli*. In preparation.

Kelley, H. H. (1967). Attribution theory in social psychology. In D. Levine (Ed.), *Nebraska Symposium on Motivation* (pp. 192–238). Lincoln: University of Nebraska Press.

Kelley, H. H. (1972). Causal schemata and the attribution process. In E. E. Jones, D. E. Kanouse, H. H. Kelley, R. E. Nisbett, S. Valins, & B. Weiner (Eds.), *Attribution: Perceiving the causes of behavior* (pp. 151–174). Morristown, NJ: General Learning Press.

Kelley, G. (1955). *The psychology of personal constructs*. New York: Norton.

Kernis, M. H. (1984). Need for uniqueness, self-schemas, and thought as moderators of the false-consensus effect. *Journal of Experimental Social Psychology, 20*, 350–362.

Klein, S. B., & Kihlstrom, J. F. (1986). Elaboration, organization, and the self-reference effect in memory. *Journal of Experimental Psychology: General, 115*, 26–38.

Kolodner, J. L. (1984). *Retrieval and organization strategies in conceptual memory: A computer model*. Hillsdale, NJ: Erlbaum.

Kulik, J. A., Sledge, P., & Mahler, H. I. M. (1986). Self-confirmatory attribution, egocentrism, and the perpetuation of self-beliefs. *Journal of Personality and Social Psychology, 50*, 587–594.

Laing, R. D., & Esterson, A. (1970). *Sanity, madness and the family*. London: Tavistock.

Laing, R. D., Phillipson, H., & Lee, A. R. (1966). *Interpersonal perception*. New York: Harper & Row.

Lehnert, W. G., & Vine, E. W. (1987). The role of affect in narrative structure. *Cognition and Emotion, 1*, 299–322.

Lennard, H. I., Beaulieu, M., & Embrey, N. (1965). Interaction in families with a schizophrenic child. *Archives of General Psychiatry, 12*, 166–183.

Lennard, H. I., & Bernstein, A. (1969). *Patterns in human interaction*. San Francisco: Jossey-Bass.

Lidz, T. (1978). Egocentric cognitive regression and the family setting of schizophrenic disorders. In L. C. Wynne, R. L. Cromwell, & S. Matthysse (Eds.), *The nature of schizophrenia: New approaches to research and treatment*. New York: Wiley.

Little, V. L., & Kendall, P. C. (1979). Cognitive–behavioral interventions with delinquents: Problem solving, role-taking, and self-control. In P. C. Kendall & S. D. Hollon (Eds.), *Cognitive–behavioral intervention: Theory, research and procedure*. New York: Academic Press.

Livesely, W. J., & Bromley, D. B. (1973). *Person perception in childhood and adolescence*. New York: Wiley.

Markus, H. (1977). Self-schemata and processing information about the self. *Journal of Personality and Social Psychology*, **35**, 63–78.

Markus, H., & Smith, J. (1981). The influence of self-schemas on the perception of others. In N. Cantor & J. Kihlstrom (Eds.), *Personality, cognition, and social interaction*. Hillsdale, NJ: Erlbaum.

Maslow, A. H. (1954). *Motivation and personality*. New York: Harper.

McDaniel, M. A., Lapsley, D. K., & Milstead, M. (1987). Testing the generality and automaticity of self-reference encoding with release from proactive interference. *Journal of Experimental Social Psychology*, **23**, 269–284.

McGuire, W. J., & McGuire, C. V. (1986). Differences in conceptualizing self versus conceptualizing other people as manifested in contrasting verb types used in natural speech. *Journal of Personality and Social Psychology*, **51**, 1135–1143.

McGuire, W. J., & McGuire, C. V. (1988). Content and process in the experience of self. In L. Berkowitz (Ed.), *Advances in experimental social psychology* (Vol. 21). New York: Academic Press.

McGuire, W. J., & Padawer-Singer, A. (1976). Trait salience in the spontaneous self-concept. *Journal of Personality and Social Psychology*, **33**, 743–754.

Mead, G. H. (1934). *Mind, self, and society*. Chicago: University of Chicago Press.

Miller, P. H., Kessel, F. S., & Flavell, J. H. (1970). Thinking about people thinking about people thinking about_____: A study of social cognitive development. *Child Development*, **41**, 613–623.

Mullen, B., Atkins, J. L., Champion, D. S., Edwards, C., Hardy, D., Story, J. E., & Vanderklok, M. (1985). The false consensus effect: A meta-analysis of 115 hypothesis tests. *Journal of Experimental Social Psychology*, **21**, 262–283.

Nelson, K. (1981). Social cognition in a script framework. In J. H. Flavell & L. Ross (Eds.), *Social cognitive development*. London: Cambridge University Press.

Nelson, K. (1986). *Event knowledge: Structure and function in development*. Hillsdale, NJ: Erlbaum.

Newell, A., Shaw, J. C., & Simon, H. A. (1963). Empirical explorations of the Logic Theory Machine: A case study in heuristics. In E. A. Feigenbaum & J. Feldman (Eds.), *Computers and thought*. New York: McGraw-Hill.

Pervin, L. A. (1983). The stasis and flow of behavior: Toward a theory of goals. In M. M. Page (Ed.), *Nebraska Symposium on Motivation, 1982*. Lincoln: University of Nebraska Press.

Piaget, J. (1965). *The moral judgment of the child*. London: Routledge & Kegan Paul. (Original work published 1932)

Pylyshyn, Z. (1984). *Computation and cognition: Toward a foundation for cognitive science*. Cambridge, MA: MIT Press.

Reiser, B. (1986). Knowledge-directed retrieval of autobiographical memories. In J. L. Kolodner & C. K. Riesbeck (Eds.), *Experience, memory, and reasoning*. Hillsdale, NJ: Erlbaum.

Reiser, B., Black, J. B., & Abelson, R. P. (1985). Knowledge structures in the organization and retrieval of autobiographical memories. *Cognitive Psychology*, **17**, 89–137.

Rieger, C. (1979). Five aspects of a full-scale story comprehension model. In N. V. Findler (Ed.), *Associative networks: Representation and use of knowledge by computers*. New York: Academic Press.

Ross, L., Greene, D., & House, P. (1977). The "false consensus effect:" An egocentric bias in social perception and attribution processes. *Journal of Experimental Social Psychology*, **13**, 279–301.

Rubin, K. H. (1973). Egocentrism in childhood: A unitary construct? *Child Development*, **44**, 102–111.

Ryle, G. (1949). *The concept of mind*. London: Hutchinson.

Salaman, E. (1982). A collection of moments. In U. Neisser (Ed.), *Memory observed: Remembering in natural contexts* (pp. 49–63). San Francisco: Jossey-Bass. (Original work published 1970)

Sarbin, T. (1954). Role theory. In G. Lindzey (Ed.), *Handbook of social psychology* (Vol. 1). Cambridge, MA: Addison-Wesley.

Schank, R. (1982). *Dynamic memory: A theory of learning in computers and people.* London: Cambridge University Press.

Schank, R., & Abelson, R. (1977). *Scripts, plans, goals and understanding.* Hillsdale, NJ: Erlbaum.

Schank, R., & Wilensky, R. (1978). A goal-directed production system for story understanding. In D. A. Waterman & F. Hayes-Roth (Eds.), *Pattern-directed inference systems.* New York: Academic Press.

Schneider, D. (1973). Implicit personality theory: A review. *Psychological Bulletin,* **79,** 294–309.

Schutz, A. (1962). *Collected papers* (Vol. 1). The Hague: Nijhoff.

Schwartz, F., & Rouse, R. O. (1961). The activation and recovery of associations. *Psychological Issues,* **3,** No. 9.

Schwartz, R. M., & Trabasso, T. (1984). Children's understanding of emotions. In C. E. Izard, J. Kagan, & R. B. Zajonc (Eds.), *Emotions, cognition, and behavior* (pp. 409–437). London: Cambridge University Press.

Selman, R. L. (1971). Taking another's perspective: role-taking development in early childhood. *Child Development,* **42,** 1721–1734.

Selman, R. L. (1980). *The growth of interpersonal understanding.* New York: Academic Press.

Selman, R. L., & Byrne, D. F. (1974). A structural–developmental analysis of levels of role-taking in middle childhood. *Child Development,* **45,** 803–806.

Shantz, C. U. (1975). The development of social cognition. In E. M. Hetherington (Ed.), *Review of child development research* (Vol. 5). Chicago: University of Chicago Press.

Shantz, C. U. (1983). Social cognition. In J. H. Flavell & E. Markman (Eds.), *Handbook of child psychology* (Vol. 3). New York: Wiley.

Sherman, S. J., Presson, C. C., & Chassin, L. (1984). Mechanisms underlying the false consensus effect: The special role of threats to the self. *Personality and Social Psychology Bulletin,* **10,** 127–138.

Simeonsson, R. J. (1973). Egocentric responses of normal and emotionally disturbed children in different treatment settings. *Child Psychiatry and Human Development,* **3,** 179–186.

Smith, A. (1976). *A theory of moral sentiments.* Oxford: Clarendon Press. (Original work published 1759)

Spence, J., & Helmreich, R. (1978). *Masculinity and femininity.* Austin: University of Texas Press.

Spence, J., & Sawin. (1985). Images of masculinity and femininity: A reconceptualization. In V. E. O'Leary, R. K. Unger & B. S. Wallston (Eds.), *Women, gender, and social psychology.* Hillsdale, NJ: Erlbaum.

Stewart, D. (1956). *Preface to empathy.* New York: Philosophical Library.

Stotland, E., & Canon, L. K. (1972). *Social psychology: A cognitive approach.* Philadelphia: Saunders.

Tagiuri, R., & Petrullo, L. (Eds.). (1958). *Person perception and interpersonal behavior.* Stanford, CA: Stanford University Press.

Taylor, S. E. (1981). The interface of cognitive and social psychology. In J. H. Harvey (Ed.), *Cognition, social behavior and the environment* (pp. 189–211). Hillsdale, NJ: Erlbaum.

Trabasso, T., Stein, N. L., & Johnson, L. R. (1981). A causal analysis of story structure. In G. H. Bower (Ed.), *The psychology of learning and motivation* (Vol. 15). New York: Academic Press.

Turiel, E. (1978). Distinct conceptual and developmental domains: Social convention and morality. In C. B. Keasey (Ed.), *Nebraska Symposium on Motivation, 1977.* Lincoln: University of Nebraska Press.

Tversky, A., & Kahneman, D. (1973). Availability: A heuristic for judging frequency and probability. *Cognitive Psychology,* **5,** 207–232.
Warr, P. B., & Knapper, C. (1968). *The perception of people and events.* New York: Wiley.
Whorf, B. L. (1956). On the connection of ideas. In J. B. Carroll (Ed.), *Language, thought, and reality: Selected writings of Benjamin Lee Whorf.* Cambridge, MA: MIT press. (Original work published 1927)
Wilkening, F., Becker, J., & Trabasso, T. (1980). *Information integration by children.* Hillsdale, NJ: Erlbaum.
Wolf, R., & Murray, H. A. (1937). An experiment in judging personalities. *Journal of Personality,* **7,** 345–365.
Worland, J., Edenhart-Pepe, R., Weeks, D. G., & Konen, P. M. (1984). Cognitive evaluation of children at risk: IQ, differentiation, and egocentricity. In N. F. Watt, E. J. Anthony, L. C. Wynne, & J. E. Rolf (Eds.), *Children at risk for schizophrenia.* Cambridge, MA: Cambridge University Press.
Wyer, R. S., & Srull, T. K. (1983). The processing of social stimulus information: A conceptual integration. In R. Hastie *et al.,* (Eds.), *Person memory* (pp. 227–300). Hillsdale, NJ: Erlbaum.
Zuroff, D. (1982). Person situation and person-by-situation interaction components in person perception. *Journal of Personality,* **50,** 1–14.

SELF-ATTENTION AND BEHAVIOR: A REVIEW AND THEORETICAL UPDATE

Frederick X. Gibbons

I. Introduction

A resurgence of interest over the last 15–20 years has seen the emergence of several new theoretical approaches to the study of the self. One theory that has contributed to this movement is self-awareness theory (Duval & Wicklund, 1972). It has now been more than 17 years since self-awareness theory was introduced. During this period the theory has been modified several times and still continues to generate a considerable amount of research. The theory has also spawned several related, but distinct, alternative models. These models have had significant impact in the area and have definitely increased understanding of the psychology of self-attention. In so doing, however, they have also shifted the focus of the theory in a different direction than that apparently intended by Duval and Wicklund (1972).

The primary purpose of this article is to review progress in the original theory since the publication of the most recent conceptual overview (Wicklund, 1980). Criticisms of the original theory and the alternative models are also discussed. In particular, the argument will be presented, contrary to the tenets of most of the alternative models, that behavioral responses to self-focused attention are intrinsically, not extrinsically, motivated and oriented. In addition, the basis for a revised model, which integrates relevant criticism and research, will be woven throughout the paper and then outlined at the end. I start with a brief review and then assess the original theory vis-à-vis alternative approaches.

II. "Original Self-Awareness Theory: A Review

According to Duval and Wicklund (1972), attention is bidirectional. At any given time, it may be focused on the self or the environment, but it cannot be directed to both at the same time. When people are reminded of themselves, for example, by a mirror or a photograph, their attention gravitates toward the dimension of self that happens momentarily to be most salient. Salience of self-dimensions is determined most often by situational factors. It may be performance on a particular task, an attitude or belief or, by default, simply physical appearance. Directing attention toward a salient self-dimension initiates a series of cognitive steps that form the basis of the theory. It is proposed that the self-focused individual will necessarily become engaged in a process of self-evaluation in which the most salient self-dimension, as it exists, is measured against a standard or ideal that the person happens to maintain for that particular dimension. The concept of standard was originally defined simply as a "criterion of correctness." Since there are few aspects of the self that are totally satisfactory (Wicklund, 1975), this comparison will eventually lead to recognition of a shortcoming or "discrepancy" between the current self and the particular ideal or standard. Recognition of this shortcoming, in turn, produces negative affect or discomfort.

At this point the theory becomes motivational in nature. Duval and Wicklund stated that the desire to reduce the negative affect, which results from recognition of a discrepancy between the "real" and the "ideal" self, is the motivating factor behind the behavioral responses that are predicted to occur. Two courses of action can result: The person might either try to avoid the self-aware state or, if possible, try to reduce the discrepancy. Thus, the application of greater effort than before into the task at hand, greater concentration, and other attempts at self-improvement are likely to occur. Little was said in the original theory about what happens cognitively while the individual is attempting discrepancy reduction, or what reaction occurs after reduction has been attempted and has either succeeded or failed.

While the real–ideal comparison and discrepancy reduction processes formed the basis of Duval and Wicklund's thinking, their theory also contained four primary corollaries and one subcorollary:

1. *Conformity.* For reasons outlined below, conformity behavior should increase when an individual is self-focused and in the presence of a group.

2. *Attribution.* Causal attributions "follow" focus of attention (cf. Duval, 1971; Storms, 1973); thus, attributions of responsibility for behavior should be more internal when attention is focused on the self.

3. *Attitude–behavior discrepancy.* Perceived inconsistency between an attitude, a personal standard (e.g., job performance), or a value (e.g., telling the

truth) and a behavior comprises a within-self discrepancy and, therefore, is likely to be acted upon when attention is self-focused; thus, attitude–behavior or attitude–attitude consistency often becomes a goal of a self-focused person.

4. *Social facilitation.* The attention of others induces a state of self-focus, which, in turn, leads to an increase in attempts at behavioral improvement. Such behavior may appear as social facilitation or amplification.

5. *Cognizance of self.* This subcorollary, although not explicitly part of the original theory, is a derivative of it and is definitely consistent with its tone (Wicklund, 1979, 1980). Specifically, a consequence of directing attention toward a salient self-dimension is that cognizance of that particular dimension is increased. Evidence of this cognizance can be seen, for example, in greater consistency between self-report and behavior, and in more accurate self-reports.

Each of the four original corollaries, plus the subcorollary added later, has been examined either directly or indirectly in experimental laboratory research, and thus provides a good basis for a review of the entire theory. Examination of that work (most of it published since 1980) and an assessment of its implications for the theory are presented in the next section. Before proceeding to that, however, a brief discussion of the unique experimental procedure used in self-awareness research is in order.

Theoretically, any stimulus that directs attention back on the self is capable of inducing a state of self-focus. In the original theory it made little difference what the stimulus happened to be, or what aspect of the self initially captured attention. Thus the "route" to introspection and self-evaluation might proceed through physical appearance (reflected in a mirror), the sound of one's voice on a tape recorder, or even the sight of one's name on a name tag. Regardless, the result was postulated to be the same: Attention will eventually gravitate toward whatever self-dimension has been made salient by the situation, and the self-evaluation process vis-à-vis that dimension will begin.

The vast majority of studies that have been conducted, however, have used mirrors as manipulations of attention in what would be considered "private" situations, that is, in the absence of an audience or observer of any kind. In retrospect, there appears to have been good reason for this. What have been termed "public" manipulations of self-attention (cf. A. H. Buss, 1980), such as live cameras, audiences, or distinguishing clothing, may be effective at focusing one's attention on the self, but they do so from a perspective that is almost always external to the self (e.g., "What are *they* expecting me to do?" or "What does *she* think of my behavior?"). Although it does limit the ecological validity of the theory somewhat, the use of introspective focusing manipulations, such as mirrors, distinguishes the state of self-awareness from other focal states that are primarily externally oriented. It also distinguishes self-awareness theory from other theories that also reflect an "other orientation" (e.g., self-consciousness theory, A. H. Buss, 1980; self-monitoring theory, Snyder, 1974). For reasons discussed more fully later in the article, research utilizing public manipulations of attention will be distinguished from those using more personal manipulations (i.e., mirrors); the difference is theoretical as well as phenomenological and empirical. The discussion here will also differentiate between situationally induced self-attention and the dispositional tendency to be self-focused as measured by the private subscale of the Self-Consciousness Scale (Fenigstein, Scheier, & Buss, 1975). Both of these, in turn, will be distinguished from the public subscale of the Self-Consciousness Scale. The reason once again has to do with the perspective on the self engendered by private vs. public self-attention.

What induces self-awareness outside of the laboratory? Consistent with the argument developed later in this article, the answer to this question is a modification of what Duval and Wicklund suggested 17 years ago. That is, any device or situation that focuses one's attention back on the self and encourages introspection and self-scrutiny is capable of inducing the state of self-focus. But the focus of the attention and the source of the evaluation must be internal to the self. What that means, ultimately, is that an individual is not likely to become self-aware in the presence of external distractions, whether they are tasks one is working on, leisure activities, or even the presence of other people. Audiences can induce self-awareness, but they are also quite capable of drawing attention away from the self (this issue is discussed more fully later in the article). In the absence of distractions, given an appropriate stimulus or simply an opportunity for introspection, then self-awareness is likely. Simply put, self-awareness occurs when aspects of the self are more salient than environmental stimuli.

III. Assessments and Modifications

A. CONFORMITY

In a detailed discussion of conformity behavior in group situations, Duval and Wicklund (1972) suggested that self-focused attention will increase conformity responses through a process mediated by attribution. Being in the minority (and therefore a target of conformity pressure) serves to direct attention back to the self, much as attention focuses on the central figure in a figure–ground contrast (Koffka, 1935). Since attributions tend to follow focus of attention, the self-aware (minority-group) individual is likely to attribute the source of any "error" (i.e., the discrepancy between one's own opinion and that of the majority group) to the self. In an attempt to reduce this discrepancy, the self-focused person(s) should try to bring behavior into line with the norm or social standard, which, as a result of the foregoing process, is now seen as correct (Duval, 1976).

1. Personal Standards

This analysis assumes that self-focused persons in a group-conflict situation will inevitably attribute the error to internal sources and accede to group pressure or anticipation of group pressure. The larger the group, the stronger the pressure (cf. Mullen, 1984) and the greater the conformity. The argument appears to be accurate when considering situations of low personal involvement, but it assigns a rather tenuous nature to personal standards. In fact, in most of the studies demonstrating this conformity reaction (e.g., Diener & Srull, 1979), it may be assumed that the subjects had little commitment to or concern with the issue in question. Those issues typically involved either verifiable beliefs (cf. Goethals & Darley, 1977) or simply estimates in ambiguous situations—the type of circumstances in which group opinion might weigh most heavily on decision making and behavior.

What this approach does not take into consideration is the fact that acceding to external pressure on an issue of some importance is likely to create a personal discrepancy of an entirely different nature. This assumption has been tested by Gibbons and Wright (1983) and indirectly by Froming, Walker, and Lopyan (1982). In both studies, a stable personal standard was pitted against opposition from a credible external source. In neither case, however, did the self-focused subjects abandon their personal standards in the face of opposition.

Froming *et al.* (1982) found that subjects maintained their belief in the usefulness of punishment as a learning tool when they were self-aware (in front of a mirror), even though they believed that others probably disagreed with them. In Gibbons and Wright (1983), a personal standard of greater significance was made salient and then contradicted by a majority. Persons who had indicated earlier that their attitudes about sexual behavior were relatively conservative were confronted with information in the form of a bogus opinion poll suggesting that the majority of their peers maintained sexual standards that were much more liberal than their own. All subjects apparently found this information credible and convincing, and when asked again how they felt about sexual issues, they modified their opinions somewhat to bring them in line with their peers. In doing so, however, the self-aware subjects maintained a relatively conservative stance within the group. As a result, their attitude–attitude correlations remained quite high ($M\ r\ =\ .79$), and they were higher than those of the non-self-focused subjects ($M\ r\ =\ .57$). Thus, the self-focused subjects did not simply abandon or ignore their personal standards and embrace those of the majority. Instead, they maintained their standards but modified them somewhat to accommodate the new information.

2. Discrepancy Prevention

In situations such as just described, where there is some pressure to behave in a manner that is not consistent with personal standards, self-focus has an effect of inhibition. That is, it reduces the likelihood of performance of behaviors that would create a personal discrepancy of some sort (e.g., lying, cf. Gibbons, 1978; harming another, Carver, 1975) even though one may not currently exist. A similar situation occurred in McCormick (1980). Self-focused subjects in that study did not capitulate to group pressure on an issue of importance after they had made some public commitment to their stance on the issue. In fact, to date there is no evidence to suggest that internally focused (self-aware) subjects will abandon a personal standard of some importance in order to conform to a group norm.

B. ATTRIBUTION

Mediating the relationship between self-focus and conformity, according to Duval and Wicklund (1972), is the impact that focus of attention has on attribution. Their contention is that attributions should be more internal when attention is internally focused. The argument is similar to that presented by other researchers (e.g., Storms, 1973) who have suggested that when people adopt the perspective of others and become observers of their own behavior, they make the same causal attributions for that behavior as do observers. Duval and Wicklund (1973) provided some evidence to support this claim. They found that self-aware subjects accepted more responsibility for a variety of hypothetical outcomes of a positive or negative nature than did subjects who were not self-focused. The latter group, in turn, has been shown to accept even less responsibility when their attention is deliberately distracted (cf. Wicklund & Duval, 1971). Similar results were reported by several other researchers, including D. M. Buss and Scheier (1976), who used the private subscale of the Self-Consciousness Scale (Fenigstein *et al.*, 1975) as a measure of dispositional self-awareness;[1] Fenigstein and Levine (1984), who enhanced subjects' self-attention by having them write stories about themselves; and Fenigstein and Carver (1978), who increased self-

---

[1]Although not identical conceptually, the theoretical similarities between the private subscale of the Self-Consciousness Scale and the state of self-awareness have been discussed many times elsewhere (e.g., Carver & Scheier, 1981; Wicklund, 1979). In fact, the private subscale was originally designed to measure a dispositional analogue to situational self-awareness (Fenigstein, 1987), as can be seen fairly clearly in the items on the scale (e.g., "I reflect about myself a lot"; "I'm generally attentive to my inner feelings"; "I'm alert to changes in my mood"). However, since I am presenting a situational rather than dispositional perspective in the current article, research employing this particular individual-difference measure will be identified in order to distinguish it from the state of self-attention as brought on by environmental factors (e.g., a mirror).

focus by having subjects listen to a tape recording that was said to be of their own heartbeat. In all of these studies, however, the outcomes were only imagined by the subjects and presumably had relatively little impact on them. It seems likely, then, that the attribution process itself occurred at a superficial level (cf. Taylor & Fiske's [1978] discussion of "top of the head" attributional responding). Under these circumstances causal ascriptions are simply reflections of where attention happens to be directed, and little thought is given to the actual consequences associated with accepting personal responsibility for one's actions.

Federoff and Harvey (1976) created a comparatively high-involvement situation by having their subjects provide therapy to a person (a confederate) supposedly suffering from a phobia and then giving the subjects false feedback suggesting that their "client" had either gotten worse or better. Information indicating that the person's condition had deteriorated led the subjects who were responding in front of a camera to deny responsibility for what had happened. The authors conclude that internal attributions in situations of this nature, with important negative consequences and implications for the subject, would be especially painful for those people who were self-focused and therefore engaged in self-evaluation (cf. also J. G. Hull & Levy, 1979, Experiment 3). Federoff and Harvey conclude that protection of the ego becomes a primary concern when attention is self-focused. Ego-defensive attributions by mirror-induced, self-aware subjects have also been reported recently by Cohen, Dowling, Bishop, and Maney (1985).

Although appealing in its parsimony, the attribution-follows-attention hypothesis seems inadequate to account for many of the attribution findings in the self-awareness literature. Based in part on the results of Federoff and Harvey (1976), Wicklund (1978) modified the theory to take into account the evidence that self-focus may sometimes increase ego protectiveness or self-esteem maintenance. Since the pain associated with embarrassment, failure, and so forth is likely to be more salient when attention is self-focused than when it is not (Scheier & Carver, 1977), the desire to avoid that pain may also be increased (Duval & Duval, 1983). Another problem with the assumption that self-aware persons automatically assume a dispositional attribution perspective similar to that of others (who happen to be observing them) is that it does not take into account the accuracy of the particular attribution. Instead, it implies that self-aware persons should consistently overestimate dispositional contributions to their actions and, like observers of their behavior, be prone to the "fundamental attribution error" (Ross, 1977). This is not the case. Self-focus does not produce an overestimation of personal involvement in specific outcomes (Stephenson & Wicklund, 1983). Instead, it encourages a more careful and thoughtful consideration of the antecedents and the consequences of behavior (cf. Gibbons, 1983). It makes sense, then, that self-attention might also increase the accuracy with which people assess their own role in a given situation or their own contribution to a particular outcome. In some situations this might produce a dispositional attribution, but in others it would not.

Several studies attest to this accurate-attribution hypothesis. In particular, self-aware subjects have been shown to be less likely than non-self-aware persons to provide inflated estimates of their own responsibility for a group activity (Stephenson & Wicklund, 1983; see also Wicklund, 1980); to accept responsibility for a change in a partner's behavior for which they were, in fact, not responsible (Ellis & Holmes, 1982); and to make inaccurate attributions of arousal (Gibbons & Gaeddert, 1984; Reisenzein & Gattinger, 1982). More recently, Gibbons et al. (1985) asked self-aware and non-self-aware psychiatric subjects (alcoholics and persons with affective disorders) to make attributions to themselves and to exogenous factors (e.g., luck, other people) for their psychiatric problems. It was assumed that this type of attribution process would certainly be involving for the subjects. Given the ambiguity in the literature, however, no clear prediction could be made as to whether self-focus would increase patients' defensiveness or else their willingness to accept responsibility. Results suggested neither was the case. Instead, the self-focused patients' attributions of responsibility were more accurate than were those of the non-self-focused patients. (Accuracy was determined by comparing their responses with actual hospital records and with evaluations provided by hospital staff.) One reason for this differential accuracy was that the non-self-focused patients underestimated the length and the severity of their problems (perhaps owing to impression management), whereas the self-aware group did not.

These results, plus those of other studies (Cohen et al., 1985; Ellis & Holmes, 1982; Franzoi & Sweeney, 1986; Nadler, 1983), all of which failed to produce evidence of enhanced dispositional attributions during self-awareness, indicate that while the self-focus–self-attribution hypothesis may be appropriately applied in situations of low personal involvement, it is inadequate to explain circumstances in which the behavior in question has important personal consequences for the actor. Taken together, these studies suggest that self-focused actors are not prone to make the fundamental attribution error as are observers of their behavior. Instead, they are more discerning in the attributions they make, taking into account not only implications for the self and self-esteem but also accuracy. The result is a more carefully considered assessment of their own role in a particular outcome. Whether the attribution itself is accurate or defensive depends on two factors: causal ambiguity and ego-involvement. Specifically, accuracy is likely when one's own contribution is determinable (e.g., Ellis & Holmes, 1986; Gibbons et al., 1985; Stephenson & Wicklund, 1983); defensiveness should occur when the outcome has potential negative implications for the self-concept and one's actual contribution is not clearly discernible (e.g., Cohen et al., 1985; Federoff & Harvey, 1976; Nadler, 1983).

C. ATTITUDE–BEHAVIOR DISCREPANCY

Duval and Wicklund (1972; see also Wicklund, 1975, 1980) claimed that recognition of inconsistency between an attitude and a behavior constitutes a within-self discrepancy, which the self-aware person is motivated to reduce. Although they did not have much empirical support for this hypothesis (cf. Wicklund & Duval, 1971), it has since generated a considerable amount of research. For example, a number of investigators (Innes & Young, 1975; Insko, Worchel, Songer, & Arnold, 1973; Scheier & Carver, 1980; Zanna & Aziza, 1976) have demonstrated that the desire to maintain cognitive consistency, as manifested in dissonance reduction, is greatly reduced when attention is externally directed. Subjects in each of these studies evidenced much less attitude change in the face of inconsistent behavior when their attention was not self-focused than when it was self-focused. Cognitive dissonance and inconsistency, like value transgressions, are much less aversive when attention is not directed on the self (cf. Wicklund, 1975). On the other hand, the discomfort of dissonance is exacerbated by self-focus. Evidence of this is provided by Greenberg and Musham (1981), who found that subjects were more likely to avoid the state of self-focus after they had been induced, through forced compliance, to engage in counterattitudinal behavior than when they had engaged in attitude-consistent behavior (cf. also Lepper, Zanna & Abelson, 1970).

Like other cognitive consistency theories, self-awareness theory assumes a consistency motive, in the sense that attitude–behavior congruence represents an ideal or standard. Moreover, there is evidence that that consistency motive can override other, conflicting response tendencies when attention is self-focused. An interesting study by Hormuth (1982) makes this point convincingly. All subjects were first trained in a particular response pattern on a paired-associate learning task. The training was extensive in this particular pattern, almost to the point of overlearning, thereby creating a "dominant response" (C. L. Hull, 1952). For half of these subjects, the dominant response that they had learned was inconsistent with a personal standard that they maintained, which was to be creative or original. For the other half, no such inconsistency existed. All subjects were then presented with single words from the original list of pairs and asked to respond to those stimuli any way they wanted. Thus they could have chosen to simply repeat the association they had learned or they could provide a new (original) association. While they were doing this, half of the subjects were seated in front of a mirror. As expected, results indicated that the self-aware subjects behaved in a manner that was congruent with their personal standards, even though that behavior was in conflict with the dominant response. That is, the self-aware subjects who maintained a standard of originality gave the most original responses. In contrast, the non-self-focused group tended to demonstrate behavior more typically associated with arousal and response amplification (and with social facilitation).[2]

D. COGNIZANCE OF SELF: AFFECT

Scheier's (1976) examination of emotional responsivity in states of self-focus represented a major theoretical extension which has been incorporated in virtually all subsequent discussions of self-awareness theory. His contention was that when an emotional state happens to be the self-dimension that is most salient, awareness of that dimension should increase, just as it would for any cognitive self-component. His dissertation research confirmed this hypothesis, as subjects who had been angered by a provocation demonstrated more retaliatory behavior when their attention was self-focused than when it was not. Subsequent research has provided evidence of similar enhanced reactions to other types of emotions (Reisenzein & Gattinger, 1982; Scheier, Carver, & Gibbons, 1979; Scheier, Carver, & Matthews, 1982). Scheier & Carver (1977), for example, found that subjects reported more negative affect, which had been enhanced via the Velten mood-induction technique (Velten, 1968), when their attention was self-focused than when it was not. In another study, Scheier, Carver, and Gibbons (1981) placed subjects in a situation in which negative affect, in the form of fear of electrical shock, conflicted with a salient behavioral standard. The standard was to help the experimenter (for the sake of science) by accepting doses of electric shock. Results indicated that self-focused subjects' behavior was influenced more by their heightened emotional states than by their desire to adhere to the behavioral standard (meaning, of course, that they accepted less shock). Finally, research by Gibbons, Carver, Scheier, and Hormuth (1979) indicated that self-focused persons' heightened cognizance of internal states includes awareness of the *absence* of emotion or arousal. In that study self-aware subjects were less influenced than were non-self-focused persons by bogus suggestions from an experimenter regarding reactions to a placebo they had ingested. The responses of the self-aware group instead reflected their actual internal states (cf. also Hansen, Hansen, & Crano, 1989; Scheier *et al.,* 1979) rather than what the experimenter had told them they would experience. In sum, the self-focused

[2]This is the only research I am aware of that examined both self-focus and social facilitation together. The results suggested no consistent relation, which is in line with Moore and Baron's (1983) discussion of the same topic. They argued that there are other social facilitation phenomena, besides facilitation of dominant responses (cf. Hormuth, 1982), that self-awareness theory or other attention-based explanations cannot account for, such as impaired complex performance and facilitation of behaviors that are not socially appropriate. They conclude that internal focus of attention is not an important variable in the social facilitation process. Given the lack of evidence of a link between self-focus and social facilitation, as well as the convincing nature of their argument, the topic will not be discussed further here.

subjects in these studies were more responsive to internal than to external cues; the non-self-focused subjects were doing the opposite.

This work represented a significant extension of the theory. By demonstrating that self-focus can influence behavior in ways that have little or nothing to do with attempted discrepancy reduction, it indicated that the self-assessment induced by self-awareness does not necessarily involve the "ideal" self. Instead, the aspect of self that happens at the moment to be most salient—whether cognitive, affective, or physical—can capture the attention of a self-aware person and become the direct focus of self-assessment. Consequently, there is less reliance on externally based information about internal states. In addition, subsequent behavior is more likely to reflect increased awareness of the self-dimension, whatever it may be.

E. COGNIZANCE OF SELF: ACCURACY

Another consequence of the increased awareness of salient self-dimensions, which is brought on by self-focus, is a corresponding increase in the accuracy of self-reports made about those salient dimensions. This newer corollary of self-awareness theory (cf. Wicklund, 1980) has come to be known as the "veracity" (or veridicality) hypothesis. The first study to examine this hypothesis (Pryor, Gibbons, Wicklund, Fazio, & Hood, 1977, Experiment 1) demonstrated that responses to straightforward questions about social behavior (e.g., "I enjoy getting acquainted with most people") were more predictive of actual social behavior when they were made while attention was focused on the self during testing than when attention was not self-focused. Consistent with Duval and Wicklund's reasoning, Pryor et al. suggested that the enhanced validity was a reflection of attempts by the self-focused subjects to reduce the potential disparity between behavior and self-report. However, subsequent research has indicated that the reasoning presented in the original theory, although entirely consistent with the validity effect, is not sufficient to explain it. For one thing, this is clearly an instance of discrepancy prevention rather than reduction. More important, however, is the fact that recent evidence indicates there is more to the self-report veracity effect than simply discrepancy reduction or prevention.

1. Attention and Motivation

In order to answer face-valid questionnaires of the kind used in Pryor et al. (1977), we can assume that the respondent must proceed, however quickly, through a series of simple cognitive steps (cf. Rogers, 1977). The process begins with a review of relevant previous behaviors. This is followed by an assessment of those behaviors relative to the particular situation, and then a report is produced based on that assessment. In discussing the veracity hypothesis, Gibbons (1983) suggested that each of these steps is facilitated by self-awareness. Specifically, it was stated that self-focus fixes attention more closely on the self-dimension being examined, thereby increasing access to relevant information (i.e., recall of previous behavioral examples). At the same time, it also enhances the motivation to report accurately about the self. In other words, self-focus facilitates self-report accuracy by combating two factors that typically reduce validity, namely, poor access to relevant information about the self (due primarily to distraction) and lack of motivation to respond accurately.

2. Inhibition of Impression Management

I would now add a third, related factor to that list, one that typically reduces the veridicality of self-reports but is also counteracted by self-focused attention. Specifically, the tendency toward embellishment or fabrication of self-report, which often reflects impression management concerns, is inhibited by self-focus. Experiment 2 in Pryor et al. (1977) offered some evidence of this inhibitory effect. Subjects were asked to report on their Scholastic Aptitude Test scores, presumably a type of information to which all of them had reasonable access. As expected, the general tendency among all subjects was to inflate their score reports, with that tendency being much stronger among those who had scored below the median on the exam than among those who had higher scores (M exaggeration = 51 points versus 16 points for high scorers). This type of embellishment was counteracted by the mirror manipulation, however. The self-aware subjects exaggerated their scores significantly less, and for this reason they ended up being more accurate.

Several other studies have demonstrated a similar inhibition of self-presentational responses among self-focused persons in favor of accurate self-report (e.g., Bernstein & Davis, 1982; Davies, 1982; Franzoi, 1983), including the study by Gibbons et al. (1985) in which self-aware subjects' willingness to report accurately about their psychiatric problems apparently overrode self-presentational concerns. In each of these examples self-focused subjects reported more accurately on previous behavior for which they had some cognitive representation. In contrast, the behavior of the externally focused subjects reflected more of a concern with others and others' impressions. This is not to suggest that self-awareness eliminates self-presentational behavior. It does not. In fact, for most people self-awareness should increase the desire to put one's "best foot forward" and present a positive image to others as well as to the self. Similarly, if the damage, or potential damage, to the ego is severe enough, self-focus can increase defensiveness or ego protection (cf. Federoff & Harvey, 1976).

What the research on self-awareness does suggest, however, is that self-presentation will stop short of misrepresentation of the self. Using a distinction suggested by several theorists in the area of self-presentation (e.g., Schlenker & Leary, 1982; Tetlock & Manstead, 1985), self-awareness may increase what has been termed "defensive impression management" (i.e., ego protection), but it inhibits "assertive impression management" (i.e., self-embellishment). More generally, self-awareness increases the correlation between internal states and observable behavior, often at the expense of external influence or pressure.

3. Limits of Self-Knowledge

Not surprisingly, more recent work has suggested that there are some limits to the veridicality effect. Gibbons and Gaeddert (1984) found that self-focused subjects were accurate in reporting their somatic states under conditions of increased arousal. They were not capable, however, of distinguishing between two equally plausible external sources of that arousal, one of which was real (evaluation apprehension), the other bogus (a placebo; cf. also Hansen et al., 1989). Similarly, self-focused attention reduced subjects' reports of placebo reactivity in Gibbons et al. (1979), but it did so only for the specific symptoms that had been ascribed to the "drug."

By the same token, there are some aspects of the self that are apparently not accessible and therefore not available to self-scrutiny, regardless of focus of attention or level of motivation. Included in this category, according to Nisbett and Wilson (1977; Wilson, Hull, & Johnson, 1981), are most thought processes, such as those associated with attributions and with decision making in general. Nisbett and Wilson make a convincing case. Nonetheless, Gibbons and Gaeddert (1984) speculated that self-focus may facilitate accessibility to such "remote" cognitive processes, and there is some preliminary evidence to support this contention. In a series of experiments, Kassin (1985) manipulated focus of attention by showing half of his subjects videotapes of themselves that had been made earlier when they were engaged in a simulated eyewitness recognition task. While viewing (or not viewing) the tape, subjects were asked to indicate how confident they now were that they had previously made the correct identification, essentially a retrospective assessment of accuracy. Correlations between self-reported level of confidence about the recognition and actual recognition accuracy were significantly higher for those subjects who viewed themselves on tape while they indicated their confidence level.

While it is probably premature to claim that Kassin's data indicate that self-focus does increase access to thought processes, it is clear that awareness of many internal states and self-dimensions is enhanced when attention is directed internally. Those dimensions include affect or emotional response (Scheier & Carver, 1977; Scheier et al., 1981); somatic condition (Gibbons et al., 1979; Gibbons & Gaeddert, 1984; Scheier et al., 1979, 1982); cognition (e.g., attitudes and values: Baldwin & Holmes, 1987; Carver, 1974, 1975; Froming *et al.*, 1982; Gibbons, 1978); and behavior (Davies, 1982; Gibbons *et al.*, 1985; Pryor *et al.*, 1977, Experiment 3). More recent work has suggested that awareness of a number of other self-dimensions may be enhanced by self-focus, such as performance capabilities (Carver, Blaney, & Scheier, 1979b; Carver & Scheier, 1981), physical symptoms (Mechanic, 1983; Pennebaker, 1982; Ruble & Brooks-Gunn, 1979), and illness (Mullen & Suls, 1982a). Understandably, more attention is currently being devoted to this question of focus of attention and the limits of self-knowledge, especially as it relates to physical and mental health (cf. Mullen & Suls, 1982b). One of the important questions here appears to be whether self-focus can help regulate self-monitoring and therefore facilitate self-care (health) or whether accurate assessment of self-condition serves to reduce what appears to be the salutary effects of self-delusion and illusion (cf. Taylor & Brown, 1988). This is clearly a question that merits further exploration and appears to be one of the directions that self-awareness research will take in the future.

F. PSYCHOLOGICAL STATE OF SELF-AWARENESS

Taken together, the studies discussed here illustrate the unique characteristics of the state of self-awareness. They present an image of the self-focused person as one who becomes more careful in deliberating his or her own behavior and its consequences and who is more concerned about the self than about others. Perhaps the psychological state of self-focus is best defined in contrast with "mindless" behavior, discussed by Langer (1978), or the "top of the head" response pattern described by Taylor and Fiske (1978). In those instances, focus of attention is the immediate environment, and people show relatively little concern for the meaning or consequences of their actions. In short, they do what the environment dictates. In contrast, the self-focused person is more concerned about what pattern of action is most appropriate—what should be done in the particular situation. If a discrepancy between a personal standard or ideal and current behavior is perceived, self-focus should enhance the motivation to reduce that discrepancy.

In many situations, however, no current discrepancy exists. That being the case, self-awareness will still affect behavior, but in a preventative manner by inhibiting standard-inconsistent actions, that is, actions that can occur with considerable regularity in the absence of self-focus (cf. Gibbons & Wicklund, 1982). For example, an adult may submit to the occasional temptation (emanating from the self or others) to lie, falsify income tax records, or slander a colleague, and the child may steal Halloween candy, all with assumed impunity. However, the self-focused adult or child (cf. Diener, Fraser, Beaman, & Kelem, 1976) is much more likely to resist such temptation. The reason is that the self-evaluation that accompanies self-focused attention will be more intense and more aversive during and after personal transgressions of this nature (cf. Carver & Scheier, 1981). In contrast, such inhibitions on behavior are theoretically nonexistent when attention is directed exclusively outward (as in the state of "deindividuation"; Diener, 1979). In other words, there are virtually no moral or ethical constraints on behavior in the absence of self-focus. Instead, behavior is controlled by exigencies of the situation or by force of habit.

G. SUMMARY

The basic premises of the theory as well as the various corollaries have each generated a considerable amount of research. That being the case, it is probably true that this brief review has not done justice to the heuristic value of the theory. Of course, not all of the research has been supportive. For example, it would appear that relationships of self-awareness to conformity and self-awareness to attribution are more complex than Duval and Wicklund thought. On the other hand, their ideas concerning reactions to within-self discrepancies, especially of the nature of attitude–behavior inconsistency, have received quite a bit of support. Among the more significant developments since 1972, however, may be the work that was prompted by the theory but not anticipated by Duval and Wicklund. That is the research on cognizance of self and the theoretical models of self-attention proposed in the decade after the original theory.

IV. Alternative Approaches: A Review

Actually several alternative models of self-focus have been proposed, each based in part on criticisms and modifications of the original theory. Two of the better known models (Carver, 1979; Carver & Scheier, 1981; J. G. Hull & Levy, 1979) will be discussed here, one briefly and the other in more depth, specifically as they relate to Duval and Wicklund's (1972) theory. In addition, some modifications of the original theory suggested by these two models will be discussed and evaluated.

A. HULL AND LEVY'S MODEL

1. Criticisms of Self-Awareness Theory

In a provocative article J. G. Hull and Levy (1979) offered four criticisms of Duval and Wicklund's (1972) theory, while proposing an alternative approach.

Their primary criticism reflects their belief that self-awareness is not associated with self-directed attention "but rather corresponds to a particular form of informational encoding" of self-relevant aspects of the environment (p. 758). Consistent with this perspective, they also argue that there is no evidence that self-awareness involves either a "naturally self-evaluative" process (i.e., comparison with standards) or an "affect-inducing" state, or that it is associated with an increase in self-attribution. I will respond to these criticisms in reverse order.

As discussed previously, the evidence does support Hull and Levy's fourth contention concerning the limits of the self-focused attention–attribution effect (Ellis & Holmes, 1982; Federoff & Harvey, 1976; Gibbons *et al.*, 1985; J. G. Hull & Levy, 1979, Experiment 3). Their third criticism (affect induction) will be discussed later. As far as their second criticism is concerned, data have now been collected that indicate people do become more concerned with matching behavior to standards when their attention is directed internally (e.g., Carver & Scheier, 1981). And these data are convincing. For example, Scheier and Carver (1983) provided evidence in a series of experiments that self-focus increases one's interest in and ability to evaluate the self. More specifically, subjects in that study were much more likely to seek out diagnostic information, which could help them evaluate their own behavior, when their attention was self-focused. These results are certainly consistent with the self-evaluative aspect of self-awareness theory and are less consistent with Hull and Levy's criticism (cf. Wicklund & Hormuth, 1981).

Regarding their primary criticism, the suggestion that self-aware persons are sensitive to self-relevant aspects of the environment is not really inconsistent with self-awareness theory. Such information should facilitate, and is sometimes necessary for, the self-evaluation process. In fact, the related argument that self-awareness increases access to the "self-schema" is also not inconsistent with the theory and is quite compatible with the approach taken here. Moreover, research cited by J. G. Hull and Levy (e.g., Turner, 1978, 1980) has demonstrated that processing of self-relevant information is facilitated when the self-schema is activated. However, the argument that this sensitivity is the result of an external (rather than internal) focus of attention is more difficult to reconcile with the theory and is not supported by the literature.

2. Self-Focus and Self-Presentation

Congruent with the argument that self-awareness involves an external focus of attention (albeit on self-relevant information), J. G. Hull and Levy also suggested that many observable self-focus phenomena are likely to disappear in the absence of an audience, or more generally, in private situations. The implication is that self-presentational concerns may motivate much of the behavior demonstrated by self-focused persons. (Actually they claim that self-awareness involves an "increased sensitivity to the evaluative connotation of the individual's relationship to the environment'' [J.G. Hull & Levy, 1979, p. 764]; cf. a similar argument by Schlenker & Leary, 1982). This claim is not consistent with self-awareness theory and, again, appears to be incongruent with much of the relevant data. As mentioned previously, several studies have demonstrated behavior instigated by self-focus that was contrary to existing self-presentational (or exogenous self-evaluation) pressures (e.g., Gibbons & Gaeddert, 1984; Greenberg, 1983; Hormuth, 1982; Pryor et al., 1977, Experiment 3). Other studies have demonstrated robust self-focus effects, such as attitude–behavior consistency, in situations that appeared to be effectively devoid of any self-presentational pressure (Carver, 1975; Gibbons & Wicklund, 1982, Experiment 4; Scheier, 1976). And in many of the self-report veridicality studies, subjects had no way of knowing that the experimenter was aware of their previously expressed attitudes or opinions (e.g., Baldwin & Holmes, 1987; Gibbons, 1978), which significantly reduces the plausibility of an impression management explanation of this accuracy–consistency effect. In short, these types of behaviors do appear to be motivated more by intrinsic than by extrinsic or other-directed concerns. In general, a self-presentation (or externally based) perspective cannot provide a systematic account of self-awareness effects.

3. Self-Focus and Sensitivity to Others' Actions

In addition, a recent study by Ellis and Holmes (1986) speaks more directly to the issue of sensitivity to self-relevant environmental information. In one of few self-awareness studies to involve interpersonal behavior, these authors had subjects interact with a confederate whose job it was to become either increasingly more positive or more negative toward the subject, regardless of what the subject actually did. Focus of attention was varied by instructing subjects to pay particular attention either to their own thoughts or feelings (self-aware condition) or to the interviewer (non-self-aware condition); there was also a control (no focus instructions) condition. Results indicated that the externally focused subjects were most affected by the confederate's unfounded behavior, whereas the self-focused subjects were least affected by it. (It is interesting to note that the same "hyperreactivity" to the self-relevant behavior of others has also been demonstrated in research by Fenigstein [1979, 1984, Experiment 3] and more recently by Major, Cozzarelli, Testa, & McFarlin [1988] among subjects high in the trait of public self-consciousness.) Ellis and Holmes concluded that self-focus (i.e., self-awareness or private self-consciousness) does not increase the tendency to view others' behavior as self-relevant, nor does it necessarily lead to greater sensitivity to external information. They state, "Private self-consciousness would be viewed as a state that attenuates an individual's sensitivity to social interdependence and reflective appraisal. It results in a self-evaluation process that usually features comparison of one's performance with personal standards'' (Ellis & Holmes, 1986, p. 75). They also qualify this claim by suggesting that "when these standards are not readily available, the individual will turn to aspects of his immediate social situation to determine an appropriate set of expectations or social comparison standards" (p. 75). In short, self-focused persons may look to the environment or other persons for information about standards that might help guide behavior, but only or primarily when internal cues are unavailable.

4. Summary

In retrospect, much of the value of the Hull and Levy paper rests not in its specific criticisms of the Duval and Wicklund theory but rather in the perspective that it has brought to, or at least promoted in, the study of self-attention. That perspective, which centers on the impact that self-attention has on the processing of information about the self, is also an important component of one of the other recent models of self-attention proposed by Carver and Scheier.

B. CARVER AND SCHEIER'S MODEL

Carver and Scheier's (1981) book on self-regulation represented one of the most significant new social psychological approaches to the study of self-attention since Duval and Wicklund (1972). This information-processing model, based on the concept of self-regulation, grew out of the Duval and Wicklund theory and relies heavily on some of the same theoretical assumptions. However, there are a number of important differences between the two approaches that include some useful extensions and modifications of the original theory. Comparison of the two models will be made first on those issues that suggest some important changes in the original theory.[3]

1. Standards

Using Scheier's (1976) work (discussed earlier) on emotional responsivity as a basis, Carver and Scheier (1981) suggested that in many situations conducive to self-focus, personal standards either do not exist, are not salient, or else are overshadowed by other self-dimensions (cf. Wicklund, 1978). In many cases,

---

[3]Carver and Scheier's model incorporates both situational and individual difference (i.e., self-consciousness; Fenigstein et al., 1975) components, which reflects their belief that both factors influence the extent to which individuals are self-attentive, as well as their reactions to self-attention. Much of their thinking regarding the disposition of self-focus was influenced by A. H. Buss's (1980) discussion of self-consciousness and social anxiety. His 1980 book presents the most thorough analysis available of the empirical and theoretical work in this area. Although I will not deal directly with his model, it should be recognized that his 1980 book and his earlier work provided the theoretical framework for much if not most of the research on the topic of personality and self-focus.

these dimensions do not involve standards of "correctness," at least not as envisioned by Duval and Wicklund (1972). Carver and Scheier use the term standard in a more generic sense. According to their definition, a standard is simply a "point of comparison," which does not "automatically connote either a sense of correctness or of excellence, although there are specific cases in which each of these connotations would be appropriate" (p. 120).

There are certainly some differences between this definition and that of Duval and Wicklund, who talk about standards in the sense of ideal or even of moralistic representations of the self (e.g., Wicklund & Frey, 1980). It would appear, however, that Carver and Scheier have expanded the notion of standard more than they have changed it. From their perspective, a "comparison point" or standard can be based on an abstract behavioral construct, such as being polite or competent, but it can also reflect a more concrete level of behavior, such as angry aggression (Scheier, 1976) or even mowing the lawn effectively. In other words, they believe that standards or reference points exist at different levels of abstraction in hierarchical structure. In each case, however, the standard is a representation of action (C. S. Carver, personal communication, February, 1987). The self-regulatory process, as they describe it, involves a sequence of comparisons between the self and a comparison point, and it occurs at increasing levels in this hierarchy. For example, shoppers who are upset because they have been cut off at the checkout counter might react to that anger more intensely were they to stop and contemplate their current state of agitation. In this case, the impulse toward retaliatory behavior would represent the comparison point at a relatively low level in the hierarchy. Alternatively, each might realize, upon further self-consideration, that restraint—reflecting a (behavioral) standard at a higher level—would be a more judicious course of action.[4]

Clearly, not all self-dimensions that can potentially become central to the focus of attention will have the same impact on behavior, especially in situations in which standards are in conflict (Carver, Blaney, & Scheier, 1979a). In this regard, the evidence does support the hypothesis that standards exist at different levels and may conflict with one another. In such circumstances, lower level "points of comparison" (e.g., self-preservation or gratification) will initially attract attention and guide response before higher level standards (e.g., values or goals) will be considered.[5] Original self-awareness theory did not discuss this

---

[4]Like Duval and Wicklund's approach, Carver and Scheier's is a discrepancy reduction model. This means that, in both instances described, irate shoppers, while engaged in self-regulation, will each attempt to reduce the discrepancy between current behavior and the related standard. In the former case, presumably the discrepancy is owing to not enough retaliation; in the latter case (which seems more likely), it would be owing to too much retaliation.

[5]Suggesting that comparison points always reflect behavior limits the Carver and Scheier approach in much the same way that they suggested that Duval and Wicklund's "moralistic" definition limited original self-awareness theory. In the revised model to be presented here, it is suggested that any aspect of the self—affective, somatic, cognitive, or whatever—can act as a comparison point.

issue of differential impact or importance of standards. In this respect, the concept of a hierarchy of self-dimensions is an appealing one. The Carver and Scheier (1981) model has proven very useful in outlining this hierarchy notion and in describing behavior in situations where several self-components may be salient simultaneously (e.g., Carver et al., 1979a, 1979b; Scheier et al., 1981).

2. Self-Schema

Carver and Scheier's approach to the study of the self draws from research in the area of social cognition as well as cybernetics. From this perspective, the self is viewed as a target of perception—just like any other target—that the perceiver comes to know through a process of information integration. That process is greatly facilitated by the presence of a schema. Schemas, typically defined as cognitive representations of members of a particular category and characteristics of those members (Bartlett, 1932), exist for objects, places, and people, including the self (Markus, 1977). The self-schema, of course, is exceptionally well developed and complex and includes numerous physical, cognitive, and dispositional characteristics. In addition, it is readily accessible (Rogers, 1977; Rogers, Kuiper, & Kirker, 1977), which means that incoming information about the self is usually processed quickly and accurately. Carver and Scheier argue convincingly that focusing attention internally upon the self helps to "access" the self-schema, thereby allowing for faster and more accurate encoding and retrieval of self-relevant information (cf. J. G. Hull & Levy, 1979; Turner, 1980). Included in this latter category would be instances of previous behaviors, as well as emotional experiences and affective reactions. Thus, one reason why self-reports are more veridical under conditions conducive to self-focus appears to be that the self-schema becomes more accessible when attention is focused on the self.

3. Expectancies

A third extension of self-awareness theory by Carver and Scheier involves their discussion of the role of outcome expectancies in determining the process of discrepancy reduction. Duval and Wicklund's theory suggested a rather straightforward sequence of events: self-focus → self-evaluation → recognition of some discrepancy → negative affect → attempted discrepancy reduction or avoidance. In response to accumulating evidence, Wicklund (1975) modified this theoretical sequence to suggest that it is possible that one may assess the self at a level that is at least temporarily superior to one's level of aspiration. Thus, self-focus does not always lead to awareness of a discrepancy and attempted reduction. Carver and Scheier agree. Moreover, they argue that it is not recognition of a real–ideal discrepancy per se that leads to behavioral change. Rather, it is the individual's assessment of the likelihood that the particular goal (or discrepancy reduction) will actually be realized that influences not only the willingness to remain in the state of self-focus but also the amount of energy expended in an attempt to match the standard (cf. Atkinson, 1957, 1964).

There is now a considerable amount of empirical support for Carver and Scheier's outcome-expectancy hypothesis. This research has demonstrated that self-focus will not be experienced as aversive if the individual is led to believe that the salient discrepancy between the self and the standard is not permanent. For example, in research by Carver and Scheier and their colleagues (Carver & Blaney, 1977; Carver et al., 1979a, 1979b; see also Steenbarger & Aderman, 1979), outcome expectancies were experimentally manipulated and subjects' reactions were assessed (cf. Duval & Duval, 1985). Consistent with their reasoning, this research indicated that self-focus does not promote attempts at discrepancy reduction and probably interferes when outcome expectancy is very low. In a related vein, Sarason (1975) and Wine (1971) have demonstrated that self-focus is a crucial component of the performance interference produced by negative outcome expectancies associated with test anxiety. Pessimism, then, is likely to lead eventually to avoidance or withdrawal from self-focus. Conversely, when outcome expectancy is favorable, self-focus will typically enhance goal-directed behavior.

The expectancy concept and the hierarchical structure of comparisons between self and comparison points represent important modifications. Logically, the perceived likelihood of attaining a particular standard or goal will influence the amount of energy, if any, that is put into attempts at reaching that standard (cf. Brehm, Wright, Solomon, Silka, & Greenberg, 1983). This will occur regardless of focus of attention, but the impact of this decision or realization is likely to be much stronger when attention is internally focused. At the same time, these are both modifications that apply primarily to those situations in which achievement or performance happens to comprise the most salient self-dimension. They are less useful in explaining or describing many value-related behaviors, such as accurate self-report, reduced aggression, or helping behaviors, where the primary consideration is typically which response is most appropriate rather than simply which (or how much) is possible.

V. Points of Distinction Between Original Theory and Others

Carver and Scheier's (1981) model does offer a number of useful modifications that appear to be essentially congruent with self-awareness theory. At the same time, there are also some other issues on which the two approaches diverge. On several of these points of contention the original theory appears to be faring well. Discussion of these points, along with the extensions and modifications mentioned earlier, can facilitate development of a revised and integrative model.

A. SELF-ASSESSMENT AND THE SELF-SCHEMA

Introduction of the schema concept and, in general, application of information-processing principles have proven especially useful in the study of the veridicality effect. In this regard, work by Higgins and his colleagues (e.g., Higgins, King, & Mavin, 1982) has suggested that there are a variety of factors that can increase accessibility of the self-schema, including frequency and recency of previous activations and level of motivation. The work of J. G. Hull and Levy (1979) and Carver and Scheier (1981) suggests that focus of attention is another variable that should be added to that list. The combination of motivational (i.e., toward self-evaluation) and attentional factors that are a part of self-awareness facilitates consideration of all aspects of the self.[6]

The concept of schema and the process of schema accessibility alone, however, are not sufficient to explain the numerous examples of enhanced self-report accuracy in the literature. For example, in the third study of Pryor *et al.* (1977), subjects were asked to indicate how much they liked a group of puzzles they had just worked on. Only the self-focused subjects provided preference reports that correlated significantly with actual time spent playing with the puzzles. In this case, it seems unlikely that any of these subjects would have completely forgotten their immediate prior behavior and its antecedents or, for that matter, that self-focus could increase access to this information. By the same token, the fact that virtually all of the non-self-aware subjects in the second experiment overestimated their SAT scores suggests that their errors did not simply reflect problems

---

[6]Higgins *et al.* (1982) also draw a distinction between schema availability (whether a particular dimension is part of the self-schema) and schema accessibility. Direction of attention would not affect the components of the schema, of course, but it would influence the extent to which those components can be brought into consideration. There is another, related question raised by this issue, and that is whether it is even possible to access the self-schema in the absence of self-focus. A complete discussion of this question is beyond the scope of this article. However, brief mention of the relevant theoretical work of Markus would be enlightening (Markus & Kunda, 1986). She has outlined two types of self-concept. The "working self-concept" is described as being comprised of a group of temporary self-conceptions that are "quite situation dependent." As she acknowledges, the structure is very similar to Mead's notion of the self (or James's concept of the "social self"). There also exists a more stable self-concept that is less responsive to situational factors and is much more enduring. It is this aspect of the self rather than the situation-dependent, working self-concept that self-awareness facilitates access to. In fact, the stable self-concept is likely to come into consideration and have an impact on behavior only when attention is self-focused.

in retrieval. A similar distortion pattern occurred among the non-self-focused psychiatric subjects in the Gibbons *et al.* (1985) research. When asked to recall their history of hospitalizations and report on their problem severity, the pattern of their mistakes was not random: They consistently underestimated both variables, which suggests that they were engaging in some form of self-presentational behavior. The self-aware subjects, in contrast, were quite accurate in their reports of the duration of their problems and much more realistic in assessing problem severity.

1. Self-Presentation

Additional evidence that self-focus involves more than just schema accessibility can be seen in studies by Gibbons and Gaeddert (1984) and Gibbons and Gerrard (1986). Prior to working on a series of math problems, Gibbons and Gaeddert's subjects were given a placebo. The drug was said to either inhibit or facilitate performance, thereby creating differential outcome expectancies in the two conditions. Further, in order to boost evaluation apprehension, the task was described as a very good predictor of academic performance in college. After they finished the math problems, subjects were asked how active the drug had been.

Our predictions were based on Kelley's (1973) augmentation principle as well as on impression management. Specifically, we expected that self-presentational concerns would lead subjects in the performance-inhibiting condition to overattribute arousal (actually produced by the evaluative task) to the drug, while those in the performance-facilitating condition would report that the drug was less active, thereby making their performance look somewhat more impressive. That is exactly what happened for the non-self-focused group. In contrast, the drug information did not influence the attributions of the self-aware group. Instead, their arousal self-reports appeared to be more in line with their actual arousal levels. In fact, we had no physiological measures to verify this interpretation; however, such information was provided in a recent replication by Hansen *et al.* (1989).

2. Truth-Telling as a Behavioral Standard

In Gibbons and Gerrard (1986) a second factor was examined that is partly responsible for the veridicality effect, namely, motivation to report accurately. According to the argument proposed in Gibbons (1983), most people maintain a standard of integrity or honesty (cf. Rokeach, 1968), which is made salient by the test-taking situation. Theoretically, self-awareness should enhance the motivation to bring behavior in line with that standard and also to avoid creating a discrepancy with it, which is what would happen if the person clearly fabricated or lied. In order to test this truth-as-standard hypothesis, it was necessary to find a sample of people who were not likely to maintain a personal standard that would inhibit lying and, therefore, whose self-reports should not be affected by self-focus. The group chosen consisted of incarcerated women who had scored very high (above the prison median) on the lie scale of the MMPI. These women, along with a comparison group of prison women who had scored below the median on the lie scale, were questioned on a number of topics, such as their participation in the rehabilitation process and how sociable they were, and then the accuracy of these reports was checked by comparing them with the prison records and evaluations provided by the prison psychologists. As expected, the mirror substantially increased the correlations of the subjects who had scored below the median on the lie scale ($M\ r = .67$), whereas it had little effect on the "high-liars." Correlations for the latter group were very comparable to the no-mirror subjects ($M\ r = -.08$).

Once again the inaccuracy of the no-mirror subjects, as well as the high-liars, appeared to be the result of externally oriented motives, namely, social desirability or impression management. Their self-descriptions tended to err in a self-serving direction (e.g., overestimation of cooperativeness and sociability, underestimation of crime severity) much more than did those of the self-aware subjects. Thus, the argument that the mirror enhanced access to self-schemas, above and beyond that triggered by the questionnaire itself, cannot adequately explain the difference between the high-liar and low-liar groups. Instead, the most obvious explanation for the difference between the two groups in the mirror condition is that the high-liar prisoners did not maintain a standard of truth telling and, therefore, were not influenced by the mirror. In short, reliance on the concept of an internal value structure is necessary in order to account for the observed effects. A similar case can be made for the results of a recent study by Wojciszke (1987), who found a significant reduction in cheating when attention was self-focused but only among persons who indicated previously that they maintained a personal value of honesty.

3. Summary

Focusing attention on the self does access the self-schema, which is why cognizance of the self increases. Which aspects of the self-schema capture attention and, therefore, which comparison points are utilized depend on situational as well as dispositional factors. Different aspects of the self have different types of comparison points (e.g., the "baseline" or unaroused self, the old or former self, or perhaps social comparison points such as a colleague's vita or teaching record), and many of these comparison points do not involve ideal representations of self-dimensions. The veridicality effect, then, is attributable in part to increased self-cognizance engendered by accessing of the self-schema. But it is also the result of increased motivation to report accurately, and this motivation does reflect a behavioral standard or ideal (cf. Duval & Wicklund, 1972). Both factors are necessary. Without the former (access to the self-schema), self-reports of behavior are less accurate simply because there is less information available on which to base them. Such was the case in the non-self-aware conditions of the veridicality-effect studies (Gibbons, 1983). Without the latter (standard of truth-telling), there is no incentive to report accurately, whether the self-schema is accessed or not (Gibbons & Gerrard, 1986; Wojciszke, 1987). In either case, the result is the same: low validity.

B. NEGATIVE AFFECT AND AFFECT AMPLIFICATION

Another argument with the Duval and Wicklund theory raised by Carver and Scheier (1981), as well as by J. G. Hull and Levy (1979) and A. H. Buss (1980), concerns the process of self-evaluation that occurs in response to self-focus. Carver and Scheier and A. H. Buss agree that some evaluation takes place, but they disagree that negative affect is a necessary result. Carver and Scheier's argument is that, while emotion can be amplified by the self-evaluation process, it is not necessarily produced by it. In support of their position, the evidence does indicate that self-reports of affect are increased by self-attention (Gibbons, 1987; Gibbons & Gerrard, 1986; Scheier & Carver, 1977; Scheier et al., 1982).[7] Whether the emotion itself is increased, however, is a different issue. Scheier et al. (1982) contend that directing attention toward an emotional reaction can "exacerbate sympathetic discharge" (p. 40; cf. A. H. Buss, 1980), thereby effectively increasing autonomic arousal. There is actually little direct evidence to either support or refute this belief, however.

On the other hand, there is considerable evidence regarding the relative impact of distraction from versus attention to pain cues on emotional distress. For the most part, this research suggests that both distraction from (Bloom, Houston, Holmes, & Burish, 1977; Epstein, Rosenthal, & Szpiler, 1978; Mullen & Suls, 1982b) and attention to a stimulus (Epstein et al., 1978; Leventhal, Brown, Shockam, & Engquist, 1979) are associated with habituation and, therefore, less reported pain or emotional intensity. In contrast, attending to one's emotional reaction (to pain) appears to retard habituation (Leventhal et al., 1979). Similarly, the studies that have directly examined somatic reactivity under conditions of self-focus have found either no change (e.g., Hansen et al., 1989) or some decrease in response (Dabbs, Johnson, & Leventhal, 1968; Lanzetta, Biernat, &

[7]An exception here is research by Lanzetta, Biernat, and Kleck (1982), who found less self-report of affect from subjects confronted by a mirror. However, in that study the self-aware subjects were also videotaped, which raises the possibility that awareness of public exposure could have aroused self-presentational concerns and affected reports of affect (cf. Carver & Scheier, 1981, p. 109).

Kleck, 1982; Paulus, Annis, & Risner, 1978). The self-focused subjects in Hansen *et al.* (1989) were significantly more accurate in their self-reports of arousal, but physiological measures provided no evidence of enhanced reactivity. This suggests that self-focus may actually work to retard the normal dissipation of arousal that occurs inevitably over time and is sped up when attention is distracted. Hence, the enhanced affect that is reported may not reflect an actual increase in somatic reactivity but rather less decline than has occurred in control conditions. This would also explain why arousal self-reports appear to be more accurate. At this point the issue remains important but unresolved.

1. Positive versus Negative Mood

More germane to the current analysis is the question of whether self-focus necessarily produces a negative emotional reaction that, in turn, is ultimately responsible for behavioral change. As indicated, a number of studies have shown increased report of affective response during self-focus; in virtually all of those studies, however, the enhanced affect has been negative. While it is true that in several cases subjects were preselected for negative affect or negative trait characteristics (e.g., Brockner, Hjelle, & Plant, 1985; Gibbons, 1986), in others they were not (e.g., Davies, 1982; Scheier, 1976; Scheier & Carver, 1977; Scheier *et al.*, 1981). But even in those latter studies the affect that was temporarily enhanced was negative in tone (fear, anger, etc.). Relatively few attempts at enhancing positive affect have been undertaken, but those that have been attempted have typically shown either marginal effects (e.g., Carver & Scheier, 1981; Fenigstein, 1979; Gibbons, 1987; Scheier & Carver, 1977, Experiment 3) or no effects (e.g., Burgio, Merluzzi, & Pryor, 1986; Davies, 1982; Gibbons, 1986; Gibbons & Wicklund, 1982; Hormuth, 1982; Reisenzein & Gattinger, 1982; Scheier & Carver, 1977). Also, in an interesting field study, Csikszentmihalyi and Figurski (1982) used a "random beeper" technique to randomly assess participants' mood states while they were engaged in various activities throughout the day. These authors found that subjects were most likely to report being self-focused when they were engaged in voluntary activity of some kind. They also tended to report experiencing negative mood states at those times when they were involved in voluntary activities and were self-focused. There was no evidence of positive mood being associated with introspection.

2. Self-Focus and Depression

Additional evidence of a link between negative affect and self-focus has come recently from a different body of literature. Noting similarities between behavior patterns characteristic of depression and reactions to self-focused attention, a number of theorists have suggested that depressed persons tend to be chronically self-focused (Ingram & Smith, 1984; Lewinsohn, Haberman, Teri, & Hautzinger, 1985; Strack, Blaney, Ganellen, & Coyne, 1985). For example, depressed persons spend more time focusing on the self after failure than do nondepressed persons (Greenberg & Pyszczynski, 1986; Pyszczynski & Greenberg, 1985). Another obvious similarity is that both states are often associated with exacerbation of affect. Similarly, there appears to be a connection between self-focused disposition, as measured by the private self-consciousness subscale, and depression, as measured by Beck's (1967) Depression Inventory (Greenberg & Pyszczynski, 1986; Ingram, Lumry, Cruet, & Sieber, 1987; Ingram & Smith, 1984). Although these correlations are typically not very strong (i.e., less than .20), they are consistent.[8] Once again, there is no evidence of dispositional self-focus being linked with improvement in mood states. Presumably, if either self-focus or self-consciousness were associated with a simple enhancement of emotional response, then polarization of mood would be demonstrated by high private self-conscious subjects—some reporting more negative mood, others more positive—with no clear linear relation discernible. It would appear, then, that while self-focus does enhance awareness of affect traits and states, it does so primarily when the mood involved is negative rather than positive. One reason why this is the case has to do with the variable of self-esteem.

C. SELF-ESTEEM AND AFFECT

Self-esteem, as either an individual-difference variable or as a motivating factor (i.e., ego protection), is not assigned much significance in the Duval and Wicklund model. Carver and Scheier (1981) see its importance primarily in terms of the impact that low self-esteem is likely to have on outcome expectancies. Brockner, however, has argued that level of self-esteem is an important factor in determining reactions to self-focused attention, and the available research evidence appears to support this contention. For example, persons who are low in self-esteem find self-focus to be more aversive (Brockner & Wallnau, 1981; Nadler, 1983) and generally appear more reactive to it than are persons moderate or high in self-esteem (Brockner, 1979b; Brockner et al., 1985; J. G. Hull & Young, 1983). For the most part, this is consistent with original self-awareness theory: People with low self-esteem would be expected to have a more significant real–ideal self-discrepancy. Consequently, the state of self-focus, which engenders a self-evaluative response, is likely to be particularly aversive for them. It is less clear, theoretically, how persons of normal self-esteem or trait affect level would respond affectively when self-aware.

[8]I have found a correlation of only .16 ($p < .001$) in a sample of more than 6000 undergraduates collected over a 4-year period.

Duval and Wicklund (1972) argued that negative affect is a natural consequence of self-focus, primarily because of the ubiquity of within-self discrepancies. Wicklund (1975) later modified this statement to acknowledge the fact that recognition of a within-self discrepancy is not inevitable. Nonetheless, he still maintained that while perception of a discrepancy might be averted temporarily, if the person remained self-focused long enough, a shortcoming at one level or another would eventually be perceived. It would appear, though, that the research evidence does not support the belief that negative affect is an inevitable byproduct of self-focused attention. For example, in the studies which involved subjects who were preselected according to level of dysphoria (e.g., Brockner *et al.*, 1985; Gibbons, 1986; Gibbons *et al.*, 1985), the nondepressed subjects did not evidence a decline in mood when self-aware. Also, although earlier research indicated that the aversiveness of self-focus could be reduced if it was preceded by positive feedback (Duval, Wicklund, & Fine, 1972; Gibbons & Wicklund, 1976), more recent work has suggested that positive feedback is not necessary for this to occur. Several studies, for example, have demonstrated that providing self-focused subjects with information that behavioral improvement on a salient self-dimension is possible (typically a dimension on which they had been previously led to believe they were deficient) can substantially reduce the aversiveness of the state (e.g., Bachtold, 1979; Carver & Blaney, 1977; Pyszczynski, Holt, & Greenberg, 1987; Strack *et al.*, 1985).

1. Within-Self Discrepancies

Once again the relationship between self-focus and a behavioral response, in this case emotion, appears to be more complex than originally thought. For persons of moderate or high self-esteem, self-focus does not have much immediate impact on mood, unless (1) mood-altering manipulations are used, (2) the perceived goal or standard for some reason is thought to be unattainable (i.e., if appropriate behavior is not possible), or (3) the person is engaging in standard-discrepant behavior of some kind. This last possibility is not the default option, however. The available research does not support the tenet that attention, when directed toward the self, automatically focuses on within-self discrepancies. There is no direct evidence in the literature of increased awareness of personal shortcomings, and perhaps more importantly there is no indirect evidence in the form of context-independent exacerbation of mood states. Most people do not automatically focus on personal shortcomings when self-aware, and so they do not typically report feeling worse. In contrast, people with low self-esteem are, in general, more cognizant of such discrepancies and are likely to become increasingly so when self-focused, which is why they do find the state to be phenomenologically aversive. This occurs whether mood states are manipulated or not, and whether specific goals or performance levels are experimentally salient (Brockner & Hulton, 1978; Brockner & Wallnau, 1981; Brockner *et al.*, 1985; Gibbons, 1987).

2. Summary

The conclusion to be reached, then, is that there is little empirical support for Duval and Wicklund's original contention that behavioral change prompted by self-focus is necessarily motivated by negative affect associated with perception of within-self discrepancies. Negative affect plays a role when self-aware individuals think they are behaving in a manner that is incongruent with personal standards, and thus a discrepancy actually exists. Under such circumstances, the desire to reduce the affect will instigate the hypothesized reaction of avoidance or attempted discrepancy reduction; in the absence of self-focus, little or no discomfort will be experienced. By the same token, anticipation of negative affect that would accompany future transgressions or the creation of a discrepancy serves to inhibit certain behaviors for the self-focused person. This inhibiting effect probably occurs with more regularity than discrepancy reduction (although this would certainly be a difficult hypothesis to test). In short, self-focus can and often does promote, change, and inhibit behavior in the absence of perceived discrepancies and any associated elevated affect, either negative or positive.

D. FOCUS OF SELF-DIRECTED ATTENTION

A final and, from the current perspective, perhaps fundamental point of disagreement between the A. H. Buss (1980) and Carver and Scheier (1981) models and that of Duval and Wicklund (1972) concerns the issue of internal versus external focus of attention. The dichotomy between public and private aspects of the self in the tradition of James (1890) is a basic component of the A. H. Buss (1980) model, and it is an important part of the Carver and Scheier (1981) model as well (cf. Greenwald, 1982; Markus & Nurius, 1986). It is also fundamental to research on dispositional self-focus that employs the Self-Consciousness Scale. It is not consistent with the theoretical perspective presented in Duval and Wicklund (1972), however. In fact, Wicklund has argued several times (Wicklund & Gollwitzer, 1987; Wicklund & Hormuth, 1981) that the distinction is essentially spurious. These objections notwithstanding, a considerable amount of evidence has been gathered suggesting that public self-consciousness and (objective) self-awareness cannot be considered identical.

A number of studies in the last 9 or 10 years have employed what A. H. Buss (1980) and Carver and Scheier (1981) have termed public manipulations of attention. Those have consisted primarily of TV or video cameras but have also included voice recordings played back in the presence of an experimenter and evaluative audiences. These studies have indicated that public manipulations are associated with (what I have termed) other-directed behaviors, such as increased conformity on low-involvement tasks (Diener & Srull, 1979; Froming et al., 1982) and less value-consistent behavior (Vallacher & Solodky, 1979). Moreover, these results have been replicated numerous times with subjects who had previously indicated they were high in the dimension of public self-consciousness (Froming & Carver, 1981; Froming et al., 1982, Experiment 3; Santee & Maslach, 1982; Scheier, 1980). In short, as A. H. Buss (1980) has suggested, the behavior of (publicly) self-conscious people is clearly distinguished from that of persons who are self-aware—a distinction that has produced some controversy of late (e.g., Carver & Scheier, 1987; Wicklund & Gollwitzer, 1987).

1. Public Self-Consciousness and Social Dependency

One of Wicklund and Gollwitzer's (1987) arguments with the concept of public self-consciousness, in particular, and the public–private distinction, in general, is that self-consciousness is essentially no different from a more general dimension of "social concern" or "social dependency." They claim that the public behavior of persons who score high on the public self-consciousness subscale is dictated primarily by concerns about others rather than the self. In fact, the public self-consciousness subscale does correlate reliably with a number of personality constructs that seem to be very similar to, if not synonymous with, social dependency, such as embarrassability (Edelmann, 1985), audience anxiousness (Leary, 1983), passivity (John, 1983), and social sensitivity (Fenigstein, 1979). It does not correlate with the use of first-person pronouns (Hoover, Wood, Wegner, & Knowles, 1982), which is a validated measure of self-focus (cf. Davis & Brock, 1975). Perhaps more important, Cheek (1982) found that the public self-consciousness subscale correlated very highly ($r = .53$) with the "other-directedness" factor (cf. Briggs, Cheek, & Buss, 1980) of Snyder's (1974) self-monitoring scale.

These correlational results should not be surprising given the fact that the creators of the scale intended it to be a measure of sensitivity to others' impressions of the self. Fenigstein (1979), for example, stated that increased concern with self-presentation is a "major consequence" of public self-consciousness (cf. A. H. Buss, 1980; Hass, 1984). Similarly, when explaining the fact that public self-consciousness tends to interfere with (rather than promote) the predictive validity of self-reports, Turner suggested it was because the trait increases self-presentational concerns (Turner & Peterson, 1977; Willerman, Turner, & Peterson, 1976). And Carver and Scheier (1981, p. 525) have also suggested that public self-consciousness is associated with the tendency to utilize the standards of others rather than those of the self. In short, these data and theories suggest that the trait of public self-consciousness reflects first and foremost a concern with others and what they think. The link to the self is primarily through an interest in self-presentation or impression management—behaviors that are, once again, essentially other- rather than self-oriented.

2. Conformity and Self-Awareness

Conformity is certainly an other-oriented response, and Duval and Wicklund (1972) did claim that self-focus is often associated with an increase in conformity behavior. In some respects this is true; however, their discussion of the relationship between conformity and self-awareness needs to be reassessed. Based on the accumulated research, I would draw two conclusions about attention and conformity and, related to these factors, the public–private distinction. First, self-attention does not promote conformity in group settings except when (1) the evidence suggests the group's opinion is valid and the individual, being in the minority, is wrong (Duval & Duval, 1983) or (2) the issue at stake is either a verifiable belief or a value of relatively little importance to the individual (Diener & Srull, 1979; Duval, 1976; Froming et al., 1982). In the former case, the group is simply a more reliable source of information than the self with regard to what behavior is appropriate or what should be done. In the latter situation, conformity increases because the individual wishes to avoid being the focus of the group (Duval & Wicklund, 1972) and realizes that conforming will have this effect. This overt behavior is likely to be accompanied by little, if any, change in personal standards or attitudes.

The second conclusion is that external focus of attention often promotes conformity. Hence, people will routinely demonstrate conformity behavior when externally oriented manipulations of attention are used, such as TV cameras (Duval, 1976) or an audience (e.g., Asch, 1951; Deutsch & Gerard, 1955; Raven, 1959). However, this latter type of conformity will occur only as long as the person is potentially the focus of group attention and is viewing the self from the perspective of others. Abandoning a personal value or commitment of some importance in the face of disagreement with a few others or even a sizable majority (cf. Gibbons & Wright, 1983) is likely to create a discrepancy even more aversive than that associated with deviance. Thus a person who succumbs to group pressure and conforms, knowing that his or her behavior is contrary to a personal standard of some importance, is likely to find the state of self-awareness very uncomfortable. Every effort will be made, then, to keep attention focused off the self.

The theoretical question still remains of whether the psychological state produced by these public types of manipulations, which involve an audience either directly or indirectly, can be considered self-awareness, at least in the same sense as that described by Duval and Wicklund (1972). As discussed earlier, their contention was that conscious attention is bidirectional and that at any given moment it may be directed outward toward the environment (e.g., a group) or inward upon the self. While it may oscillate back and forth from self to environment, sometimes very rapidly, it cannot focus on both targets simultaneously. As Duval and Wicklund (1972) point out, there is considerable historical precedent in the attention literature for this dichotomy assumption (Mason, 1961; Polanyi, 1958; Wylie, 1968). In addition, the idea that the self has a reflexive capacity, which is fundamental to self-awareness theory, has been suggested by a number of theorists, beginning with James (1890) and including Mead (1934) and others of the symbolic interactionist school (Cooley, 1902/1964; Shibutani, 1961). In fact, the work of the symbolic interactionists is very relevant to the study of self-focused attention in general, and specifically to the issue of the public versus the private self.

3. Self-Awareness and Symbolic Interactionism

The work of Mead and Shibutani helped shaped some of Duval and Wicklund's original ideas about the influence of a value system on behavior. More recent discussions by Wicklund (1979, 1980; see also Gibbons & Wicklund, 1982; Stephenson & Wicklund 1983, 1984) have maintained this conceptual link. At the same time, however, Duval and Wicklund (1972) highlight an important point of departure from the theorizing of Mead and other sociologists, which concerns the nature of the self-concept and involves the public–private distinction. According to Mead (1934), the existence of a self-concept is contingent on the individual's ability to adopt the perspective of another toward oneself. In a similar vein, Cooley (1902/1964) talks about the "looking glass self" as being a simple reflection of how we think others view us. And Goffman (1959) describes the self as consisting of characteristics associated with particular roles that one assumes vis-à-vis other people.

In contrast to this sociological orientation, Duval and Wicklund argue that the perspective of others is important in the development of the self-concept and the personal value structure. However, self-definition, that is, what monitors behavior during self-awareness, comes from within and is not dependent on others: "In no way do we assume that the individual is dependent upon the point of view of the other in the sense that Mead intends" (Duval & Wicklund, 1972, p. 31). Thus the behavior brought forth by self-focused attention is endogenous by definition, specifically in reaction to personal standards, and it is not dictated by the interests or desires of others: "The individual is not seen by us as using the values of the other as the criteria for his self-evaluation" (p. 8).

4. Self-Awareness, Groups, and Public Self-Consciousness

The psychological state described by Duval and Wicklund (1972) differs from that reflected in the self-presentational behavior of persons who are high in the trait of public self-consciousness, or the behavior of persons responding to an evaluative audience or a TV camera. A person can become self-aware in group situations, to be sure, but that is more likely to occur when she or he feels alienated or somehow isolated from the group. In contrast, feelings of group cohesion or unity help keep attention focused externally, thereby promoting conformity with group norms and, when carried to an extreme, resulting in deindividuation. The deindividuated state, then, is characterized by a more or less constant absence of self-focus. When this happens, behavior essentially comes under control of the group (Diener, 1979; Prentice-Dunn & Rogers, 1982).

Self-awareness may occur if the person believes that he is the focus of others' attention. But the oscillation of attention from self to environment and back is likely to be rapid, thereby inhibiting the assessment and evaluation of the private self (involving values and standards) that is the defining characteristic of the self-aware state. Maximum self-focus is likely to occur immediately after the attention of the group has shifted from the self onto something or someone else. This inhibition is precisely why the behavior of publicly self-conscious persons reflects virtually none of the hypothesized and observed reactions to self-awareness that have been noted in the literature, such as enhanced self-report validity, affect or somatic awareness, accurate attribution, or value-consistent behavior. In fact, in many cases, the behavior of publicly self-conscious persons is in direct opposition to these hypothesized and observed reactions (e.g., self-presentation, increased suggestibility, enhanced concern with others' opinions, less independence.)

5. Summary

It would be illogical, of course, to argue that self-conscious persons are oblivious to their own presence; a glance at the items on the public self-consciousness subscale indicates that cannot be the case (e.g., "I'm concerned about what other people think of me"; "I'm self-conscious about the way I look"). Instead, it is suggested that the primary focus of concern of self-conscious persons is not the self but rather others and what they think. In this regard the reasoning of Wegner and Giuliano (1982) is very helpful. They suggest that people who are engaging in impression management (and the argument can easily be extended to publicly self-conscious persons) have a "tacit awareness" of other people when behaving, meaning they view the self from the perspective of other people. Self-conscious persons, then, are certainly aware of themselves.

But what controls (or regulates) their actions is external to the self. Akin to self-monitors (Snyder, 1974), they look outside the self for direction to guide behavior. Self-aware persons, on the other hand, look to the self. This being the case, it is hard to understand how two such diverse states as self-awareness and self-consciousness could be emanating from the same psychological construct.[9] Whether the concept of public self-awareness is entirely redundant in relation to that of "social dependency" is certainly debatable. It seems clear, though, that it is not the same as objective self-awareness.

VI. The Nature of Standards

A more basic issue involved in the discussion of public versus private self-attention is the question of where standards originate. For J. G. Hull and Levy (1979) the concept of behavioral standards is superfluous, much as is the concept of motivation. A. H. Buss (1980) also argues against the self-evaluation process but is much less clear on the specific notion of standards. As suggested previously, Carver and Scheier's notion of a hierarchy of self appears to be quite useful in explaining situations in which different standards, sometimes in competition with one another, are made salient simultaneously. Moreover, their ideas probably come closest to Duval and Wicklund's with regard to the role of behavioral standards. In fact, higher level comparison points, according to their definition(s), do bear a strong resemblance to the concept of standards outlined by Duval and Wicklund. For example, Carver and Scheier use the terms "behavior-specifying information," "specifications of qualities of states or of actions," and the basic term "goals." Low-level comparison points, on the other hand, such as muscle reactions and routine behavioral activity, as Carver and Scheier point out, do not require self-attention. Hence they would generally fall outside the realm of concern of a theory of self-awareness.

In the Carver and Scheier model, what causes the individual to want to compare and then bring behavior in line with superordinate or higher level personal standards is the desire or need to regulate behavior. They eschew the concept of motivation, calling it "metatheoretical baggage." And yet, when looking at

---

[9]Further evidence of the distinction between self-awareness and public self-consciousness comes from physiological research. As noted previously, internal focus of attention is typically associated with a decrease in arousal (Paulus, Annis, & Risner, 1978; Dabbs, Johnson, & Leventhal, 1968); the obvious exception is when internal conflict (e.g., dissonance) or arousal draws attention inward. In contrast, the presence of audiences or TV cameras usually produces an increase in arousal (Cohen & Davis, 1973; Martens, 1969), which in turn is indicative of an external focusing of attention (cf. Lacey & Lacey, 1970).

what they identify as the higher levels of the standard hierarchy, what "controls" behavior at that level seems a lot like what other theorists might call motivation. For example, when the desire to regulate the self encourages actions that are consistent with a moralistic value or what Carver and Scheier (1981) consider higher level standards, such as sympathizing with or helping others even at one's own expense (e.g., Berkowitz, 1987; Mayer, Duval, Holtz, & Bowman, 1985; Stephenson & Wicklund, 1983, 1984), then the self-regulatory process begins to sound like it is somehow motivated. Moreover, the points of comparison at this level appear to be very similar to what Duval and Wicklund called ideals.

A. SELF AND THE GENERALIZED OTHER

The question remains, where do guiding standards of behavior originate? In an attempt to answer this question, I again look to the symbolic interactionist school and, specifically, to the concept of the generalized other. Mead (1934) describes the generalized other as the internalized reflection of an externally based value system. As Wicklund and Gollwitzer (1987) point out, the development of this value system reflects an "*accumulation* of perspectives," which are garnered from "broad reference groups" (p. 497). By definition, others are instrumental in its development, and it certainly is susceptible to change. The system itself is internally based, however, and is not dependent on external or social influence. It is this accumulation of values that gives direction and continuity to behavior when attention is self-focused.

Evidence of the generalized other's influence can be seen in the research on truth telling (Gibbons & Gerrard, 1986) and honesty (Wojciszke, 1987), and perhaps most clearly in the studies on attention and helping behavior. This research has indicated that self-focused persons will help more, provided they believe that helping is the appropriate response within the situational context, and they will allocate rewards in a more equitable manner, even when such behavior is counter to their own personal interests or unpopular in the immediate social milieu (Greenberg, 1980, 1983; cf. Kernis & Reis, 1984). Invoking an elaborate hierarchical structure of self-regulation to explain this behavior seems supererogatory. The same is true for the concept of discrepancy reduction. It is more parsimonious to suggest simply that self-focus under these circumstances promotes a rather straightforward and immediate reaction to an internal value structure. Current behavior (i.e., an existing real–ideal discrepancy) is not a primary concern; instead, attention is directed toward future behavior. The decision process, then, is just as simple: "What should be done?" and, in some instances, "Can I do it?"

1. Values and Standards

A similar argument can be made for a variety of other phenomena from the self-awareness literature. Examples include less aggressive behavior or more, depending on the subject's perception of what is most appropriate in the situation (Carver, 1974, 1975; Scheier, Buss, & Buss, 1978); more veridical assessment of one's performance in a group (Stephenson & Wicklund, 1983); less cheating by persons who value honesty (Wojciszke, 1987); more accurate self-report (Pryor *et al.*, 1977); and less impression management (Pryor *et al.*, 1977, Experiment 2; Gibbons & Gaeddert, 1984; Gibbons *et al.*, 1985). Some of these examples clearly are of a moralistic nature. They were chosen in order to illustrate the concept of values, however, and not to suggest that all standards are necessarily value laden. Performance goals or aspirations, for example, are often of primary concern when attention is self-focused. Even in that case, however, the argument remains essentially the same: Self-focus promotes behavior that the individual believes should be done, whether it is value related, such as telling the truth, or simply the best performance possible on an exam. More generally, I would agree with Duval and Wicklund that moralistic values may be seen as a subset of the larger category of behavioral standards.

2. Private Audiences

Before continuing, it is worth noting that recent research by Baldwin and Holmes (1987) has indicated that situational circumstances can affect which particular components of the value structure are influential—that is, utilized as comparison points—at a particular time. More specifically, their research has suggested that values associated with certain significant others (who have presumably contributed to the development of the personal value structure) can be made salient in a particular context. As a result, the impact of those individuals' values on behavior is amplified during self-awareness. In their first study, Baldwin and Holmes asked subjects to visualize either older members of their family or else a couple of their campus friends. The subjects were then asked to evaluate pornography. The assumption was that the standards of the former "private audience" would be perceived by the subjects as less accepting of the pornography than would those of the latter group, and that this would have an effect on subjects' reported enjoyment of the literature. As expected, the self-aware subjects did report less enjoyment of the pornography if they had been asked to visualize family members than if they were thinking about their friends. Of additional interest, however, was the fact that the correlation between previously reported attitudes and enjoyment of the pornography remained very high among the self-aware subjects ($r = .61$), and it was higher than that of the non-self-focused group ($r = .17$; cf. Gibbons, 1978).

These results and this research illustrate effectively the manifold nature of the personal value structure. As suggested earlier, the structure itself is the reflection of an accumulation of internalized values from different external sources. At any given time one or more of these particular sources can become influential, which raises an interesting question: What would happen if the assumed value of a particular significant other conflicted with a personal standard, a situation that undoubtedly is currently confronting the conservative children of more liberal baby-boomer parents, raised during the 1950s and early 1960s? Unfortunately, the Baldwin and Holmes research cannot answer that question since they did not have such a conflict condition. This situation is similar to that of the conformity research discussed earlier (e.g., Gibbons & Wright, 1983), which leads me to essentially the same prediction: Opposition from particularly important external sources may encourage self-focused individuals to scrutinize and question their own standards more carefully, but, ultimately, strong personal standards will tend to predominate. Presumably, subsequent research in this area will help clarify this empirical question.

B. CONFLICT

With one important exception, then, the behavior of self-aware persons does reflect a compelling influence from an internal value system of the nature of a generalized other. The exception occurs in those instances in which a particular standard is faced with substantial opposition. That opposition may take one of several different forms, including salient, competing self-dimensions, such as pain or fear; conflicting values or behavioral standards (internal or external); or else a perceived inability to attain the standard. In the first instance, Carver and Scheier's (1981) model is very helpful. It would suggest that lower level standards or points of comparison would predominate. Only in this case the comparison point is a particular experience rather than a behavior. Thus, fear interferes with attempts at matching an experimental standard of cooperativeness (e.g., Carver *et al.*, 1979a; Scheier *et al.*, 1981). Similarly, self-concern may prevent the self-focused person from considering appropriate prosocial behavior or else lead the individual to the conclusion that standard-consistent behavior is, at least momentarily, less appropriate than self-protection (Vallacher & Solodky, 1979). In general, dysphoria—originating either within the individual or from the environment—or pain, or fear, or self-concern are all likely to interfere with value recognition as well as with attempts to bring behavior in line with those values.

By the same token, those persons who believe they cannot do what they feel they should are likely to experience an increase in negative affect when they are self-aware. Hence, people who are low in self-esteem and therefore generally pessimistic in terms of self-efficacy will find the state of self-focus to be phenomenologically aversive (Brockner, 1979b; Brockner *et al.*, 1985; Brockner & Wallnau, 1981). Presumably, the most common reaction to self-focus for those people would be either to avoid the self-focusing stimulus or simply to divert attention elsewhere (cf. Carver & Scheier, 1981; Duval & Wicklund, 1972).

VII. Revised Model

Reviewing the accumulated self-attention research from the last 9 or 10 years leads to two basic conclusions: (1) There is support for many of Duval and Wicklund's initial conceptualizations as well as the basic structure of the theory, and (2) as this review has suggested, a number of changes in the theory are called for. In response to the criticisms presented by alternative models, as well as by research generated by them and by original self-awareness theory, a revised model is described here and outlined in Fig. 1. The model is similar to that of Duval and Wicklund but includes a number of modifications, two of which are primary: (1) the inclusion of the concept of self-schema and (2) the theoretical assumption that there are different levels of self and that reactions to self-focus will vary as a function of which level happens to be momentarily salient.

A. SELF-ASSESSMENT AND THE SELF-SCHEMA

The basis of most models of self-focus is essentially the same: Attention is bidirectional, and at any given time it can be focused on either the self or the environment. Attention may oscillate back and forth between the two foci, and the presence of others can help direct attention back to the self; however, one cannot be self-focused and other focused at the same time. Thus, the latter category of attention, which includes as focal targets other individuals, groups, and the like, is not considered self-awareness. By the same token, paying attention to peripheral self-components, such as gross motor activity, in order to facilitate interaction with the environment is also not considered self-awareness. Focusing on the self will facilitate access to the self-schema, much as consideration of a particular ethnic group will activate a schema for that group. Since the schema incorporates all aspects of the self-concept, from physical to cognitive to moral, almost by definition, people who are self-aware are going to become more attuned to and more cognizant of themselves. In addition, when the self-schema is accessed, self-assessment is inevitable. Just as the museum visitor evaluates artwork, or the prospective home buyer evaluates property, the self-

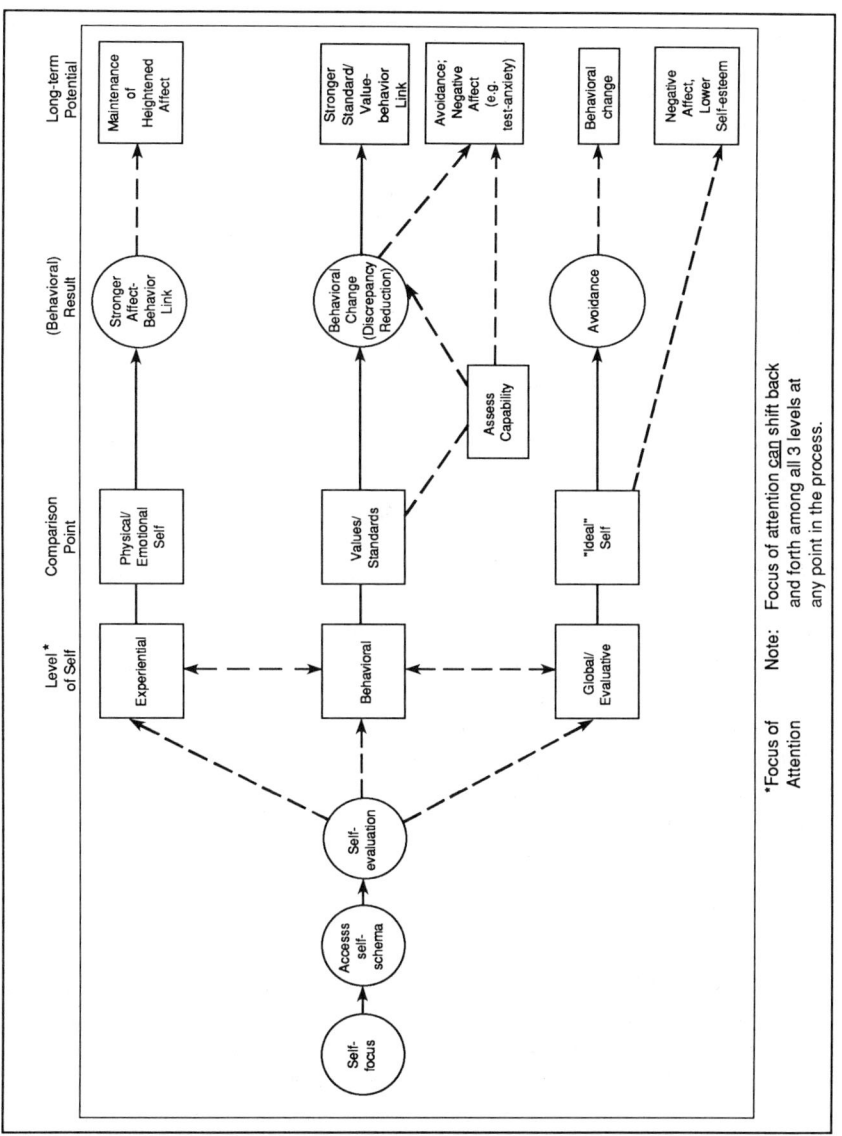

Fig. 1. A revised model of self-awareness.

aware person is going to engage in an assessment of the object that she or he is contemplating.

B. SELF-DIMENSIONS

There are many different aspects of the self that can become the focus of this evaluative self-assessment. Sometimes these self-dimensions may attain salience sequentially and sometimes simultaneously, which raises the question of which standard is likely to predominate when several are salient at the same time. This question is particularly important (and interesting) when the dimensions happen to conflict with one another, as would be the case, for example, for the chaste college freshman who is debating the imminent loss of virginity, or for the squeamish editor contemplating donating blood in response to an urgent request on the radio. In this respect the evidence supports Carver and Scheier's (1981) model of a self-structure with multiple levels.

In the current model three general levels of self are identified (see Fig. 1): experiential, behavioral, and global–evaluative. These dimensions exist in hierarchical structure in terms of abstraction, and in each instance the point of comparison (i.e., the standard in Duval & Wicklund's terms) is different. Which level, and therefore which comparison point, happens to be salient is determined primarily by situational factors. The level of focus, in turn, determines the type of behavioral response. In sum, it is hypothesized that the process of assessment, once initiated, can involve one or more of several different components of the self. The process does not, however, immediately invoke perceptions of the ideal self, nor does it necessarily result in the recognition of a personal discrepancy. The following discussion presents further description of the three levels, including related comparison points and behavioral reactions.

1. Experiential

If mood states or arousal, or any corporal aspect of the self, happen to be elevated when the individual is self-aware, then attention will initially focus on that dimension. This will lead to heightened awareness of the affect or arousal (cf. Scheier *et al.*, 1982), and it will also strengthen the link between affect and related behaviors, such as retaliation after provocation (Scheier, 1976) or avoiding or retreating from a feared stimulus (Scheier *et al.*, 1981). At this level, standards are in fact simply points of comparison (cf. Carver & Scheier, 1981), such as vocal accent, hair color or presence, or weight. They have little to do with either values or motivation and may have nothing to do with behavior, but they do involve self-assessment. If an autonomic response is involved, then as long as it remains elevated it will attract attention, and thus consideration of an appropriate or standard-based behavioral response is at least delayed and may not occur at all.

2. Behavioral

If the individual is free of psychological or physiological distractions, even momentarily, and a response of some kind is called for, then the self-assessment will focus initially on consideration of relevant behavioral standards or values (cf. Duval & Wicklund, 1972). These standards serve as a guide, informing the individual what behavior is appropriate within the current situation, that is, what should and, just as important, what should not be done. The result typically is a stronger relation between internal standards and behavior. The values and standards come from within. But that does not preclude the possibility that the self-focused person may sometimes look to others for information about what behavior is appropriate. That information will then be considered when deciding on a particular response. If the standard evoked by the situation involves some kind of performance (e.g., an exam, ability to resist temptation, bravery), then the self-evaluation process will include an assessment of one's ability to attain that standard (cf. Carver & Scheier, 1981). Low expectations will be accompanied by negative affect (exacerbated by self-focus); high expectations will be associated with heightened optimism and determination. This is one of the reasons why persons with low self-esteem and low self-efficacy find the state of self-focus especially aversive (Brockner, 1979b). Finally, if self-focused attention should happen to disrupt an ongoing behavior (cf. Carver & Scheier, 1981), then it is possible that attention could focus on the perceived discrepancy between the appropriate and the current behavior, leading to attempts at reducing the discrepancy.

a. Value Structure. The value structure that is involved at the behavioral level reflects the accumulated learning of socialization experience. Although many individual standards have little to do with morality, the general nature of the value structure certainly has a civilizing effect on behavior, as Wicklund (1980) suggested. Conceptually, it is analogous to the generalized other (Mead, 1934; Cooley, 1902/1964), or to what James (1890) called the "spiritual" self. This structure is unique to the individual, however, and is not dependent on the presence of the others who were instrumental in its development (cf. Baldwin & Holmes, 1987; Duval & Wicklund, 1972). External sources can effect change in this value structure. Once a particular value is internalized, however, social influence on that dimension will be minimized when attention is self-focused. In contrast, in the absence of self-focus, values will have little or no influence on behavior.

b. Self-Esteem. If, in fact, external influence is minimized during self-focus, then why does a person respond to the dictates of this independent value system?

The answer is simply that to do otherwise would have a negative impact on self-esteem. Transgressing against a personal value or ignoring a behavioral standard while attention is self-focused will lead the individual into an evaluative level of self-assessment. And at this level one is especially sensitive to the self-esteem implications of his or her behavior. Thus, protection of self-esteem is the ultimate motivating force behind the self-aware response process at the behavioral level in this model.

3. Evaluative

If the situation does not call for a particular behavioral response, or if attempts at matching the standard have succeeded or failed, then self-focus will elicit a global evaluation of self at a more abstract level ("How well am I doing in attaining these standards?"). Once again, others may be used as a source of information, via social comparison, in assessing the self. Ultimately, however, the comparison point at this level, and this level only, is the ideal self. Consequently, attempts at improving behavior, including reducing perceived discrepancies with the ideal self, are likely to occur. For example, the parent who verbally abuses a son or daughter may resolve to change that behavior or perhaps may just placate the self by vowing "to do better in the future." In the absence of a resolution of some sort, the urge to avoid self-focus is likely to be very compelling. Reactions to this evaluation will generally reflect self-esteem. Those who are most self-critical will find the state aversive; those with higher self-esteem usually will not (cf. Shibutani, 1961). Since no specific behavioral standards are involved, no immediate behavioral responses, other than avoidance, are likely to occur, even though long-term behavioral change is a possible outcome.

It is often the case that more than one dimension of the self becomes salient at one time. When that happens, lower levels in the hierarchical structure—the experiential and then the behavioral levels—are likely to predominate in terms of attentional focus.[10] It is also possible that neither experiential aspects of the self nor behavior would be salient in a given situation, which would result in (self-directed) attention being focused almost immediately on a global evaluation of the self vis-à-vis the ideal. This is essentially the process outlined by Duval and Wicklund (1972). In other words, a self-aware person may focus on one level (e.g., an emotional state at the experiential level) and never consider self-components from another level (e.g., behavioral standards at the behavioral level). By the same token, just as attention can oscillate back and forth from the environ-

---

[10]The belief that affective dimensions of the self are more dynamic and therefore more likely to capture attention than are "cooler" dimensions, such as cognition, has a long history in psychology, beginning with James (1890) and continuing to the present (e.g., Weinstein, 1988; Wicklund, 1980).

ment to the self, it can also shift from any one of the different levels to another and is likely to do so quite rapidly. I agree with Wicklund (1980), however, that prolonged self-focus will eventually uncover some perceived personal shortcoming, causing discomfort and attempted distraction to the environment. People seldom stay self-focused for very long.

4. Individual Differences

There are likely to be individual differences in the extent to which attention is focused on the three aspects of self. For example, persons with low self-efficacy should spend relatively more time assessing behavioral standards than those with higher self-efficacy. Depressed persons tend to be preoccupied with (negative) affective states (cf. Beck's, 1967, discussion of the depressive triad), whereas people high in the trait of private self-consciousness (Fenigstein *et al.*, 1975) will generally spend more time at all three levels. Since frequent self-reflection will serve to strengthen the link between the standard and behavior, people who are dispositionally inclined toward self-focus (i.e., "high privates") are either going to demonstrate significant standard–behavior consistency, or else they are going to feel quite bad about not being able to do so. Finally, the tendency to avoid self-focus is probably also a characteristic of the sociopathic personality.

C. INTERNAL CONFLICT

There are also going to be individual differences in the extent to which people maintain a particular standard. Someone who values intellectual performance more than integrity, for example, may be even more likely to cheat when attention is self-focused within an evaluative context than when it is not (Vallacher & Solodky, 1979). Assessing the relative importance or centrality of values has been and most likely will continue to be problematic, which makes predictions of behavior in situations of conflicting standards difficult at best (cf. Wicklund, 1980), tautological at worst.[11] Unfortunately, no solution to the problem can be offered here, except to suggest that accurate prediction is theoretically possible, if individual differences in value structure are assessed when attention is self-focused. One thing is clear in situations of internal conflict, such as those of competing standards, and that is eventually either the situation will attract atten-

---

[11]The issues of salience of standards and competition among conflicting standards are generally difficult ones for self-awareness theory or related theories to handle (cf. Wicklund & Gollwitzer, 1987). In many situations where universal values or norms hold, the prediction of behavior is not a difficult task. Where that is not the case, however, personal standards and values are likely to reflect considerable individual differences. This means that the prediction of *individual* responses in these instances is difficult.

tion away from the self or else the perceived threat to self-esteem will encourage the person to divert attention to the environment. A similar situation is likely to develop should the person feel incapable of doing what should be done. In this case, self-aware persons will usually attempt to avoid the self-focused state either physically or cognitively (as both Duval and Wicklund and Carver and Scheier suggest). Perseveration on the self is likely to be debilitating, as can be seen in the research on test anxiety (Wine, 1971) and depression (Greenberg & Pyszczynski, 1986).

D. DIFFERENCES FROM PREVIOUS MODELS

Although the two fundamental assumptions of the current approach (i.e., bidirectional attention and self-evaluation) are the same as those of the two major models discussed above, the current approach does differ from each of those two in a number of ways. First, I would agree with Carver and Scheier (1981) that focusing attention on the self results in accessing the self-schema. However, I would argue in addition that the self-schema incorporates an internalized structure of values and personal standards analogous to the generalized other. That value structure, if invoked, can both promote and inhibit behavior. When the value structure is absent, then focus of attention will usually have little effect on behavior (cf. Gibbons & Gerrard, 1986; Wojciszke, 1987).

Second, persons who are reacting to an audience (or a TV camera) are primarily concerned with others and not the self. Attention is often directed back on the self in a public situation, but this involves a view of the self from the perspective of others. In the current model, that is not considered self-awareness. On the other hand, feelings of alienation or distinction from the group are likely to promote self-awareness. When that happens, the impact of the group and its members is reduced to a single source of information to be considered by the individual in deciding appropriate behavior. In most cases personal standards ultimately will prevail, even though the discomfort associated with being the focus of the group may temporarily promote behavior that is out of line with personal standards. This reflects a fundamental difference in emphasis (i.e., on the self) in the current model as opposed to those generated since Duval and Wicklund's original theory.

Third, the current model categorizes self-components into a hierarchical structure containing three levels. Self-assessment occurs at each level, from the physical, including emotion or illness, to the behavioral (i.e., behavioral standards), to the level of general evaluation of the self. Personal standards are relevant only at the behavioral level. At the global/evaluative level (and only at this level), self-assessment occurs vis-à-vis the ideal self and therefore is likely to reflect self-esteem.

Fourth, behavioral change evidenced in response to self-focus is not necessarily or even usually motivated by negative affect, at least not directly. Rather, it is motivated by a desire to maintain self-esteem and avoid the self-esteem damage associated with a realization that personal values or standards have been transgressed or ignored. Similarly, self-regulation at low levels of the response hierarchy (cf. Carver & Scheier, 1981) does not involve self-assessment and thus should not be considered self-awareness. At higher levels the self-regulatory process resembles Duval and Wicklund's (1972) model very closely, and Carver and Scheier's reasoning seems quite congruent with the approach taken here—with addition of the concept of a value structure and recognition of the importance of motivational involvement.

Fifth and related to the point just mentioned, outcome assessment, which is an integral part of the self-regulatory model, is appropriate for performance situations (and involves estimates of self-efficacy). But in many instances outcome assessment does not occur; it is irrelevant. Instead, attention focuses almost immediately on the particular self-dimensions that happen to be salient, and assessment at that level occurs automatically. Once again, the important point here has to do with where attention is focused during self-awareness. Both the Carver and Scheier and the Duval and Wicklund theories claim that perceived discrepancies are most salient during self-focus and prompt behavioral reaction—what might be termed a "deficit" or reactive model. As mentioned earlier, however, there is very little support for the discrepancy hypothesis, except perhaps when considering performance assessment. Thus, increased accuracy of self-reports made by self-focused persons, greater attitude–behavior consistency, and value-consistent behavior in general are not the result of attempts at reducing perceived discrepancies.

To the extent that there is concern about discrepancies, it is from an anticipatory perspective, that is, a desire to prevent them from developing. I would argue, then, that the self-aware individual is usually goal oriented, trying to bring behavior in line with a standard; and that occurs whether a discrepancy exists or not. Put simply, attention is fixed on the goal more than on the discrepancy. Similarly, self-assessment at the evaluative level may result in a personal commitment to improve behavior (e.g., become a better Catholic or a better spouse). Although this involves admission of an existing shortcoming, nonetheless focus is on the future as much as it is on the past. More often than not, self-focus either inhibits discrepancy-producing behavior or simply facilitates behavior in a direction that is thought to be appropriate.

Finally, and perhaps most important, according to the current, revised approach, the unique characteristic of self-awareness that distinguishes it from other psychological states is the careful consideration of all aspects of the self—physical, behavioral, and cognitive—that it engenders. This consideration is manifest in a stronger relation between attitudes and behavior, in more veridical attributions and self-reports, and in most instances less conformity and less ("assertive") self-presentation. More generally, it increases what might simply be called self-knowledge. Conversely, in the absence of self-focus the link between values and overt behavior is theoretically nonexistent; likewise, the link between the internal self and all its components (attitudes, feelings, beliefs) and behavior is minimal.

E. SUMMARY

1. Research Directions

It is probably a fair assessment to suggest that the heuristic value of the model proposed here rests primarily in its integration of previous research. Nonetheless, many unresolved issues have been highlighted by the current discussion, some of which remain from previous models. Most of those issues revolve around two fundamental topics: conflict and accuracy. A number of questions remain about the issue of conflicting standards, for example, the conflict associated with ego protectiveness versus accurate attribution. Similarly, relatively little is known about the mechanics of self-focus in group settings or social interactions, or about how personal standards affect self-presentation in a group. In addition a number of related issues and questions are raised by the current, revised model: to what extent does self-awareness occur in a public setting, when is behavior directed toward discrepancy reduction, what circumstances prompt consideration of the global–evaluative level of self, what is the impact of self-focus on defensive versus assertive impression management, and what is the effect of self-focus on self-esteem, and vice-versa?

Of late much of the work stimulated by self-awareness theory (or theories) has headed in a more applied direction. Some of the as yet unanswered questions associated with this recent work have already been discussed briefly, such as the impact of self-focus on awareness of physical health and on mental health, including depression, and the effect of self-attention on abstract thought processes (cf. Wilson *et al.*, 1981). I suspect that this trend toward applications of self-attention theory will continue, with increasing emphasis on the limits of self-knowledge, including the extent to which attention can facilitate access to more or less remote aspects of the inner self. Finally, there is still much to be learned about the basic question of what the consequences of accurate self-knowledge are in terms of physical, psychological, and emotional well-being (cf. Taylor & Brown, 1988).

2. Conclusion

The current model includes a number of modifications of self-awareness theory (Duval & Wicklund, 1972), based on research generated by the theory as well as alternative models of self-attention prompted by it. That research has been interpreted in a manner that is thought to be more congruent with the original theory and thus reflects a different orientation than that promoted by the other models. In essence, an attempt has been made to reemphasize the self in self-awareness theory. At the same time, it is recognized that the original theory maintained a rather monolithic concept of the self, consistent with the invariant process of reactions to the self that it proposed. The process described here is more divergent, reflecting a belief that there are in fact different types of self-awareness. Each type has a different focal point and can promote very different behavioral responses. In short, the current model is both an expansion and a contraction of the original—a sign that the theory is evolving and will continue to do so.

Acknowledgments

I thank Charles Carver, Meg Gerrard, Jeff Greenberg, Stefan Hormuth, Jay Hull, Teddy Warner, and Robert Wicklund for their comments on the manuscript.

References

Asch, S. E. (1951). Effects of group pressure upon the modification and distortion of judgment. In H. Guetzkow (Ed.), *Groups, leadership, and men*. Pittsburgh, PA: Carnegie Press.
Atkinson, J. W. (1957). Motivational determinants of risk-taking behavior. *Psychological Review*, **64**, 359–372.
Atkinson, J. W. (1964). *An introduction to motivation*. New York: Van Nostrand.
Bachtold, L. M. (1979). Objective self-awareness as a non-aversive state: Effect of anticipating discrepancy reduction. *Journal of Personality,* **47**, 330–339.
Baldwin, M. W., & Holmes, J. G. (1987). Salient private audiences and awareness of the self. *Journal of Personality and Social Psychology,* **52**, 1087–1098.
Bartlett, F. C. (1932). *Remembering: A study in experimental and social psychology*. Cambridge, England: Cambridge University Press.
Beck, A. T. (1967). *Depression: Clinical, experimental and theoretical aspects*. New York: Hoeber.
Berkowitz, L. (1987). Mood, self-awareness, and willingness to help. *Journal of Personality and Social Psychology,* **52**, 721–729.
Bernstein, W. M., & Davis, M. H. (1982). Perspective-taking, self-consciousness, and accuracy in person perception. *Basic and Applied Social Psychology,* **3**, 1–19.
Bloom, L. J., Houston, B. K., Holmes, D. S., & Burish, T. G. (1977). The effectiveness of attentional diversion and situational redefinition for reducing stress due to nonambiguous threat. *Journal of Research in Psychology,* **11**, 83–94.
Brehm, J. W., Wright, R. A., Solomon, S., Silka, L., & Greenberg, J. (1983). Perceived difficulty, energization, and the magnitude of goal valence. *Journal of Experimental Social Psychology,* **19**, 21–48.

Briggs, S. R., Cheek, J. M., & Buss, A. H. (1980). An analysis of the self-monitoring scale. *Journal of Personality and Social Psychology,* **38,** 679–686.

Brockner, J. (1979). The effects of self-esteem, success–failure, and self-consciousness on task performance. *Journal of Personality and Social Psychology,* **37,** 1732–1741.

Brockner, J., Hjelle, L., & Plant, R. (1985). Self-focused attention, self-esteem, and the experience of state depression. *Journal of Personality,* **50,** 425–434.

Brockner, J., & Hulton, A. J. B. (1978). How to reverse the vicious cycle of low self-esteem: The importance of attentional focus. *Journal of Experimental Social Psychology,* **14,** 564–578.

Brockner, J., & Wallnau, L. B. (1981). Self-esteem, anxiety, and the avoidance of self-focused attention. *Journal of Research in Psychology,* **15,** 277–291.

Burgio, K. L., Merluzzi, T. V. & Pryor, J. B. (1986). Effects of performance expectancy and self-focused attention on social interaction. *Journal of Personality and Social Psychology,* **50,** 1216–1221.

Buss, A. H. (1980). *Self-consciousness and social anxiety.* San Francisco: W. H. Freeman.

Buss, D. M., & Scheier, M. F. (1976). Self-consciousness, self-awareness, and self-attribution. *Journal of Research in Personality,* **10,** 463–468.

Carver, C. S. (1974). Facilitation of physical aggression through objective self-awareness. *Journal of Experimental Social Psychology,* **10,** 365–370.

Carver, C. S. (1975). Physical aggression as a function of objective self-awareness and attitudes toward punishment. *Journal of Experimental Social Psychology,* **11,** 510–519.

Carver, C. S. (1979). A cybernetic model of self-attention processes. *Journal of Personality and Social Psychology,* **37,** 1251–1281.

Carver, C. S., & Blaney, P. H. (1977). Perceived arousal, focus of attention, and avoidance behavior. *Journal of Applied Psychology,* **86,** 154–162.

Carver, C. S., Blaney, P. H., & Scheier, M. F. (1979a). Focus of attention, chronic expectancy, and response to a feared stimulus. *Journal of Personality and Social Psychology,* **37,** 1186–1195.

Carver, C. S., Blaney, P. H., & Scheier, M. F. (1979b). Reassertion and giving up: The interactive role of self-directed attention and outcome expectancy. *Journal of Personality and Social Psychology,* **37,** 1859–1870.

Carver, C. S., & Scheier, M. F. (1981). *Attention and self-regulation: A control-theory approach to human behavior.* New York: Springer-Verlag.

Carver, C. S., & Scheier, M. F. (1987). The blind men and the elephant: Selective examination of the public–private literature gives rise to a faulty perception. *Journal of Personality,* **55,** 525–541.

Cheek, J. M. (1982). Aggression, moderator variables, and the validity of personality tests: A peer-rating study. *Journal of Personality and Social Psychology,* **43,** 1254–1269.

Cohen, J. L., & Davis, J. H. (1973). Effects of audience status, evaluation, and time of action on performance with hidden word problems. *Journal of Personality and Social Psychology,* **27,** 74–85.

Cohen, J. L., Dowling, N., Bishop, B., & Maney, W. (1985). Causal attributions: Effects of self-focused attention and self-esteem feedback. *Personality and Social Psychology Bulletin,* **11,** 369–378.

Cooley, C. H. (1902/1964). *Human nature and the social order.* New York: Scribners.

Csikszentmihalyi, M., & Figurski, T. J. (1982). Self-awareness and aversive experience in everyday life. *Journal of Personality,* **50,** 15–28.

Dabbs, J. M., Jr., & Johnson, J. E., & Leventhal, H. (1968). Palmar sweating: A quick and simple measure. *Journal of Experimental Psychology,* **78,** 347–350.

Davies, M. F. (1982). Self-focused attention and personality validation. *Current Psychological Research,* **2,** 87–93.

Davis, D., & Brock, T. C. (1975). Use of first-person pronouns as a function of increased objective self-awareness and performance feedback. *Journal of Experimental Social Psychology,* **11,** 381–388.

Deutsch, M., & Gerard, H. B. (1955). A study of normative and informational social influence upon individual judgment. *Journal of Abnormal and Social Psychology,* **51,** 629–636.

Diener, E. (1979). Deindividuation, self-awareness, and disinhibition. *Journal of Personality and Social Psychology,* **37,** 1160–1171.

Diener, E., Fraser, S. C., Beaman, A. L., & Kelem, R. T. (1976). Effects of deindividuating variables on stealing by Halloween trick-or-treaters. *Journal of Personality and Social Psychology,* **33,** 178–183.

Diener, E., & Srull, T. K. (1979). Self-awareness, psychological perspective, and self-reinforcement in relation to personal and social standards. *Journal of Personality and Social Psychology,* **37,** 413–423.

Duval, S. (1971). *Causal attribution as a function of focus of attention.* Unpublished manuscript, University of Texas, Austin.

Duval, S. (1976). Conformity on a visual task as a function of personal novelty on attitudinal dimensions and being reminded of the object status of self. *Journal of Experimental Social Psychology,* **12,** 87–98.

Duval, S., & Duval, V. H. (1983). *Consistency and cognition: A theory of causal attribution.* Hillsdale, NJ: Erlbaum.

Duval, S., & Duval, V. H. (1985). *Level of perceived coping ability and attribution for negative events.* Paper presented at the Conference on Attribution and Personality, California School of Professional Psychology.

Duval, S., & Wicklund, R. A. (1972). *A theory of objective self-awareness.* New York: Academic Press.

Duval, S., & Wicklund, R. A. (1973). Effects of objective self-awareness on attribution of causality. *Journal of Experimental Social Psychology,* **9,** 17–31.

Duval, S., Wicklund, R. A., & Fine, R. L. (1972). Avoidance of objective self awareness under conditions of high and low intra-self discrepancy. In S. Duval & R. A. Wicklund *A theory of objective self awareness.* New York: Academic Press.

Edelmann, R. J. (1985). Individual-differences in embarrassment, self-consciousness, self-monitoring, and embarrassability. *Personality and Individual Differences,* **6,** 223–230.

Ellis, R. J., & Holmes, J. G. (1982). Focus of attention and self-evaluation in social interaction. *Journal of Personality and Social Psychology,* **43,** 67–77.

Epstein, S., Rosenthal, S., & Szpiler, J. (1978). The influence of attention upon anticipatory arousal, habituation, and reactivity to a noxious stimulus. *Journal of Research in Personality,* **12,** 30–40.

Federoff, N. A., & Harvey, J. H. (1976). Focus of attention, self-esteem, and the attribution of causality. *Journal of Research in Personality,* **10,** 336–345.

Fenigstein, A. (1979). Self-consciousness, self-attention, and social interaction. *Journal of Personality and Social Psychology,* **37,** 75–86.

Fenigstein, A. (1984). Self-consciousness and the overperception of self as a target. *Journal of Personality and Social Psychology,* **47,** 860–870.

Fenigstein, A. (1987). On the nature of public and private self-consciousness. *Journal of Personality,* **55,** 543–554.

Fenigstein, A., & Carver, C. S. (1978). Self-focusing effects of false heartbeat feedback. *Journal of Personality and Social Psychology,* **36,** 1241–1250.

Fenigstein, A., & Levine, M. P. (1984). Self-attention, concept activation, and the causal self. *Journal of Experimental and Social Psychology,* **20,** 231–245.

Fenigstein, A., Scheier, M. F., & Buss, A. H. (1975). Public and private self-consciousness: Assessment and theory. *Journal of Consulting and Clinical Psychology, 43,* 522–527.

Franzoi, S. L. (1983). Self-concept differences as a function of private self-consciousness and social anxiety. *Journal of Research in Psychology, 12,* 275–287.

Franzoi, S. L., & Sweeney, P. D. (1986). Another look at the relation between private self-consciousness and self-attribution. *Journal of Research in Personality, 20,* 187–206.

Froming, W. J., & Carver, C. S. (1981). Divergent influences of private and public self-consciousness in a compliance paradigm. *Journal of Research in Personality, 15,* 159–171.

Froming, W. J., Walker, G. R., & Lopyan, K. J. (1982). Public and private self-awareness: When personal attitudes conflict with societal expectations. *Journal of Experimental Social Psychology, 18,* 476–487.

Gibbons, F. X. (1978). Sexual standards and reactions to pornography: Enhancing behavioral consistency through self-focused attention. *Journal of Personality and Social Psychology, 36,* 976–987.

Gibbons, F. X. (1983). Self-focused attention and self-report validity: The "veridicality" hypothesis. *Journal of Personality, 51,* 517–542.

Gibbons, F. X. (1986). Social comparison and depression: Company's effect on misery. *Journal of Personality and Social Psychology, 51,* 140–148.

Gibbons, F. X. (1987). Mild depression and self-disclosure intimacy: Self and others' perceptions. *Cognitive Therapy and Research, 11,* 361–380.

Gibbons, F. X., Carver, C. S., Scheier, M. F., & Hormuth, S. E. (1979). Self-focused attention and the placebo effect: Fooling some of the people some of the time. *Journal of Experimental Social Psychology, 15,* 263–274.

Gibbons, F. X., & Gaeddert, W. P. (1984). Focus of attention and placebo utility. *Journal of Experimental Social Psychology, 20,* 159–176.

Gibbons, F. X., & Gerrard, M. (1986). *Self-awareness and the truth-as-standard hypothesis.* Paper presented at the American Psychological Association Convention, Washington, DC.

Gibbons, F. X., Smith, T. W., Ingram, R. E., Pearce, K., Brehm, S. S., & Schroeder, D. J. (1985). Self-awareness and self-confrontation: Effects of self-focused attention on members of a clinical population. *Journal of Personality and Social Psychology, 48,* 662–675.

Gibbons, F. X., & Wicklund, R. A. (1976). Selective exposure to self. *Journal of Research in Personality, 10,* 98–106.

Gibbons, F. X., & Wicklund, R. A. (1982). Self-focused attention and helping behavior. *Journal of Personality and Social Psychology, 43,* 462–474.

Gibbons, F. X., & Wright, R. A. (1983). Self-focused attention and reactions to conflicting standards. *Journal of Research in Personality, 17,* 263–273.

Goethals, G. R., & Darley, J. M. (1977). Social comparison theory: An attributional approach. In J. M. Suls & R. L. Miller (Eds.), *Social comparison processes.* New York: Wiley.

Goffman, E. (1959). *The presentation of self in everyday life.* New York: Doubleday.

Greenberg, J. (1980). Attentional focus and performance causality as determinants of equity behavior. *Journal of Personality and Social Psychology, 38,* 579–585.

Greenberg, J. (1983). Overcoming egocentric bias in perceived fairness through self-awareness. *Social Psychology Quarterly, 46,* 152–156.

Greenberg, J., & Musham, C. (1981). Avoiding and seeking self-focused attention. *Journal of Research in Psychology, 15,* 191–200.

Greenberg, J., & Pyszczynski, T. (1986). Persistent high self-focus after failure and low self-focus after success: The depressive self-focusing style. *Journal of Personality and Social Psychology, 50,* 1039–1044.

Greenwald, A. G. (1982). Ego-task analysis: An integration of research in ego-involvement and self-awareness. In A. H. Hastorf & A. M. Isen (Eds.), *Cognitive social psychology*. New York: Elsevier/North-Holland.

Hansen, R. D., Hansen, C. H., & Crano, W. D. (1989). Sympathetic arousal and self attention: The accessibility of interoceptive and exteroceptive arousal cues. *Journal of Experimental Social Psychology,* in press.

Hass, G. (1984). Perspective taking and self-awareness: Drawing an E on your forehead. *Journal of Personality and Social Psychology,* **46,** 788–798.

Higgins, E. T., King, G. A., & Mavin, G. H. (1982). Individual construct accessibility and subjective impressions and recall. *Journal of Personality and Social Psychology,* **43,** 35–47.

Hoover, C., Wood, R., Wegner, D. M., & Knowles, E. (1982). *Self-focused attention and empathy.* Unpublished manuscript, University of Wisconsin, Green Bay.

Hormuth, S. E. (1982). Self-awareness and drive theory: Comparing internal standards and dominant responses. *European Journal of Social Psychology,* **12,** 31–45.

Hull, C. L. (1952). *A behavior system.* New Haven, CT: Yale University Press.

Hull, J. G., & Levy, A. S. (1979). The organizational functions of the self: An alternative to the Duval and Wicklund Model of self-awareness. *Journal of Personality and Social Psychology,* **37,** 756–768.

Hull, J. G., & Young, R. D. (1983). Self-consciousness, self-esteem, and success–failure as determinants of alcohol consumption in male social drinkers. *Journal of Personality and Social Psychology,* **44,** 1097–1109.

Ingram, R. E., Lumry, A. E., Cruet, D., & Sieber, W. (1987). Attentional processes in depressive disorders. *Cognitive Therapy and Research,* **11,** 351–360.

Ingram, R. E., & Smith, T. W. (1984). Depression and internal versus external focus of attention. *Cognitive Therapy and Research,* **8,** 139–152.

Innes, J. M., & Young, R. F. (1975). The effects of presence of an audience, evaluation apprehension, and objective self-awareness on learning. *Journal of Experimental Social Psychology,* **11,** 35–42.

Insko, C. A., Worchel, S., Songer, E., & Arnold, S. E. (1973). Effort, objective self-awareness, choice, and dissonance. *Journal of Personality and Social Psychology,* **28,** 262–269.

James, W. (1890). *The principles of psychology.* New York: Holt.

John, O. (1983). *Selbstaufmerksamkeit und Selbstprasentation: Moderator-variablen in der Personlickheit serfassung [Self-consciousness and self-monitoring: Moderator variables in personality assessment]?* Unpublished Diplomarbeit, Universitat Bielefeld.

Kassin, S. M. (1985). Eyewitness identification: Retrospective self-awareness and the accuracy-confidence correlation. *Journal of Personality and Social Psychology,* **44,** 878–893.

Kelley, H. (1973). Processes of causal attribution. *American Psychologist,* **28,** 107–128.

Kernis, M. H., & Reis, H. T. (1984). Self-consciousness, self-awareness, and justice in reward allocation. *Journal of Personality,* **52,** 58–70.

Koffka, K. (1935). *Principles of gestalt psychology.* New York: Harcourt, Brace.

Lacey, J. I., & Lacey, B. C. (1970). Some autonomic-central nervous system relationships. In P. Black (Ed.), *Physiological correlates of emotion.* New York: Academic Press.

Langer, E. J. (1978). Rethinking the role of thought in social interaction. In J. Harvey, W. Ickes, & R. Kidd (Eds.) *New directions in attribution theory* (Vol. 2). Hillsdale, NJ: Erlbaum.

Lanzetta, J. T., Biernat, J. J., & Kleck, R. E. (1982). Self-focused attention, facial behavior, autonomic arousal, and the experience of emotion. *Motivation and Emotion,* **6,** 49–63.

Leary, M. R. (1983). Social anxiousness: The construct and its measurement. *Journal of Personality Assessment,* **47,** 66–75.

Lepper, M. R., Zanna, M. P., & Abelson, R. (1970). Cognitive irreversibility in a dissonance-reduction situation. *Journal of Personality and Social Psychology,* **16,** 191–198.

Leventhal, H., Brown, D., Shockam, S., & Engquist, G. (1979). Effects of preparatory information about sensations, threat of pain, and attention on cold pressor distress. *Journal of Personality and Social Psychology, 37,* 688–714.

Lewinsohn, P. M., Hoberman, H., Teri, L., & Hautzinger, M. (1985). An integrative theory of depression. In S. Reiss & R. Bootzin (Eds.), *Theoretical issues in behavior therapy.* New York: Academic Press.

Major, B., Cozzarelli, C., Testa, M., & McFarlin, D. B. (1988). Self-unification vs. expectancy confirmation in social interaction: The impact of self-focus. *Personality and Social Psychology Bulletin, 14,* 346–359.

Markus, H. (1977). Self-schemata and processing information about the self. *Journal of Personality and Social Psychology, 35,* 63–78.

Markus, H., & Kunda, Z. (1986). Stability and malleability of the self-concept. *Journal of Personality and Social Psychology, 51,* 858–866.

Markus, H., & Nurius, P. (1986). Possible selves. *American Psychologist, 41,* 954–969.

Martens, R. (1969). Palmar sweating and the presence of an audience. *Journal of Experimental Social Psychology, 5,* 371–374.

Mason, R. E. (1961). *Internal perception and bodily functioning.* New York: International Universities Press.

Mayer, F. S., Duval, S., Holtz, R., & Bowman, C. (1985). Self-focus, helping request salience, felt responsibility, and helping behavior. *Personality and Social Psychology Bulletin, 11,* 133–134.

McCormick, T. F. (1980). *An investigation of standards of correctness by inducing conformity and consistency pressures within the framework of objective self-awareness.* Unpublished doctoral dissertation, University of Texas, Austin.

Mead, G. H. (1934). *Mind, self, and society.* Chicago: University of Chicago Press.

Mechanic, D. (1983). Adolescent health and illness behavior: Review of the literature and a new hypothesis for the study of stress. *Journal of Human Stress, 9,* 4–13.

Moore, D. L., & Baron, R. S. (1983). Social facilitation: A psychophysiological analysis. In J. T. Cacioppo & R. E. Petty (Eds.), *Social psychophysiology* (pp. 454–466). New York: Guilford Press.

Mullen, B. (1984). Participations in religious groups as a function of group composition: A self-attention perspective. *Journal of Applied Social Psychology, 14,* 509–518.

Mullen, B., & Suls, J. (1982a). "Know thyself": Stressful life changes and the ameliorative effect of private self-consciousness. *Journal of Experimental Social Psychology, 18,* 43–55.

Mullen, B., & Suls, J. (1982b). The effectiveness of attention and rejection as coping styles: A meta-analysis of temporal differences. *Journal of Psychosomatic Research, 26,* 43–49.

Nadler, A. (1983). Objective self-awareness, self-esteem, and causal attributions for success and failure. *Personality and Individual Differences, 4,* 9–15.

Nisbett, R. E., & Wilson, T. O. (1977). Telling more than we can know: Verbal reports on mental processes. *Psychological Review, 84,* 231–259.

Paulus, P. B., Annis, A. B., & Risner, H. T. (1978). An analysis of the mirror-induced self-awareness effect. *Bulletin of the Psychonomic Society, 12,* 8–10.

Pennebaker, J. W. (1982). *The psychology of physical symptoms.* New York: Springer-Verlag.

Polanyi, M. (1958). *Personal knowledge: Towards a post-critical philosophy.* New York: Harper & Row.

Prentice-Dunn, S., & Rogers, R. W. (1982). Effects of public and private self-awareness on deindividuation and aggression. *Journal of Personality and Social Psychology, 43,* 503–513.

Pryor, J. B., Gibbons, F. X., Wicklund, R. A., Fazio, R., & Hood, R. (1977). Self-focused attention and self-report validity. *Journal of Personality, 5,* 513–527.

Pyszczynski, T., & Greenberg, J. (1985). Depression and preference for self-focusing stimuli following success and failure. *Journal of Personality and Social Psychology, 49,* 1066–1075.

Pyszczynski, T., Holt, J., & Greenberg, J. (1987). Depression, self-focused attention, and expectancies for positive and negative future life events for self and others. *Journal of Personality and Social Psychology,* **52,** 994–1001.

Raven, B. H. (1959). Social influence on opinions and the communication of related context. *Journal of Applied Social Psychology,* **58,** 119–128.

Reisenzein, R., & Gattinger, E. (1982). Salience of arousal as a mediator of misattribution of transferred excitation. *Motivation and Emotion,* **6,** 315–328.

Rogers, T. B. (1977). Self-reference in memory: Recognition of personality items. *Journal of Research in Personality,* **11,** 295–305.

Rogers, T. B., Kuiper, N. A., & Kirker, W. A. (1977). Self-reference and the encoding of personal information. *Journal of Personality and Social Psychology,* **35,** 677–688.

Rokeach, M. (1968). *Beliefs, attitudes, and values.* San Francisco: Jossey-Bass.

Ross, L. (1977). The intuitive psychologist and his shortcomings: Distortions in the attribution process. In L. Berkowitz (Ed.), *Advances in experimental social psychology* (Vol. 10). New York: Academic Press.

Ruble, D. N., & Brooks-Gunn, S. (1979). Menstrual symptoms: A social cognition analysis. *Journal of Behavioral Medicine,* **35,** 515–534.

Santee, R. T., & Maslach, C. (1982). To agree or not to agree: Personal dissent amid social pressure to conform. *Journal of Personality and Social Psychology,* **42,** 690–700.

Sarason, I. G. (1975). Anxiety and self-preoccupation. In I. G. Sarason & C. D. Spielberger (Eds.), *Stress and anxiety* (Vol. 2, pp. 27–44). New York: Wiley.

Scheier, M. F. (1976). Self-awareness, self-consciousness, and angry aggression. *Journal of Personality,* **44,** 627–644.

Scheier, M. F. (1980). Effects of public and private self-consciousness on the public expression of personal beliefs. *Journal of Personality and Social Psychology,* **39,** 514–521.

Scheier, M. F., Buss, A. H., & Buss, D. M. (1978). Self-consciousness, self-report of aggressiveness, and aggression. *Journal of Research in Personality,* **12,** 133–140.

Scheier, M. F., & Carver, C. S. (1977). Self-focused attention and the experience of emotion: Attraction, repulsion, elation, and depression. *Journal of Personality and Social Psychology,* **35,** 625–636.

Scheier, M. F., & Carver, C. S. (1980). Private and public self-attention, resistance to change and dissonance reduction. *Journal of Personality and Social Psychology* **39,** 390–405.

Scheier, M. F., & Carver, C. S. (1983). Self-directed attention and the comparison of self with standards. *Journal of Experimental Social Psychology,* **19,** 205–222.

Scheier, M. F., Carver, C. S., & Gibbons, F. X. (1979). Self-directed attention, awareness of bodily states, and suggestibility. *Journal of Personality and Social Psychology,* **37,** 1576–1588.

Scheier, M. F., Carver, C. S., & Gibbons, F. X. (1981). Self-focused attention and reactions to fear. *Journal of Research in Psychology,* **15,** 1–15.

Scheier, M. F., Carver, C. S., & Matthews, K. A. (1982). Attentional factors in the perception of bodily states. In J. Caccioppo & R. Petty (Eds.), *Social psychophysiology* (pp. 510–542). New York: Guilford Press.

Schlenker, B. R., & Leary, M. R. (1982). Social anxiety and self-presentation: A Conceptualization and model. *Psychological Bulletin,* **92,** 641–669.

Shibutani, T. (1961). *Society and personality: An interactionist approach to social psychology.* Englewood Cliffs, NJ: Prentice-Hall.

Snyder, M. (1974). Self-monitoring of expressive behavior. *Journal of Personality and Social Psychology,* **30,** 526–537.

Steenbarger, B. N., & Aderman, D. (1979). Objective self-awareness as a nonaversive state: Effect of anticipating discrepancy reduction. *Journal of Personality,* **4,** 330–339.

Stephenson, B., & Wicklund, R. A. (1983). Self-directed attention and taking the other's perspective. *Journal of Experimental Social Psychology,* **19,** 58–77.
Stephenson, B., & Wicklund, R. A. (1984). The contagion of self-focus within a dyad. *Journal of Personality and Social Psychology,* **46,** 163–168.
Storms, M. D. (1973). Videotape and the attribution process: Reversing actors' and observers' points of view. *Journal of Personality and Social Psychology,* **27,** 165–175.
Strack, S., Blaney, P. H., Ganellen, R. J., & Coyne, J. C. (1985). Pessimistic self-preoccupation, performance deficits, and depression. *Journal of Personality and Social Psychology,* **49,** 1076–1085.
Taylor, S. E., & Brown, J. D. (1988). Illusion and well-being: A social psychological perspective on mental health. *Psychological Bulletin,* **103,** 193–210.
Taylor, S. E., & Fiske, S. T. (1978). Salience, attention, and attribution: Top of the head phenomena. In L. Berkowitz (Ed.), *Advances in experimental social psychology* (Vol. 10). New York: Academic Press.
Tetlock, P. E. & Manstead, A. S. R. (1985). Impression management vs. intrapsychic explanations in social psychology: A useful dichotomy? *Psychological Review,* **92,** 59–77.
Turner, R. G. (1978). Self-consciousness and speed of processing self-relevant information. *Personality and Social Psychology Bulletin,* **4,** 456–460.
Turner, R. G. (1980). Self-consciousness and memory of trait terms. *Personality and Social Psychology Bulletin,* **6,** 273–277.
Turner, R. G., & Peterson, M. (1977). Public and private self-consciousness and emotional expressivity. *Journal of Consulting and Clinical Psychology,* **45,** 490–491.
Vallacher, R. R., & Solodky, M. (1979). Objective self-awareness, standards of evaluation, and moral behavior. *Journal of Experimental Social Psychology,* **15,** 254–262.
Velten, E. (1968). A laboratory task for induction of mood states. *Behaviour Research and Therapy,* **6,** 473–482.
Wegner, D. M., & Giuliano, T. (1982). The forms of social awareness. In W. J. Ickes & E. S. Knowles (Eds.), *Personality, roles, and social behavior.* New York: Springer-Verlag.
Weinstein, N. D. (1988). The precaution adoption process. *Health Psychology,* **7,** 355–386.
Wicklund, R. A. (1975). Objective self-awareness. In L. Berkowitz (Ed.), *Advances in experimental social psychology* (Vol. 8). New York: Academic Press.
Wicklund, R. A. (1979). Three years later. In L. Berkowitz (Ed.), *Cognitive theories in social psychology.* New York: Academic Press.
Wicklund, R. A. (1979). The influence of self-awareness on human behavior. *American Scientist,* **67,** 187–193.
Wicklund, R. A. (1980). Group contact and self-focused attention. In P. B. Paulus (Ed.), *Psychology of group influence.* Hillsdale, NJ: Erlbaum.
Wicklund, R. A., & Duval, S. (1971). Opinion change and performance facilitation as a result of objective self-awareness. *Journal of Experimental and Social Psychology,* **7,** 319–342.
Wicklund, R. A., & Frey, D. (1980). Self-awareness theory: When the self makes a difference. In D. M. Wegner & R. R. Vallacher (Eds.), *The self in social psychology.* New York: Oxford University Press.
Wicklund, R. A. & Gollwitzer, P. M. (1987). The fallacy of the private–public self-focus distinction. *Journal of Personality,* **55,** 491–523.
Wicklund, R. A., & Hormuth, S. E. (1981). On the functions of the self: A reply to Hull and Levy. *Journal of Personality and Social Psychology,* **40,** 1029–1037.
Willerman, L., Turner, R. G., & Peterson, M. A. (1976). A comparison of the predictive validity of typical and maximal personality measures. *Journal of Research in Personality,* **10,** 482–492.
Wilson, T. D., Hull, J. G., & Johnson, J. (1981). Awareness and self-perception: Verbal reports on internal states. *Journal of Personality and Social Psychology,* **40,** 53–70.

Wine, J. D. (1971). Test anxiety and direction of attention. *Psychological Bulletin,* **76,** 92–104.
Wojciszke, B. (1987). Ideal-self, self-focus, and value–behaviour consistency. *European Journal of Social Psychology,* **17,** 187–198.
Wylie, R. C. (1968). The present status of self-theory. In E. F. Borgatta & W. W. Lambert (Eds.), *Handbook of personality theory and research.* Chicago, IL: Rand McNally.
Zanna, M. P., & Aziza, C. (1976). On the interaction of repression-sensitization and attention in resolving cognitive dissonance. *Journal of Personality,* **44,** 577–593.

COUNTERFACTUAL THINKING AND SOCIAL PERCEPTION: THINKING ABOUT WHAT MIGHT HAVE BEEN

Dale T. Miller
William Turnbull
Cathy McFarland

I. Introduction

The evaluation of experience is relative. Reactions to events depend not only on what the events are but on what they are not. The mental representations to which an event is compared may be precomputed and exist prior to the occurrence of the event. Expectancies provide the clearest example of this class of representations. Consider students' reactions to their exam scores. One important determinant of their reactions will be their expectancies. Students generally will be satisfied if their scores are close to or higher than the scores they expected but dissatisfied if the scores are significantly lower. Students' conceptions of what constitutes a fair score is another type of precomputed representation that can affect their reactions. Even scores that exceed students' expectations may still disappoint them if they fall below those that the students felt they deserved.

Reality is also compared to postcomputed representations, those that are neither consciously nor unconsciously held prior to an event but which are generated post hoc by the event itself (Kahneman & Miller, 1986). Whereas precomputed representations focus on thoughts of what was expected to be or what should have been, postcomputed representations focus on counterfactual thoughts of what might have been. The postcomputed or counterfactual representations that are evoked by experience can shape people's reactions every bit as powerfully as the precomputed ones they bring to the experience. For example, students who receive a score that falls one short of that required for a higher grade may still be disappointed even though that score met both their expectations and their perceptions of fairness. The disappointment, in this case, would stem from the contrast between what happened and postcomputed counterfactual thoughts of what almost happened.

The precomputed representations that exist prior to an event, combined with the postcomputed counterfactual thoughts, images, and scenarios that are evoked by the event itself, comprise what Kahneman and Miller (1986) have termed the event's *norm*. The discrepancy between an event and the norm that it evokes defines the event's normality. The more discrepant an event is from the representations (precomputed or postcomputed) that it evokes, the less normal (more abnormal) the event is said to be.

The norm to which an event is compared may be dominated by precomputed representations or by postcomputed representations. In this article we examine how norms dominated by postcomputed representations influence perceptions of social events. Our aim is not to deny the importance of anticipation and expectation in social perception but simply to encourage consideration of the role that counterfactual thinking plays in this process. To accomplish this, we will show that people's reactions to social events that evoke the same precomputed representations will vary if those events evoke different postcomputed counterfactual representations. Our discussion focuses on three factors that influence the relation between the target event and the postcomputed representations it evokes. These factors are (1) the ease with which actions leading to the event can be undone mentally, (2) the ease with which the event itself can be undone mentally, and (3) the ease with which the event can be replicated mentally.

II. Mentally Undoing Actions

Consider the fate of an individual who is killed in the crash of a commercial airliner after switching from another flight only minutes before takeoff. If your reactions are similar to our own, you will find it difficult to resist the thought that this passenger would not have been killed "if only" he or she had not switched flights. You might also feel that the fate of this person is more poignant or tragic than the death of a passenger who had been booked on the fatal flight for some weeks. What prompts these reactions? After all, the outcome is identical in both cases. And the two fates surely do not differ in their probability or foreseeability. Switching flights is neither perceived to increase nor decrease one's probability of crashing. Nor do moral prescriptions concerning what one ought to do account for the different affective reactions in the two cases. What then is the difference?

We propose that the differential reactions arise because of the differential ease of mentally simulating or imagining a more positive alternative in the two cases (Kahneman & Miller, 1986; Kahneman & Tversky, 1982b). The counterfactual world in which the victim escaped the actual fate is imaginatively "closer" or more available in the "changed flight" version of the scenario. The reason for this, we propose, is that it is so easy to imagine the victim having not changed flights. It is true that the victim's fate in the "unchanged flight" version of the scenario would have been avoided if he or she had switched flights, but there is little tendency in this case to say "if only the flight had been switched" because that counterfactual alternative is not easily imagined (Kahneman & Tversky, 1982b; Wells, Taylor, & Turtle, 1987).

Following Kahneman and Miller (1986), we use the term *abnormal* to refer to actions that can easily be imagined otherwise. Outcomes that follow from abnormal actions, and thus are themselves easily imagined otherwise, we will refer to as abnormal outcomes. The readiness with which people say "if only" in referring to an action is one way of estimating the normality of both the action and the outcome to which it leads.

A. NORMALITY AND EMOTIONAL AMPLITUDE

The normality of an outcome is reflected in the intensity of the reaction it provokes. The more strongly an event evokes imagined representations that are dissimilar to it, the stronger will be the emotional response evoked by that event (Kahneman & Miller, 1986). Because the crash victim who switched flights evokes a contrasting scenario more powerfully than does the crash victim who did not switch, the former's fate evokes a stronger reaction than does the latter's. In this respect, postcomputed representations function similarly to precomputed representations. In both cases, emotional reaction intensifies as a function of the availability and discrepancy of the evoked alternative. But what are the determinants of normality? Why is it easier to imagine or mentally simulate some actions being different than it is others? The determinants of an action's normality are not well understood but we will consider three potential candidates.

1. Exception versus Routine

In a seminal analysis of counterfactual thinking, Kahneman and Tversky (1982b) proposed that when people generate alternatives to outcomes they generally do so by imagining routine or default actions in the place of exceptional ones rather than the converse. This proposition is illustrated by the plane crash example. Because switching flights at the last minute is more exceptional than not switching flights, it is easier to imagine a victim not switching than it is to imagine a victim switching.

In another test of the hypothesis that fates preceded by exceptional actions will generate stronger affective reactions than fates preceded by routine actions, Kahneman and Tversky (1982b) presented subjects with the following scenario:

> Mr. Adams was involved in an accident when driving home after work on his regular route. Mr. White was involved in a similar accident when driving on a route that he only takes when he wants a change of scenery.

Even though the fates of the two individuals in this scenario were identical, the majority of subjects (82%) predicted that the victim whose fate was preceded by an exceptional action (Mr. White) would be more upset than the victim whose fate had been preceded by a routine action (Mr. Adams).

Further support for the link between the routineness of an action and the normality of the ensuing outcome comes from studies conducted by Johnson (1986) and Miller and McFarland (1986). These studies demonstrate that observers' reactions to victims of misfortune are also stronger when the victim's actions are exceptional than when they are routine. Johnson (1986) presented subjects with a scenario that described various aspects of the life of a college student named Debbie. In the most relevant condition, the scenario ended by relating the following event:

> Attending a rock concert, Debbie momentarily occupied seat 2047, but moved when a tall person sat in front of her. At intermission, the person sitting in seat 2047 was randomly chosen (by number of seat currently occupied) to win a trip around the world for two.

Subjects who read the description of Debbie that included the fact that she narrowly missed receiving a positive outcome rated her more negatively on both semantic differential scales and on various other measures than did subjects who read a description that omitted the information about the "near miss." Johnson's (1986) research indicates that it is not only people who have bad things happen to them who are derogated (Lerner & Miller, 1978) but also people who come close to having good things happen to them.

Miller and McFarland (1986, Study 1) also probed observers' reactions to victims. The cover story in their study described subjects' task as that of helping provide information to a victim compensation board on the public's reaction to various types of victims. The description of the victim and the circumstances of the victimization were identical across two versions of a scenario, with the only difference being the normality of the victim's fate. Normality was manipulated by describing the action leading to the victimization as being either an exception to or in accordance with the victim's routine actions. The victim was a man who had been severely injured during a robbery. In one condition, the robbery took place in the store he most commonly frequented. In a second condition, the robbery took place in a store the victim did not commonly frequent but had decided to go to "for a change of pace." The conditions were designed to parallel the example of the crash victim who had or had not engaged in the exceptional action of switching flights. Miller and McFarland (1986) predicted that subjects would experience the fate that befell the victim in the "unusual" store condition as more abnormal, and hence more deserving of sympathy, than the fate that befell the victim in the "usual" store condition. Consistent with this hypothesis, subjects recommended significantly more compensation (over $100,000 more) for the same injury in the exceptional context than they did in the routine context.

The latter study demonstrates that even morally charged judgments such as those involving compensation can be influenced by the normality of the outcome. It is as though a negative fate for which a more positive contrast is highly available is worse, or more unfair, than one for which there is no highly available positive alternative (cf. Folger, 1986). Before leaving this example, note that the different reactions to the two victims are not owing to differences in the perceived probabilities of their fates. Subjects' judgments of the probabilities of being shot in the two stores were low and indistinguishable from one another.

2. Omission versus Commission

A second asymmetry in counterfactual thinking noted by Kahneman and Tversky (1982a) concerns the distinction between acts of commission and acts of omission. They propose that it is usually easier to imagine oneself abstaining from actions that one has carried out than carrying out actions that were not in fact performed. Or to put it somewhat differently, it is easier to generate alternatives to outcomes that follow from actions than it is to generate alternatives to outcomes that follow from inactions. One way to test this hypothesis is to see if the negative consequences of actions evoke stronger emotional responses than do the negative consequences of failures to act. Kahneman and Tversky (1982a) performed this test with the following vignette:

> Mr. Paul owns shares in company A. During the past year he considered switching to stock in company B, but decided against it. He now finds that he would have been better off by $1200 if he had switched to the stock of company B. Mr. George owned shares in company B. During the past year he switched to stock in company A. He now finds that he would have been better off by $1200 if he had kept his stock in company B.

Although both men lost the same amount of money, most of the subjects predicted that Mr. George, who lost his money by switching stocks, would experience more regret than Mr. Paul, who lost his money by not switching stocks (92 vs. 8%). The finding that acts of commission produce greater regret than acts of omission was replicated in a series of studies conducted by Landman (1988).

3. Constrained versus Unconstrained Behavior

The number of alternatives available to the actor at the time of his or her action also seems to affect the normality of both the action and its consequences. The greater the number of predecision options available in a situation, the less normal the action taken is perceived to be. A study by Wells and Gavanski (1989, Experiment 1) offers strong support for this hypothesis. Subjects read a story about a woman, Karen, who went to lunch with her boss, Mr. Carlson. Unaware that Karen was allergic to wine, Mr. Carlson ordered a dish for her that contained wine. As a consequence of eating that dish, Karen died. There were two versions of the story. In the "one wine" version, the vignette described Mr. Carlson as first having considered some other dish that did not contain wine before he decided to order the fatal one. In the "two wine" version, the vignette described Mr. Carlson as first having considered another dish that also contained wine before he decided to order the fatal one. When asked to list things in the story that, had they been different, would have prevented Karen's death, 36% of the subjects in the "one wine" condition listed the ordering decision, whereas only 11% of the subjects listed that decision in the "two wine" condition. An additional finding of this study was that 85% of the subjects rated the ordering decision as a cause of Karen's death in the "one wine" condition, whereas only 48% listed that decision as a cause of her death in the "two wine" condition. The findings of Wells and Gavanski (1988) indicate that people are more likely to mentally undo actions the greater the number of alternative courses of actions considered by or available to the actor.

A study by Turnbull and Mawhinney (1986) indicates that victims who experience negative outcomes following unconstrained (and hence undoable) actions may be especially predisposed to self-blame. Subjects were presented with a vignette depicting a woman who parked in a shopping mall lot in either the only spot available or in one of many available spots. On leaving the lot, both the protagonist and another driver backed out at the same time and bumped into one another, causing minor damage to both cars. The protagonist was covered by a no deductible insurance policy, but the other drive had a $200 deductible. Subjects were asked to predict how much money the protagonist would pay toward the other person's deductible as well as the amount of self-blame the protagonist would accept for the accident. There were significant differences on both measures: The protagonist was expected to pay more money and blame herself more when there had been many parking spots available than when there had been only one. Subjects apparently reasoned that a person who need not have taken the "accident-destined" spot would feel more responsible for the accident than would the person who had no choice but to take that spot. As with the protagonist in the Johnson (1986) "rock concert" scenario, responsibility appears to be assigned as a consequence of the ease with which the protagonist can be imagined having engaged in an alternative action that would have led to an alternative outcome—a more positive outcome in the Johnson (1986) study and a less negative one in the Turnbull and Mawhinney (1986) study.

B. UNDOING ACTIONS AND BLAME ASSIGNMENT

As well as identifying features of actions that affect the strength with which alternative actions (and hence alternative outcomes) are evoked, the studies we have reviewed explore the role that postcomputed thoughts plays in reactions to misfortune. At this point we consider the more general significance of this research for an understanding of reactions to victimization.

1. Victim Reactions

How does the normality of a victim's fate affect his or her reaction to it? We saw that the more abnormal the victim's actions preceding misfortune (1) the more upset the victim was expected to be (Kahneman & Tversky, 1982b), (2) the more regret the victim was expected to experience (Kahneman & Miller, 1986), and (3) the more self-blame the victim was expected to accept (Turnbull & Mawhinney, 1986). Why should victims be harder on themselves when their misfortunes are preceded by abnormal actions? Any perceived differences in responsibility cannot be accommodated by conventional analyses of responsibility, such as those pertaining to the five levels of responsibility identified by Heider (1958) and elaborated by Shaw and Sulzer (1964). Of these various levels—responsibility by association, commission, foreseeability, intention, and the absence of justification—only the responsibility of foreseeability seems even superficially relevant to the variable of normality.

Foreseeability and normality are importantly different, however, as a close examination reveals. The ascription of responsibility by virtue of foreseeability requires that the perceiver believe that Y would not have occurred if the target had not done X *and* that the target should have known that X could have led to Y. By way of illustration, consider the familiar refrain, "If only I had been more careful, this wouldn't have happened." The speaker of this statement is accepting responsibility for a misfortune not only because of the acknowledgment that his or her carelessness played a causal role in the occurrence of the misforutne but also because of the acknowledgment that there is a positive correlation between amount of carelessness and the probability of experiencing a misfortune.

Intelligent people know that carelessness can lead to misfortunes, just as they know that cheaters never prosper, that people should look before they leap, and so forth. For this reason, foreseeable fates can be expected to be more easily imagined otherwise than unforeseeable fates. If the victim had followed the dictates of rationality and morality, the misfortune would have been avoided. On the other hand, not all highly abnormal fates will qualify as foreseeable. A man who has an accident after taking an unusual route home might say, "If only I had taken my usual route, this would not have happened.'' But we need not assume that he believes he ''should have known'' that the action he took would increase the probability of having an accident. Yet in some important sense he may feel very similar to people who bring their misfortune upon themselves by careless or foolish actions. Because people say ''if only'' when unintended negative consequences were foreseeable, it may be difficult for them to not hold themselves responsible in other circumstances in which they find themselves saying ''if only.''

2. Observer Reactions

The two studies (Miller & McFarland, 1986, Study 1; Johnson, 1986) that we presented pertaining to observers' reactions to misfortunes both demonstrated that the ease of mentally undoing a negative fate affects how observers react to the victim. However, the nature of the link between normality and sympathy that the two studies revealed was quite different. Suffering a fate that could be undone easily elicited higher derogation from subjects in Johnson's (1986) study, whereas it elicited higher compensation from subjects in Miller and McFarland's (1986) study. How can these conflicting reactions to victims who were very close to being nonvictims be resolved? At least two possibilities exist. First, Miller and McFarland's subjects may have recommended greater compensation to the victim of the easily undone fate because they realized that this victim would be tortured more by self-blame and ''if only'' thoughts. A second, and we think more likely, possibility emerges from a consideration of the well-established finding that observers will derogate innocent victims only if the victims cannot be compensated (Lerner, 1970; Lerner & Miller, 1978). A sense of injustice generally will elicit efforts to restore justice, but if this proves impossible, observers may attempt to reduce their sense of injustice by derogating the victim. Thus, Johnson's (1986) subjects might have compensated the woman who narrowly missed winning the trip around the world if they had been given the opportunity to do so, and Miller and McFarland's (1986) subjects might have derogated the robbery victim if they had not been provided with the opportunity to compensate him.

This last point suggests a caveat concerning the application of Kahneman and Miller's (1986) model of counterfactual thought to the victim domain. This model predicts the amplitude of emotional reactions to victims, but it does not constitute a theory of justice per se. It makes predictions about the factors that influence the intensity of people's reactions to morally charged events, not the direction of these reactions. Still, as our literature review suggests, the affective reactions elicited by an event can guide a wide array of responses that bear directly on moral reactions. The precise means by which this occurs remains a question for future research, as does the more preliminary question of why it is easier to generate counterfactual alternatives to some events (e.g., acts of commission and exceptions) than to others (e.g., acts of omission and routines).

III. Mentally Undoing Outcomes

In their original discussion of undoing, Kahneman and Tversky (1982b) provided the following vignette:

> Mr. Crane and Mr. Tees were scheduled to leave the airport on different flights, at the same time. They travelled from town in the same limousine, were caught in a traffic jam, and arrived at the airport 30 minutes after the scheduled departure of their flights. Mr. Crane is told that his flight left on time. Mr. Tees is told that his flight was delayed and just left five minutes ago.

The fates of Mr. Tees and Mr. Crane were identical, as was the relation between their expectancies and their fates (they both expected to miss their flight). Nevertheless, the fate of Mr. Tees seems worse. Indeed, subjects overwhelmingly predicted that Mr. Tees would be more upset than would Mr. Crane (96 vs. 4%). Why? In this case, the impact of Mr. Tees' fate does not seem to depend on the ease of modifying any particular action in the causal chain that preceded his fate. There is no specific factor that led Mr. Tees to arrive 5 minutes after the departure of his flight. Still, the perception that Mr. Tees would be more upset does appear to be tied to the differential availability of a postcomputed rather than a precomputed representation. It is the discrepancy between what did happen and what easily might have happened, not what was expected to happen or what should have happened, that produces the variations in affective reaction. But if it is not the greater abnormality of the actions leading to Mr. Tees fate that produces the stronger reaction to it, what then is it?

A. MENTAL MODELS AND NORMALITY

We suggest that people's differential reactions to Mr. Tees and Mr. Crane reflect the relative ease with which they can mentally revise the parameters of the mental model they apply when analyzing the fates of these men. By the term mental model, we refer to content-based rules of thumb about the ways that systems operate. These rules specify the ways that systems can be transformed from one state to another, as well as the critical range of values around which parameters in the model can be manipulated or set. Any particular value that falls within this critical range is easily imagined changed to some other value within that range (see Rip's [1985] discussion of "figurative" mental models for an elaboration of this concept). As a general proposition, we contend that the smaller the imagined change one has to make to the causal model of an event in order to imagine or mentally simulate an alternative outcome, the more available that alternative will be, and the greater, in turn, the affective reaction to the event will be.

A close examination of the case of Mr. Tees and Mr. Crane will help clarify this proposition. The relevant mental models in this example are those pertaining to traffic flow and plane delays. From the vantage point of these mental models, it is easier to imagine Mr. Tees making his flight than it is to imagine Mr. Crane making his. Most people can easily imagine a traffic jam that impeded a person for 25 minutes impeding him for only 20 minutes instead. The parameters that control traffic jams are such that fluctuations of 5 minutes in either direction are easily imagined, at least much more easily imagined than fluctuations of 25 minutes. For this reason, one is more likely to say, "If only the driver had made up 5 minutes," than "If only the driver had made up 25 minutes." A similar argument can be extended to the case of plane delays. A plane delay can be caused by many factors, but most of the scenarios in which a plane was delayed for 25 minutes would require very little parametric alteration for them to accommodate a 30-minute delay. It is not necessary to know what caused the delay to believe that it easily could have extended another 5 minutes.

Although 5 minutes is easily undoable in the "missed plane" example, there are many other instances of temporal misses in which the same difference would not create a sense of a "near miss." Five minutes in a scenario involving a traffic jam or plane delay is a psychologically short time, but 5 minutes in scenarios involving competitors in a mile run is not. One would not say that a runner who was 5 minutes behind the winner of a mile race was close to winning. One's understanding of competitive running might permit one to say, "If only he had cut his time down by 5 seconds he would have won," but almost certainly not, "If only he had cut his time down by 5 minutes he would have won." Thus, whether a temporal miss of a particular duration is perceived to be a "near miss" depends on the observer's mental model of the event in question.

Because people may have different mental models of traffic jams and plane delays, not everyone will find it equally easy to imagine a counterfactual world in which a person who missed a plane by 5 minutes actually caught it. Neither will people have a single model of events such as traffic jams or plane delays. A plane delay of 25 minutes will elicit different imagined scenarios than will one of 2 hours. Furthermore, the particular scenario that is imagined or accessed when one hears of a plane delay will affect the ease of imagining an additional delay of 5 minutes.

Analyses of people's characters appear to function similarly to mental models. The ease with which observers mentally undo a person's fate will depend on the model they have of that person as well as of the circumstances (system) affecting the person. This fact is frequently exploited for dramatic effect by skilled playwrights. In the world of drama one frequently encounters events, which from a material or physical perspective need not have happened but which from a characterological or dramatic perspective were ineluctable. What makes *King Lear* a successful tragedy, for example, is the tension between the audience's understanding that there is sufficient time between Lear's regaining of his senses and Cordelia's execution for her to be saved and its understanding that the dramatic momentum initiated by Lear's character makes her death inevitable. Shakespeare's genius succeeds in creating a dramatic context in which a fate that easily could be imagined different in another world is not easily imagined different in Lear's world. If the audience could too easily imagine Cordelia's life being saved, *King Lear* would fail as a tragedy.

B. MENTAL MODELS AND EMOTIONAL AMPLITUDE

The route by which a postcomputed alternative is elicited in the Mr. Tees and Mr. Crane example may be different than the one involved in the previously described "undoing action" studies, but the link between the availability of the imagined alternative and the aroused affect is the same. The more available the counterfactual scenario is, the more intense is the affective response. As another illustration of this principle, consider the following scenario from Miller (1984):

> Mrs. Nelson and Mrs. Thomas each held winning lottery tickets. Mrs. Nelson bought her ticket 8 weeks before the draw. Mrs. Thomas bought her ticket an hour and a half before the draw.

When asked who would be the happier of the two winners, the vast majority of subjects (93%) designated Mrs. Thomas. This was despite the fact that the fates of the two women were the same, as were their expectancies. (One's subjective probability of winning a lottery is not affected by when the ticket is bought.) The only difference between the two individuals is how close they came to missing their good fortune. The shorter the time between the purchase of the ticket and the close of the draw, the greater the number of different events one can imagine preventing the act of purchasing the winning ticket. As a consequence of this, people assume Mrs. Thomas will have the sense that she came very close to not buying the winning ticket and, consequently, the feeling that she was particularly lucky to have possessed the winning ticket.

The reader will note that this last example involves the positive emotion of happiness, whereas our previous examples all have involved negative emotions. The positive reaction occurs in this example because the counterfactual world that was almost experienced is the negative one of not buying the winning lottery ticket.

Miller and McFarland (1986, Study 2) also explored outcome undoing in one of their "victim compensation" studies. The victim in this study had died from exposure after surviving a plane crash in a remote area. He had made it to within 75 miles of safety in one condition and to within $\frac{1}{4}$ mile of safety in a second condition. Based on the assumption that it is easier to imagine an individual continuing another $\frac{1}{4}$ mile than another 75 miles, Miller and McFarland predicted that the fate of the "close" victim would be perceived to be more abnormal, and hence more deserving of sympathy, than the fate of the "distant" victim. The results supported the prediction inasmuch as subjects once again recommended significantly more compensation for the family of the victim whose fate seemed closer to having been avoided.

1. Rational versus Irrational Models

In the studies of outcome undoing that we have described so far, the models that people are bringing to bear on the events seem to be rational. After all, it is physically easier to save 5 minutes than 25 minutes in a traffic jam and it is easier to walk $\frac{1}{4}$ mile than 75 miles. The postcomputed scenario construction that subjects are engaging in, therefore, is grounded in reality. This may not always be the case, however, as is illustrated in a study conducted by Turnbull (1981). This study focused on subjects' reactions to the outcome of a staged lottery. Subjects knew they were one of 500 participants in the lottery and thus, not surprisingly, expressed little optimism of winning. Consistent with their low expectations, the participants generally expressed little disappointment when they discovered they had not won. The only exceptions to this were those subjects who held ticket numbers that were countably close to the number of the winning ticket. Apparently, the countable closeness of a lottery ticket to the winning ticket led to a sense of being close to winning. Being one number away from the winning ticket may leave a person with a sense of a near miss that is similar to that experienced by Mr. Crane, who missed his flight by 5 minutes, but there is an important difference between the two cases. There is a rational account of why a person who misses a plane by 5 minutes could be said to be closer to having caught it than a person who misses a plane by 25 minutes, but there is no rational account for why a person who misses a winning lottery ticket by one number could be said to be closer than a person who misses it by four numbers. The procedure by which the person drew his or her particular number was a random one, hence the chances of the person having drawn any other particular number were not affected by the closeness of that number to the one actually drawn.

The disappointment of those ticket holders with close numbers possibly arose because they mistakenly viewed their fate from the perspective of a nonrandom model. For instance, they may have reacted to holding a number that was close to the winning number as they would to receiving an exam score that was close to a higher grade. A person who receives a score one short of that required for an *A* also can be expected to have the sense of a near miss, but in this case the reaction would be grounded in rationality. An exam score is not determined by random forces (despite what students may sometime think), and those causal factors that are believed to have produced a score one short of the total required for an *A* could reasonably be viewed as having required little variation to have yielded one more mark.

2. Social Knowledge and Sympathy Reactions

A controversial incident that occurred some years ago in France illustrates how knowledge structures relating to social relations can also influence the availability of alternatives to an event and, in turn, reactions to the event. The incident was a bomb attack on a synagogue that left a number of people injured. France's prime minister at the time publicly denounced the attack and expressed his sympathy for both the Jews who were inside the synagogue and the innocent passersby. The prime minister's differentiation of the victims into Jews and innocent passersby provoked considerable controversy because many interpreted it as implying that he did not consider the Jews to be as innocent as the passersby.

Certainly, the term innocent has a clear moral connotation, but should we assume that the prime minister's remarks reflect anti-Semitism? Not necessarily. According to the present model of counterfactual thought, his failure to apply the term innocent to the Jews inside the synagogue may simply reflect the fact that his mental model of a synagogue enabled him to mentally remove passersby from the vicinity more easily than the attending Jews. That the Jews were the intended victims of the attack also makes their injuries more difficult to undo (although no more deserved) than those of the passersby. The principle of psychologic operating here appears to be the following: What need not have been, ought not have been. The closer a misfortune is to not having happened, the more unfair or tragic it will appear.

A similar principle may help explain at least some of the public reaction evoked by the death of Christa McAuliffe in the Challenger shuttle explosion in 1986. There were seven people (including another female) killed by the explosion, but it was the nonastronaut—the school teacher, Christa McAuliffe—who became the focus of the nation's sympathy and public grieving. That McAuliffe was a school teacher, a mother, and an engaging person undoubtedly contributed to the response she evoked, but there also may have been something else at work here. As was the case with the injured passersby in the synagogue attack, she need not have been there. If she had been killed by a freak explosion in her classroom, her fate would not have been so abnormal and, we suspect, not nearly as tragic.

As another example of the role that social models play in reactions to victims, consider the fate of a policeman killed by a drug dealer in a New York City housing project a few years ago. The policeman was killed as he searched what he thought was an empty apartment for a young girl who was reported missing. The day following his death, the police commissioner publicly expressed sympathy to the victim's family, noting that the tragedy of his death was especially great because the little girl had been playing at a neighbor's house and was not actually lost. Why does the fact that the target of the victim's search was not lost make his brutal murder more tragic? One is surely no more deserving of being killed if one is looking for a child who is actually lost than if one is looking for a child who is only reported to be lost, any more than one is more deserving of being killed in a space shuttle explosion if one is a professional astronaut than if one is a teacher.

This reaction also cannot be accounted for in terms of any precomputed thoughts. People might justify their relatively muted reactions to the deaths of the professional astronauts by saying that "danger comes with the territory," and they may even say this in the case of Jews who live in a country with a history of anti-Semitic violence, but how does this line of reasoning help explain the reaction to the policeman's fate? We would argue that it does not. What does help is a consideration of the counterfactual possibilities that the relevant mental model makes available to us. The relevant model in this case specifies that people need not look for people who are not lost. Accordingly, anything that happens to someone who is searching for someone who is not lost need not (and thus ought not to) have happened. Searching for a child who is not lost seems senseless, and being killed during the search also seems senseless. By referring to his actions as senseless, we of course do not mean that the policeman was doing anything that deviated from his duties when he searched for the girl who was mistakenly reported as lost. He simply was engaging in an unnecessary action, one that is easy to imagine not having been undertaken.

In summary, reactions to misfortunes depend not only on their expectedness and their perceived deservedness but also on their normality. The closer one's mental model suggests a misfortune was to not happening, the more abnormal that misfortune will seem and the stronger one's affective reaction to it will be.

IV. Mentally Replicating Outcomes

The research described in the previous two sections shows that an event's normality—as assessed by affective reaction to it—depends on the strength with which it evokes constructions of alternative events. In this section we present research that demonstrates that an event's normality also depends on the strength with which it evokes constructions of similar events. Events evoke counterfactual thoughts not only of how things might have been different but also of how things might have been the same. We propose that the more difficult it is to mentally replicate an event, the less normal the event will be, and the stronger, in turn the affective reaction it evokes will be. To illustrate this principle, we present a series of studies on judgments of suspiciousness (Miller, Turnbull, & McFarland, 1989). In each of these studies, subjects read one of two versions of a scenario in which a highly improbable event occurred or was alleged to have occurred. The a priori probability of the target event was kept constant across the two versions, but the normality of the event was varied by manipulating the number of ways the event could have occurred. The hypothesis that guided these studies is that two equally improbable outcomes will seem differentially surprising (suspicious) if the occurrence of one of them is more easily replicated mentally than is the occurrence of the other.

A. NORMALITY AND SUSPICION

1. Suspicion about the Luck of the Draw

To begin, imagine that you have a young child who loves chocolate chip cookies. Imagine further that you buy your cookies in packages that include oatmeal as well as chocolate chip cookies. Your child's practice is to go to the cookie jar and select the chocolate chip cookies, leaving the oatmeal cookies to go stale. One day you think of a strategy to cope with the problem. You tell your child to close his or her eyes before reaching into the jar and to take whichever cookie is grabbed first. The child agrees to this and heads for the kitchen and the cookie jar. Returning shortly thereafter, the child exclaims that just what you said to do was done and a chocolate chip cookie was selected.

How would you react to the child's announcement? Would you accept your child's claim that, by coincidence, a coveted chocolate chip cookie was selected or would you be suspicious that the child had peeked? What factors might affect your judgment in this regard? Information you had about the child's prior behavior would be one obvious candidate for consideration. A prior history of honesty would leave you less suspicious than a prior history of dishonesty. Knowledge you had concerning the strength of the child's preference for chocolate chip over oatmeal cookies probably also would be relevant. Suspicion would be expected to increase as the child's assumed motivation to cheat increased. In addition to your knowledge of the protagonist, your level of suspicion may well be influenced by your knowledge of the contents of the cookie jar. If 50% of the cookies were chocolate chip, you almost certainly would not be as suspicious as you would be if only 5% were. Indeed, an event could not even appropriately be termed a coincidence, let alone be expected to generate suspicion, if it were not at least moderately improbable.

The present model of counterfactual thought suggests that the relative frequency of the two types of cookies may not be the only feature of the jar's contents that would affect your suspicion. Contrast the levels of suspicion you would anticipate experiencing in two slightly different versions of the scenario. In version A there are 1 chocolate chip and 19 oatmeal cookies in the jar; in version B there are 10 chocolate chip and 190 oatmeal cookies in the jar. The relative frequency of the two types of cookies is the same in the two versions of the scenario (1 to 19), but—if you are like us—we suspect that you would be more suspicious when the child had claimed to draw the only remaining chocolate chip cookie than merely 1 of 10 remaining chocolate chip cookies.

To test this intuition, Miller, Turnbull, and McFarland (1989) presented subjects with one of the two versions of the vignette and asked them, "How suspicious would you be that the child had peeked before selecting the cookie?" As expected, subjects presented with version A of the scenario indicated that they would be significantly more suspicious than did subjects presented with version B of the scenario.

To assess whether the two versions produced different a priori subjective probability estimates as well as differences in suspiciousness, two independent groups of subjects were presented with the two versions of the scenario (omitting the alleged outcome) and were asked to indicate the likelihood that the child would select a chocolate chip cookie. Subjects answered the question on a 10-point scale that ranged from 0% to 100% The responses of these two groups did not differ.

Why should reactions to the two scenarios be different? Basing feelings of suspicion on factors such as the actor's past behavior, his or her motivation, and the likelihood of the event occurring by chance seems fair and rational. But what is fair or rational about considering the absolute number of desired cookies in the jar? The differential reactions generated by the two scenarios may not be accounted for by naive theories of suspicion, but the present model of counterfactual thought does offer a possible account. The event of selecting a chocolate chip cookie may have been equally probable in the two scenarios (5%) but it was not equally normal or surprising. When there were 10 chocolate chip cookies, and hence 10 similar ways for the event to occur, the purported selection of a chocolate chip cookie was more normal than when there was only 1 chocolate chip cookie, and hence only one route by which the event could have occurred. In short, we propose that the selection of the chocolate chip cookie in the 10 to 190 cookies case generates less surprise (suspicion) than it does in the 1 to 19 cookies case because there are more ways to imagine the event happening in the former than in the latter case.

These results indicate that the shadow of reasonable doubt accorded to the target of suspicion extends as the normality of the event increases. The more easily subjects could imagine something happening by one route (chance), the less suspicious they were that it occurred by some other route (peeking). Subjects' perceptions of the child's honesty were no doubt also affected by the probability that they assigned to the event. If 50% of the cookies were chocolate chip, the subjects surely would have expressed less suspicion. Moreover, consideration of probability in this manner would both be psychologically sensible and comport with legal philosophy. Exhortations to juries not to convict someone unless they are sure "beyond a reasonable doubt" invites them to consider the likelihood that a set of occurrences could have come about without the accused being guilty of the offense as charged. However, neither cultural nor legal dictates would seem to justify a consideration of the ease of mentally replicating the event when determining the probability that the target violated the prohibition against peeking.

2. Suspicion about the Fairness of a Contest

Subjects in the Miller *et al.* (1989) Study 1 were more suspicious about the legitimacy of the procedure that yielded a desired outcome the more difficult it was for them to simulate the outcome emerging by means of that procedure. Making judgments about the coincidental nature of outcomes is not restricted to contexts involving random draws. We are rarely certain that any outcome reflects only one particular cause, and thus we are constantly having to decide whether an outcome that is consistent with one particular hypothesis constitutes evidence for that hypothesis or simply represents a coincidence. Researchers are able to utilize statistics to help them make these decisions but the layperson must rely on personal intuitions.

The Miller *et al.* (1989) Study 2 examined how the normality of an outcome affected subjects' judgments in one such situation. Subjects were asked to complete a questionnaire that presented them with one of two scenarios that were identical in all respects except for the normality of the target event. The scenario appears below with the manipulated information in italics:

> John S. is a supervisor in a local manufacturing firm. John is responsible for promoting the employees in his department. In the past he has been accused of being against equal rights and opportunities for women. There is (are) *1 (10)* male(s) and *9 (90)* females in his department who are potential candidates for promotion. John decides to give these employees a written examination to help with his decision. John grades these exams himself and reports that the highest mark was obtained by a man, whom he promotes.

Consistent with the prediction, subjects expressed significantly greater suspicion that the promotion decision reflected an antifemale bias when there was only 1 male who could have received the highest score than when there were 10 different males who could have received the highest score. Once again, this effect did not appear to stem from different a priori subjective probability estimates. The response of two independent groups of subjects who simply were asked to estimate the likelihood that the highest score would be obtained by a male did not differ.

3. Suspicion about the Representativeness of an Unexpected Event

The studies we have described thus far manipulated the number of legitimate ways a low-probability event could have occurred in an attempt to affect subjects' suspiciousness about the fairness of the process that generated the event. The subjects' task was to determine whether an event, which was both improbable and consistent with the protagonist's wishes, constituted a fortuitous coincidence or reflected a nonrandom and hence illegitimate procedure. By specifying the exact nature of the relevant population, these studies precluded subject suspicion about another feature of the scenario, the alleged frequency of the target attribute in the population. For example, subjects in the Miller et al. (1989) Study 1 were not asked whether the purported random selection of the chocolate chip cookie affected their suspicion that there were more than the alleged number of chocolate chip cookies in the jar. Similarly, subjects in the Miller et al. Study 2 were not asked how the fact that a male had achieved the highest score on the exam affected their suspicion that there were more than the alleged number of male employees in the department. Had the scenarios not stipulated the frequency of the event in the distribution, it is conceivable that the differential normality of the event would have resulted in differential suspicion about the event's frequency.

A third study conducted by Miller et al. (1989) pursued this possibility. The specific hypothesis tested was that the fewer similar instances there are purported to be in the population from which an improbable event springs, the more inclined people are to believe that the event was actually more probable than they had been led to believe. Subjects were asked to complete a questionnaire that presented them with one of two versions of a scenario that were identical in all respects except for the normality of the target event. The scenario appears below with the manipulated information in italics:

> Imagine that you rented a car from a company called "Rent a Clunker." You went to this company because its rates were much cheaper than other car rental companies but you were worried about the reliability of the cars. The manager assured you that his cars were very reliable, claiming that only *2 (20)* of his *20 (200)* cars had ever had problems. You choose a car and leave for a long trip. Within an hour the car breaks down.

We predicted that subjects would express more suspicion about the manager's integrity when he alleged there were only 2 unreliable cars in his fleet than when he alleged there were 20. Guiding this prediction was the assumption that encountering 1 of 2 possible unreliable cars would seem a less normal event than encountering 1 of 20 possible unreliable cars, even though the probability of encountering an unreliable car in the two cases was the same (10%). The results supported the hypothesis. Subjects expressed significantly more suspicion that the manager had lied in the small-fleet condition than in the large-fleet condition.

Following the practice of the previous studies, we presented two independent groups of subjects with the scenarios (omitting the outcomes) and asked them to indicate the likelihood that someone would get an unreliable car if they were to rent one from this company. The estimates did not differ across the two conditions.

4. Suspicion and Stereotype Revision

The previous study has an intriguing implication for the process of stereotype revision. By way of illustration, consider the following thought experiment. Imagine that you visit a city in which there are members of an ethnic group with which you are not familiar. Assume that you have been given conflicting accounts of the group's social manner. One of these accounts suggests that the majority of the members of this group are extremely rude. The other account suggests that only a small minority (no more than 5%, say) of the group members are extremely rude and that the vast majority are very courteous. Now imagine that you have your first encounter with a member of the group and find this individual to be extremely rude. This experience obviously would be consistent with the negative account and inconsistent with the positive account that you heard. Nevertheless, it remains possible that the positive account was the correct one and that the first member of the group you encountered was atypical. Before you reflect on how prepared you would be to entertain the "atypical instance" hypothesis, consider an additional piece of information. Imagine that you know that the size of the ethnic group in the town was either small (less than 20) or very large (more than 50,000). How do you think your knowledge of the absolute number of rude group members would affect your inclination to reject the low-incidence (positive) hypothesis on the basis of an encounter with one rude member? Would you be equally willing in the two cases to dismiss your experience as unrepresentative and to continue to entertain the hypothesis that the vast majority of the group members are courteous?

The hypothesis guiding the Miller *et al.* (1989) Study 4 suggests that your confidence in the accuracy of the high-incidence (negative) account would be higher when the group was small than when it was large. The larger the group, the more rude individuals there are for you to meet, even if they are a minority, and hence the more normal it is for you to encounter one. To test this hypothesis subjects were asked to complete a questionnaire describing one of two versions of a scenario that were identical in all respects except for the normality of the target event. The scenario appears below with the manipulated information in italics:

> Imagine that you are an anthropologist who decides to study a tribe living in a remote area of South America. Two other anthropologists, who have investigated the tribe previously, provide you with differing views of the friendliness of the tribe members. One investigator says that at least *20 (200)* of the *40 (400)* members are hostile and unfriendly, whereas the other investigator claims that only *2 (20)* of the *40 (400)* tribe members are hostile and unfriendly. You visit the tribe and the first tribe member you encounter is hostile and unfriendly.

After subjects had read the scenario, they were asked to answer the following question: "On the basis of your first encounter with a member of the tribe, how confident would you be that the investigator who had claimed that at least 20 (200) of the tribe members were hostile and unfriendly had provided the more accurate of the estimates?"

We predicted that subjects would be more inclined to believe in the validity of the high-incidence hypothesis the less normal the target event appeared to be. This prediction was confirmed. Subjects were more confident that a hypothesis specifying a high incidence of the observed characteristic (hostility) was correct when the low-incidence hypothesis specified that there were only 2 members of the population who had that characteristic than when it specified that there were 20 members who had that characteristic.

B. SUMMARY AND IMPLICATIONS

In each of the four studies we have described, subjects expressed differential suspicion about the coincidental or chance origins of equally unexpected outcomes. The reason for this, we argued, is that people do not decide whether or not an event occurred by chance solely on the basis of its a priori probability; they do so also on the basis of the ease with which they can imagine or mentally simulate the event. To be sure, a high-probability event will evoke representations of similar outcomes more strongly than will a low-probability event. But the probability of the event is not the only factor that guides the generation of the evoked norm. The absolute number of similar ways in which the same outcome could be achieved is also important. The fewer ways it could happen, the less normal it is and thus the more surprising is its occurrence.

The most obvious implication of the present findings is that people will have more difficulty convincing others that an event that confirms a suspicion is "just a coincidence" in some circumstances than in others, even when the probabilities of the events occurring are the same. This fact could influence, among other things, the way in which the person associated with the coincidence responds to an audience. So, for example, one might expect especially defensive posturing from the child who draws the last chocolate chip cookie, or from the employer who reports that the employee who received the highest grade from him was the only male employee. Similarly, the manager of the car rental company might be especially vehement in protesting his honesty when a customer returns one of only two allegedly unreliable cars.

The findings of Miller *et al.* (1989, Study 4) also have implications for relations with outgroups. From this study it appears that an unexpected experience with a member of a small outgroup will be more likely to lead people to revise their beliefs than will an equally unexpected experience with a member of a large outgroup. People's willingness to change their beliefs in the face of evidence depends not only on how probable that evidence appears to be in light of their belief but also on how normal it appears to be. Subjects in the Miller *et al.* Study 4 found it hard to believe that they "just coincidentally" encountered one of two hostile members in a tribe, and thus they assumed that there must be more than two. The more numerous the members of an outgroup, the easier it is to believe that the "rotten apple" one has encountered is not representative of the rest of the barrel.

V. Discussion

The theme of this article is that experience is evaluated in relation to both the precomputed knowledge structures that we bring to the experience and the counterfactual representations that the experience brings to mind. The research we have reported illustrates that the availability of postcomputed representations plays an important role in many domains of social perception. One of these domains is that of reactions to negative life events. We argued that a person's reaction to his or her own misfortune, or to that of another, is not determined solely by the expectancies, prescriptive standards, or moral schemas that the person holds. The counterfactual alternatives or representations evoked by the misfortune itself are also important. Victims whose fates are easily imagined otherwise evoke more sympathy and sometimes less sympathy than those whose fates are more normal. A second domain we explored was suspicion concerning the randomness of low-probability events. Across a diverse set of situations, we demonstrated that people's suspicion that an event was not random, or that it had a probability of occurring that was higher than that alleged, depended at least partly on the ease of imagining or mentally simulating that event. In each of the judgment domains explored, we observed the same pattern: The more abnormal an event, the more intense the reaction (e.g., sympathy, suspicion) it evoked.

A. NORMALITY AND HEURISTIC PROCESSING

An event's normality appears to have its effect on social judgment through its effect on heuristic processing. When people decide how much blame or compensation to assign a victim, or how suspicious they are that an individual misrepresented the probability of an event, it appears that they are guided by the strength of their reaction to the outcome. The stronger the reaction evoked by a victim's fate, the more intense are the blame and sympathy reactions. Similarly, the greater one's surprise about an outcome, the greater is one's suspicion that the outcome was not random. As with other forms of heuristic processing (Kahneman & Tversky, 1973), this process generally serves people well. Because people's perceptions of a victim's deservedness generally will influence their emotional reaction to the victim's fate—the less deserving, the stronger the reaction—their feelings generally will serve as a reliable index of how deserved they perceive the victim's misfortune to be, and hence how much blame or compensation they should assign. Emotional reactions, however, are not determined solely by the fit between the victim's fate and beliefs about what is just. They also are affected by the normality of his or her fate. A similar process appears to be at work in the suspicion studies we reported. Feelings of surprise constitute and ecologically valid clue to one's a priori subjective probability estimates (cf. Tversky & Kahneman, 1973) and hence to the likelihood that an occurrence was in fact random. The correspondence between surprise and subjective probability estimates will not always be perfect, however, because feelings of surprise may also reflect the event's normality.

Basing reactions to an event on its normality may be more justified in some circumstances than in others. If people's naive theories of the determinants of regret were probed, it is possible that, along with actions that were immoral or foolish, people would identify ill-fated actions that could have been otherwise. At the very least, people are unlikely to see anything irrational or inexplicable about regretting abnormal actions (e.g., taking an unusual route home from work) more than normal actions (e.g., taking one's customary route home from work). The emotional state of regret appears to be one that is recognized as highly dependent on postcomputed thought. Indeed, the relation between regret and postcomputed thought is celebrated in John Greenleaf Whittier's famous line, "For all sad words of tongue or pen, the saddest are these: 'It might have been!'"

In other domains, the case for considering the normality of an event is harder to make. For example, a list of factors that people think should influence compensation recommendations for victims is unlikely to include reference to the ease of imagining the victim escaping his or her fate. Indeed, 90% of the more than 100 subjects whom we questioned explicitly stated it would be unfair to consider this factor in determining the amount of compensation to award a victim. The case of suspicion is similar. What do our naive theories point to as critical determinants of suspicion? Many factors probably influence how suspicious we are about the accuracy of a person's account of how something happened (e.g., the selection of a desired cookie). It is not clear, however, that included among the factors people identify as relevant would be the ease of imagining the event occurring. Indeed, in light of the judgmental connotation attached to suspicion, people may explicitly exclude this factor as being pertinent to judgments of suspiciousness. Could one really defend feeling differentially suspicious about the honesty of two children as a function of the size of their family's cookie jar? Here, then, is a situation in which a particular judgment, suspicion, is affected by a factor that—far from being explicitly incorporated into naive theories pertaining to the judgment—almost certainly would be unanimously rejected as pertinent to the judgment.

B. BIASING EFFECTS OF NORMALITY

One path through which an event's normality could affect the reaction it evokes is by influencing other factors that more proximally mediate reactions to the event. In the case of reactions to misfortunes, for example, normality may have its influence by guiding perceptions of responsibility. The more abnormal the misfortune, the more responsibility the victim may be assigned. Analogously, normality may affect suspiciousness about alleged coincidences by guiding perceptions of their subjective probability. The more abnormal the "coincidence," the lower its a priori probability may be assumed to be. As plausible as this link may sound, we found no evidence for it in our research. In our suspicion studies, for example, probability estimates were not affected by the normality of an alleged coincidence, even though suspicion judgments were. Nor, we suspect, would ratings of foreseeability, or any other form of responsibility, have been affected by the normality of a victim's fate, even though sympathy reactions were.

We do not wish to claim that normality would never lead to such effects, however. If subjects in the suspicion studies had not had algorithms for calculating the probability of the target events, they may very well have relied on the event's normality to estimate both its probability and the degree of suspicion it warranted. The easier it is to imagine the event occurring, the more probable it may be assumed to be. Normality, in this sense, would be functioning similarly to the availability heuristic in the memory process. On this point, Tversky and Kahneman (1973) have shown that estimates of an event's probability are often dependent on the availability of similar events in memory. The more available similar events are in memory, the more probable they are assumed to be.

The fact that normality does not have its influence on reactions to events, exclusively, at least, through the biasing of other relevant factors (e.g., attributed foreseeability, subjective probability estimates), suggests that there may not always be an isomorphic relation between the strength of these other factors and the reaction that the event evokes. For example, one might believe that there was a reasonable probability that an event could occur by chance and still be suspicious that it did not occur by chance. Or one might believe that a person could not reasonably have foreseen that changing seats might cost her a trip around the world and still believe that she is foolish for having done so. The absence of such an isomorphism can spell trouble for unsuspecting researchers who unwittingly use dependent measures that are sensitive to postcomputed thoughts.

To illustrate the potential problems that can arise in this regard, consider the relation between those studies that measure the causal responsibility that the self accepts for negative events and those that measure the guilt that the self experiences following transgressions. For example, subjects induced to "accidentally" perpetrate a negative event, such as the destruction of some experimental equipment, have been found to display an enhanced willingness to comply with subsequent, experimentally unrelated requests for help (Carlsmith & Gross, 1969; Freedman, 1970). The transgression–compliance effect, as it is called, is presumably mediated by the guilt-reducing effects of compliance. There is a puzzling aspect to this phenomenon. The puzzle is not that the act of helping relieves feelings of guilt, but rather that the people in these experiments experience any guilt at all (Lerner, 1980; Lerner & Miller, 1978; Ross & DiTecco, 1975). Research on the attribution of responsibility shows over and over again that people are extremely hesitant to accept responsibility for any negative outcome if doing so would threaten their self-image (Shaver, 1985). So why would people accept responsibility for the outcomes that occur in the transgression–compliance studies, ones with which they have only the most tenuous connection?

One way of resolving this puzzle is to question the extent to which attributions of personal responsibility for negative outcomes are isomorphic with, and causally related to, the guilt aroused by such outcomes. The experience of guilt, or at least the affective state that predisposes individuals to comply with requests for favors, is assumed to reflect the internalization of responsibility for the accident. But it may not, just as high suspiciousness in our cookie jar study did not reflect a low-probability assignment. The point to keep in mind is that the attribution of responsibility literature and the transgression–compliance literature employ different dependent measures. The former tradition measures attributions of responsibility directly, the latter measures them indirectly. To pursue further the parallel with the cookie jar study, it is possible that the affective state experienced by transgressing subjects may not reflect high feelings of responsibility but rather the high availability of "if only" thoughts. When people can easily imagine not engaging in action that had harmful actions, they may experience guilt even if they recognize that they did nothing wrong by engaging in those actions.

C. FUTURE DIRECTIONS

The research we have described in this article demonstrates that the contrasts that exist between an experience and the perceiver's thoughts about what might have been can have effects similar to those produced by the contrasts between an experience and a perceiver's expectancies or thoughts about what ought to have been. One task for future research is to compare more closely the effects of these two types of contrasts to assess the extent and form of their similarity (cf. Abelson, 1983).

The general question to be answered here concerns the functional similarity of norms dominated by precomputed representations and those dominated by postcomputed representations. For example, how does affect generated by contrasts between events and precomputed alternatives differ from affect generated by contrasts between events and counterfactuals? Consider two students who experience disappointment at not getting an *A* on an exam. The first student is disappointed because she expected an *A* and thus had her expectation violated. The second student is disappointed not because he expected an *A* but rather because he came within one mark of receiving one. How, if at all, will the affective states of these two students differ? Will the disappointment be more intense or long-lasting in one case than the other? A similar question can be posed with respect to the differences between the negative feelings that follow from the commission of ill-fated, foolish, or immoral actions and those that follow from the commission of actions that are highly mentally undoable but neither foolish nor immoral. Does counterfactual guilt persist a greater or shorter time than moral guilt, for example? And will base rate information have comparable effects on the two types of guilt? That is, does telling a guilty person that many people committed the same foolish act have effects equivalent to those produced by telling a guilty person that many people committed the same undoable act?

Much of our discussion has focused on reactions to victims of misfortunes, and here too a great deal more research is needed. Particularly useful would be research addressing the issue of how reactions arising from highly available counterfactual thoughts differ from reactions arising from the application of various precomputed knowledge structures. Contrast a person who is the victim of a highly improbable misfortune and one who is a victim of a highly undoable misfortune that is not especially improbable. Let us say that the first victim was the only member of a platoon to be seriously wounded in battle and the second victim was a member of a casualty-ridden platoon who was seriously wounded only minutes before a cease-fire went into effect. In the first case, both the victim and observers can be expected to dwell on the contrast between the victim's fate and the more fortunate fates of others. Victims of such misfortunes are inclined to ask, "Why me?" (Janoff-Bulman & Lang-Gunn, 1988; Silver & Wortman, 1980). Without a satisfactory account of how the victim differs from the nonvictims, the victim's fate will seem devoid of meaning both to observers and to the victim. The reaction to the second, highly abnormal fate seems somewhat different. The "Why me?" question does not seem appropriate in a case such as this. In some sense, the psychological closeness of the event to its counterfactual nonoccurrence suggests its own explanation—it was meant to be.

Future research might profitably probe the hypothesis that fate is more likely to be implicated in the account of a near miss than an improbable outcome. Because something need not have been and could easily have been otherwise, one may be tempted to believe that it was meant to be. Pointing to bad luck seems psychologically more satisfying when discussing the case of a crash victim who was killed on his or her first airplane flight than it does when discussing the case of a crash victim who was killed after changing flights at the last minute.

Finally, it is important for future research to explore the ways in which people resolve or cope with the cognitive and affective incoherence that an event's normality can produce. For example, how do people cope with feeling guilty over an undoable action that they know was neither foolish nor immoral? Does feeling guilty when one knows one should not feel guilty intensify the dysphoria? And how does one reconcile feelings of differential sympathy for victims whose fates cannot be discriminated on moral or rational grounds? These are just some of the fascinating questions that we hope future research will address.

References

Abelson, R. P. (1983). Whatever became of consistency theory? *Personality and Social Psychology Bulletin,* **9,** 37–54.

Carlsmith, J. M., & Gross, A. E. (1969). Some effects of guilt on compliance. *Journal of Personality and Social Psychology,* **11,** 232–239.

Folger, R. (1986). A referent cognitions theory of relative deprivation. In J. M.Olson, C. P. Herman, & M. P. Zanna (Eds.), *Relative deprivation and social comparison: The Ontario Symposium* (Vol. 4, pp. 33–56). Hillsdale, NJ: Erlbaum.

Freedman, J. L. (1970). Transgression, compliance, and guilt. In J. Macaulay & L. Berkowitz (Eds.), *Altruism and helping behavior.* New York: Academic Press.

Heider, F. (1958). *The psychology of interpersonal relations.* New York: Wiley.

Janoff-Bulman, R., & Lang-Gunn, L. (1988). Coping with disease, crime, and accidents: The role of self-blame attributions. In L. Y. Abramson (Ed.), *Social cognition and clinical psychology: A synthesis* (pp. 116–147). New York: Guilford Press.

Johnson, J. T. (1986). The knowledge of what might have been: Affective and attributional consequences of near outcomes. *Personality and Social Psychology Bulletin,* **12,** 51–62.

Kahneman, D., & Miller, D. T. (1986). Norm theory: Comparing reality to its alternatives. *Psychological Review,* **93,** 136–153.

Kahneman, D., & Tversky, A. (1973). On the psychology of prediction. *Psychological Review,* **80,** 237–251.

Kahneman, D., & Tversky, A. (1982a). The psychology of preferences. *Scientific American,* **246,** 160–173.

Kahneman, D., & Tversky, A. (1982b). The simulation heuristic. In D. Kahneman, P. Slovic, & A. Tversky (Eds.), *Judgment under uncertainty: Heuristics and biases* (pp. 201–208). New York: Cambridge University Press.

Landman, J. (1988). Regret and elation following action and inaction. *Personality and Social Psychology Bulletin,* **13,** 524–536.

Lerner, M. J. (1970). The desire for justice and reactions to victims. In J. Macaulay & L. Berkowitz (Eds.), *Altruism and helping behavior.* New York: Academic Press.

Lerner, M. J. (1980). *The belief in a just world: A fundamental delusion.* New York: Plenum Press.

Lerner, M. J. & Miller, D. T. (1978). Just world research and the attribution process: Looking back and ahead. *Psychological Bulletin,* **85,** 1030–1051.

Miller, D. T. (1984). Unpublished data.

Miller, D. T., & McFarland, C. (1986). Counterfactual thinking and victim compensation: A test of norm theory. *Personality and Social Psychology Bulletin,* **12,** 513–519.

Miller, D. T., Turnbull, W., & McFarland, C. (1989). When a coincidence is suspicious: The role of mental simulation. *Journal of Personality and Social Psychology,* **57,** in press.

Rips, L. (1985). Mental muddles. In M. Brand & G. R. M. Harmish (Eds.), *The representation of knowledge and belief.* Tucson: University of Arizona Press.

Ross, M., & DiTecco, D. (1975). An attributional analysis of moral judgment. *Journal of Social Issues,* **31,** 91–109.

Shaver, K. G. (1985). *The attribution of blame: Causality, responsibility, and blameworthiness.* New York: Springer-Verlag.

Shaw, M., & Sulzer, J. (1964). An empirical test of Heider's levels of responsibility. *Journal of Abnormal and Social Psychology,* **69,** 39–46.

Silver, R. L., & Wortman, C. B. (1980). Coping with undesirable life events. In J. Garber & M. E. P. Seligman (Eds.), *Human helplessness: Theory and applications.* New York: Academic Press.

Turnbull, W. (1981). Naive conceptions of free will and the deterministic paradox. *Canadian Journal of Behavioural Science,* **13,** 1–13.

Turnbull, W., & Mawhinney, M. (1986). *Counterfactual thinking and self-blame.* Unpublished manuscript.

Tversky, A., & Kahneman, D. (1973). On the psychology of prediction. *Psychological Review,* **80,** 237–251.

Wells, G. L., & Gavanski, I. (1989). Mental simulation of causality. *Journal of Personality and Social Psychology,* **56,** 161–169.

Wells, G. L., Taylor, B. R., & Turtle, J. W. (1987). The undoing of scenarios. *Journal of Personality and Social Psychology,* **53,** 421–430.

INDEX

A

Abnormal conditions focus model, PEAT attributions and, 203–205
Accessibility
  attitude–behavior processes and, 104
  mixed models, 98, 99
  moderation, 85–88
  spontaneous processing model, 81–85
  transformation rule model for prediction and, 226
Accuracy, self-attention and, 259–262, 294
Achievement, impression formation and, 28, 29
Adaptation, impression formation and, 14, 15, 19, 62
Adjectives, attitude–behavior processes and, 83, 84
Affect
  counterfactual thinking and, 330
    normality, 328
    replicating outcomes, 318, 319
    undoing actions, 306, 307, 312
    undoing outcomes, 313–315, 318
  impression formation and, 7
  self-attention and
    alternative approaches, 264, 268
    assessment, 258, 259
    modification, 273–275
    revised model, 288, 289, 291, 293
    self-esteem, 275–277
    standards, 285
Agent, PEAT attributions and, 113
Aggression, self-attention and, 284
Anxiety, self-attention and, 269
Argumentation, PEAT attributions and, 154, 155

Arousal, self-attention and
  assessment, 256, 258, 261
  negative affect, 273, 274
  revised model, 288
  self-schema, 271
Assessment
  attitude–behavior processes and, 77
  impression formation and, 8, 9, 56
  self-attention and, 252–263
    revised model, 270, 286, 288–293
    self-schema, 270
Association, self-attention and, 257
Attention, see also Self-attention
  attitude–behavior processes and, 82, 101
  impression formation and, 2, 3, 6, 9, 60, 61
    alternatives, 58, 59
    attributes, 30, 33, 35
    category-based processes, 14, 17, 18, 20, 21
    motivation, 36, 47–54, 56, 57
Attitude-behavior processes, 75–78, 102–105
  deliberative processing model, 88–91
  integrative model, 91
  motivation, 91–94
  supporting evidence, 94–96
  mixed models, 96, 97
    deliberative process, 97–100
    spontaneous process, 100–102
  spontaneous processing model, 78–81
    memory, 81–85
    moderation, 85–88
Attitudes
  impression formation and, 15, 34, 41, 43–45
  self-attention and
    alternative approaches, 265
    assessment, 253, 257, 258, 261

focus, 279
revised model, 293
self-awareness theory, 250
standards, 284
Attributes, impression formation and, 1, 2, 4, 6–10, 12, 61, 62
alternatives, 59, 60
category-based processes, 14–17, 20
interpretation, 22–36
motivation, 36, 45–48
motivational influences, 49, 51–53, 56
Attribution
PEAT, *see* PEAT attributions
self-attention and
alternative approaches, 264
assessment, 254–256, 263
focus, 281
self-awareness theory, 250
Augmentation
PEAT attributions and, 206
correspondent inference theory, 168, 192, 196
Kelley's theories, 154–158, 160–162
self-attention and, 271
Authority, impression formation and, 41, 49
Automatism, attitude–behavior processes and, 104, 105
deliberative process, 97–100
spontaneous processing model, 83, 84
Avoidance
attitude–behavior processes and, 84
self-attention and, 268, 269, 277, 288, 290

B

Bayes' theorem, PEAT attributions and, 201, 202
Beck's Depression Inventory, self-attention and, 275
Behavior
attitude and, *see* Attitude-behavior processes
self-attention and, *see* Self-attention
Belief revision, PEAT attributions and, 201, 202
Beliefs, impression formation and, 15, 16
Bias
attitude–behavior processes and, 81, 92
counterfactual thinking and, 321, 327–329
impression formation and, 14, 41, 42, 44, 53

PEAT attributions and, 204
Blame, counterfactual thinking and, 310–313, 326
BOMDAS, transformation rule model for prediction and, 220
Brewer, PEAT attributions and, 200, 201

C

Carelessness, counterfactual thinking and, 311
Carver, self-attention and
alternative approaches, 264, 266–269
focus, 277, 278
negative affect, 273
revised model, 292, 293
self-schema, 270
standards, 282, 283, 285
Categories
attitude–behavior processes and, 101, 102
impression formation and
alternatives, 57–62
attributes, 22–36
individuation, 16–19
motivation, 36–39, 43–47
motivational influences, 49–56
priority, 19–22
responses, 15, 16
social categorization, 13–15
PEAT attributions and, 198, 199, 205
self-attention and, 268, 284
transformation rule model for prediction and, 214, 223, 229, 231, 232
Category-based expectancies, PEAT attributions and, 177–184, 186, 189, 190, 193
Characteristics
PEAT attributions and, 206
Bayes' theorem, 202
correspondent inference theory, 167, 168, 182, 192, 194, 196
Kelley's theories, 128, 150, 152–154, 158, 160–162
propositions, 116, 119–121, 124–128
self-attention and, 268
Cognition
attitude–behavior processes and, 77, 79, 93, 101
counterfactual thinking and, 330
impression formation and, 2, 4, 7, 8, 62
alternatives, 57, 58
attributes, 32

category-based processes, 14, 17, 18, 20
  motivation, 36, 42, 45
  PEAT attributions and, 118, 121, 199
  self-attention and
    alternative approaches, 268
    assessment, 257–261
    revised model, 286, 292, 293
    self-awareness theory, 250
  transformation rule model for prediction
    and, 211–213, 215–218, 241
    declarative knowledge, 228, 232
    procedural knowledge, 220, 224, 226, 227
    self-knowledge, 234, 235, 237
Commission, counterfactual thinking and, 309
Comparison, self-attention and
  alternative approaches, 266, 267, 269
  revised model, 288, 290
  self-schema, 272
  standards, 282–285
Compensatory causes, PEAT attributions and, 149–154, 161, 162, 196
Competition, impression formation and, 40, 41
Compliance, counterfactual thinking and, 328
Configuration theory, PEAT attributions and, 146–161, 177
Conflict
  impression formation and, 44
  self-attention and
    alternative approaches, 267
    assessment, 257
    revised model, 291, 292, 294
    standards, 285, 286
Conformity, self-attention and
  assessment, 252–254, 263
  focus, 278–281
  revised model, 294
  self-awareness theory, 250
Consensus, PEAT attributions and
  correspondent inference theory, 164–170, 172, 173, 175, 176
  covariation, 128–131, 134–141, 143, 145, 146
  Jones and McGillis, 177, 178, 181–183, 186, 188–193
  Kelley's theories, 153, 161, 194, 195
Conservatism, PEAT attributions and, 126
Consistency
  PEAT attributions and, 206
    Bayes' theorem, 201

correspondent inference theory, 170, 177, 178, 184–186, 193–196
  covariation, 128, 131–146
  Jaspars, 197, 198
  Kelley's theories, 153, 161
  self-attention and, 251
    alternative approaches, 265
    assessment, 254, 257
    revised model, 291, 293
Constraint
  attitude–behavior processes and, 76, 102
  counterfactual thinking and, 309, 310
  PEAT attributions and
    correspondent inference theory, 167–173, 176, 192, 193, 195
    Kelley's theories, 150, 156
    propositions, 115, 116, 119
  self-attention and, 263
Construction, attitude–behavior processes and, 93
Context
  attitude–behavior processes and, 97, 101, 104
  counterfactual thinking and, 309
  impression formation and, 4, 9–12, 61
  self-attention and, 283, 284, 291
  transformation rule model for prediction
    and, 216, 218
    declarative knowledge, 227, 231
    procedural knowledge, 219–221, 227
    self-knowledge, 234
    situational influences, 239
Continuum model of impression formation, see Impression formation
Contrast
  counterfactual thinking and, 309, 329, 330
  PEAT attributions and
    abnormal conditions focus model, 204
    correspondent inference theory, 182, 183, 186–196
    Jaspars, 198
Contrast interpretation, PEAT attributions and, 130
Control, attitude–behavior processes and, 90
Coping, transformation rule model for prediction and, 236
Correspondent inference theory, PEAT attributions and, 162–164, 206
  fundamental concepts, 164–176
  Kelley's theories, 193–196

later developments, 176–193
Counterfactual thinking, 305, 306, 325, 329, 330
  normality
    biasing effects, 327–329
    heuristic processing, 326, 327
    replicating outcomes, 318, 319
    implications, 324, 325
    suspicion, 319–324
  undoing actions, 306, 307
    blame assignment, 311–313
    normality, 307–310
  undoing outcomes, 313
    emotional amplitude, 315–318
    normality, 313–315
Covariation theory, PEAT attributions and, 128–147, 152–154, 161, 206
  abnormal conditions focus model, 203–205
  correspondent inference theory, 170, 177, 178, 180–182, 193–196
  Jaspars, 197–199
Cues
  attitude–behavior processes and, 76, 79, 93, 98, 101
  impression formation and, 4, 11
    attributes, 23, 24, 28
    motivation, 43
  self-attention and, 259, 273
  transformation rule model for prediction and, 215, 230
Culture, transformation rule model for prediction and, 221, 232

D

Davis, PEAT attributions and, 111, 112, 172, 177, 201
Declarative knowledge, transformation rule model for prediction and, 213, 216, 217, 219, 220, 226–228, 241
  individual differences, 240
  self-knowledge, 238, 239
  situational influences, 239
Defenses, self-attention and, 255, 256, 260, 261, 294
Deliberative process, 88–91, 102, 103
  integrative model, 91–93, 95
  mixed models, 96, 99, 100
Dependency, self-attention and, 278, 279, 282
Depression, self-attention and, 274, 275, 291, 292

Desirability
  PEAT attributions and, 164–171, 173–177, 186–188, 190–194
  self-attention and, 272
Discounting, PEAT attributions and
  correspondent inference theory, 192, 195, 196
  Kelley's theories, 154, 156–162
Discrepancy
  counterfactual thinking and, 306, 307, 313
  self-attention and
    alternative approaches, 268, 269
    assessment, 254, 257, 258, 261
    negative affect, 275
    revised model, 286, 290, 293, 294
    self-awareness theory, 250, 251
    self-esteem, 276, 277, 279
    standards, 283
Disposition
  PEAT attributions and, 112
    correspondent inference theory, 162–164, 168–170, 172, 173
    Jones and McGillis, 177–179, 186
    Kelley's theories, 150, 152, 195, 196
    propositions, 115–117, 119, 122, 125, 126
    Reeder and Brewer, 200
  self-attention and
    alternative approaches, 268
    assessment, 254, 256
    focus, 277
    negative affect, 275
    revised model, 291
    self-awareness theory, 252
    self-schema, 272
  transformation rule model for prediction and, 211, 212, 236
Dissonance, self-attention and, 257
Distinctiveness, PEAT attributions and
  abnormal conditions focus model, 204
  Bayes' theorem, 201
  correspondent inference theory, 177–181, 183–187, 190–193, 195
  covariation, 128, 131–146
  Jaspars, 197, 198
  Kelley's theories, 153, 161
  propositions, 127
Distortion, self-attention and, 271
Distraction, self-attention and, 252, 254, 273, 289, 291
Distress, self-attention and, 273

Dominance
  PEAT attributions and, 199
  self-attention and, 257
Duval, self-attention and, 249
  alternative approaches, 263, 266–268
  assessment, 252, 263
  focus, 277, 279–281
  negative affect, 273
  revised model, 286, 290, 292, 293
  self-awareness theory, 250, 252
  self-esteem, 275–277
  standards, 282–284

E

Ego, self-attention and, 255, 260, 294
Egocentricism, transformation rule model for prediction and, 212, 214, 215, 241
Entity, PEAT attributions and, 113, 204, 206
  configuration, 152, 153
  correspondent inference theory, 164, 167, 169–173, 175, 176
  covariation, 128–132, 134–137, 141, 142, 145, 146
  Kelley's theories, 194, 195
  later developments, 181, 183, 185, 186, 189–193
  propositions, 115
Environment
  attitude–behavior processes and, 80
  impression formation and, 13, 14, 20, 36
  PEAT attributions and, 112, 126
  self-attention and
    alternative approaches, 264
    assessment, 262
    focus, 280, 281
    revised model, 286, 291, 292
    self-awareness theory, 250, 252
    standards, 285
Episodic experience, transformation rule model for prediction and, 212, 214, 240, 241
  declarative knowledge, 228, 230
  procedural knowledge, 222, 223
  self-knowledge, 234, 236
Exception, counterfactual thinking and, 307–309, 313
Expectancy
  counterfactual thinking and, 305–307, 315, 325, 329
  impression formation and, 19, 44, 48, 50, 52

PEAT attributions and, see PEAT attributions
  self-attention and, 268, 269, 271
Expectations
  attitude–behavior processes and, 90
  self-attention and, 289

F

Facilitation
  attitude–behavior processes and, 83, 92
  PEAT attributions and
    abnormal conditions focus model, 203–205
    configuration, 152–160
    correspondent inference theory, 167–169, 172, 191, 192
    covariation, 131–133, 137, 141–144
    Jaspars, 199
    Kelley's theories, 161, 162, 194–196
    propositions, 118, 119, 121–124, 126
  self-attention and
    alternative approaches, 264
    assessment, 258, 260, 262
    revised model, 293, 294
    self-awareness theory, 251
    self-schema, 271
False consensus, transformation rule model for prediction and, 238, 239
Feedback
  impression formation and, 50, 51
  self-attention and, 255, 276
Flavell's model, transformation rule model for prediction and, 215
Foreseeability, counterfactual thinking and, 311, 312, 327
Frequency, impression formation and, 11

G

Generalized other, self-attention and, 283–285, 289
Goals
  impression formation and, 60–62
  motivation, 36–40, 43, 44, 46, 47
  motivational influences, 48–50, 52–54, 56, 57
  self-attention and, 269, 276, 282, 284
  transformation rule model for prediction and
    declarative knowledge, 229, 232

338 INDEX

procedural knowledge, 221, 222, 224, 227
Guilt, counterfactual thinking and, 328–330

H

Habituation, self-attention and, 273
Heuristic processing, counterfactual thinking and, 326, 327
Hierarchy
  self-attention and
    alternative approaches, 267–269
    revised model, 288, 290, 292, 293
    standards, 282, 283
  transformation rule model for prediction and, 241
    declarative knowledge, 231–233
    individual differences, 239, 240
    procedural knowledge, 218, 220, 221, 223–226
    self-knowledge, 234, 237
    situational influences, 239
Hostility, attitude–behavior processes and, 80
Hull, self-attention and, 263–266, 270

I

Impression formation, attitude–behavior processes and, 92
Impression formation, continuum model of, 1–5, 60–62
  alternatives, 57
    parallel operation, 59, 60
    representations, 57–59
  assessment, 8, 9
  attention, 6
  attributes, 22, 23, 32, 33
    confirmation, 24–27
    initial categorization, 23, 24
    mediation, 33–36
    piecemeal integration, 31, 32
    recategorization, 27–31
  category-based processes, 13
    individuation, 16–19
    priority, 19–22
    responses, 15, 16
    social categorization, 13–15
  clarification, 9–12

confirmatory categorization, 6, 7
initial categorization, 4
motivation, 36–38
  category-based impressions, 43–46
  goals, 46, 47
  individuation, 38–43
motivational influences, 47, 56, 57
  attention, 52, 53
  category-based responses, 51, 52
  individuation, 47–51
  stages, 53–56
personal relevance, 4, 6
piecemeal integration, 8
public expression, 8
recategorization, 7, 8
Impression management, self-attention and
  alternative approaches, 265
  assessment, 260, 261
  focus, 279, 281
  revised model, 294
  self-schema, 271, 272
  standards, 284
Individual differences, transformation rule model for prediction and, 239, 240
Individuation, impression formation and, 1–3, 6, 7, 12, 60–62
  alternatives, 57–60
  attributes, 22, 27, 30–35
  category-based processes, 13, 16–22
  motivation, 38–43, 46
  motivational influences, 46–55
Inference
  attitude–behavior processes and, 93
  impression formation and, 16, 19, 24, 32, 48
  PEAT attributions and
    Bayes' theorem, 202
    configuration, 151, 153, 154, 159
    correspondent inference theory, 196
    covariation, 146
    propositions, 120, 125
    Reeder and Brewer, 200
  transformation rule model for prediction and, 211, 212, 228, 236, 239
Information, impression formation and, 2, 3, 6, 7, 9, 60
  attributes, 22, 35
  category-based processes, 14, 16, 18, 19, 22
  motivation, 36, 47, 49–52, 55, 56

Inhibition
  PEAT attributions and
    configuration, 152–158, 160
    correspondent inference theory, 168, 173, 181, 183, 185 189, 195
    covariation, 121, 129, 141–145
    Kelley's theories, 162
    propositions, 118, 119, 122–126
  self-attention and
    assessment, 260, 261
    focus, 281
    revised model, 292
    self-esteem, 277
    self-schema, 271
Integration
  impression formation and, 4, 7–9, 12
    alternatives, 58, 59
    attributes, 23, 28, 31–33, 35
    motivation, 55, 56
  PEAT attributions and, 152, 162, 206
  transformation rule model for prediction and, 215, 227, 228, 240
Integrative model, attitude–behavior processes and, 91–96
Interdependence, impression formation and, 3, 6, 61
  motivation, 46, 47, 50–52, 56, 57
Internal responses, impression formation and, 8
Interpretation
  impression formation and, 3, 7, 12, 60, 61
    attributes, 22–36
    motivation, 47, 50–53, 55, 57
  PEAT attributions and
    covariation, 130, 131, 140, 144, 146
    Kelley's theories, 147, 161
    propositions, 117, 119
Introspection
  self-attention and, 251, 252, 274
  transformation rule model for prediction and, 214

J

Jaspars, PEAT attributions and, 197–199
Jones, PEAT attributions and, 111, 112
  Bayes' theorem, 201
  correspondent inference theory, 162, 172, 176–193

K

Kelley
  PEAT attributions and, 111, 112, 128, 161, 162, 206
  Bayes' theorem, 201
  configuration, 146–161
  correspondent inference theory, 162–164, 176–178, 181, 185–187, 192–196
  covariation, 128–146
  Jaspars, 197
  self-attention and, 271
Knowledge, counterfactual thinking and, 317–319

L

Labels
  impression formation and, 6, 9, 10
    attributes, 23–31, 34, 35
    motivation, 39, 52, 54
  PEAT attributions and, 115, 116, 150, 151, 172
  transformation rule model for prediction and, 234, 235
Levy, self-attention and, 263–266, 270

M

Markus's model, transformation rule model for prediction and, 233
McGillis, PEAT attributions and, 162, 176–193
Memory
  attitude–behavior processes and, 104
    integrative model, 91, 94–96
    mixed models, 97–100
    spontaneous processing model, 79–88
  counterfactual thinking and, 327
  impression formation and, 4, 10, 11, 16–19
  PEAT attributions and, 117
  transformation rule model for prediction and
    declarative knowledge, 228
    procedural knowledge, 219, 227
    self-knowledge, 233–235, 237, 238
MODE model, attitude–behavior processes and, 92–96, 105
Mood
  impression formation and, 11, 12
  self-attention and, 274–276, 288

340 INDEX

Motivation
  attitude–behavior processes and, 89, 91–94, 96, 103
  counterfactual thinking and, 319, 320
  impression formation and, 2, 3, 6, 12, 36–38, 61
    attributes, 31–33
    categories, 19–21, 43–46
    goals, 46, 47
    individuation, 38–43
    influences, 59
  self-attention and, 249
    alternative approaches, 265
    assessment, 257, 259–262
    revised model, 288, 290, 293
    self-awareness theory, 250
    self-esteem, 275
    self-schema, 270, 271, 273
    standards, 282, 283
  transformation rule model for prediction and, 212, 228
Motives, transformation rule model for prediction and, 213

N

Negative affect, self-attention and, 273–275
  revised model, 291, 293
  self-awareness theory, 250
  self-esteem, 276, 277
  standards, 285
Normality, counterfactual thinking and, 306, 330
  biasing effects, 327–329
  heuristic processing, 326, 327
  replicating outcomes, 318–324
  undoing actions, 307–311
  undoing outcomes, 313–315, 318
Norms
  attitude–behavior processes and, 89, 90
  self-attention and, 281
  transformation rule model for prediction and, 235
Novelty, impression formation and, 4, 10, 11

O

Ommission, counterfactual thinking and, 309
Opportunity, attitude–behavior processes and, 91–94, 96

P

Parsimony, PEAT attributions and, 126, 144
PEAT attributions, 111–113, 205, 206
  abnormal conditions focus model, 203–205
  Bayes' theorem, 201, 202
  correspondent inference theory, 162–164
    concepts, 164–176
    Kelley, 193–196
    later developments, 176–193
  Jaspars, 197–199
  Kelley's theories, 128, 161, 162, 193–196
    configuration, 146–161
    covariation, 128–146
    propositions, 113–128
  Reeder and Brewer, 200, 201
Peers
  impression formation and, 41, 42
  self-attention and, 253
  transformation rule model for prediction and, 212
Perception, counterfactual thinking and, see Counterfactual thinking
Personal standards, self-attention and
  alternative approaches, 266, 267
  assessment, 253, 254, 257, 262
  nature, 282, 285
  revised model, 292, 294
  self-esteem, 277, 279
Personality
  attitude–behavior processes and, 78, 103
  impression formation and, 10, 19, 42
  self-attention and, 278, 291
  transformation rule model for prediction and, 216, 227, 229, 240
Phobia, self-attention and, 255
Piaget, transformation rule model for prediction and, 212
Placebo, self-attention and, 258, 261, 271
Prediction, transformation rule model for, see Transformation rule model for prediction
Prejudice, impression formation and, 1, 46, 50
Priming
  attitude–behavior processes and, 82–84, 100
  PEAT attributions and, 140
  transformation rule model for prediction and, 237, 238
Probability
  counterfactual thinking and, 325
  normality, 326–328

replicating outcomes, 320–324
undoing actions, 306, 309
PEAT attributions and, 205, 206
Bayes' theorem, 201, 202
configuration, 147–151, 159, 160
correspondent inference theory, 165–167, 169, 171, 176
covariation, 128, 131–140, 142–144, 146
Jaspars, 198
Jones and McGillis, 176–181, 183, 185, 188, 189
Kelley's theories, 161, 194, 195
propositions, 113–119, 122, 123, 126, 127
Reeder and Brewer, 200
Procedural knowledge, transformation rule model for prediction and, 213, 216–218
individual differences, 240
model, 219–224
postulates, 218, 219
situational influences, 239
studies, 224–227
Projection, transformation rule model for prediction and, 214
Prototypes
attitude–behavior processes and, 102
PEAT attributions and, 117
transformation rule model for prediction and, 213, 216
declarative knowledge, 228, 229
procedural knowledge, 227
self-knowledge, 234–236
Psychiatry, self-attention and, 256, 260, 271

R

Rationality, counterfactual thinking and, 316, 317, 320
Recency
impression formation and, 11
transformation rule model for prediction and, 226
Reciprocity, transformation rule model for prediction and, 217, 218
Reeder, PEAT attributions and, 200, 201
Reinforcement, impression formation and, 26, 30, 31, 38
Relevance
attitude–behavior processes and, 93, 100, 103

counterfactual thinking and, 327, 328
impression formation and, 4, 6
alternatives, 57, 58
category-based processes, 15
motivation, 36–38, 45, 54
PEAT attributions and, 125
self-attention and, 260, 264, 268
transformation rule model for prediction and, 230, 233, 238
Retrieval
attitude–behavior processes and, 103
integrative model, 93, 96
mixed models, 98
spontaneous processing model, 79
self-attention and, 268, 271
transformation rule model for prediction and, 228
Role, impression formation and, 10, 61
attributes, 29
category-based processes, 13, 17
motivation, 51, 53
Role taking, transformation rule model for prediction and, 214, 216, 217, 241
individual differences, 240
self-knowledge, 233
Routine, counterfactual thinking and, 307–309

S

Scheier, self-attention and
alternative approaches, 264, 266–269
focus, 277, 278
negative affect, 273
revised model, 292, 293
self-schema, 270
standards, 282, 283, 285
Schema, *see also* Self-schema
counterfactual thinking and, 325
impression formation and, 13, 61
PEAT attributions and
correspondent inference theory, 196
Kelley's theories, 147–154, 161
Reeder and Brewer, 200
Schizophrenia
impression formation and, 39, 53, 54
transformation rule model for prediction and, 240
Script
PEAT attributions and, 203–205
transformation rule model for prediction and, 222, 235, 238

Self-attention, 249
  alternative approaches, 263
    Carver and Scheier's model, 266–269
    Hull and Levy's model, 263–266
  assessment, 263
    accuracy, 259–262
    affect, 258, 259
    attitude–behavior discrepancy, 257, 258
    attribution, 254–256
    conformity, 252–254
    psychological state, 262, 263
  focus, 277–282
  negative affect, 273–275
  revised model, 286, 287, 294, 295
    internal conflict, 291, 292
    previous models, 292–294
    research, 294
    self-dimensions, 288–291
    self-schema, 286, 288
  self-awareness theory, 250–252, 269, 270
  self-esteem, 275–277
  self-schema, 270–273
  standards, 282, 283
    conflict, 285, 286
    generalized other, 283–285
Self-awareness theory, 249–252, 269, 270
  alternative approaches, 263–265, 267
  assessment, 255–263
  focus, 277–282
  revised model, 286, 290, 292–295
  self-esteem, 275–277
  self-schema, 270–272
  standards, 282, 284, 285
Self-concept, 280
Self-consciousness, 275, 277–279, 282, 291
  scale, 252, 254, 277
Self-dimension, 250
  alternative approaches, 267–269
  assessment, 258–262
  revised model, 288–291, 293
  self-esteem, 276
  standards, 286
Self-esteem
  impression formation and, 45, 46, 54
  self-attention and
    affect, 275–277
    assessment, 255, 256
    revised model, 289, 290, 292–294
    standards, 285
  transformation rule model for prediction and, 238

Self-focus, 277, 279–281
  alternative approaches, 264–269
  assessment, 253–260, 262, 263
  negative affect, 273–275
  revised model, 286, 289–294
  self-awareness theory, 250–252
  self-esteem, 275–277
  self-schema, 270–272
  standards, 283–286
Self-knowledge
  self-attention and, 261, 262
  transformation rule model for prediction and, 233–239
Self-report
  alternative approaches, 265, 269
  assessment, 259, 260
  focus, 278, 281
  negative affect, 273, 274
  revised model, 293, 294
  self-schema, 270, 271
  standards, 284
Self-schema
  impression formation and, 7, 55
  self-attention and
    alternative approaches, 264, 268
    assessment, 270–273
    revised model, 286, 288, 292
  transformation rule model for prediction and, 233, 238 239
Semantics
  attitude–behavior processes and, 80, 82
  counterfactual thinking and, 308
Sensitivity, self-attention and, 265
Signal detection theory, PEAT attributions and, 200, 201
Situation
  PEAT attributions and, 113
  self-attention and, 250, 252, 283–285
  transformation rule model for prediction and, 239
Social dependency, self-attention and, 278, 279, 282
Social perception, counterfactual thinking and, see Counterfactual thinking
Spontaneous processing model, attitude–behavior processes and, 78–81, 102–104
  memory, 81–85
  mixed models, 96, 100–102
  moderation, 85–88
  motivation, 91–93

Standards, *see also* Personal standards
  counterfactual thinking and, 325
  self-attention and, 282, 283
    conflict, 285, 286
    generalized other, 283–285
    revised model, 289–291, 294
Stereotypes
  attitude–behavior processes and, 92
  counterfactual thinking and, 323, 324
  impression formation and, 1–4, 6, 10, 62
    alternatives, 57, 59
    attributes, 24–28, 30, 33, 35
    category-based processes, 13, 14, 17, 18, 20, 21
    motivation, 42, 43, 45, 46
    motivational influences, 48, 49, 53, 56
  PEAT attributions and, 117, 178–181
  transformation rule model for prediction and, 221, 229 232
Stimulus onset asynchrony, attitude–behavior processes and, 83
Storage-bin model, transformation rule model for prediction and, 226
Stress, transformation rule model for prediction and, 239
Subcategories, impression formation and, 4, 7, 29, 55
Subjective scaling model, PEAT attributions and, 198, 199
Suspicion, counterfactual thinking and, 325
  normality, 326–328
  replicating outcomes, 319–324
Symbolic interaction, self-attention and, 280, 283
Symbols, PEAT attributions and, 155, 157

T

Target-based expectancies, PEAT attributions and, 177–186
Traits
  impression formation and, 10, 16, 24, 31, 52
  PEAT attributions and, 115
  self-attention and, 274, 275, 278, 279
  transformation rule model for prediction and, 230
Transformation rule model for prediction, 211–213, 241
  critique, 215–217
  declarative knowledge, 227, 228
    hierarchy, 231–233
    intersections, 229–231
    types, 228, 229
  extant approaches, 213–215
  individual differences, 239, 240
  procedural knowledge, 218
    model, 219–224
    postulates, 218, 219
    studies, 224–227
  self-knowledge, 233
    false consensus, 238, 239
    Markus's model, 233
    self-as-distinct view model, 234–238
  situational influences, 239
  visual experiences, 217, 218
Transgression, counterfactual thinking and, 328

U

Undoing actions, counterfactual thinking and, 306, 307, 315
  blame assignment, 311–313
  normality, 307–310
Undoing outcomes, counterfactual thinking and, 313
  emotional amplitude, 315–318
  normality, 313–315

V

Valence, PEAT attributions and
  correspondent inference theory, 169, 170, 177, 186, 193 194
  Kelley's theories, 160
Values
  impression formation and, 43, 46, 49
  self-attention and
    focus, 278, 279, 281
    revised model, 288–290, 292–294
    standards, 283–285
Victims, counterfactual thinking and, 325, 329, 330
  normality, 326
  undoing actions, 308, 311, 312
  undoing outcomes, 316
Visual experiences, transformation rule model for prediction and, 217, 218

W

Wicklund, self-attention and, 249, 250, 252, 263

alternative approaches, 263, 266–268
focus, 277, 279–281
negative affect, 273
revised model, 286, 289–293

self-esteem, 275, 277
standards, 282–284
Withdrawal, self-attention and, 269

CONTENTS OF OTHER VOLUMES

Volume 1

Cultural Influences upon Cognitive Processes
  Harry C. Triandis
The Interaction of Cognitive and Physiological Determinants of Emotional State
  Stanley Schachter
Experimental Studies of Coalition Formation
  William A. Gamson
Communication Networks
  Marvin E. Shaw
A Contingency Model of Leadership Effectiveness
  Fred E. Fiedler
Inducing Resistance to Persuasion: Some Contemporary Approaches
  William J. McGuire
Social Motivation, Dependency, and Susceptibility to Social Influence
  Richard H. Walters and Ross D. Purke
Sociability and Social Organization in Monkeys and Apes
  William A. Mason
Author Index—Subject Index

Volume 2

Vicarious Processes: A Case of No-Trial Learning
  Albert Bandura
Selective Exposure
  Jonathan L. Freedman and David O. Sears
Group Problem Solving
  L. Richard Hoffman
Situational Factors in Conformity
  Vernon L. Allen
Social Power
  John Schopler
From Acts to Dispositions: The Attribution Process in Person Perception
  Edward E. Jones and Keith E. Davis
Inequality in Social Exchange
  J. Stacy Adams
The Concept of Aggressive Drive: Some Additional Considerations
  Leonard Berkowitz
Author Index—Subject Index

Volume 3

Mathematical Models in Social Psychology
  Robert P. Abelson
The Experimental Analysis of Social Performance
  Michael Argyle and Adam Kendon
A Structural Balance Approach to the Analysis of Communication Effects
  N. T. Feather
Effects of Fear Arousal on Attitude Change: Recent Developments in Theory and Experimental Research
  Irving L. Janis
Communication Processes and the Properties of Language
  Serge Moscovici
The Congruity Principle Revisited: Studies in the Reduction, Induction and Generalization of Persuasion
  Percy H. Tannenbaum
Author Index—Subject Index

Volume 4

The Theory of Cognitive Dissonance: A Current Perspective
  Elliot Aronson
Attitudes and Attraction
  Donn Byrne
Sociolinguistics
  Susan M. Ervin-Tripp
Recognition of Emotion
  Nico H. Frijda
Studies of Status Congruence
  Edward E. Sampson
Exploratory Investigations of Empathy
  Ezra Stotland
The Personal Reference Scale: An Approach to Social Judgment
  Harry S. Upshaw
Author Index—Subject Index

Volume 5

Media Violence and Aggressive Behavior: A Review of Experimental Research
  Richard E. Goranson
Studies in Leader Legitimacy, Influence, and Innovation
  Edwin P. Hollander and James W. Julian
Experimental Studies of Negro-White Relationships
  Irwin Katz
Findings and Theory in the Study of Fear Communications
  Howard Leventhal
Perceived Freedom
  Ivan D. Steiner
Experimental Studies of Families
  Nancy E. Waxler and Elliot G. Mishler
Why Do Groups Make Riskier Decisions than Individuals?
  Kenneth L. Dion, Robert S. Baron, and Norman Miller
Author Index—Subject Index

Volume 6

Self-Perception Theory
  Daryl J. Bem
Social Norms, Feelings, and Other Factors Affecting Helping and Altruism
  Leonard Berkowitz
The Power of Liking: Consequences of Interpersonal Attitudes Derived from a Liberalized View of Secondary Reinforcement
  Albert J. Lott and Bernice E. Lott
Social Influence, Conformity Bias, and the Study of Active Minorities
  Serge Moscovici and Claude Faucheux
A Critical Analysis of Research Utilizing the Prisoner's Dilemma Paradigm for the Study of Bargaining
  Charlan Nemeth
Structural Representations of Implicit Personality Theory
  Seymour Rosenberg and Andrea Sedlak
Author Index—Subject Index

Volume 7

Cognitive Algebra: Integration Theory Applied to Social Attribution
  Norman A. Anderson
On Conflicts and Bargaining
  Erika Apfelbaum
Physical Attractiveness
  Ellen Berscheid and Elaine Walster
Compliance, Justification, and Cognitive Change
  Harold B. Gerard, Edward S. Connolley, and Roland A. Wilhelmy
Processes in Delay of Gratification
  Walter Mischel
Helping a Distressed Person: Social, Personality, and Stimulus Determinants
  Ervin Staub
Author Index—Subject Index

Volume 8

Social Support for Nonconformity
  Vernon L. Allen
Group Tasks, Group Interaction Process, and Group Performance Effectiveness: A Review and Proposed Integration
  J. Richard Hackman and Charles G. Morris
The Human Subject in the Psychology Experiment: Fact and Artifact
  Arie W. Kruglanski
Emotional Arousal in the Facilitation of Aggression through Communication
  Percy H. Tannenbaum and Dolf Zillman

The Reluctance to Transmit Bad News
    Abraham Tesser and Sidney Rosen
Objective Self-Awareness
    Robert A. Wicklund
Responses to Uncontrollable Outcomes: An Integration of Reactance Theory and the Learned Helplessness Model
    Camille B. Wortman and Jack W. Brehm
Subject Index

Volume 9

New Directions in Equity Research
    Elaine Walster, Ellen Berscheid, and G. William Walster
Equity Theory Revisited: Comments and Annotated Bibliography
    J. Stacy Adams and Sara Freedman
The Distribution of Rewards and Resources in Groups and Organizations
    Gerald S. Leventhal
Deserving and the Emergence of Forms of Justice
    Melvin J. Lerner, Dale T. Miller, and John G. Holmes
Equity and the Law: The Effect of a Harmdoer's "Suffering in the Act" on Liking and Assigned Punishment
    William Austin, Elaine Walster, and Mary Kristine Utne
Incremental Exchange Theory: A Formal Model for Progression in Dyadic Social Interaction
    L. Lowell Huesmann and George Levinger
Commentary
    George C. Homans
Subject Index

Volume 10

The Catharsis of Aggression: An Evaluation of a Hypothesis
    Russell G. Geen and Michael B. Quanty
Mere Exposure
    Albert A. Harrison
Moral Internalization: Current Theory and Research
    Martin L. Hoffman
Some Effects of Violent and Nonviolent Movies on the Behavior of Juvenile Delinquents
    Ross D. Parke, Leonard Berkowitz, Jacques P. Leyens, Stephen G. West, and Richard J. Sebastian
The Intuitive Psychologist and His Shortcomings: Distortions in the Attribution Process
    Lee Ross
Normative Influences on Altruism
    Shalom H. Schwartz
A Discussion of the Domain and Methods of Social Psychology: Two Papers by Ron Harre and Barry R. Schlenker
    Leonard Berkowitz
The Ethogenic Approach: Theory and Practice
    R. Harre
On the Ethogenic Approach: Etiquette and Revolution
    Barry R. Schlenker
Automatisms and Autonomies: In Reply to Professor Schlenker
    R. Harre
Subject Index

Volume 11

The Persistence of Experimentally Induced Attitude Change
    Thomas D. Cook and Brian F. Flay
The Contingency Model and the Dynamics of the Leadership Process
    Fred E. Fiedler
An Attributional Theory of Choice
    Andy Kukla
Group-Induced Polarization of Attitudes and Behavior
    Helmut Lamm and David G. Myers
Crowding: Determinants and Effects
    Janet E. Stockdale
Salience: Attention, and Attribution: Top of the Head Phenomena
    Shelley E. Taylor and Susan T. Fiske
Self-Generated Attitude Change
    Abraham Tesser
Subject Index

Volume 12

Part I. Studies in Social Cognition

Prototypes in Person Perception
    Nancy Cantor and Walter Mischel
A Cognitive-Attributional Analysis of

Stereotyping
  David L. Hamilton
Self-Monitoring Processes
  Mark Snyder

Part II. Social Influences and Social Interaction

Architectural Mediation of Residential Density and Control: Crowding and the Regulation of Social Contact
  Andrew Baum and Stuart Valins
A Cultural Ecology of Social Behavior
  J. W. Berry
Experiments on Deviance with Special Reference to Dishonesty
  David P. Farrington
From the Early Window to the Late Night Show: International Trends in the Study of Television's Impact on Children and Adults
  John P. Murray and Susan Kippax
Effects of Prosocial Television and Film Material on the Behavior of Viewers
  J. Phillipe Rushton
Subject Index

Volume 13

People's Analyses of the Causes of Ability-Linked Performances
  John M. Darley and George R. Goethals
The Empirical Exploration of Intrinsic Motivational Processes
  Edward I. Deci and Richard M. Ryan
Attribution of Responsibility: From Man the Scientist to Man as Lawyer
  Frank D. Fincham and Joseph M. Jaspars
Toward a Comprehensive Theory of Emotion
  Howard Leventhal
Toward a Theory of Conversion Behavior
  Serge Moscovici
The Role of Information Retrieval and Conditional Inference Processes in Belief Formation and Change
  Robert S. Wyer, Jr. and Jon Hartwick
Index

Volume 14

Verbal and Nonverbal Communication of Deception
  Miron Zuckerman, Bella M. DePaulo, and Robert Rosenthal
Cognitive, Social, and Personality Processes in the Physiological Detection of Deception
  William M. Waid and Martin T. Orne
Dialectic Conceptions in Social Psychology: An Application to Social Penetration and Privacy Regulation
  Irwin Altman, Anne Vinsel, and Barbara B. Brown
Direct Experience and Attitude–Behavior Consistency
  Russell H. Fazio and Mark P. Zanna
Predictability and Human Stress: Toward a Clarification of Evidence and Theory
  Suzanne M. Miller
Perceptual and Judgmental Processes in Social Contexts
  Arnold Upmeyer
Jury Trials: Psychology and Law
  Charlan Jeanne Nemeth
Index

Volume 15

Balance, Agreement, and Positivity in the Cognition of Small Social Structures
  Walter H. Crockett
Episode Cognition: Internal Representations of Interaction Routines
  Joseph P. Forgas
The Effects of Aggressive-Pornographic Mass Media Stimuli
  Neil M. Malamuth and Ed Donnerstein
Socialization in Small Groups: Temporal Changes in Individual–Group Relations
  Richard L. Moreland and John M. Levin
Translating Actions into Attitudes: An Identity-Analytic Approach to the Explanation of Social Conduct
  Barry R. Schlenker
Aversive Conditions as Stimuli to Aggression
  Leonard Berkowitz
Index

Volume 16

A Contextualist Theory of Knowledge: Its Implications for Innovation and Reform in Psychological Research
  William J. McGuire
Social Cognition: Some Historical and

Theoretical Perspectives
Janet Landman and Melvin Manis
Paradigmatic Behaviorism: Unified Theory for Social-Personality Psychology
Arthur W. Staats
Social Psychology from the Standpoint of a Structural Symbolic Interactionism: Toward an Interdisciplinary Social Psychology
Sheldon Stryker
Toward an Interdisciplinary Social Psychology
Carl W. Backman
Index

Volume 17

Mental Representations of Self
John F. Kihlstrom and Nancy Cantor
Theory of the Self: Impasse and Evolution
Kenneth J. Gergen
A Perceptual-Motor Theory of Emotion
Howard Leventhal
Equity and Social Change in Human Relationships
Charles G. McClintock, Roderick M. Kramer, and Linda J. Keil
A New Look at Dissonance Theory
Joel Cooper and Russell H. Fazio
Cognitive Theories of Persuasion
Alice H. Eagly and Shelly Chaiken
Helping Behavior and Altruism: An Empirical and Conceptual Overview
John F. Dovidio
Index

Volume 18

A Typological Approach to Marital Interaction: Recent Theory and Research
Mary Anne Fitzpatrick
Groups in Exotic Environments
Albert A. Harrison and Mary M. Connors
Balance Theory, the Jordan Paradigm, and the Wiest Tetrahedon
Chester A. Insko
The Social Relations Model
David A. Kenny and Lawrence La Voie
Coalition Bargaining
S. S. Komorita
When Belief Creates Reality
Mark Snyder
Index

Volume 19

Distraction–Conflict Theory: Progress and Problems
Robert S. Baron
Recent Research on Selective Exposure to Information
Dieter Frey
The Role of Threat to Self-Esteem and Perceived Control in Recipient Reaction to Help: Theory Development and Empirical Validation
Arie Nadler and Jeffrey D. Fisher
The Elaboration Likelihood Model of Persuasion
Richard E. Petty and John T. Cacioppo
Natural Experiments on the Effects on Mass Media Violence on Fatal Aggression: Strengths and Weaknesses of a New Approach
David P. Phillips
Paradigms and Groups
Ivan D. Steiner
Social Categorization: Implications for Creation and Reduction of Intergroup Bias
David A. Wilder
Index

Volume 20

Attitudes, Traits, and Actions: Dispositional Prediction of Behavior in Personality and Social Psychology
Icek Ajzen
Prosocial Motivation: Is It Ever Truly Altruistic?
C. Daniel Batson
Dimensions of Group Process: Amount and Structure of Vocal Interaction
James M. Dabbs, Jr. and R. Barry Ruback
The Dynamics of Opinion Formation
Harold B. Gerard and Ruben Orive
Positive Affect, Cognitive Processes, and Social Behavior
Alice M. Isen
Between Hope and Fear: The Psychology of Risk
Lola L. Lopes
Toward an Integration of Cognitive and Motivational Perspectives on Social Inference: A Biased Hypothesis-Testing Model
Tom Pyszczynski and Jeff Greenberg
Index

Volume 21

Introduction
Leonard Berkowitz

Part I. The Self as Known

Narrative and the Self as Relationship
Kenneth J. Gergen and Mary M. Gergen
Self and Others: Studies in Social Personality and Autobiography
Seymour Rosenberg
Content and Process in the Experience of Self
William J. McGuire and Claire V. McGuire
Information Processing and the Study of the Self
John F. Kihlstrom, Nancy Cantor, Jeanne Sumi Albright, Beverly R. Chew, Stanley B. Klein, and Paula M. Niedenthal

Part II. Self-Motives

Toward a Self-Evaluation Maintenance Model of Social Behavior
Abraham Tesser
The Self: A Dialectical Approach
Carl W. Backman
The Psychology of Self-Affirmation: Sustaining the Integrity of the Self
Claude M. Steele
A Model of Behavioral Self-Regulation: Translating Intention into Action
Michael F. Scheier and Charles S. Carver
Index

Volume 22

On the Construction of the Anger Experience: Aversive Events and Negative Priming in the Formation of Feelings
Leonard Berkowitz and Karen Heimer
Social Psychophysiology: A New Look
John T. Cacioppo, Richard E. Petty, and Louis G. Tassinary
Self-Discrepancy Theory: What Patterns of Self-Beliefs Cause People to Suffer?
E. Tory Higgins
Minding Matters: The Consequences of Mindlessness–Mindfulness
Ellen J. Langer
The Tradeoffs of Social Control and Innovation in Groups and Organizations
Charlan Jeanne Nemeth and Barry M. Staw
Confession, Inhibition, and Disease
James W. Pennebaker
A Sociocognitive Model of Attitude Structure and Function
Anthony R. Pratkanis and Anthony G. Greenwald
Introspection, Attitude Change, and Attitude–Behavior Consistency: The Disruptive Effects of Explaining Why We Feel the Way We Do
Timothy D. Wilson, Dana S. Dunn, Dolores Kraft, and Douglas J. Lisle
Index